THIRD EDITION

THE HUMAN DIRECTION

An Evolutionary Approach to Social and Cultural Anthropology

JAMES PEACOCK

University of North Carolina

A. THOMAS KIRSCH

Cornell University

PRENTICE-HALL, INC., Englewood Cliffs, N.J. 07632

Library of Congress Cataloging in Publication Data

Peacock, James L
   The human direction.

   Bibliography: p.
   Includes index.
   1. Ethnology. 2. Social evolution. I. Kirsch,
A. Thomas, joint author. II. Title.
GN316.P33 1980   301.2   79-17854
ISBN 0-13-444851-0

Printed in the United States of America

10 9 8 7 6 5 4 3 2 1

Editorial/production supervision
  and interior design by Scott Amerman
Cover photograph by Stan Wakefield
Manufacturing buyer: John Hall

PRENTICE-HALL INTERNATIONAL, INC., *London*
PRENTICE-HALL OF AUSTRALIA PTY. LIMITED, *Sydney*
PRENTICE-HALL OF CANADA, LTD., *Toronto*
PRENTICE-HALL OF INDIA PRIVATE LIMITED, *New Delhi*
PRENTICE-HALL OF JAPAN, INC., *Tokyo*
PRENTICE-HALL OF SOUTHEAST ASIA PTE. LTD., *Singapore*
WHITEHALL BOOKS LIMITED, *Wellington, New Zealand*

Contents

5. Primitive Society and Culture   135

6. Archaic Society and Culture   166

Preface

Although there are as many ways of teaching introductory cultural or social anthropology as there are teachers of anthropology, two strategies are common. Either the instructor covers an aggregate of topics—kinship, technology, religion, language—or he presents a mélange of portraits depicting the myriad "ways of mankind." In both instances, anthropology is presented as a set of fragmented segments. While a good teacher can render such a course rewarding, he is handicapped by the lack of focus and by the absence of a framework that encourages systematic comparison and leads by logical progression toward synthesis. Students who begin the course enthusiastically often lose interest as it fails to progress and resolve chaos into order.

The Human Direction is designed to contribute focus and system to introductory courses in cultural or social anthropology. We have tried to retain the great virtue of the orthodox strategies—diversity of exotic immersions—and at the same time organize these experiences within a broad evolutionary framework that will logically progress toward synthesis, encourage the student to compare the societies and cultures of the world systematically, relate anthropology to significant social issues, and ultimately lead to the broadest of questions: What is the future of man?

After three opening chapters aimed at sensitizing the student to the anthropological view and to certain crucial anthropological concepts, the text moves into its evolutionary analysis. Chapter 4 sets forth the main dimensions of the evolutionary scheme and asks the question: In what direction is the world evolving? The next four chapters portray, in detail, selected societies—the Australian aborigines, the Swazi of Africa, the Buddhists of Thailand, the medieval Christians, the modernizing Japanese, and others—in order to expound the evolutionary theory as well as to encourage systematic understanding and comparison of these particular societies. Chapter 10 treats contemporary America, which the student can approach with fresh insight and objectivity derived from the comparative and evolutionary perspective of the first six chapters. The final chapter briefly considers the dynamics of sociocultural evolution, and speculates about the future shape of human society and culture.

In constructing the evolutionary framework that provides the skeleton for the text, we classify all the societies of the world, past and present, in terms of a scale whose levels, following Robert N. Bellah, we label as primitive, archaic, historic, early-modern, and modern.[1]* These stages represent different levels of sociocultural complexity, of which each allows a greater potential for change and a greater degree of freedom in dealing with the environment than the preceding level. The progression from the primitive to the modern is charted along a number of dimensions: specialization of social units, functional specificity of social relations, centralization, and autonomy of religious systems in relation to social systems.

We recognize that not every society of the world fits neatly and unambiguously into any single level of our scheme. Many a society is at one level along certain dimensions, at another level along others. Despite the admitted difficulty of neatly classifying all societies, however, the portrayal of a number of the world's societies as cases logically ordered in a general scheme can be highly instructive. Such portrayal highlights contrasts and correlations. For example, society *A* may be classed as *archaic* in its religion because it possesses a pantheon of gods clearly distinguished from men, whereas society *B* is classed as *primitive* in its religion because it possesses not gods, but rather spirits who are not clearly distinguished from men. Similarly, society *A* may be classed as archaic in its government because it has kings, whereas society *B* is classed as primitive because it possesses elders and chiefs, rather than kings. This simple example illustrates how an evolutionary scheme can display not only contrasts between societies, but also correlations between institutions (in this case, correlations between kingship and

*The notes are on page 296.

theism, chieftainship and animism) within any single society. Alerting the student to such contrasts and correlations between and within societies is an important goal of anthropology.

Our evolutionary scheme can be viewed not only as a convenient framework for classifying societies, but also as a world history. Although there are societies (for example, some in Southeast Asia) whose histories closely follow the sequence from primitive to modern outlined by our scheme, we make no attempt to periodize the history of any one society, much less of all societies, and we do not maintain that every society necessarily develops in the sequence we outline. Rather, our scheme plots world history by dividing it into periods each bearing the label of the most advanced sociocultural pattern—primitive, archaic, historic, early-modern, or modern—achieved during that period.

Thus, prior to the emergence of the great Near Eastern civilizations, which are dated from such archaeological sites as Jarmo (6700 B.C.), it appears that there existed no societies more advanced than the primitive type; hence, the period prior to 7000–6000 B.C. is called *primitive*. During this era, the most advanced societies were those that had undergone what V. Gordon Childe has called the Neolithic Revolution.[2] Technologically, these societies had passed from the stage of hunting and gather food to that of raising food and breeding stock. Although they produced food, these Neolithic communities were socioculturally primitive.

By 7000–6000 B.C., archaic society had come into being, and it remained the most advanced form of society until about 1000 B.C. Archaic societies flourished in the Indus River region of India and Pakistan, in China, and in the Near East, and (much later) in the New World. Capitalizing on the farming and stockraising techniques developed by Neolithic primitive man, archaic societies achieved certain important advances, such as the creation of cities, writing (which was, however, restricted to a few craft specialists), and political centralization.

Two to three thousand years ago, the first historic societies appeared, stimulated by the rise of the great world religions—Buddhism, Christianity, and Islam. The central achievement of historic societies was spiritual: a more universal definition of man than that found in primitive and archaic culture. Universalistic conceptions encouraged numerous social and material developments, such as the spread of literacy to a sizable religio-political elite, the development of bureaucracy, and the creation of kingdoms and empires far more extensive than those of the archaic era.

Early-modern society appeared only some three or four hundred years ago during the time of Western religious reformation, political revolution, and industrial development. Early-modern patterns of industrialism, nationalism, and science are still spreading throughout the world. Until recently such patterns were, in terms of our scheme, the most advanced yet achieved by man.

We hypothesize the eventual appearance of a modern pattern that goes beyond the early-modern one. This hypothesis is based partly on the notion that sociocultural evolution is an unending process and partly on observation of trends and events occurring primarily in the West and especially in America. Whether current trends are true signs of an emerging pattern or are simply abortive reactions to current strains is unclear, and our speculations about the future form of modern society and culture are necessarily very tentative.

While our evolutionary scale can be viewed as a world history, every one of the sociocultural levels or types distinguished by that scale is represented by some contemporary society. That is, primitive, archaic, historic, and early-modern societies all exist in the *contemporary* world. To underline this point, a contemporary society has been chosen as a central illustrative case for each of the evolutionary levels. Although the contemporary world tolerates a diversity of societies, all of these are apparently converging into a single type, a world-wide pattern that emphasizes early-modern and modern features. At every point of world history, the trend has been for the less advanced societies to absorb, either willingly or reluctantly, the patterns of the more advanced societies. During the modern era this trend has accelerated. The less advanced societies are changing in the direction of the most advanced pattern extant more rapidly today than every before in human history.

Implicit in our evolutionary scheme is a philosophy of history—one that tries to be flexible rather than dogmatic, suggestive rather than definitive. At various points, we alert the student to alternative interpretations, to unresolved theoretical and methodological issues, and to possible lines of speculation that go beyond this book. Since the book focuses on a process whose end result no one can predict precisely, we emphasize the open-endedness of the evolutionary process. The final chapter, on the future shape of human culture and society, is frankly speculative.

The Human Direction does not exhaust the entire field of anthropology, and the instructor will doubtless wish to incorporate supplementary materials. Many such materials—on kinship, on peasant societies, on New World ethnography, or on Old World prehistory, for example—will fit nicely into certain rubrics of the evolutionary scheme. The Suggested Readings at the end of the chapters propose sources for this kind of elaboration of the text. The book does not attempt a systematic treatment of physical anthropology, linguistics, or archaeology, and the instructor who assigns this text for a course that covers these fields as well as sociocultural anthropology will presumably treat them with the help of additional texts. A few suitable and readily available works in these fields are proposed in the Suggested Readings of Chapter 1.

Certain traditional materials even of sociocultural anthropology have been omitted, and some materials not ordinarily deemed anthropological, such as Max Weber's studies of India, China, and the West, have been incorporated. With the accelerating pace of modernization and the resulting rapid transformation of non-modern societies, social and cultural anthropology is increasingly training its sights on the problems of transition to modernity, on the new nations, on the great traditions of the Near and Far East, on complex societies generally, and on our own society in particular. These trends have brought anthropology into closer touch with the other social sciences—history, political science, sociology. A text that did not reflect this movement would fail to reflect one of the most dynamic features of contemporary anthropology. Nor could a text be considered truly contemporary if it failed to consider a related and equally important movement within current anthropology: the revival of interest in the process of sociocultural evolution.

A final characteristic of this book is its emphasis on *culture*, especially religion, and its deliberately limited treatment of technology, environment, and economics. This is not meant to imply that techno-economic factors are unimportant in sociocultural evolution, for clearly they are of great importance. But since certain anthropological schools have treated such factors as the prime movers of evolution, we strive to correct the bias by emphasizing the contribution of religion. Religion is a kind of gyroscope that sustains the stability of a wide range of social activities and institutions; it can also become the generator of widely ramifying social changes. Analysis of religion is therefore remarkably revealing of the values and operation of society and of broad-scale social change.

Recognizing the difficulties of analyzing subjective phenomena such as religion, we acknowledge the advantages of concentrating on more objective factors such as technology and economics. We are reluctant, however, to de-emphasize a fundamental facet of human life and sociocultural evolution simply because it is difficult to measure and dissect objectively. The temptation to concentrate on the easily discernible, and for that reason to assign it the status of prime mover in the evolutionary process, is great. The fallacy in such a procedure is illustrated by the following parable, recounted by the philosopher Abraham Kaplan.[3] A drunk, having dropped his keys in the gutter, proceeded to search for them on the sidewalk under a street light. A passerby, noting that the gutter was the place the drunk had dropped his keys, asked him why he did not search there instead of on the sidewalk. The drunk replied, "There's more light up here." The moral is that the place most easily lighted is not necessarily the place to find what one is searching for.

In revising this book, we have been led by comments from readers to add certain sections—for example, a discussion of the dynamics of modernization in Chapter 4 and additional materials on peasantry in Chapter 7. We have slightly elaborated or up-dated some of our remarks on contemporary America, but retain a discussion of certain writings that have ceased to be faddish. An example is the school which proclaimed the Death of God. Dissection of this image and its wider implications remains a powerful means to grasp fundamental directions of modern religious life, and no recent symbols distill so dramatically what we take to be the essence of contemporary religious thought. Certain now-classic notions of American society (e.g., *The Organization Man*) have been retained because they signal the advent of a major era in American life—one which later years and recent analyses continue to elaborate. The major additions to the previous edition of this work are two new Chapters, 2 and 3. Chapter 2 sketches the history of social and cultural anthropology, and Chapter 3 expounds the anthropological view of social patterning (exemplified by systems of kinship) and of cultural patterning (exemplified by religious systems). The object of these new chapters is to initiate a general understanding of social and cultural anthropology before elucidating the evolutionary perspective.

We would like to express our deep appreciation for the comments, suggestions, and encouragement of Ingrid Kirsch, Lucy Milner, Jeannette Mirsky, Florence Peacock, and Amelie Rorty, and for the scholarly assistance of Mark Leone and Martin Silverman. Professors Arthur Vidich, Robert Smith, and Robert Bellah read the manuscript, provided helpful advice, and, in the case of Professor Bellah, provided an orienting scheme for the entire work. We should also express our gratitude for the assistance of the Prentice-Hall editors and staff.

J. L. P.
A. T. K.

SECTION

I

SOCIETY
AND CULTURE
IN ANTHROPOLOGICAL
PERSPECTIVE

The objective of this section, which comprises chapters 1, 2, and 3, is to introduce the central anthropological notion of social and cultural patterning. Chapter 1 treats the concept of pattern, modes of interpreting patterns, types of pattern, and, finally, introduces social and cultural patterning. Chapter 3 deepens the analysis by the extended examples of kinship and religious systems—analyzed to display, respectively, the logic of social and of cultural patterning. Chapter 2 provides historical background for appreciation of contemporary anthropological views concerning social and cultural patterning.

Section I, then, should provide basic understanding of what is perhaps the central perspective of social and cultural anthropology. One is then prepared to apply this perspective in addresssing various issues and questions. One such application is the concern of the remainder of the book: What is the direction in which societies and cultures evolve?

1

On the Study
of Society and Culture

As Raymond Firth's ship neared the beach of the tiny Pacific island Tikopia, he saw a crowd of natives bustling about in response to his visit. Firth, a British anthropologist, later reflected:

> Even with the pages of my dairy before me it is difficult to reconstruct the impression of that first day ashore—to depersonalize the people I later came to know so well and view them as merely a part of the tawny surging crowd.... In his early experience in the field the anthropologist is constantly grappling with the intangible. The reality of native life is going on all around him, but he himself is not yet in focus to see it. He knows that most of what he records at first will be useless: it will be either definitely incorrect, or so inadequate that it must later be discarded. Yet, he must make a beginning somewhere. He realizes that at this stage he is incapable of separating the patterns of custom from the accidentals of individual behavior, he wonders if each slight gesture does not hold some meaning which is hidden from him.... He is conscious of good material running to waste before him moment by moment: he is impressed by the vastness of the task that lies before him and of his own feeble equipment for it in the face of a language and custom to which he has not the key.... At the same time, he is experiencing the delights of discovery, he is gaining an inkling of what is in store; like a gourmet walking round a feast that is spread, he savors in anticipation the quality of what he will later appreciate in full.[1]

Cast into the midst of this "tawny surging" crowd, the anthropologist finds himself in a world whose laws and dimensions he cannot yet fathom. Confused by the shock of strangeness, he hungers after understanding; in Firth's word, he "savors" the quality of that which he will someday appreciate and comprehend. This appreciation and comprehension will perhaps yield intense insight, similar to that of psychoanalysis, Zen meditation, or some other deep emotional/intellectual quest. But to put all of this less mystically: The anthropologist craves, even as he is absorbed in the concrete events of native life, to *formulate* a *pattern* in terms of which events can be explained. After that pattern is formulated the events appear logical and comprehensible.

The term *formulate* is important. The anthropologist in the midst of an exotic milieu does not see, hear, or touch a pattern—any more than a physicist in the laboratory sees, hears, or touches, a thermodynamic law. The pattern, like the law, is an intellectual construct rather than a perceived event. Patterns and laws are formulated to explain perceived events, and conversely perceived events furnish a basis for formulating patterns and laws. But the events he experiences are not the only basis on which the anthropologist formulates patterns. Along with his camera and notebook, the anthropologist brings prior concepts to his field experience, and these concepts influence his formulation of pattern perhaps as much as the experience itself.

Some of the concepts that the anthropologist brings to the field are specific. He may arrive with a hypothesis in mind, for example, that a system of marriage has political effects, and in the field he may collect data relevant to this hypothesis. Other concepts that he brings are more general. Some are so general, in fact, that together they comprise an *anthropological view,* a broad perspective on human behavior that most, although perhaps not all, anthropologists share as a result of their training and experience. Just as there is the historical view of human behavior, the statistical, the psychological, and the economic, so there is the anthropological view, which, when combined with these other views, yields a sharpened vision of human affairs. The purpose of this chapter is to introduce the reader to the anthropological view.

Patterns

A pattern is more than the list of its parts. To describe the parts that compose a pattern is not sufficient to describe that pattern; the relations between the parts must also be described. Thus, if one went no further than describing each of the four sides of a square, one would fail to achieve a description of a square; the four sides could also form a rhombus. To make clear that one refers to a square and not to a rhombus, one must define the relations between the sides. In this case, that means defining the angle of the corner formed by the joining of any two sides. To describe both the parts and their relations to each other is to describe a pattern.

Formulating patterns rather than just listing parts is one practice essential to the role of the anthropologist. The explorer, by contrast, often simply recounts the various parts of a group's life without going very deeply into the relations between these parts. From an explorer we might learn that society X lives in a marshy plain, that it grows rice, and that it enjoys the custom of polygyny, in which ideally each man possesses many wives. We would not expect to learn much about how these customs interrelate since analysis of this sort is not the explorer's purpose. The anthropologist, on the other hand, feels compelled not only to describe these separate customs but also to grope toward an understanding of the way they interlock. He might succeed in showing that the custom of polygyny allows a distribution of labor, for example, that allows rice to be grown under the particular conditions imposed by the marshy plain setting. Thus, the anthropologist would formulate a simple pattern.

Imagine that some anthropologist were to take a liking to Mae West's classic remark that the important thing is "not the man in your life, but the life in your man." If he then happened to recall the exhortation of President Kennedy that one should ask not about "what your country can do for you," but about "what you can do for your country," the anthropologist would realize that the West and Kennedy remarks follow a single pattern. Trying to formulate that pattern, he would observe that both remarks are based on the rule, "Restate a phrase or clause, reversing the position of certain words in the original statement." The anthropologist would thereby have formulated a simple pattern.

Modes of Formulating Patterns

The perceptive reader may have sensed a difference in the manner of formulating patterns illustrated by the example dealing with Mae West and President Kennedy, and that illustrated by the example dealing with rice and polygyny. In the rice/polygyny example, the anthropologist formulated what we call a *functional pattern*. In the West/Kennedy example, he formulated what we call a *logical pattern*. A functional pattern reveals working relations between elements of a group's life; a logical pattern reveals symbolic relations.

To describe the logical relations among the elements of a group's life, one simply shows that the various elements derive from a single principle or rule. Thus, both the Kennedy and the West remarks were derived from a single rule. Another example of a logical pattern in language concerns the rule of English grammar, "Add -ed to form the past tense." The child who has not yet learned the exceptions to this rule often applies it inappropriately by saying "comed" or "bringed" for the past tense of "come" or "bring." These errors are derivations from a rule. By formulating the rule and listing its behavioral derivatives, the anthropologist formulates a logical pattern pervading an area of American life. Such logical patterning is not restricted to the realm of language. For example, Americans are legally bound to stay on the right-hand side of the road while driving, and they also tend to stay on the righthand side of the sidewalk while walking. These two behaviors can be derived from a single rule, "Stay on the right."[2]

The key relationship in a logical pattern is the relationship between rules and derivations. The key relationship in a functional pattern is the relationship between conditions and consequences. Thus, the anthropologist tried to show that polygyny is a social condition that prompts an agricultural consequence—rice growing in a marshy terrain. A folk saying offers an excellent illustration of the condition/consequence relationship.

> For want of a nail, the shoe was lost; for want of the shoe, the horse was lost; for want of the horse, the rider was lost; for want of the rider, the battle was lost; for want of the battle, the kingdom was lost, and all for the want of a horseshoe nail.

This saying could be diagrammed as a chain, with each element a condition of the next element on the chain and a consequence of the previous element.

A functional chain is often circular, as in the case of a certain kind of electric circuit. When this electric circuit is activated, the switch makes contact with a magnet, but in doing so breaks the circuit. The magnet loses power and the switch moves out of contact. This, of course, again closes the circuit, with the result that the switch reestablishes contact with the magnet. Again the circuit is broken . . . and so on. Similar circular systems are found in society.

It is usually a mistake to think of a chain or circle of functionally related elements as a row of billiard balls—each imparting motion to the next upon contact. The relationships are often less direct. For example, the first American consul in Japan, Townsend Harris, was visited by a Japanese officer who asked if he could borrow Harris's horse. Harris said yes. A few days later he discovered that the horse of the Japanese prime minister, as well as the horses of all his officers, had been shod.[3] Now, introducing the horseshoe to Japan did not cause a sudden appearance of Japanese men talented at copying the mechanical inventions of the West. Men with the capacity already existed, as fully matured adults, at the time the horseshoe was introduced. But the presence of such men was functionally related to the introduction of the horseshoe. Because such talent was already present, the horseshoe could be copied; because it was copied successfully, new opportunities for developing such talent were generated; because such talent was then utilized, a favorable atmosphere for other technological innovations emerged. Thus, a system of complicated functional interrelationships must be unraveled to explain the historical process, and one must avoid the temptations to think in terms of the simple, slam-bang causality of the billiard ball example. It is not as though horseshoes were thrown at the heads of the Japanese men, thereby causing mechanical talent to spring full-blown from those heads.

No matter where they are or what they are analyzing, anthropologists tend to interpret their observations and experiences in logical patterns, in functional patterns, or in a combination of these two. Broadly speaking, when the anthropologist analyzes or synthesizes he formulates the logical or functional relationships among elements of a system.

Interpreting Events in Terms of Patterns

As he struggles to formulate the patterns expressed by native life, the anthropologist is also trying to interpret each particular custom or event in terms of that pattern. The task is surprisingly difficult, especially since everyone, layman and anthropologist alike, tends to perceive particular events as if they were not part of the native's society and culture, but, by some sorcery, a part of the society and culture of the observer.

A Western audience looks at films depicting the behaviors of certain non-Western peoples. African Masai are shown spitting on one another; African Basuto, hissing at each other; African Bi Rom, shaking clenched fists at one another; and the Toda of South India are shown thumbing their noses at one another.[4] The audience's natural impulse is to conclude that in each case war is imminent. Yet studies of the Masai, Basuto, Bi Rom, and Toda indicate that all the gestures depicted are meant kindly. The Masai spit on each other to express their feelings of benediction. The Basuto hiss to express respect. The Toda and the Bi Rom express friendly feelings by fist shaking and nose thumbing. Thus, the audience's initial intuition proves wrong. The spectator is interpreting, more or less unconsciously, the native actions as if they were Western actions. He is ascribing familiar meanings to foreign behaviors, not realizing that the same physical act may assume different meanings in different cultures. Thus emerges the simple but important principle: *Interpret native actions in terms of native patterns.*

This principle can have some very practical consequences. Among the many reports issuing from anthropologists who served as World War II advisers to the armed forces came one from the late Clyde Kluckhohn. Discussing the American military's interpretation of Japanese behavior during World War II, Kluckhohn writes:

> Most of our top military men reasoned this way: We know that the Nazis are fanatics, but the Japanese have proved themselves still more fanatical. How can leaflets and broadcasts possibly affect soldiers who will go readily into a Banzai charge or fight under hopeless conditions in a cave, finally blowing themselves to pieces with a hand grenade? Why should the lives of our men be risked in attempting to secure more prisoners when it is obvious that Japanese prisoners will not provide us with intelligence information?
>
> The generals and admirals who argued in this fashion were highly intelligent men. In common-sense terms their picture was perfectly sound. Common-sense was not enough, for it assumed that all human beings would picture the same situation to themselves in identical terms. An American prisoner of war still felt himself to be an American and looked forward to resuming his normal place in American society after the war. A Japanese prisoner, however, conceived of himself as socially dead. He regarded his relations with his family, his friends, and his country as finished. But since he was physically alive he wished to affiliate himself with a new society. To the astonishment of their American captors, many Japanese prisoners wished to join the American army and were, in their turn, astonished when they were told this was impossible. They willingly wrote propaganda for us, spoke over loud speakers urging their own troops to surrender, gave detailed information on artillery emplacements and the military situation in general. In the last six months of the war some Japanese prisoners flew in American planes within forty-eight hours after their capture, spotting Japanese positions. Some were allowed to return within the Japanese lines and brought back indispensable information.[5]

Kluckhohn's explanation for the inability of Americans to predict or understand how Japanese could so easily shift allegiance, yet display fanatical courage during a Banzai charge, is oversimplified (as are many anthropological sermons), but it is still suggestive. The Americans, says Kluckhohn, were raised in the Judeo-Christian tradition of absolute morality: the same code is demanded for all situations. By contrast, Japanese morality is situational.

> As long as one was in situation A, one publically observed the rules of the game with a fervor that impressed Americans as "fanaticism." Yet the minute one was in situation B, the rules for situation A no longer applied.[6]

The Americans, perceiving Japanese behavior in terms of the principles of absolute morality, found it difficult to shake the conviction that any soldier who responded with fanatical loyalty in one situation, as the Japanese soldier did, could assume a totally different loyalty in another situation. The Americans perceived the fanaticism of the Japanese in their caves as if it were an event in the life of Americans. They did not analyze it as an event in the life of the native himself.

Ethnocentrism and Grand Theory

Violation of the principle *Interpret native action in terms of native patterns* is called *ethnocentrism*. Even the anthropologist, whose professional creed and training sensitize him to the dangers of ethnocentrism, never wholly escapes this bias. The field anthropologist, whose task is only to record accurately what he observes, is plagued enough with the disease of ethnocentrism; the grand theorist is doomed to even more suffering. The analyst of a single society can at least try to record the behaviors of the natives in terms of their own concepts; the grand theorist, who wishes to compare many different societies, can never do so in terms of the concepts or categories of any one society. Rather, he must strain to define a single set of categories that will apply to all the societies he compares. And since his categories inevitably derive from his own society's intellectual traditions, he is even more likely to commit the crime of ethnocentrism than is the analyst of a single society.

To illustrate the conflict between the grand theorist and the field anthropologist, suppose that each is confronted with the transcript of a commercial reportedly heard over All India Radio:

> Use Jayanti Miracle Oil internally for cancer and externally for eczema. Jayanti Miracle Oil brings furniture to a high polish, removes rust stains from metal, and is an excellent cooking substitute for ghee. Use Jayanti Miracle Oil on your hair, on the floor, and in the kitchen....[7]

The broadcast prompts the grand theorist to speculate excitedly that lack of specialization in Indian social roles is paralleled by their unspecialized material substance. Just as an Indian Brahman can be both priest and cook, so Indian oil can be used for both eczema and furniture. By contrast, in America roles are specialized and so is material substance. Priests specialize in being priests, cooks in being cooks, and similarly cooking oil specializes in being cooking oil, hair tonic in being hair tonic. The field anthropologist objects to such comparison on the grounds that it is ethnocentric. *Role* is a concept of Western social science, as is *speciali- zation,* and even *priest* and *cook.* To be properly understood, the Indian must be described in terms of his own categories. "But how can you compare India and America if not in terms of some abstract category such as *role* that applies to both societies?" asks the grand theorist. Com- parison of societies poses a dilemma for the anthropologist who would avoid ethnocentrism.

Silent Patterns

The anthropologist does not expect to find a native word for every significant unit of the native pattern, nor does he expect to meet a native who can fully verbalize that pattern. It is the anthropologist who has the task of formulating the native pattern. Those facets of the pattern which the anthropologist formulates, but which the native cannot or ordinarily does not verbalize, are called *silent patterns.*

Formal, Informal, and Technical Patterns

Edward T. Hall, in his engaging book *The Silent Language,*[8] suggests the distinction between *formal patterns* and *technical patterns.* If a pattern is formal, the group adhering to it feels that it defines *the way* its members, or certain of its members, should act. If a pattern is technical, the group adhering to it feels that it defines *a means* to achieve a desig- nated goal. A group of scientists might regard precise thought as the way to think—as a custom valuable in itself regardless of any purpose that it might or might not serve. By contrast, they might regard any given mathematical technique as merely a means to achieve precision of thought, and if a new technique came along that promised to achieve this goal more efficiently than did the old technique, they would happily drop the old in favor of the new.

In all societies, including our own, ideas about time are part of formal patterns; that is, without stopping to think about it, we and other natives simply assume that time is what we have been brought up to believe it is. *Year* is a formal unit in the Western time system. For Westerners, year means 365 days plus one fourth day that is accounted for by adding an extra whole day to the year every fourth (leap) year. Although Westeners take it for granted that time is measured in years, the year once was more a technical unit than a formal one. Egyptian priests who created the year as a device for calculating the annual Nile floods perhaps saw it in a technical way since for them the year was simply a means to achieve a designated goal. Yet today the year is part of a formal pattern in the West.

Americans assume without question that time is like a straight line. Every event can be imagined as occurring between two points on this line. The age of dinosaurs lies some distance back on the line; the American Revolution is much nearer to our present position. Gestation stretches for nine months along the line, death is no broader than a point. All events of our lives and of history or prehistory can be plotted on this one universal line we perceive as time. For those who have grown up thinking linearly it is completely natural to assume that this is just the way the universe is built.

Yet Hopi Indian tradition apparently did not include the concept of a universal time line along which all events could be located and measured. Each event had a shape of its own, unrelated to any other. Corn matured. Women gestated. Lambs became sheep. It did not occur to the Hopi to measure obviously different processes or events in terms of the constant units—minutes, weeks, months, years—that would make up a universal time line. Some claim that even today the Hopi find following a schedule or meeting a deadline difficult and unnatural. Thinking in terms of schedules requires classifying a wide variety of events by placing them sequentially on a single abstract line. In Hopi tradition the notion of such a line would be meaningless.

Americans think formally of time sequence as evidence of causality. *Post hoc, ergo propter hoc* ("after the fact, therefore because of the fact") may be a fallacy in logic, but it is very much a part of American thinking. The occurrence of one event immediately after another leads us to look quite naturally for a causal relationship between the events. Our thinking follows the billiard ball pattern: The cue ball is the cause, and when the ball it slams into moves, that is the effect. It is natural for us to think this way since the idea of *causation* is part of our formal culture, built into the structure of English grammar and elaborated in the world of science and technology. But this is not the way all men think. As early as 1890, Sir James George Frazer, in *The Golden Bough*,[9] advanced the notion that some men think sympathetically rather than causally. According to sympathetic belief, if one native were in the jungle hunting, and another native back in the village touched oil, then the hand of the hunter would turn slick on his spear. This would not be attributed to any direct causal relationship between the two events. It is not that the hand touching oil at home somehow would set up a conduction through ground or air that would eventuate in the hand getting greasy in the jungle. Rather, hand-at-home and hand-in-jungle are alike, hence in sympathy. Therefore, it is believed that one greasy hand *becomes* the other.

Americans, assuming that time is a straight line with a beginning and an end, have traditionally viewed work as an activity directed toward an end, with the proper path toward that end being the "straight and narrow." To allow onself to stray from that path is sinful. Thus, Americans resent interruptions. Very different are the Trobriand islanders of the Western Pacific who, it is said, do not particularly mind interruptions; to them, time is not a line along which one moves, but a puddle in which one wallows.[10]

Probably the American's formal assumptions about time affect even his biological behaviors such as sleep. Americans are brought up to believe that a certain space along the daily time line, eight hours, should be devoted to uninterrupted sleep, yet observers of those tribal cultures which are not obsessed by a time line have remarked on the ability of the natives to miss sleep with no evidence of harm.[11]

Assumptions about time are good examples of formal patterns, for we naturally assume that the way time seems to us is objectively the way it is. All formal patterns carry such assumptions—they are taken to be universal truths. Precisely because we do not question them, we do not think about them, and so they are *silent patterns:* It is difficult or impossible for us to put them into words. But the anthropologist is in a position to dissect such patterns even if, as in these last examples, he is actually dissecting himself.

Informal patterns are yet another type of social pattern the anthropologist may discern. They differ from the formal in that they are less absolute a definition of the way a society's members should act, yet they resemble the formal patterns in that they are hard to verbalize, and therefore silent. To illustrate informal patterns, Edward T. Hall[12] analyzed the punctuality rules of American businessmen. He concluded that American businessmen adhere to the following informal code: Being three minutes late for a business appointment is not serious enough to require comment; being four minutes late calls for an unintelligible remark; and being five minutes late requires a short apology. By contrast, Hall cites a country where an hour's tardiness is equivalent to five minutes in America, where fifty minutes equals our four minutes. The American ambassador to this unnamed country was once visited by local diplomats, who arrived at a time such that they were not so punctual as to be obsequious, yet not so late as to be insulting: they arrived fifty minutes late. The meeting did not go well, and the ambassador later remarked to his colleagues, "How can you depend on these people when they arrive an hour late for an appointment, then just mutter something?" The ambassador felt this way, Hall maintains, because he was governed by American rules of punctuality. Not warned of the native patterns, he became annoyed when, after a fifty-minute wait, he received only the muttered equivalent of the American apology for a four-minute tardiness.

Ideal Patterns and Actual Patterns

Every anthropologist who has lived with and observed the natives of foreign society has discovered not only that the natives have trouble describing some of their patterns of behavior but also that some of their descriptions differ markedly from their actual behavior. Certain Brazilian Indians, for example, are fond of telling anthropologists that they live in villages laid out in the form of a bisected circle, but flying over such a village shows that this is not so. The Chinese provided a more complicated example. For centuries they have reported that they live in what anthropologists call *extended households* (households that, in addition to parents and children, include grandparents, aunts, uncles, and cousins). Even high school world history texts now dutifully report that the Chinese, before the Communist Revolution, lived in such households. But analysis of the way the Chinese actually lived reveals that only a tiny percentage of Chinese households, mainly those of the elite, were of this extended type.[13] Thus, a native stereotype of native society can mislead the unwary observer into assuming that native behavior follows a pattern that, in actual fact, it does not follow.

Linguistically Codified Patterns

One of the most provocative ideas about silent patterns is that a language structures the patterns of thinking and perceiving of those who speak it whether they are aware of it or not. Just as the artist and the geologist who look at the Grand Canyon may see it differently, so speakers of different languages preceive the world in different ways. Each language codifies its own distinctive perceptual pattern. A language's grammar is particularly important for such codification. This theory, still a center of debate, is most clearly illustrated by comparing English grammar to the grammars of languages outside the Indo-European family. Because the languages we are accustomed to call foreign, such as Greek, Latin, Italian, Spanish, French, German, and even Sanskrit, are all of the Indo-European family, they display grammatical patterns—and therefore perceptual patterns—that are similar to those of English. But the Hopi and Navaho languages, spoken by Indians of the American southwest, belong respectively to the Uto-Aztecan and Athabaskan families, and they seem to codify perceptual patterns that are radically different from those of English.[14]

Whereas English verbs change form to distinguish past, present, and future, Hopi changes form to distinguish fact, expectation, and law among events. When an English speaker sees a man running, he says "he runs" or "he is running" (both signifying "now"), but the Hopi speaker says *"wari"* ("running occur")—a statement of fact. When the runner has passed out of sight or has finished running, in English we say "he ran," "he has run," "he was running," but the Hopi would still put it *"wari"* ("running occur")—a statement of fact, if the speaker actually saw the runner. For future events, we say "he will run" (a statement of confidence in a future event) or "he shall run" (a statement of the speaker's compelling insistence that he *will* run in the future). The Hopi verb changes to *"warikni"* ("running occur I daresay"), a statement of expectation.

If an English speaker wishes to make a statement of law or regularity, such as "he runs on the track team," and even though such running could be placed in the past or the future, he would say "he runs." To express regularity, English simply uses the common present tense, but in Hopi, the verb must change its form to *"warikngwe"* ("running occurs characteristically").

In sum, English changes the verb form to express changes in tense: present ("he runs"), past ("he ran"), and future ("he will run"). Hopi changes the verb form to express changes in the epistemological state of events, that is, to indicate how sure the speaker is about the occurrence of the events in question. If the event is a fact, the speaker says *"wari";* if it is expected, he says, *"warikni";* if it is law, he says, *"warikngwe."* Hopi grammar is, therefore, radically different from English grammar: It lacks tense.

Navaho verbs, like Hopi verbs, differ from English and from other Indo-European verbs in that they do not necessarily express tense by their forms. The Navaho speaker is not compelled to indicate tense every time he utters a verb, as is the speaker of English. But the Navaho is forced by the grammatical structure of his language to indicate other categories. For example, Navaho verbs change their form according to the shape of the object involved in the action expressed by the verb. To simulate this pattern we might pretend that the English speaker must add a different shape of object. He would speak of "handlefying" poles (objects of a long rigid type); of "handleating" snakes (objects that are slender and flexible); of "handleificating" a cup of tea (objects of the container-with-content type; of "behandling" salt (objects of granular mass); and of "behandleificating" hay (objects which are bundled). The Navaho is forced to make just such distinctions by varying his verb forms.

How strongly do a language's rules of grammar affect the way its speakers think and act? This is the controversial question which anthropologists and linguists have debated for decades. On the face of it, it is hard to believe that the pattern of categorizing the world, forced upon a person by his language, would not affect his world view. The question is, how much does it affect it? And is the effect significant enough to warrant our attention? Evidence indicates that the grammatical rules do have significant effects on world view. As anecdotal evidence, Edward T. Hall recounts experiences with the traditional Navaho that illustrate how little the "future" meant to him—so little, in fact, that schedules and promises were irrelevant to Navaho culture. The reader will recall a similar comment regarding Hopi culture. Other evidence comes from an experiment by Carroll and Casagrande,[15] based on the Navaho pattern of changing the form of a verb according to the shape of the verb's object.

The experimenters hypothesized that, because the Navaho were brought up to categorize shape of objects by choice of verb form, Navaho speakers would learn to discriminate between the shapes of objects at an earlier age than English speakers—whose grammar does not force them to make such shape discriminations. Thus, since Navaho grammar forces discrimination between such objects as string or rope (long, flexible), paper or cloth (flat, flexible), and sticks or poles (long, rigid), Navaho speakers should perceptually and manually distinguish such objects earlier than English speakers. The subjects were 135 Navaho children. Some spoke only Navaho, some spoke both Navaho and English, and some spoke only English. The experiment was conducted in the Navaho language or, when appropriate, in English. Each child was presented with a series of pairs of objects, one pair at a time. After being shown a pair of objects, the child was shown a third object and asked to say which object of the pair most closely matched the third object. For instance, one of the pairs was a yellow stick and a piece of blue rope of comparable size. The child was then shown a yellow rope, and asked whether it went better with the yellow stick or with the blue rope. Thus he could choose to match similar shapes (ropes) that fall into a single Navaho verb-shape class (long flexible object), or he could match similar colors (yellow). It turned out that children who spoke only Navaho matched objects on the basis of shape with greater frequency than did children who spoke only English. Thus Navaho grammatical categories apparently do influence the way Navaho children perceive and manipulate the physical world. This experiment, coupled with other evidence, suggests that in spite of the controversy about precisely how much impact language has on perception of the world, there can be little doubt that grammatical categories do introduce some bias in perception and action, and that this bias is greater than most people realize.

Invisible Functions

Not only can we either fail to see the patterns that guide our lives, or assert as gospel patterns that aren't actually followed, but we may also overlook ramified functions of our social patterns: The ways in which these patterns contribute to our social and personal lives. The assumption that every pattern that serves a function was deliberately designed by somebody to serve that function is known as the *teleological fallacy*. Formerly, that "somebody" who was supposed to have created the patterns and completely understood their functions was God. Benjamin Franklin argued:

> God clearly wants us to tipple, because he has made the joints of the arm just the right length to carry a glass to the mouth, without falling short of or overshooting the mark: let us adore then, glass in hand, this benevolent wisdom: let us adore and drink.[16]

Franklin's argument is that because the arm serves the function of conveying drink to the mouth, God intended it to do so and knows that it does so. Teleologists more recent than Franklin impute such intention to agents other than God. Thus some students of biological evolution have written as if the ancient lungfish deliberately developed the rudiments of hands in order that, millions of years later, the primates could use those hands for grasping trees or tools. Similarly, some historians have written as if Calvinism could not have provided the cultural basis for capitalism unless the Calvinists had intended that it do so. Teleological arguments often confuse intention and consequence, purpose and function. They assume that if X serves a function, it must have been intended that it do so. Stated baldly, the argument is unfounded, but teleological thinking is still pervasive.

Anthropologists not only reject the notion that if a pattern serves a function some agent created it for that purpose, but they also—as a task central to their discipline—endeavor to contradict the notion that the agents involved in a pattern are necessarily aware of its function. They try to reveal ways in which patterns serve functions that are "invisible" to the natives. George Herbert Mead's analysis of crime and punishment nicely exemplifies such invisible functions.[17] The cry "thief" or "murderer," says Mead, unites the community in anger against the criminal, its common enemy. Yet, the criminal does not commit the crime with the conscious intent of uniting the community against him; nor do the people who become aroused against the criminal and scream for his execution do so with the conscious purpose of uniting themselves. In fact, if the community were aware of the positive function (the community's unification) served by the crime, their anger against the criminal might cool. But if the community failed to unite in anger against the criminal, the criminal would fail to serve his positive social function. Here apparently is a case where ignorance is useful to society; if society recognized and appreciated the benefits of crime and punishment, then crime and punishment could no longer supply those benefits.

The denial that a pattern serves a social function may, in some cases, actually increase the pattern's social effectiveness. For example, some artists in Western society insist that their art has no social function—that it exists for its own sake. (Humphrey Bogart, upon being asked if he thought art should carry a moral message to influence society, replied, "You got a message? Send it Western Union.") But this very claim perhaps enhances art's ability to affect society. People are often averse to being proselytized or inundated with propaganda. Such an attempt brings up their guard, and they tend to resist the message. Artists, disarming their audience of its resistance by denying that they want to preach or propagandize, may increase their actual power to do so.

A provocative theory set forth by George Devereux suggests that the silent function of art is to express socially unacceptable thoughts or acts in socially acceptable ways.[18] According to Devereux, an art form that is socially acceptable because of its beauty, refinement, or cleverness may express with impunity socially exceptionable content. As the saying goes, "I'm willing to listen to a dirty story if it's really funny." When the artist emphasizes form, argues Devereux, he is free to claim that the content really does not matter. For example, a youth who expresses his love for a girl by writing a poem can repudiate the poem's content if it becomes embarrassing by saying that it is just a poem and not really a declaration of love. By emphasizing form, the poet is able to express content that he could not express otherwise.

And conversely Devereux reasons that if art sanctions the illicit by means of refined form and beauty, then wherever form and beauty are emphasized there is an illicit message to be found. Accordingly, Devereux suggests that brilliantly scored staccato passages for bass instruments are really the composer's method of flatulating in public. Devereux wants to unveil the animal urges that he believes are served by high culture—whether we admit it or not. If nothing else, his theory is a useful part of the anthropological outlook: It prods the anthropologist into seeking out the illicit functions that respectable natives would often prefer not to see.

Shifting from a psychological to a sociological orientation, consider this notion: Many idea patterns that to the natives are formal—"the way," "God-given"—can be shown by the analyst to serve social functions that the natives do not ordinarily recognize. Natives are not brought up consciously to admit, for example, that beliefs which they hold sacred serve to support the *status quo;* yet analysis can often show that this is the case. For instance, the Hindu notion of cyclical time bolstered the position of the Indian elite, for this time concept involved belief in a cycle of rebirths according to which the status of a person—high or low—in his next life depended on how well he followed the law (*dharma*) in this life. Following the *dharma* required his being contented with the caste into which he was born. To rise from his caste in this life endangered his existence in the next; one overly ambitious might even be reborn an animal. Thus Hindu beliefs discouraged members of the low castes from competing with members of the elite castes for power and prestige. In a similar way, the Western notion of linear time may reinforce the class and society system peculiar to the West. The concept of time as moving in a straight line, made sacred in the Judeo-Christian notion of history, supports the idea of progress. And the idea of progress justifies the position of all progressives.

Like the psychiatrist, the anthropologist preaches the value of assuming, on proper occasions, an objective stance toward one's own behavioral patterns. The psychiatrist hopes to alleviate his patient's neurosis by forcing him to dredge from his subconscious those painful early experiences that presumably provoke his suffering, and to dissect those experiences coldly, as if they were specimens on a laboratory bench. The psychiatrist tries to lead his patient to a degree of objectivity that will enable him to analyze his own actions with the detachment of a man who is examining not himself but a character in a movie. In much the same way, the anthropologist would like to teach some of the natives (including himself) to view their entire society as if it were depicted on a movie screen—with all of its silent patterns and invisible functions in sharp focus.

Shared Patterns

All right, girls, into your stretch nylon denims! You know the ones—the ones that look like they were designed by some leering, knuckle-rubbing old tailor with a case of workbench back who spent five years, like da Vinci, studying nothing but the ischia, the gemelli, and the glutei maximi. Next, hoist up those bras, up to the angle of a Nike missile launcher. Then get into the cable-knit mohair sweaters, the ones that fluff out like a cat by a projecting heating duct. And then unroll the rollers and explode the hair a couple of feet up in the air into bouffants, beehives, and Passaic pompadours. Stroke in the black makeup all around the eyelids, so the eyes look as though Chester Gould, who does Dick Tracy, drew them on. And then put those patient curls in your lips and tell Mother—you have to spell it out for her like a kid—that yes, you're going out with some of your girlfriends, and, no, you don't know where you're going, and yes, you won't be out late, and for God's sake, like don't panic all the time, and then, with an I-give-up groan, tell her that "for God's sake" is not cursing.

At least that is the way it always seemed, as if some invisible force were out there. It was as though all these girls, all these flaming little Jersey teen-agers, had their transistors plugged into their skulls and were taking orders, simultaneously, from somebody like the Ringleader Deejay.

Simultaneously, all over Plainfield, Scotch Plains, Ridgefield, Union City, Weehawken, Elizabeth, Hoboken, and all the stretches of the Jersey asphalt, there they went, the Jersey teen-agers . . .[19]

This passage from Tom Wolfe's *The Kandy-Kolored Tangerine-Flake Streamline Baby*—a bit dated but still useful—vividly catches the idea of a shared pattern.

Obvious as it may be that teen-age conformists share a pattern, we are perhaps less accustomed to emphasizing the sharing of patterns by creative individualists. Devotees of an author such as James Joyce, for instance, stress his uniqueness—the individuality of his twists of language and his idiosyncratic perceptions. But if an anthropologist were to analyze the patterns that Joyce has in common with the rest of his society, the great mass of shared conventions and beliefs contained in his writings would loom into prominence, overshadowing the idiosyncratic elements in his image. For instance, a rough calculation would surely reveal that in spite of Joyce's liberties with the English language, he abides by more rules than he breaks. It would be most surprising, for example, to discover that he begins numerous words with *ng*. No such words exist in English, but more important, when native speakers of English are invited to coin new sound combinations, these rarely turn out to begin with *ng*. One of the unspoken but iron laws of English is "Never start a word with *ng*," and although speakers of English do not realize that they are doing so, they learn this rule early and follow it faithfully—so faithfully that they find it difficult even to pronounce words from foreign languages (such as the Malayo-Polynesian languages) that do start with *ng*. (Pronounce the Thai word *nguang* "to be sleepy" or the Javanese word *ngamang* "to speak.") If one were to list all the rules of English grammar and of literary form, and then all the laws, morals, conventions, and patterns of thought to which any creative artist unthinkingly conforms even when he is at his most creative, one might well conclude that we overemphasize the uniqueness of genius and we underemphasize the extent to which even the thought of a genius reflects patterns that he shares with others in his society. Doubtless, in the time of Cervantes or Pope (when authors were regarded as spokesmen for society) and in primitive societies today (where artists are regarded as conveyors of tradition to such a degree that they do not even sign their works), the public was and is not so entrapped by a faddish preoccupation with the unique.

Assuming a broad view helps one see similarities between what had previously appeared as idiosyncratic behaviors: One perceives shared patterns. Jazz aficionados will emphasize the originality, the uniqueness, of each inspired improvisation. Yet a broad comparative perspective can bring into sharp relief the patterns common to all the supposedly unique improvisations. Thus all jazz improvisations are based on the Western scale of seven tones separated by equal intervals, a feature that contrasts with all Balinse *gamelan* (percussion orchestra) improvisations, since these are based on a scale of five tones separated by unequal intervals.

There is yet another way in which the jazz musician expresses a shared pattern. Consider the hero in *Young Man with a Horn*.[20] He strains to hit a note on his trumpet that has never been heard before. In other words, he is a conformist. He conforms to the American tradition that each individual should strive to transcend tradition, should strive to create something new. The mandate for change is the central unchanging value of American ideology, and the young man with the horn is simply expressing a pattern that he shares with countless other tradition-bound revolutionaries.

Just as the physicist who stands back and surveys the universe as a whole perceives similarities between swinging pendulums and orbiting planets, so the anthropologist observing a society as a whole finds similarities among parts that are missed by narrower disciplines. The problem of narrow viewpoint is nicely illustrated by the Russian story about the worker who left the factory every afternoon with an empty wheelbarrow. Since the factory guards never found anything inside the wheelbarrow, the worker was always allowed through the gate. But weeks later it was discovered that the worker had been stealing wheelbarrows.

Culture and Society

We come now to two perspectives or concepts of particular importance: *culture* and *society*. *Personality* is a third concept that must be distinguished from both of these. Culture is a system of logically related ideas and values shared by participants in a social system, which in turn is a system of interacting roles and groups. Society is a particular type of social system. Personality is the system of behavioral components of an individual person.*

Returning to the crowd of natives that Firth encountered on the Tikopia beach, consider the cultural, social, and personality patterns that the anthropologist might abstract from his observations of a group of this kind. The anthropologist might treat such a group as a social system, *i.e.,* a system of interacting roles or groups. From this perspective, he would formulate the manner in which leaders relate to followers, old men to young men, men to women, members of clan *Z* to members of clan *Y*. The anthropologist might also treat the group as a cultural system, a system of logically related ideas and values: He might formulate the group's shared concepts of honesty and fair play, of good and evil, and go on to show how these ideas and values relate logically to each other. Finally, the anthropologist might depict the personality of each member of the group, laying bare the components that compose each person. He could, for example, portray the leader of the group on the beach as compensating for a sexual frustration by his domineering behavior. What must be remembered is that these three types of pattern—culture, society, and personality—are analytical, not concrete. They are formulated by the anthropologist. Although not themselves observable events in the group's life, they are based on the anthropologist's observation of such events. Nor are these patterns necessarily formulated by the natives, although the natives may well formulate patterns like those formulated by the anthropologist.

An important question is to what extent can a given analytical formulation explain concrete, observed behavior. We would say, for example, that one can go a long way in explaining the concrete, observed behaviors of Firth's beach group by considering it as a social system, while ignoring for the moment the idiosyncratic personalities of the individuals in the group. Obviously, varied personalities will be found in this group. Some will be boisterous, others reserved. Yet all members of the group will share certain traits. They are all there to greet Firth; they all display similar gestures in greeting; and they are all dressed similarly. Furthermore, many of the variations that do appear among the different individuals can be explained by the roles they play in the group; thus, the leader is domineering because he is the leader. And the assignment of each individual to a role often is influenced by other roles he plays in

---

*Our view of culture, society, and personality derives from Talcott Parson's action theory as first expressed in his *The Structure of Social Action,* chapter 19, more recently in his Introduction to Part IV of *Theories of Society.*

the society rather than by any unique talent he possesses; thus, the leader may have been chosen because he is the son of a chief. No amount of depth analysis of each personality within the group, by itself, would explain the group's concerted behavior. The considerable independence of the group's functioning from the functioning of any of the individual personalities that compose it would be revealed if a beach group of the same island in 1930 and one in 1940 were to display similar patterns (as is likely) even though the members have changed.

It is not only a small group, whose members are periodically collected within the sight of a single observer during a flash of time, that can be viewed as a social system; a more ramified system of social interactions can also be viewed in this way. For instance, the system of exchanges of money, goods, and services that we analytically define as the American economy can be viewed as a social system. As in the case of the beach group, the role a person plays in the American economy is not the only role he plays in life: He may be a son, father, husband, and hobbyist, as well as producer, buyer, and seller. No man, not even the dedicated captain of industry, plays a purely economic role every moment of his life. Therefore, when an economist analyzes an economy, he is not analyzing a system of total personalities. He is investigating relations among specialized roles, in this case economic roles. A social system such as the economy is thus treated as if it existed apart from the personalities who play specialized roles in it. The beach group continued to be the same group (in the sense that its patterns of interaction remained the same) even when its members changed; similarly, the American economy continues to exist through the years even though its personnel changes.

A society, like an economy, is large and ramified, but a society differs from an economy—which is a subsystem of a society—in that it encompasses all, or virtually all, aspects of its members' lives. Since a society includes economies, governments, families, schools, churches, and other subsystems, it includes the economic, political, familial, educational, religious, and other strands of the lives of its members. And because a society includes all of these subsystems, it is more self-sufficient than any one of its subsystems. The American economy, for example, cannot produce its own new members, but American society can. The American economy must recruit its members from another subsystem of American society: the family system, which has the means to give birth to new individuals. On the other hand, American society includes the family system, and is therefore self-regenerative. Although a society may recruit some of its members from outside, by adoption, conquest, enslavement, or immigration, it replenishes itself mainly from within.

Maintaining considerable control over its own territory is one way a society sustains its self-sufficiency. This does not imply that the boundaries of every society are clearly defined geographically. Such clear-cut boundaries—marked by fences, guards, and customs officials—followed the rise of modern national states, and are not found in primitive societies. An Australian aboriginal tribe, for instance, roams about a vaguely defined territory which, for religious more than governmental or legal reasons, it regards as its own. But however loosely defined this territory is, the tribe still considers itself to be in control of its own territory.

A society's members share a common culture—a pattern of ideas and values. A shared culture allows and encourages members of a society to get along well enough so that the society is not destroyed by civil war or anarchy. But since the shared culture in itself can hardly assure harmony, society also sets forth laws, customs, and procedures which control conflict and competition. The court trial, a means to resolve conflict, is one obvious example.

What is the relationship between culture and society? The distinction between a cultural system and a social system is analytical, not concrete, which means that by viewing a single episode of behavior, such as the behavior of the Tikopia beach group, the analyst can formulate either a social system, or a cultural system, or both. The same is true of all the behavior that passed before the observer's eyes during his stay on Tikopia. All the observations amassed might form the basis for two separate books. One, *The Culture of Tikopia,* would delineate logical linkages between the Tikopian conceptions of the cosmos, of society, of beauty. The second, *The Society of Tikopia,* would illustrate the way in which chiefs relate to followers, parents punish children, clans exchange wives, and other customary social relations. Some of the same observations would appear in both books, but each book would analyze these observations from its own perspective.

Although the cultural/social distinction is analytical in the sense that it is formulated by an analyst, it is also helpful in illuminating many concrete real divisions within behavioral systems. One can say, for instance, that universities are more culturally oriented than governments, and conversely that governments are more socially oriented than universities. American universities are more oriented toward maintaining the system of ideas and values that constitute Western culture, whereas American government agencies are more oriented toward maintaining the system of social relations that constitute American society. The distinction rests in the degree or emphasis; for although each organization is both culturally and socially oriented, each emphasizes one of these orientations to a greater degree than the other.

This notion of concrete analogues to the analytical cultural/social distinction raises questions about the concept of cause and effect. Since *cultural system* and *social system* (or *culture* and *society*) are different concepts which the analyst employs in viewing the same behaviors, we cannot logically speak of the cultural system as "affecting" the social system, or vice versa. This would be like saying that the volume of a body affects its weight, for *volume* and *weight* are two different analytical perspectives on the same physical body. Similarly, it would not be logical to say that a cultural system affects an observed group of persons, any more than one can say that a physics formula fires a rocket, for the formula is an analytical formulation which possesses no physical power in itself. On the other hand, by the so-called comparative method, we can show that if statements $x, y, z \ldots n$ regarding a group's cultural system are defensible, then statements $a, b, c \ldots n$ regarding that group's social system are likely to be defensible too. In other words, by surveying numerous societies, we can show that where ideas and values of a particular type are present, social patterns of a particular type are likely to be present also. Therefore, we *infer* that certain ideas and values are necessary for the existence of a particular type of social life, and vice versa.

One reason for emphasizing the distinction between social systems and cultural systems is the tendency of members of many societies to distinguish phenomena that are more cultural from those that are more social. As will be seen later, the more radically members of a society distinguish between their social institutions and relationships and a system of symbols representing cosmic or religious (cultural) ideas and values, the more dynamic, complex, and adaptive their society and culture are likely to be.

Overview

For the anthropologist, all men in all societies, including his own, are a "surging crowd" of natives. Entering any society for field study is much like Firth's experience upon arriving at Tikopia. Embarking on his study, the anthropologist resembles an infant: He must painfully learn to make sense out of the "booming, buzzing confusion" into which he has been thrust. To his task the anthropologist brings a kit of concepts, such as *culture, society,* and *personality.* In terms of these, he sorts and classifies his observations, his raw data, and order gradually emerges. The anthropologist formulates the patterns—logical and functional—that underlie observed behaviors.

Anthropologists are especially attuned to cultural differences. They must be aware of the difference in the meaning of shaking a clenched fist for Americans and for Bi Rom, of military action for Americans and for the Japanese, and of the more subtle differences in such things as perception of space and time that are codified differently in different languages. Their awareness of these differences cautions them against ethnocentrism—the interpretation of native actions in terms of the observer's culture. More positively, it sensitizes them to the need for interpreting the native's actions in terms of the native's world view. Among other things, this implies that key statements gleaned directly from native informants are very important anthropological data. Yet the anthropologist cannot base his formulations exclusively on the native's statements about his society and culture. The native's statements must be measured against the anthropologist's observations. The native often perceives his own society and culture as more closely approximating his ideals or his utopian visions than it really does. For this reason and also because the native is so accustomed to his way of life that he takes it for granted, an outside observer may perceive many native patterns that are "silent" to the native himself, many functions that are invisible to him. Although the anthropologist strives to see native behavior from the native viewpoint, he must also strive to see even more in native life than the native sees.

A more compelling reason for the anthropologist to transcend the native viewpoint is that he can never stop with analyzing a single society. The ultimate aim of anthropology is to understand the entire range of social and cultural phenomena—past, present, and future. Therefore, the anthropologist must analyze many societies and their cultures. Just as he formulates patterns that explain diverse (and apparently chaotic) behaviors within a particular society, so he must formulate the patterns that give order to the diversity among societies. Such formulation requires a conceptual framework that encompasses the features of many societies and cultures and is not restricted to the features of any one society or culture. We will turn later to a consideration of such a framework: a theory of sociocultural evolution.

Topics for Discussion

A basic fact confronted by the anthropologist is that of deep-seated cultural differences—most conspicuously, as we have seen, differences in world view and in perception of space and time. From the existence of such differences, the anthropologist must conclude that culture is not immediately given in the human biological structure and that it is not simply an induction from the encounters of individuals with the external world. And yet there is a powerful evidence that mankind is fundamentally one: Men are a single biological species and display basic psychic similarities. How is it possible to reconcile cultural differences with the unity of man? And what is the bearing of this question on the dilemma of the anthropologist who seeks to understand native society in native terms while of necessity remaining bound to his own culture? What assumptions must he make in order to believe that he can bridge the cultural gap between his own society and some other society?

Suggested Readings

Anthropological Fieldwork

Tristes Tropiques (paperback, English translation, 1964) by Claude Lévi-Strauss. Poetic, philosophical, written by the anthropologist who has supposedly usurped Sartre's throne as France's leading intellectual.

Return to Laughter (paperback, 1964) by Elenore S. Bowen. A novel providing a down-to-earth portrait of field experience.

"Curt Nimuendaju, 1883–1945" (1946) by H. Baldus. Life story of an anthropologist who went native, told in an obituary of Curt Nimuendaju.

In the Company of Man: Twenty Portraits of Anthropological Informants (paperback, 1964) edited by Joseph B. Casagrande. Vivid descriptions of the anthropologist in the field.

Women in the Field (1970) by Peggy Golde. Field experience of women anthropologists.

---

*Full facts of publication for each work cited in the Suggested Readings are provided in the bibliography. Information on distributors of films cited is provided in the film bibliography.

Methods and Styles in the Study of Culture (1974) by Robert Edgerton and L. L. Languess. Good general guide to fieldwork.

Field Projects in Anthropology: A Student Handbook (1974) by Julia Crane and Michael Angrosino. Outlines projects for learning fieldwork.

The Cultural Experience (1972) by James Spradley and David McCurdy. Field method illustrated by projects carried out in American society by undergraduates.

Patterning

Language (1921, paperback available) by Edward Sapir. Influential in the development of the concept of patterning in language and culture.

Language (1933) by Leonard Bloomfield. Provides a clear and detailed exposition of Grimm's Law, a convincing formulation of linguistic patterning which predicts patterned sound changes in Indo-European language (pp. 347 ff.).

The Silent Language (paperback, 1961) by Edward T. Hall. On the problem of inferring "silent" patterns.

Language, Thought, and Reality: Selected Writings of Benjamin Lee Whorf (paperback, 1956) edited by John B. Carroll. Provocative analysis of the relationship between the Hopi language and thought patterns.

The Navaho (paperback, 1956) by Clyde Kluckhohn and Dorothea Leighton. Analysis of the relationship between the Navaho language and thought patterns (chapter 8).

Language in Culture and Society: A Reader in Linguistics and Anthropology (1964) edited by Dell Hymes. Includes perspectives of the Whorfian as well as the newer ethnoscience school which is concerned with methodologies for formulating cultural patterns in terms of the native's own categories.

"Residence Rules" (1956) by Ward H. Goodenough. An example of the ethnoscience approach and a particularly precise statement of the difference between native categories and those used for the purpose of comparing societies.

Culture, Society, and Personality

Culture: A Critical Review of Concepts and Definitions (paperback, 1963) by Alfred L. Kroeber and Clyde Kluckhohn. On the concept of culture.

Sociology: A Systematic Introduction (1960) by Harry M. Johnson. On the concept of society and social systems. Provides the best simplified exposition of Talcott Parson's ideas, on which this book bases its discussion of society, culture, and personality (chapters 1 and 2).

Personality in Culture (1967) by John J. Honigmann. On the notion of personality, especially as conceived by the anthropological culture-and-personality school. An exhaustive treatment.

Culture, Personality, and Behavior (1973) by Robert Levine. An effort at theoretical integration of cultural and psychological studies.

Biology and Culture

The Evolution of Man's Capacity for Culture (paperback, 1959) edited by James N. Spuhler.

The Human Animal (paperback, 1960) by Weston LaBarre.

"The Human Revolution" (1964) by Charles F. Hockett and Robert Ascher.

Evolution and Human Behavior: An Introduction to Darwinian Anthropology (1973) by Alexander Alland.

These four suggestive discussions deal with the biological characteristics of man that allow (or force) him to develop culture.

Introductory Texts

In the Beginning: An Introduction to Archaeology (1975) by Brian M. Fagan.

Prehistoric Archaeology: A Brief Introduction (1969) by Frank Hole and Robert Heizer.

Physical Anthropology: A Perspective (1973) by John Buettner-Janusch.

Human Evolution (1972) by J. B. Birdsell.

An Introduction to Language (1974) by Victoria Fromkin and Robert Rodman.

In an introductory course on general anthropology, these texts may suitably supplement *The Human Direction,* in order that the four major fields of anthropology (physical, archaeological, and linguistic, as well as sociocultural anthropology) may be covered.

Films

The Hunters. A compelling portrait of a Kung bushman hunting expedition in the northern Kalahari desert.

Dead Birds. A poetic interpretation of the Dani of West New Guinea.

Dynamics of Male Dominance in a Baboon Troop. Caricatures human society and thus encourages an objective view of that society.

The Baboon Troop (Amboseli Reserve). Caricatures human society.

Four Families. Dramatizes social perspective by portraying Indian, French, Japanese, and Canadian patterns side by side.

The Loon's Necklace. Depicts exotic gods and myths.

Glooscap County. Depicts exotic gods and myths.

Trance and Dance in Bali. A Balinese dance-drama-trance featuring an oedipal struggle between witch and dragon.

Bear and the Hunter. A lyrical account of a bear hunt in northern Lapland.

The Navaho as Filmmaker. A series of seven films made by the natives themselves.

The Nuer. A beautiful visual portrait of a society classic in ethnographic writing.

The films are selected for their ability to sensitize the viewer to exotic patterning. For descriptions of other ethnographic films as well as information on reviews of films and readings pertaining to them see Karl G. Heider's *Films for Anthropological Teaching* (1968).

chapter 2

The Development of Anthropological Thought Concerning Society and Culture

In order to appreciate both the possibilities and limitations of contemporary anthropological thought, it is useful to trace its history. Among the insights thus gleaned is a sense of the movement in anthropology from a preoccupation with origins to a concern with patterns. Yet the logic of this history points also to a reemergence of anthropological interest in social and cultural evolution, perhaps with special focus on the future.

When did anthropology begin? There are almost as many answers to this question as there are anthropologists. In part this variety is due to the different ways that anthropologists define their discipline. For some, anthropology is the discipline that asks the broadest and most general questions concerning human beings: What is the nature of human nature? This question leads to more specific ones: What is the significance of the biological, social, and cultural differences and similarities of human groups? What is the place of human beings in the natural order? To pursue such questions anthropologists have developed some distinctive ways of studying human groups. However, the broad inquiry into the nature of man is certainly not the exclusive property of anthropologists; it is the concern of biologists, theologians, philosophers, psychologists, and many others. Indeed, this inquiry is not confined to scholars—it is endemic in human life and has been addressed by every culture since the beginning of human existence, crystallized in world views that define the meaning and significance of the natural, social, and supernatural world.

A narrower view of anthropology is that it is a scholarly discipline, which is to say that it boasts a distinctive body of problems, methods, and knowledge which is closely tied to formal organizations such as professional associations and academic departments that bear the discipline's name. This view emphasizes the roots of anthropology in the Western cultural tradition (but recognizes its spread into the non-Western world) and thus can pinpoint more precise origins. Even so, there are ambiguities. Some historians of anthropology seek the beginnings of anthropological thinking in the philosophies of ancient Greece (such as those of Plato and Aristotle), and even more specifically in the writings of the fifth century (B.C.) Greek writer Herodotus whose extensive travels resulted in rather modern ethnographic descriptions of the environment, artifacts, beliefs, and behaviors of peoples of the eastern Mediterranean. Other historians of anthropology stress the contributions of the Italian Renaissance, for scholars of this epoch introduced a comparative dimension by their fascination with the differences between their own culture and that of classical antiquity. Still others have stressed the influence of social philosophers of the European enlightenment of the seventeenth and eighteenth centuries, invoking the writings of men such as Thomas Hobbes, John Locke, and Jacques Rousseau. These writings culminated in a social *science,* a conception of inductively verified laws of social pattern and development. And, finally, some would emphasize that it was only in the nineteenth century, with the advent of scholars ranging from Bachofen to Sir Edward Tylor and Sir James Frazer, that anthropology became a clearly delineated field of study, addressing the problem of formulating the similarities and differences among the entire universe of human groups worldwide and throughout history. It was this epoch that marked the first formal recognition of anthropology in Western academic institutions: Sir Edward Tylor was appointed Reader of Anthropology at Oxford University in 1884, and Franz Boas' appointment at Clark University in 1888 marked the first such recognition in the United States.

It would be fascinating to accept the broad view of anthropology and attempt to track its antecedents and parallels throughout human history and the human scene. One would have to consider the fact that many societies conceive themselves to be the only people, or the only true people, as is reflected in their groups names. For example, the Navaho call themselves *dene* which can be translated as "the people," and the Ancient Jews termed themselves "the chosen people." That this kind of ethnocentrism, which is probably at some level universal in human groups, can give rise to anthropology is illustrated by the ancient Chinese. China saw itself as the Middle Kingdom, the center of the human universe and civilization. Non-Chinese, no matter how highly developed their culture or how complex their society, were considered "barbarians" who automatically owed subservience to the innately superior Chinese civilization. This perceived discrepancy between Chinese and barbarians resulted in the appointment of officials—ancient anthropologists—whose duty it was to record the customs and characteristics of those barbarians who suffered the misfortune of living beyond the borders of China or in its hinterlands.

Reflecting on the Chinese example is sufficient to remind us of our own Western ethnocentric assumption, less blatant than in the past perhaps but still present, that *we* are the center of the universe and the corollary that, therefore, it is legitimate to support a group of specialists (i.e., anthropologists) whose task is to record the customs of others. Accepting the truths in this diagnosis of the origins of anthropology in the ethnocentrism of a culture, we shall proceed to examine in more detail the history of the discipline conceived in the narrower perspective sketched above. That is, we define here anthropology as an outgrowth of Western culture, and we shall endeavor to track the major developments within this specific Western context that gave rise to the field as we now know it. Narrowing the compass still more, we shall trace anthropology back to the transformation from the medieval to the modern sociocultural order in Europe. Since various aspects of that transformation are discussed in detail in chapter eight, here we highlight only major factors.

Anthropology and the Transformation of Medieval Europe

The medieval social order was basically feudal and hierarchical, and its political and religious hierarchies were intertwined and mutually supporting. Latin, the language of education, was known only by a small elite who were preoccupied with ideas defined by the religious orthodoxy. Scientific advances certainly did occur, but as the experiences of Copernicus (1473-1543) and Galileo (1564-1642) attest, knowledge of the world was subordinate to theology. If this was true of the physical world, it was even more true of the human realm. The metaphor of the "great chain of being" hypothesized that the animate world was a gradation from God to the lowliest creature, and that all peoples were positioned within this theologically defined framework.[1] The spatial expanse of the world was believed to be known in broad outline, as were the temporal dimensions. Thus, the Bishop of Armagh, James Ussher (1581–1656) concluded after painstaking biblical research that the creation recounted in Genesis had occurred in 4004 B.C. This date was incorporated into the authorized Bible and scriptural commentaries and was widely accepted. For medieval man, then, the world was stable and small and its history short. All of this was to change dramatically with the religious reformation that was to come in the sixteenth century.

With the Age of the Reformation the feudal order was eroded and replaced by the nation-state, either monarchical or republican. Serfs became peasants, and industrialization produced cities that turned peasants into tradesmen and workers. Both vernacular languages (instead of Latin) and expanded literacy were encouraged by the fifteenth-century invention of the printing press and by religious reformers who required personal knowledge of Holy Scripture to guide individuals' lives. The dominance of the Church and hierarchy was destroyed and Western society became more diverse. These changes in life were connected to a transformation in world view. Medieval assumptions based mainly on religious orthodoxy were questioned, producing an intellectual vacuum that eventually was to stimulate the ideas of the Enlightenment.

Francis Bacon (1561–1626) and Isaac Newton (1642–1727) were two among many who challenged the medieval assumptions about the physical world and initiated the Enlightenment approach which was more empirical and inductive. Newton's demonstration of uniform laws of gravitation was especially influential in proving the power of an experimental-inductive inquiry and suggesting that it could be generalized to social phenomena as well.

Enlightenment thinkers sought to rethink fundamentally the question of human nature and society, and they rejected such medieval assumptions as Aristotle's dictum that social life is given and fixed by natural law and man need only assume his proper place. On the contrary, Thomas Hobbes (1588–1679) concluded, social life is not given by nature but voluntarily entered by man to alleviate his continual state of fear. According to Hobbes, the original state of nature was a war of all against all in which human life was "nasty, poor, brutish and short." Each individual gave up some of his natural liberty and vested it in a central state apparatus, a Leviatnan, which used this delegated power to enforce social rules and provide security for all. John Locke (1632–1704) and David Hume (1711–1776) were other thinkers who denied that human qualities were innately given by nature; they argued that the individual entered the world like a blank sheet of paper; human qualities were imprinted through experience. Though his views were diametrically opposed, Jean Jacques Rousseau (1712–1778), like Hobbes, speculated on the state of nature prior to man's creation of a social order through a "social contract."

The views of these Enlightenment figures illustrate the ferment and questioning concerning the nature of human nature that pervaded the postmedieval era, and these thinkers established orientations still fundamental in social science and philosophy, not to mention ideology. Thus, Hobbes classically articulated the problem of how order can exist in society and the relationship of the individual to his society. (Emile Durkheim's subsequent study, *The Elementary Forms of the Religious Life,* published in 1915 directly addresses Hobbes' formulation.) And Locke's views were absorbed in the political ideologies of subsequent generations, including the founding fathers of the United States, whose notions that all men are created equal and endowed with certain inalienable rights and that governments derive their just powers from consent of the governed were incorporated almost word for word from Locke into the Constitution and the Declaration of Independence. For anthropology, a specific influence derived from the Enlightenment thinkers' use of evidence drawn from the exotic peoples of the world. Thus, Locke's view that the right to own property was fundamental to man in a state of nature drew on his readings about the American Indians. And Rousseau's view of the idyllic state of man in nature was influenced by reports of life in Tahiti based on Captain James Cook's voyages in the South Seas. Also important for freeing thought were the satires of Jonathan Swift and Voltaire; the satirical sense that one's social life is arbitrary was honed by the knowledge of variety in human societies which came with discoveries of exotic peoples. Such influences reveal relations between the Age of Enlightenment and the Age of Discovery.

The great voyages of discovery were initiated by Prince Henry of Portugal (1390–1460) in an effort to break the Arab sranglehold on trade with the Orient. Initially the early voyagers, such as Columbus (1451–1506), simply believed they had found a new way to the already known world. But gradually the explorers realized they had encountered a world quite different from that known to medieval Europe; Amerigo Vespucci (1451–1512), for whom America is named, is credited with first stating that the voyagers were encountering a *new* world.

The West was gripped with excitement as each new voyage discovered new lands and peoples, and accounts of these discoveries were immensely popular. Some were by the voyagers themselves; others were summarized by such scholars as Richard Hakluyt (1552–1616) and Samuel Purchas (1557–1626) or in tomes such as the Jesuit *Relaciones'* twenty-three volumes published between 1610–1791. Missionaries such as Garcilasso de la Vega wrote on the Inca, Bartolome de las Casas on the

Aztecs, Jean Francoise Lafitau on the Indians of North America, and others on the peoples of South Asia and Polynesia.

Proliferating knowledge concerning peoples of the world not only provided material for the Enlightenment thinkers but raised perplexing problems for the theologians. Were these newly discovered peoples fully human, comparable to the peoples of Europe? The high civilization of the Inca and Aztecs suggested yes; the rude state of the Tierra Del Fuegans and Australian aborigine seemed to say no. Pope Paul III resolved the question at least for Catholics in his encyclical *Sublimus Deus* issued in 1537, which decreed that these peoples were indeed human and, moreover, capable of conversion to Catholicism. Yet, the Pope's decree by no means assured benign treatment much less equality among Europeans and others. The concept of the "great chain of being" permitted the others to be conceived as a lower level, and Christian theology could see their customs and beliefs as deserving obliteration because they were the work of the devil.

Yet another dilemma was posed by the sheer diversity of the newly discovered peoples. Although the Reformation had attacked much Christian orthodoxy, it had by no means undermined all. Indeed, scripture had gained in importance as the influence of the established Church hierarchy waned. What, then, could be said of the Biblical account of creation and the peopling of the earth in light of the new discoveries? Bishop Ussher's date of 4004 B.C. for creation provided little time to account for the emergence of so varied a lot, and certainly the Near Eastern confines of the Bible did not encompass the Pacific and the New World. Striving to accommodate discoveries to scripture, scholars hailed the Indians as descendents of Noah, dispersed after the Flood, or one of the lost tribes of Israel. Such queries crystallized in two opposing viewpoints regarding creation, known as monogenesis and polygenesis. Supporters of monogenesis—which included such figures as the great French naturalist Buffon (1707–1788) and Samuel Stanhope Smith (1750–1819), a president of Princeton University—held that the Biblical account of Genesis was literally correct and that the great variety of peoples would be explained by differing environmental conditions into which the first men had rapidly spread. Supporters of polygenesis included such men as Count Joseph Arthur de Gobineau (1816–1882), whose views later influenced Nazi racial theories, and Samuel George Morton (1799–1851), a Philadelphia physician and professor of anatomy. They held that each race of man had been specially created by acts of divine intervention, hence each had its own immutable God-given characteristics. Mixing was therefore sinful and detrimental.

The dispute between monogenists and polygenists in the human arena had its counterpart in the field of nonhuman biology. Cuvier

(1769-1832) argued for the immutability of all species of plants and animals, while his opponent Lamarck (1744-1829) argued for the inheritance of acquired characteristics. Lamarck theorized that environmental change could rapidly produce change in form, even from one species to another. Lamarck's experiments could not be replicated and he fell into disrepute (though his views were subsequently given official sanction in Soviet biology for a time). Not until 1859 did a kind of variation on Lamarck's concept become widely accepted, and this was Charles Darwin's (1809-1882) theory of evolution. Darwin's theory was based on detailed observations of variations in flora and fauna that he had made during the voyage of *H.M.S. Beagle* (1831-1836), particularly on the Galapagos Islands off the coast of western South America. Observing that the adjacent islands and mainland had similar but slightly varying forms, Darwin concluded that all these forms must have had common ancestors, and that variation had come about as an adaptation to varying conditions. He reasoned further that less adaptive varieties became extinct while adaptive ones flourished and reproduced. This theory of "natural selection" was able to explain how, over a period of time, a species could be transformed. While Darwin reflected for many years on his findings, A. R. Wallace (1823-1913) had arrived at similar conclusions based on lengthy research in Malaysia and Indonesia. Darwin and Wallace published their views jointly in the *Journal of the Linnean Society* in 1859. In this same year Darwin published his book *The Origin of Species by Means of Natural Selection, or the Preservation of Favored Races in the Struggle for Life.* Although Darwin did not systematically pursue his ideas to explain human variety, such Darwinians as Thomas Huxley did, and ever since the revolution in scientific thought introduced by Darwin has had profound repercussions for anthropology.

As the Industrial Revolution developed in Europe there was growing interest in the physical structure of the earth as a source of coal and other raw materials for industry. This interest encouraged the development of geology and that field experienced issues similar to those confronting biology.[2] During the eighteenth and nineteenth centuries a major geological dispute concerned which forces had shaped the surface of the earth. The dominant view was set out by Abraham Gottlob Werner, professor of mineralogy at Freiburg in Saxony. Werner held that all rock formations were precipitates, either chemically or mechanically, from aqueous solution. Originally, he believed, the earth had been covered entirely by water, and the rock formations that formed the earth's surface could be correlated with different stages when the earth had been innundated by floods. Hence, Werner's followers were known as Neptunists; their adversaries were known as Vulcanists. The Vulcanist position was set out by James Hutton in *Theory of the Earth* published in

1795. Hutton argued that geology should emphasize processes observable today rather than speculate about those no longer operable, and he stressed the role of heat rather than floods. The Vulcanists believed the pressures of heat had caused the rise and fall of mountains and continental masses. Neither Vulcanists nor Neptunists questioned the accepted Biblical chronology and for both a key event was the Biblical flood. Discovery of aquatic fossils remote from existing bodies of water was interpreted as confirming the Biblical account.

The view that the surface of the earth had been formed by such catastrophic events as the Biblical flood was definitively undermined by the publication of Sir Thomas Lyell's *Principles of Geology, Being an Attempt to Explain the Former Changes of the Earth's Surface by Reference to Causes Now in Operation,* based on the views of Hutton. Lyell gathered all available evidence on the formation of the earth's surface through presently observable processes and dynamics and showed that for these forces to shape the earth would require a considerably longer time span than was widely accepted through Biblical chronology. Lyell's book, published in three volumes between 1830 and 1833, helped to broaden the time frame in which the earth was to be viewed just as the voyages of discovery had broadened the spatial frame.

A related development in geology had to do with methods of dating rock strata and fossilized life forms. William Smith, a hydraulic engineer concerned with reclaiming farmland from the sea, investigated the fossils found in various rock formations. He observed that some fossil forms found in lower rock strata disappeared in higher strata, being replaced by other life forms. Smith also observed that mammalian remains did not occur in lower strata but did in higher ones. Smith concluded that higher strata were geologically more recent than lower and that the various fossils contained in the strata demonstrated the evolution of life forms. Using strata and fossils one could date, at least relatively, the successive levels at any particular site or other sites where the same strata and fossils were found. The significance of this point had previously been obscured by the debates about the significance of cataclysmic events in forming the surface of the earth. This stratigraphic view was important not only for geologists, but also it subsequently became a key tool of archaeological research when they came to study prehistoric populations. The stratigraphic view seems to have provided an implicit model for nineteenth-century anthropologists as well, for they saw cultural evolution in terms of levels of development. Primitive peoples were "living fossils."

While these developments were occurring in biology and geology, parallel ones emerged in archaeology. Here too scholars were becoming aware that the Biblical chronology was too short to include their discoveries. C. J. Thomsen, the curator of the Museum of Northern Antiquities at Copenhagen, arranged and classified various prehistoric discoveries in a sequence of Stone, Bronze, and Iron Ages. This sequence, which had been anticipated by the Roman poet Lucretius (ca. 91–51 B.C.), came to be accepted for most of the prehistory of Europe and extended to other areas of the world as well.

In France, a customs officer and amateur archaeologist named Jacques Boucher de Perthes (1783–1868) discovered roughly chipped stone axes imbedded in rock formations near the town of Abbeville. Such stone implements had been found before but were popularly believed to be accidents of nature, and there was also a superstition that they were the thunderbolts of the gods. Boucher de Perthes concluded that these stone axes had been produced by human populations of far greater antiquity than had been dreamed of before. Though de Perthes' findings were ridiculed by some, the British geologist Falconer persuaded Lyell to visit the Abbeville sites and observe the great age of the rock formations in which the axes were embedded. Lyell did so in 1859, the year of Darwin's publication of *Origin of Species,* and his support helped gain recognition of de Perthes' chronology.

The final realm in which ancient prehistory was demonstrated was that of fossil man. Fossilized skeletal material was found in a limestone cave in the Neanderthal region of Germany in 1857. The skull of this skeleton was much larger than that of the modern human, with a low forehead, a flattened dome, and large, nearly fused brow ridges. The significance of the find was debated. Virchow declared the skull was merely that of an idiot, but in 1863 the Darwinian Thomas Huxley agreed with the German pathologist Schaafhausen that the Neanderthal skeleton was that of a primitive human race that had occupied western Europe in prehistoric times long past.

In sum, the transformation of the medieval world view broadened the West's perspective on the origin and history of humankind. From an essentially static, theologically and scripturally defined view, scholarship moved toward a more inductive and dynamic perspective based on the findings of biology, geology, archaeology, and paleontology, and on the remarkable discoveries of the explorers. Mankind was now seen to boast a long history, a wide expanse, and great variety—longer, wider, and greater than was portrayed in the literally interpreted Bible. Furthermore, the formulations of scholars such as Darwin set the stage for viewing human nature and human history in an evolutionary perspective, to see life as moving through gradual transformations spurred by the need to adapt to a changing environment. While this evolutionary perspective has thus far been reviewed primarily as it emerged with reference to man's physical and biological existence, the viewpoint was seminal also among those who found an anthropology that addresses society and culture.

The Formative Era

From the mid-1800s, anthropological and ethnological societies were founded in Europe and the United States and there appeared publications that marked the emergence of anthropology as a discipline. A sampling of these works includes: *Allgemein Kulturgeschichte der Menschheit (Universal Culture History of Man)* published in seven volumes from 1843 to 1851 by Gustav Klemm, then followed by other significant volumes in the German language during the years 1859–1861; Waitz' *Anthropology of the Natural Peoples;* Bastian's works on ancient history and psychology; and Johann Bachofen's *Das Mutterrecht (The Mother-right)*. During the next forty years were published the classic works in the English language, largely by Britishers: *Primitive Marriage. An Inquiry into the Origins of the Form of Capture in Marriage Ceremonies* by John McLennan, and Sir Henry Maine's *Ancient Law, Its Connection with the Early History of Society and its Relation to Modern Ideas,* both in 1861; John Lubbock, Lord Avebury's *The Origin of Civilisation and the Primitive Condition of Man* in 1865, and Sir Edward Tylor's *Researches into the Early History of Mankind and the Development of Civilization* the same year; Lewis Henry Morgan's *Systems of Consanguinty and Affinity of the Human Family* in 1871, and his *Ancient Society, or Researches into the Lines of Human Progress* in 1877; Sir James Frazer's multivolumed *Golden Bough* beginning in 1890; and Alfred Haddon's *The Study of Man* in 1898. Lucien Levy-Bruhl published his *Les fonctions mentales dans les societies inferieures (How Natives Think)* in 1910.

Many of the points in these works had been anticipated by writers of antiquity and the Enlightenment, but what is significant about these formative works is that, taken together, they signal the emergence of a coherent and distinctive anthropological world view. Indeed, one can now speak of a discipline, for this body of thought identified a set of problems or inquiries (largely directed to explaining cultural and social similarities and differences among the world's peoples), developed methods (e.g., comparative history), and coined standard technical terminologies (such as "endogamy," "exogamy," "couvade," and "totemism"). Significantly the discipline cut across national and linguistic boundaries, uniting an otherwise disparate group of individuals into a common program of scholarship. What was the world view of this formative discipline, and what were the points of difference and dispute?

Broadly speaking, the formative scholars agreed that all of humankind in all times and all places was the subject of anthropology, and that the approach to understanding this vast subject should be holistic— including biological, psychological, social, cultural, linguistic, and historical dimensions. Furthermore, the method should be naturalistic and inductive, divorced from the speculative deductions and theological presuppositions that had characterized previous reflections on mankind. The expanded temporal and spatial dimensions that were the fruits of the voyages of discovery and of the findings of geology, biology, and paleontology provide a framework within which formative anthropology could treat all human groups everywhere and in all epochs.

Within this overarching consensus lurked differences of opinion. Some emphasized the role of biological factors, such as "race," to explain why some peoples appeared more advanced than others. Klemm, for example, believed that there were "active" and "passive" races, the former being populations which significantly contributed to the progress of human civilization, the latter merely copying and transmitting traditions received from the activists. Others emphasized environment. Bastian, for example, believed that all humans had the same basic mental makeup (*Elementargedanken* or "elementary ideas"), and that differences among groups came from differences in environment, what he termed "geographic provinces." Already, then, the perennial "nature/nurture" debate was apparent: How much of human variation is due to genetic inheritance, how much to adaptation and learning in an environment?

Even more pervasive than this nature/nurture division was that between evolution and diffusion. Evolutionists emphasized the inventiveness of each society, the adaptive innovations that goaded them to move through different stages of development. Diffusionists emphasized the borrowing of one society from another, and they argued that similarities and differences among societies could best be explained by mixing and mingling that resulted from differential borrowing. At the extreme, diffusionists insisted that humans were uninventive, that progressive elements are invented only once then transmitted by diffusion from their point of origin. Grafton Elliot Smith and W. J. Perry, for example, believed that the fundamental elements of world civilization had been invented in ancient Egypt; thus they explained such elements as writing, astronomy, pyramids, and divine kings that were found unevenly distributed but in far-flung areas, such as the Near East, Middle America, and Southeast Asia. Less extreme diffusionists included Fritz Graebner (1877–1934) and Father Wilhelm Schmidt (1868–1954) who formed the *Kulturkreis* or "culture circle" school that plotted the spread of certain elements, such as art motifs, languages, and tools through waves of migration or diffusion. In America, such anthropologists as Clark Wissler (1870–1947) used a moderate version of this perspective by mapping the distribution of such traits as house types, clothing styles, and types of weapons within distinctive "culture areas."

Cultural evolutionism was perhaps the dominant point of view adopted by the most influential of the formative anthropologists. Evolutionary ideas had been explored by such Enlightenment writers as Saint Simon and Comte; however, the formative scholars were probably more influenced by the Darwinian synthesis of biological evolution and by geological and paleontological studies of extinct fossil forms and the earth's antiquity. Many cultural evolutionists thought that various cultures were stratified into different "levels" of progress and that contemporary primitives represented "living fossils" which told much about extinct and ancient ways of living. Despite differences of emphasis, the evolutionists broadly agreed that their task was to account for the development of human culture from its most primitive and ancient origins to its culmination in the institutions of the nineteenth-century West. This development was viewed as part of a temporal framework that encompassed all manifestations of human life in all times and places.

Three major stages of evolution were widely recognized: *savagery, barbarism,* and *civilization.* The nineteenth-century evolutionists rather took it for granted that their own society represented the most advanced civilized state, and hence their primary task was to examine the diverse variants from their own and place them in the sequence. Especially were they concerned to identify the most primitive traits, for these would reveal the origins of civilization.

Lewis Henry Morgan's evolutionary scheme illustrates facets of this early anthropological view. Morgan's work is interesting in part because he developed a comprehensive framework, but also because Morgan's views were adopted by Karl Marx and Fredrich Engels and became a part of accepted Communist ideology. Then, too, Morgan's formulations grew in part from fieldwork, for he became interested in anthropology through association with the Seneca Indians who lived nearby his home in Rochester, New York. The Seneca were part of the great Iroquois Confederacy of tribes, on which Morgan published a book in 1851. He became intrigued with the Iroquois manner of reckoning kinship which was "matrilineal," that is, children were considered part of the kinship group of their mother, but not that of their father. Morgan discovered that this type of kinship was found among other Indian groups and also in Asia, and this supported the diffusionist view that the Indians had originated from Asia. Morgan then sent questionnaires to traders, missionaries, and colonial officers throughout the world, inquiring about forms of kinship. This research, published in 1871 under the title *Systems of Consanguinity and Affinity of the Human Family,* demonstrated that the matrilineal type of kinship was widely distributed throughout the world—so widely that Morgan concluded that it represented a distinct stage in the evolution of civilization.

Morgan then sought to formulate a universal scheme of social and cultural evolution. This work was published in 1877 as *Ancient Society*. Here he showed how such features as subsistence, government, family, and property evolved through the phases of savagery, barbarism, and civilization. He de-emphasized religion, which he felt dealt with the irrational and among primitives was "grotesque and to some degree unintelligible" but he emphasized the family, a preoccupation found amongst other nineteenth-century evolutionists.

Morgan was convinced that the monogamous family of Western society was the most civilized known. Seeking to determine the least civilized, he postulated an ur-period, lost in the mists of ancient prehistory, when there was no family. In this dim twilight of mankind, he felt, people mated indiscriminately, "like animals," without regard to kin or other ties. This stage was known as that of "primitive promiscuity." He then set about determining how humans got out of this wretched state, and three family forms were especially strategic. These were the *consanguine* family, which was based on the "intermarriage of brothers and sisters in a group;" the *punaluan* family, which was based on the "intermarriage of several brothers to each other's wives in a group, and of several sisters to each other's husbands in a group;" and finally, the *monogamous* family of civilization. Thus, society progressed from a disorderly promiscuity through an ordered but incestuous group marriage to the nongroup, nonincestuous virtues of monogamy, a state for which "Morgan had a warm reverence," believing that "the whole previous experience and progress of mankind culminated in this one institution."[3]

Parochial and speculative as Morgan's arguments may seem today, they were based on imaginative and shrewd interpretation of existing data. For example, he assumed that kinship terminologies change more slowly than family forms, hence existing terminologies reflected *past* family forms. Thus, in the Malayan kinship terminology brothers, sisters, and their kinsmen of the same generation called all the children of the others by the same kin term as they used for their own children. Morgan interpreted this practice as reflecting a past stage of the consanguine family when brothers, sisters, and their various cousins mutually cohabited. Under this condition, paternity would not be known, hence all children of the group would be identified simply as "our children."

Despite numerous disagreements (for example, whether a matriarchial or a patriarchial stage came first in human history), the evolutionists shared certain fundamental perspectives that united them in a community of scholarship. For example, they typically treated each type of institution—kinship, religion, etc.—as a discrete entity isolated from the other institutions in society. Thus, Morgan singled out seven institutions and traced their evolution separately and did not systematically pursue the linkages of each to the others. Precisely such linkages between institutions were to become the dominant concern of a later generation of anthropologists who focused more on particular societies rather than the universal evolution of civilization that concerned the nineteenth-century evolutionists.

A second and related trait of the evolutionists was a lack of interest in fieldwork. Given their concern for painting vast panoramas, the evolutionists found themselves relying on synthesis of the materials gathered by travelers, missionaries, colonial officials, and embedded in historical accounts, rather than engaging in intensive "participant observation" of particular communities. The evolutionists have been criticized by later generations for indulging in "armchair speculation" and "conjectural history;" they sat in the study or library and drew together the various reports on peoples they had never seen (Sir James Frazer reportedly replied, when asked if he had ever met one of the savages to which he had devoted thirteen hefty volumes, "God forbid!"). It is said that had they had direct experience in the field they would not have stumbled as they did into their parochial and sweeping dicta. This criticism is not entirely just, for many of the evolutionists did engage in some field investigation. Tylor, for example, had visited the Caribbean and Mexico; Maine had been a colonial officer in India; Morgan had contact with the Iroquois; and Bastian was an inveterate traveler who visited Africa and Asia for long periods. It is true that the evolutionists did not suffer through the prolonged "participant observation" in a single community which, in later anthropology, was to drive home a sense of the complexity and subtlety in the way societies and cultures are patterned. It is also true that such intensive field experience was largely irrelevant for the vast issues that the evolutionists tackled.

As anthropology developed, it became clear that information was needed which was not present in the reports of nonanthropological observers, or which needed to be collected more systematically. Hence, anthropologists began to make field trips of their own, typically, at first, in group expeditions that resembled those of explorers who sought new areas of the physical world. Thus, in 1898–1899 the Torres Straits expedition set out from Cambridge University. The party included psychologists and physiologists who were equipped to measure differences in primitive and civilized peoples in such areas as perception, intelligence, and the ability to withstand pain and heat or cold. W. H. R. Rivers (1864-1939), who was a member of this expedition, published an article in 1910 that formulated a standard method for systematically collecting data on kinship organization, and this kind of technique was used in subsequent field trips. But these were still expeditions—short visits to out-of-the-way peoples to gather standardized data before moving on to another group—rather than intensive long-term fieldwork in the manner of later anthropologists.

A final focus of the formative anthropologists was on the past. They looked backward, from the vantage point of the civilized, at the savage past where humanity was believed to have begun. Even diffusionists started with a contemporary distribution of elements or traits and traced that distribution to its origin. And even as anthropology moved out of the formative era, this focus on the past remained. Thus, Franz Boas, a pioneer in moving anthropology beyond the formative stage by rejecting the sweeping conjectures of both evolutionism and diffusionism and emphasizing firsthand fieldwork, geared his work to reconstructing the "memory culture" of American Indians.

In sum, the last half of the nineteenth century saw anthropology in its formative years as a discipline. Encompassing all humankind in space and time, this formative anthropology shared a holistic and naturalistic approach. The era saw the synthesis of a vast body of information on humankind, the development of methods to delineate similarities and differences manifested by human beings throughout the world, and a technical vocabulary for describing these features. With the advent of the twentieth century, however, anthropology experienced a shift in perspective so significant that the formative anthropologists would now doubtless find much that is unfamiliar in the discipline which they themselves had created.

The Transition to Classical Sociocultural Anthropology

The transition from formative to classical anthropology was not sudden or decisive. Such formative features as the commitment to investigating the entire human spectrum and to holistic methods remained. Specialization was, however, apparent. Just as each anthropologist began to specialize intensively in particular areas of the world, so did each specialize in some facet of study—linguists in language, archaeologists in material culture, physical anthropologists in biology, and ethnologists in society and culture. Still, all anthropologists were expected to have some knowledge of all specialties and of all peoples.

If any single occurrence signals the transition from formative to classical anthropology, it was Bronislaw Malinowski's extended period of intensive field work in the Trobriand Islands during World War I.[4] Malinowski (1884–1942) was born in Poland. He had originally planned to become a physicist but he chose anthropology after an illness that set him to reading Frazer's *Golden Bough*. Malinowski first went to Leipzig where he studied with Wilhelm Wundt (1832–1920), the great German experimental psychologist who also had an interest in folk culture. He then went to England and studied with Edward Westermarck (one of the early opponents of the notion of primitive promiscuity) at the London School of Economics. There Malinowski attracted the interest of C. G. Seligman (1873–1940) who had participated in the Torres Straits exped- ition and was a firm believer in firsthand anthropological research. Seligman arranged for Malinowski to accompany him to Australia for a meeting of the British Association in 1914. World War I broke out while they were there, and Malinowski, as a citizen of the Austro-Hungarian Empire, was technically an enemy alien. The Australian authorities permitted Malinowski to sit out the war in New Guinea and the Trob- riand Islands. After a brief expedition to New Guinea, Malinowski spent the period from 1915 to 1918 living intimately with the Trobrianders, learning their language and sharing their lives. He was not the first anthropologist to spend an extended period with a non-Western group (A. R. Radcliffe-Brown had carried out research in the Andaman Islands from 1906 to 1908; many Americans had experienced extended contacts with Indian groups; and of course such travelers as Burton and Doughty had lived for long periods with foreign societies). But the type of inten- sive fieldwork that Malinowski reported in his publications beginning in 1922 became the dominant way to conduct anthropological research. The shift in method from armchair theorizing to first-hand research also marked a transformation of the anthropological perspective: the choice of problems to be researched, data to be gathered, and mode of explana- tion.

This shift can be illustrated by comparing Malinowski's Trobriand studies with the research interests of formative anthropology. For the formative evolutionists, kinship and marriage were among the several strategic institutions employed to map the evolution from primitive to civilized. To do this evolutionary analysis, anthropologists would abstract kinship systems from any particular setting and locate them on an evolu- tionary scale for comparative purposes. Thus, matrilineal kinship was taken by Morgan and other evolutionists to symptomize an intermediate stage between "group marraige" (Morgan's consanguine family) in which paternity was difficult to establish, and a later patrilineal stage.

Living among the matrilineal Trobrianders, Malinowski discovered dimensions of matrilineality that had escaped the evolutionists. For example, he discovered that rights to land for horticulture among the Trobrianders were vested in matrilineal clans as was political power. Such relations between economics, politics, and matrilineage had been recognized by Morgan in his study of the Iroquois but he had not pursued this aspect in his evolutionary theories. And Malinowski discovered interesting living arrangements. The Trobrianders had a complicated residence rule which required that siblings of different sex separate as they approached maturity. As children, brothers and sisters lived with their mother and her husband (i.e., their father), but as they grew up, the male child was expected to live with his mother's brother in another village while the female child would go to live with her husband in his village when she married (and this would be the village of *his* mother's brother, while this girl's brother would bring his wife to live with them when he married). That is, men, once they matured, stayed put in the villages of their mother's brothers, while their wives moved in with them. All of this meant that the men were always living in villages whose land was controlled by their own matrilineage, whereas married women were always living on land controlled by their husband's matrilineage. Thus, even though rights to land were traced through women, it was the men and not the women who had rights to the land on which they were residing: matrilineality certainly did not mean matriarchy. Had an evolutionist observed such a pattern, he might have labeled it "transitional" between matriarchy and patriarchy. Malinowski saw instead that the complex of kinship, marriage, land holding, and politics constituted a stable, enduring, functionally integrated system.

Myth was another important focus of formative anthropology. Diffusionists had tracked the distribution of myths to reveal histories of routes of past migration and contact, for example. Malinowski saw myth differently, not as a reflection of past history but as a charter for present life: "a reality lived, not a story told." Drawing on his extensive knowledge of Trobriand kinship and society, Malinowski was able to discern that myths served as charters to testify to the land rights of particular clans for example, as when a myth telling of a clan's origins in a given site proved its rights to that site. Again, Malinowski's field experience helped him see institutions and forms, customs and beliefs not as discrete and isolated elements that "evolved" or "diffused," but as parts of living systems.

After World War I, intensive fieldwork like that of Malinowski became the preferred method for cultural and social anthropological research and was in fact virtually required for a doctorate in these fields. A monograph describing a particular tribe or village known through at least a year of intensive "participant observation" was the typical result of such research, and the list of classic monographs is too long to repeat. A few examples are Richard Thurnwald's (1869–1954) *Economics in Primitive Society;* A. R. Radcliffe-Brown's (1881–1955) *The Andaman Islands;* Melville Herskovits' (1895–1963) *Rebel Destiny, Among the Bush Negroes of*

Dutch Guiana; Robert Redfield's (1897–1957) *Tepoztlan, a Mexican Village;* E. E. Evans-Pritchard's (1902–1973) *Witchcraft, Oracles and Magic Among the Azande;* Margaret Mead's (1903–1978) *Coming of Age in Samoa;* Raymond Firth's (1901–   ) *We, The Tikopia;* and the various monographs by Malinowski.

These works and others of their type signalled that a new consensus had emerged in anthropology. Fieldwork, not armchair speculation, was the desideratum. Analysis of how elements of a social and cultural system fit together in a particular habitat and community, rather than the formative comparison of institutions abstracted from their ethnographic context, was the norm. This shift was fundamental.

Despite commonalities in the new perspective, notable differences were also apparent. Thus, in the emerging classical British anthropology Radcliffe-Brown rivaled Malinowski for leadership and Radcliffe-Brown's perspective clashed in one important respect with Malinowski's. Malinowski saw culture as an adaptive response to biologically and psychologically based human needs. Technology was a response to the need for food and shelter, kinship and marriage to the drive toward reproduction and sex. Radcliffe-Brown held that social anthropology was an autonomous discipline which required social rather than biological and psychological explanation; rather than tracing technology to hunger or kinship to sex, Radcliffe-Brown emphasized that the task of the anthropologist was to analyze the relation of such forms and institutions to the social structure in which they were embedded.

A second difference was between British and American social anthropology. The transition from evolutionism to "structural-functionalism" whether of the Malinowskian or Radcliffe-Brownian variety is clear among the British, while it is less so among American anthropologists. Franz Boas had already been encouraging field studies to reconstruct disappearing Indian cultures so that the fieldwork tradition to a degree existed already in America. At the same time, considerable interest in historical reconstruction remained as well. As Americans broadened their sphere of interest beyond American Indians to the rest of the world, they overlapped often with the British and other Europeans, who were also working in these areas. Yet, Americans preserved a somewhat distinctive orientation. They tended to emphasize the study of "culture" instead of "society," to look for "configurations" rather than "structures," and to stress relations between parts (e.g., great and little traditions, language and culture, and culture and personality) rather than a monolithic social structure.

Despite these and other differences, an overarching consensus did characterize the new epoch. Fieldwork was virtually the only acceptable mode of carrying out anthropological research. This involved analysis of how elements of a single society and culture fit together in an integrated and enduring *system,* in contrast to the formative emphasis on comparison of elements abstracted from their context. This consensus had important implications.

Viewing societies as integrated and bounded systems to be observed in the present through fieldwork encouraged the view that they were also in equilibrium. Thus, classical anthropologists displayed a certain conservative bias in that they wrote as though the status quo observed during fieldwork always had been and always would be. This style of reporting observations in the "ethnographic present" lifted a community out of its specific context in time and reified it into an eternal structure: "the Nuer," "the Australian aborigines," or "We, the Tikopia."

Viewing cultures and societies as integrated systems also discouraged efforts at systematic comparison between one society or culture and another, for one's primary task was to show how parts of a given system related to the whole. This approach led to the philosophical doctrine of cultural relativism. Such practices as infanticide, cannibalism, and headhunting, which had drawn the condemnation of formative anthropologists as signs of savagery were analyzed by the classical anthropologists as elements in a larger social and cultural pattern. They might not condone such practices, but they could not, without admitting ethnocentrism, condemn them either; instead, they must explain them as *relative to* the local context.

Although they emphasized stability, the classical anthropologists could not deny change. However, change was viewed as abnormal, an intrusion into the system from some external source—conquest, natural disaster, or cultural contact. Any change might upset the delicate integration of social and cultural systems, but the classical anthropologists also held that change could be beneficial if properly introduced. For example, the introduction of improved health delivery systems or improved agricultural technology might improve the lives of the natives. Applied anthropology originated as a way of studying directed change of this sort and finding ways to smooth the introduction of such changes in the least disruptive way.

In sum, the post-World War I classical consensus differed in fundamental ways from that of the formative era. Social and cultural anthropologists concentrated on the study of social and cultural systems through intensive fieldwork, and this focus encouraged several features: a view of society and culture as an integrated whole; an emphasis on the present instead of the past, and on equilibrium instead of change, except where change must be "relieved" as in applied anthropology; and finally, the doctrine of cultural relativism. In many ways, the classical paradigm still dominates social and cultural anthropology, and much of its viewpoint is reflected in our first and third chapters.

World War II and Its Aftermath

World War II suddenly made areas of Asia, Africa, and the Pacific strategic, and anthropologists were called on to use their expertise concerning the peoples and cultures of these regions. Though wartime conditions did not permit classical fieldwork in these strategic areas, anthropologists carried out studies of "culture at a distance." Drawing on the holism and functionalism learned through field experience, anthropologists synthesized published materials, interviews, and other data to construct integrated pictures of the foreign cultures of concern. Probably the best known of such studies is Ruth Benedict's *The Chrysanthemum and the Sword* which presented an insightful though biased view of the Japanese. Other anthropologists aided in the establishment of training programs by the military which aimed to upgrade the language and area knowledge of those involved is the war effort overseas.

Prior to World War II there had not been many professional anthropologists in Europe and the United States, and few universities provided such training. After the war, American colleges and universities expanded as a response to the interest of returning servicemen in gaining advanced education supported by the G.I. Bill. Anthropology benefitted from this expansion, as new departments were established and many, including servicemen who had been involved in the foreign area and language training, sought advanced degrees in anthropology. With the Cold War, the government as well as private foundations also contributed to this expansion by providing support for area programs that would insure that the expertise needed to understand the various strategic parts of the world would be available for any emergency. A further rationale was to train experts who could assist in the economic development and modernization of the newly independent countries of the non-Western world and who could provide aid in the administration of those parts of the world assigned to the United States for U.N. Trusteeship. As beneficiary of these trends anthropology grew and so did the number of anthropologists.

As the world changed following the war, so did anthropology. Yet the classical paradigm continued, including the emphasis on structural-functional analysis of social and cultural systems through intensive fieldwork. Many postwar developments, only a few of which will be sketched here, elaborated this classic mode.

The relation between culture and personality became a focus for some postwar American anthropologists. Studies demonstrated that types of child rearing, personality, and values or beliefs were correlated. For example, cross-cultural studies found that a strong emphasis on achievement goes with early training for independence and with a father who is not overly dominant. Although this kind of relationship has been fairly convincingly documented, numerous studies have demonstrated the enormous difficulty of formulating any personality or character type which characterizes an entire nation, region, class, or other sociocultural unit; the system usually permits a considerable variation of personalities—as we say, "it takes all kinds."

Postwar British anthropologists realized that the sociocultural systems they studied were not the "seamless webs" of neatly integrated roles and statuses they had classically assumed. Conflict became an important topic, and ritual was seen to have as much to do with conflict as with solidarity. Thus, ritualization was understood as marking off one role from another in order to avoid conflict between them; the political role of a king might be ritually segregated from his kinship role, for example. Other types of ritual have been shown to permit the expression of tension and discontent, still others to seemingly cure diseases that derive from such stresses. Following on the insights of Dutch anthropologist Arnold van Gennep, who wrote on "rites of passage" in 1909, anthropologists such as Victor Turner have deepened insight into the way ritual initiates the person into the system in which he lives. Thus, initiation ceremonies always have a "liminal" period when the initiates are permitted to behave contrary to the normal structure into which they are passing but have not yet joined. Pilgrimages, movements, communes, and sects are among the other examples of liminal "antistructures" that Turner has analyzed to reveal how the established structure and antistructure are delicately balanced in each society—a relationship more complex than that envisioned by the classical model of the neatly integrated homogeneous system.

Dynamic process has become a focus. Kinship groups, for example, are no more seen as fixed structures but as undergoing "developmental cycles." Families develop and change as they move from marriage to the birth and maturation of children, who in turn marry and begin their own cycle. The social system may remain stable, but that stability is sustained through dynamic process. This principle is demonstrated on a larger scale by E. R. Leach's study, *Political Systems of Highland Burma,* which will also be considered in our discussion of primitive society. Leach had begun his fieldwork with the Kachin of Burma prior to the outbreak of World War II which brought him into action in the highland area for the duration of the War. He had been trained by Malinowski and had planned a classic type of field research, but the interruption by the war forced him to supplement his limited field data with historical materials. Viewing the Kachin over a span of a century Leach concluded that the Kachin system is composed of two variant subsystems between which individual communities oscillate. One variant is relatively egalitarian and democratic, the other more hierarchical and autocratic, and movement from one to the other is triggered by individual Kachin who seek power through manipulating ambiguities within Kachin culture.

Some anthropologists turned their attention to the cultural system seen as distinct from the social. Symbolic anthropologists have analyzed the structure of such forms as myth, rite, and games to reveal ways that cultures process information and bestow meaning. Cognitive anthropologists have drawn on the insights of linguistics to carry out precise and detailed analyses of native schemes of classification and labeling the world in which they live. Both these approaches have deepened the understanding of cultural systems beyond that achieved by the classical anthropologists who tended to perceive culture either as unsystematized "shreds and patches" (a term used by Robert Lowie, one of Boas' early students), or as too neatly systematized within the structure of society (as did Malinowski). Also worthy of mention in this regard is the way in which postwar anthropologists have approached the relationship between sociocultural systems and the environment. Whereas classical anthropology tended to ignore the environment or included it as an implicit part of the seamless web of the social order, modern ecological anthropologists have sharpened the distinction between society and environment to investigate the dynamic interplay between social arrangements, rituals, technological systems, and physical resources. They have investigated the ways that such forces as energy harnessing, population concentration, and mode of production in dialectical interplay prod societies toward change.

Some cultural anthropologists have formulated the way that discrepancies between cultural definitions and social actualities elicit change. This approach is best illustrated by the anthropology of movements. As early as the late nineteenth century the American anthropologist George Mooney had observed the Ghost Dance of the American Indians, and not too long after that, F. E. Williams reported on the "Vailala Madness" of Melanesia. These movements were similar despite their geographic separation in that both required the natives to radically transform their traditional culture while revitalizing other parts, and both expected benefits to come if the whites who exploited them could be made to go. After World War II, Melanesia exhibited numerous similar movements known as Cargo Cults, in which giving up old traditions was associated with the coming of ships that would disgorge wonderful cargos for the natives to enjoy. Anthony F. C. Wallace attempted to generalize these phenomena under the term "revitalization movements." Wallace's theory, which we discuss in a different context later, saw the origin of the movements in a perceived discrepancy between the cultural system or "cognitive map" and the actual situation in which the natives found themselves. The thrust of these movements was to bring about a match between the two by formulating a new cultural system, usually articulated by a prophet through a vision, and mobilizing the social system to activate that vision in real life. In this way the discrepancy between cultural expectations and actual experiences would be reduced and a state of equilibrium would be restored.

The end of World War II signaled the beginning of the end of Western colonial control of the non-Western world. Former colonial societies were transformed into new states. On the whole, these sought not to return to their precolonial condition but to modernize. Since anthropologists had been involved in these societies, many of them were caught up in trying to understand this effort at modernizing change. They addressed such questions as the relation between the urban and rural areas, "primordial" sentiments and nationalistic ideologies, ethnic and tribal identities and cosmopolitan values. And since these "new nations" were frequently heirs of complex civilizations, those who studied them could hardly follow the lead of classical anthropology and ignore history.

In sum, post-World War II anthropology has adhered to the major tenets of the classical era: systemic analysis achieved by intensive fieldwork. Where postwar anthropology has gone beyond the classicists is, broadly speaking, in an awareness of differentiation within systems and potentials for change. The seamless web has become segmented into detailed studies of personalities, cultural and environmental substructures; and the equilibrium in terms of which the isolated classical community was viewed has been replaced by a focus on conflict, dynamics, change, and history, as well as the movements and struggles of contemporary society.

Anthropology—Past, Present, Future

Formative anthropology had its beginnings in the last half of the nineteenth century and it concentrated on those elements of culture, viewed as discrete entities, which could help us understand the origins of contemporary civilization. It looked backward to the past. Classical anthropology dominated the first half of the twentieth century, and it emphasized the relations among elements of particular societies and cultures that could be observed at first hand, seen as operating "right now" as a system. Classical anthropology positioned itself firmly in the present. By the logic of its history so far, should we expect that it will turn toward study of the future? Certain trends suggest that this orientation is stronger today than in former epochs, but the picture is not clear or simple.

Contemporary anthropology displays considerable flux, so much as to suggest that the discipline is on the verge of a shift as significant as that which marked the movement from formative to classical. Although there have been several calls to "rethink" the discipline, a recent work calls for an even more radical "reinvention" of anthropology—scrapping present assumptions and starting over, with a clean slate.[5] Current trends do indeed suggest a search for a new synthesis. Some appear to regress to interests of the nineteenth-century formative anthropology. For example, the new field of sociobiology[6] parallels in many respects nineteenth-century biological determinism, and certain ecological studies parallel nineteenth-century environmental determinism. Historical studies return to the historical particularism of Boasian American anthropology. Interest in modernization and acculturation is similar to nineteenth-century diffusionism, and new cultural evolutionism is in some ways like the old.

Despite these parallels, the retention of classical patterns prevents a return to the formative state of mind. The focus on systemic analysis by intensive fieldwork, for example, seems too firmly embedded to be easily cast aside and that focus transforms the mode of addressing the formative issues. Analysis of cultures, environments, societies, and personality systems and structures has become too elaborate to easily slip into the oversimplified molds of the nineteenth century. Most important, perhaps, contemporary anthropology emphasizes dynamic *process* as much as static structure, and this emphasis should give a healthy awareness of the flexibility of existence, the potential for variety and change. Such awareness is crucial if anthropology is indeed to turn its attention to trends and patterns that lead toward the future of an increasingly complex world.

Overview

One's view of when and where anthropology originated depends on one's definition of the subject. Defined as a discipline within the Western intellectual tradition, anthropology is most directly traced to the breakdown of the Middle Ages and the emergence of Enlightenment. After sketching these developments, this chapter focuses on the three major stages of anthropology's development as an identifiable discipline.

The first stage, which we term *formative,* spanned the period from 1850 to 1920. It concentrated on discovery of the human past and on evolutionary development. The primary method was comparative history, exemplified by such scholars as Lewis Henry Morgan who subsumed the world's societies and cultures under schemes that postulated universal sequences of evolution.

The second stage, which we term *classical,* lasted from 1920 to 1950. It concentrated on ethnographic patterning of the human present. The primary method was intensive fieldwork, exemplified by Bronislaw Malinowski's years among the Trobriands of the Western Pacific. Eschewing what was now seen as a vain effort to trace origins and universal development, the classic objective was to formulate the principles by which each society and culture was organized, and eventually to generalize these principles to explain the functioning of all human societies and cultures.

The third stage, which is *contemporary,* has emerged since World War II. It does not display a shape so coherent as hindsight suggests for stages one and two. The anthropological view has become more complex. Social and cultural life is seen now as a delicately balanced arrangement of competing components rather than as a harmonious whole. The sense of conflict has encouraged an interest in change, and the interest in change directs attention toward the future. Can one speak, then, of the one hundred years of development of anthropological thought as a movement from concern with past, then present, and, finally, future? The pattern is not that simple, though certainly the future—the human direction—is one of the emerging concerns.

Topics for Discussion

Every culture probably has some sort of implicit view of human nature, the characteristics of various groups, and the significance of social and cultural differences. For example, the traditional Chinese viewed themselves as the civilized center of the universe surrounded by "barbarians." Such informal anthropological views can often be seen in stereotypes relating to the sexes ("passive" versus "aggressive"), to young versus old ("irresponsible" versus "conservative"), to ethnic or racial groups ("clannish"), and to social classes ("snooty"). Try to identify some of these stereotypes you have encountered in your own experience and discuss the implicit views contained in them.

In recent years a number of books (e.g., Van Daniken's *Chariot of the Gods*) has attempted to attribute prehistoric edifices and constructions in various parts of the world to visits to earth by advanced beings from outer space who showed human beings how to build these structures. Compare this notion with that of the extreme diffusionists of the nineteenth century such as G. Elliot Smith and W. J. Perry who attempted to explain the appearance of such creations as Pyramidal structures and writing as the result of the spread of these elements from a single point of invention throughout the world.

Suggested Readings

General Treatments of the History of Anthropology

Origins and Growth of Archaeology (paperback, 1971) by Glyn Daniel. A synthesis of the development of archeology.

The Rise of Anthropological Theory (1968) by Marvin Harris. A comprehensive discussion from a particular point of view.

From Ape to Angel (paperback, 1964) by H. R. Hays. An informal history of social anthropology.

The Development of Anthropological Ideas (1976) by John Honigmann. A sophisticated treatment with an excellent bibliography for further reading.

The Studied Man (paperback, 1963) by Abram Kardiner and Edward Preble. Brief vignettes of a number of influential figures.

Images of Man (paperback, 1974) by Annemarie de Waal Malefijt. A readable overview.

A Hundred Years of Anthropology (paperback, 1974) by T. K. Penniman. A thorough treatment including all subfields of anthropology.

A History of Ethnology (1975) by Fred W. Voget. Detailed study focusing mainly on sociocultural anthropology.

The Preformative Era and the Impact of Darwin

The Age of Reason Reader (paperback, 1973) edited by Crane Brinton. Short
selections on a variety of topics by influential seventeenth- eighteenth-
century writers.

Darwin's Century (paperback, 1961) by Loren Eiseley. A readable account of the
major contributors to evolutionary thought.

From Genesis to Geology (paperback, 1959) by Charles C. Gillispie. The interplay
between geological discovery and religious thought before Darwin.

The Death of Adam (paperback, 1961) by John C. Greene. The impact of the idea
of evolution on religious belief.

Early Anthropology in the Sixteenth and Seventeenth Centuries (paperback, 1971) by
Margaret T. Hodgen. Precursors of formal anthropology.

The Leopard's Spots (1960) by William R. Stanton. Scientific attitudes toward race
in America.

The Formative Era

Evolution and Society (paperback, 1970) by J. W. Burrow. Social evolutionary
thought in Victorian England, including discussion of Maine, Spencer, and
Tylor.

Social Anthropology, and Other Essays (paperback, 1964) by E. E. Evans-Pritchard.
Chapter Two includes a discussion of social evolutionary thought.

A History of Anthropology (1910) by Alfred C. Haddon. Includes classical and
European contributions.

Pioneers of American Anthropology (1966) edited by June Helm. The founders of
American anthropology.

The History of Ethnological Theory (1937) by Robert Lowie. For many years the
standard text.

American Anthropology: The Early Years (paperback, 1976) edited by John Murra.
Essays on early American anthropology.

Race, Culture and Evolution (1968) by George Stocking, Jr. Essays in the history of
anthropology.

The Shaping of American Anthropology: 1883–1911 (1974) by George Stocking, Jr.
The formative era in American anthropology, particularly the influence of
Boas.

The Classic Era

Man and Culture (paperback, 1964) edited by Raymond Firth. An assessment of
Malinowski's contributions.

Theories of Man and Culture (paperback, 1973) by Elvin Hatch. Comparison of the views of a number of leading British and American anthropologists.

The Revolution in Anthropology (1967) by I. C. Jarvie. A discussion of the significance of the shift in anthropology to fieldwork and functional theory.

Anthropologists and Anthropology (paperback, 1974) by Adam Kuper. The classic British school of anthropology.

Ruth Benedict (paperback, 1974) by Margaret Mead. An evaluation of an influential American figure.

Alfred Kroeber (paperback, 1973) by Julian Steward. An assessment of the contributions of one of the leading post-Boasian anthropologists in America.

Selections of Readings on the History of Anthropology

High Points in Anthropology (paperback, 1973) edited by Paul Bohannon and Mark Glazer. Selections from the works of influential anthropologists.

Readings in the History of Anthropology (1974) edited by Regna Darnell. Essays on the history of anthropology.

Readings in Early Anthropology (1965) edited by J. S. Slotkin. Selections from early anthropological writings.

chapter 3

Sociocultural Systems and Subsystems

The quote from Raymond Firth's *We, the Tikopia* which opened chapter 1 evokes a common anthropological experience—the encounter with an exotic and unfamiliar situation. Firth initially experienced Tikopia as a strange mob, a "tawny, surging crowd." Later he would begin to tease out regular and recurrent patterns—functional and logical, explicit and implicit, actual and ideal. Eventually he would synthesize such patterns into a coherent formulation of the Tikopian society and culture. Ultimately he and other scholars move to an even wider view as they endeavor to connect the Tikopian way of life to the entire range of life styles, past and present, which human beings have invented to bestow order and meaning on their existence.

Investigation of unfamiliar cultures is essential to the anthropological endeavor, but encounter with the unfamiliar is not confined to anthropologists. That experience occurs for everyone. Imagine, for example, walking down the street of a city, sitting on a bench in a college campus, or riding a bus or plane and overhearing a conversation in a language that is entirely foreign:

A. "aâ . . . khunthawm . . . khyynníica'painăi"
B. "oô . . . thaâmiingeunphawaw . . . phŏmtâwngkaanpaiduunăng"

For most of us this conversation would be a meaningless stream of strange noises but a speaker of Thai would recognize that these sounds were a part of a conversation between A and B in which A asked B what he would be doing that evening, and B replied that if he could afford it he wanted to go to the movies. Without knowing the "code" which unravels the meanings of the Thai language the listener could not grasp what was being said.[1]

The anthropologist's encounter with the exotic and unknown resembles the linguist's encounter with an unfamiliar language. Their mode of investigation is similar too. The anthropologist attempts to "decode" the unfamiliar culture he encounters in his fieldwork just as the linguist attempts to decode the unknown language. The linguist first tries to break up the stream of speech sounds into its constituent elements, the minimal units of meaningful sound. Linguists call these units "phonemes" and they are represented in the Thai conversation by the various symbols we refer to as consonants and vowels. Each symbol represents a unit of sound in Thai. The symbols /p/ and /ph/ and /t/ and /th/ indicate, for example, that in Thai "aspiration"—a puff of breath after a consonant—makes a difference in meaning. The various diacritical symbols over the consonants and vowels reveal one important difference between Thai and English. These diacritical marks (ˆ, ´, ˇ) show that Thai, like some other languages such as Chinese, is a "tonal" language. Rising or falling pitch of sound makes a difference in meaning. For example, the sounds represented by /maa/ spoken with an "even" tone (unmarked) means "to come," spoken with a "rising" tone means "dog," and spoken with a "high" tone means "horse." Also, in contrast to English the "doubled vowels" signs, for example /aa/ versus /a/, /ii/ versus /i/, /yy/ versus /y/ indicates that "vowel length"—how long the vowel sound is intoned—also makes a difference of meaning in Thai. For example, /can/ means "moon" while /caan/ with the /a/ held longer means "plate." Every language has a small number of meaningful sound units and these are distinctive to it; thus Thai phonemes are not identical with those of English.

Once the linguist has uncovered the meaningful units of sound in a language he attempts to discover the rules that govern how these phonemes can or cannot be combined to form larger units called "morphemes," roughly the equivalent of "words" in English. For example, the sound represented more or less by the letter /l/ can appear in any position in a Thai syllable except at the end. Hence, there are *no* Thai morphemes that end with an /l/ sound as in English /jail/. Every language has a set of rules which governs the way its sounds are meaningfully combined.

Having formulated the "morphophonemic rules" of a language, the linguist then attempts to discover the rules that govern how the various morphemes of a language can be combined to form larger utterances similar to what in English we would call "sentences." These are the rules of "grammar." The linguist would discover that Thai grammar differs in many ways from English. For example, Thai does not have "articles" such as /the/ and /a/ and Thai verbs do not have "declensions" or "tense," so there does not have to be "agreement" between "subject," "verb," and "object" in a Thai sentence. Nor is it obligatory in Thai to indicate "gender" in speech. Yet some categories are obligatory in Thai. Thus Thai "nouns" are classified in a variety of categories and in some instances, such as counting objects, the noun class must be expressed. For example, Buddhist monks /phra/ are counted as falling into one noun class /ong/ whereas ordinary laymen are counted in another /khon/. And, although most animals such as dogs and horses are counted in one noun class /tua/, elephants, which have a sacred connotation among Thai, are counted in another class /chyâg/. In order to speak Thai grammatically the proper noun class of each object must be known and expressed in speech.

The raw data with which the linguist works are a single continuous stream of speech sounds, similar to the stream of behavior that the anthropologist encounters. In actual research, the linguist must analyze these various levels—phonemic, morphophonemic, grammatical—simultaneously. Having analytically sorted out these various aspects of the language, the linguist endeavors to put them back together again for a total description. He hopes that his formulation of the language is so accurate and complete that a nonnative speaker could use it to learn to speak the language correctly, to communicate with native speakers. And ultimately he wishes to go beyond this particular language, to compare it with the entire range of languages past and present which human beings have invented to form communities of speech and meaning.

Anthropologists have not agreed upon some simple "minimal unit of sociocultural behavior" like the linguist's phoneme, but the types of problems they investigate and the analytical procedures they use are similar to those of the linguist. The raw material with which the anthropologist (like the linguist) has to work is a single continuous stream of observed behavior. Although anthropology ultimately seeks a holistic analysis and understanding of that stream of behavior, anthropologists have found it useful to differentiate the flow into categories. For example, some anthropologists distinguish the social system from the cultural system. As was explained previously, these are analytical perspectives that emphasize different aspects of existence. The social system can be seen as a network of roles and groups, the cultural system as a schema of shared values, symbols, and beliefs.

The distinction between social system and cultural system is a very basic and useful one. Conventionally, however, anthropologists have differentiated sociocultural systems into finer units of analysis. Sociocultural systems are subdivided into such subsystems as kinship and marriage, religion and art, economics and politics. And these subsystems are then related to their environmental and technological bases and to the media of communication, such as language, through which they operate. The divisions are somewhat arbitrary, yet each type of subsystem displays a distinctive kind of patterning and has given rise to a distinctive set of investigations and formulations which elucidate the logic of that patterning.

To exemplify some of the recurrent patterns discovered by anthropology, this chapter will treat two subsystems—kinship and religion. The reasons for selecting these subsystems as extended examples are several. First, kinship and religion have been of central significance of anthropological thought, hence understanding of the anthropological view of these subsystems is critical for understanding of anthropology. Second, the analysis of kinship and religion is central to this book's evolutionary study. Both the general and the evolutionary concern with kinship and religion derive from the central role that the two subsystems play in traditional societies and cultures; whether to comprehend traditional life per se or evolution away from that life, it is necessary to grasp the systematics of kinship and religion. A final reason for treating these subsystems is that they exemplify social and cultural patterning. Though both kinship and religion partake of both cultural and social aspects, it is convenient to emphasize kinship as an example of social patterning and religion as an example of cultural patterning. Accordingly, in discussing kinship we shall stress social patterning (though necessarily treating also the cultural), and in discussing religion we shall stress cultural patterning (though necessarily also involving the social).

Social Systems and Kinship

The reasons for the centrality of kinship for sociocultural anthropology are many. For one thing, the family is the one institution common to all societies throughout history, in contrast to the relatively recent development of such institutions as market economies and governmental or religious bureaucracies. Kinship is also one of the major connections between man's biological roots and the sociocultural order; the family is, after all, the unit within which the person is gestated, born, and socialized; and, finally, in those societies of small scale and simple technology which loom large in anthropological studies, the kinship system is essentially *the* structure that organizes social relationships of all kinds.

The anthropological literature on kinship systems is immense and exceedingly complex.[2] Here we cannot comprehensively survey kinship. Instead, we wish to lay out the basic logic that operates within such systems, to give some idea of the range of types of kinship systems anthropologists have investigated, and especially to give some sense of the kinds of connections that integrate kinship systems into a working social arrangement. In order to do this we shall begin by contrasting two major ways of tracing descent—bilateral and unilineal—and sketch some of the implications each has for the rest of social life. To illustrate the principles involved we will simplify the way such systems operate in reality.

In most modern societies, kinship is reckoned bilaterally, whereas in many nonmodern societies, especially primitive societies, kinship is reckoned unilineally. To reckon descent bilaterally is to trace one's kinsmen more or less equally through both paternal and maternal lines. To reckon descent unilineally is to trace kinsmen through only one parent, or at least to emphasize one line more than the other. If the emphasis is on the father's side of the family, we speak of patrilineal descent; if the emphasis falls on the mother's side, we speak of matrilineal descent.*

Unilineal Descent

Patrilineal or matrilineal reckoning of kinship involves the notion that only one parent is regarded as a kinsman. The other parent is considered an affine or in-law, i.e., a person married to a kinsman, rather than a blood kinsman. The Trobrianders, who trace descent matrilineally, are said to believe that the "mother's husband" plays no part in procreation. The mother is the procreator. From her comes the life substance. From her blood the child is created, so the child is blood kin to her. The "mother's husband" is a kind of in-law to the child, a person who happens to be married to that kinswoman of the child termed "mother."

The Kachin of Burma, who reckon descent patrilineally, hold an opposite view. The Kachin believe that the child is created from the bone of the father. The "father's wife" is regarded as a kind of in-law, a person who happens to be married to that kinsman of the child termed "father."

The experience of growing up in a family founded on notions of

---

*Ward H. Goodenough, in his "Residence Rules," demonstrates the crudity of such categories as "patrilocal" and "matrilocal." The point could be extended to "patrilineal" and "matrilineal." For the purpose of introducing the notion of variability of patterning in kinship and for broad-scale comparison, these categories are adequate, but for technical and refined analysis of any single society more subtle distinctions would have to be made.

this kind is far different from the experience of growing up in the bilineal Western family. It appears that the much discussed Oedipus complex takes another course among the Trobrianders than among Westerners. The Oedipus complex in the West involves father, mother, and son. The theory is that the son is jealous of the father's sexual relationship with the mother. He fears that the powerful father will castrate him as punishment for his forbidden desire for the mother. He therefore represses his sexual yearnings for the mother and enters a period of latency, during which he shows little interest in girls. According to Freud, this latency period lasts until puberty.

The Trobriand boy does not have a father in the Western sense. He spends his childhood in the company of his "mother's husband," but, as the term suggests, the man has little authority over the boy. Instead, authority is vested in the boy's kinsmen, and since the boy's father is clearly not a kinsman, it falls to the boy's maternal uncle—as his closest senior male kinsman—to exercise disipline, to punish him for childhood wrongs. The uncle is also the breadwinner; among the Trobrianders it is customary for a man to support not his own wife and her household, but his sister and his sister's household. It is the boy's uncle, not his father, who provides the yams. In effect, the Trobriand uncle serves almost all the functions of the Western father.

But there is one crucial difference: The brother of the boy's mother has no access to her sexually. She is, after all, his sister, and among the Trobrianders the taboo on incest is strong. Thus, what in the West is the single role of "father," in the Trobriand Islands is split into two roles: the role of "mother's husband" and the role of "mother's brother." With the object of Oedipal anger thus splintered, the Trobriand boy's conflicts are also splintered—he cannot play them out so directly against a single father figure as can his counterpart in the West. Although we have greatly simplified the Trobriand situation, it seems clear that variations in patterns of tracing descent may have deep implications for human experience.

Where descent is traced unilineally one typically finds corporate descent groups. A descent group is a set of kinsmen linked by common descent counted exclusively through either the male or the female line. Among descent groups one can distinguish broader and narrower types. The broader, which can be termed a clan, includes the total group of kinsmen who trace their descent from some common ancestor whether the actual genealogical connections can be demonstrated or not. For example, Chinese clans may include thousands of people living throughout the world, who share the same patrilineal surname even though they may not be able to demonstrate their common ancestor. The narrower includes only those persons who can demonstrate their actual relatedness. These are called lineages and are often localized including kinsmen who live nearby, jointly control property, and do other things in common. For example, the *tarvarad* of the matrilineal Nayar in India holds property jointly, acts jointly with respect to territorial and property matters, assembles together on ceremonial occasions, and has a formal head.

Myths of the Amazons to the contrary notwithstanding, two conditions appear to hold for all descent groups: First, women are responsible for the care of children; and, second, men have ultimate authority. These conditions hold for both patrilineal and matrilineal descent groups, and they imply an important difference of pattern between the two. In patrilineal descent groups the line of descent and the line of authority coincide, both identified with men. In matrilineal descent groups the line of authority runs through men but the line of descent through women. This difference implies significant consequences.

A man does not occupy an important position within his wife's matrilineal group. The men who hold authority in the matrilineage are not the husbands of its members but the brothers, cousins, and uncles of the women through whom the line is traced. Speaking grossly, we might say that the husbands are like studs only. The matrilineage uses the men to reproduce its members by permitting them to copulate with its women, but it does not bestow on them positions of authority and responsibility. As a result, husbands in a matrilineal society have a rather weak and narrowly specialized link to the mother and her children. The husbands need not even live with their wives. As traditional among the Minangkabau of Sumatra, they may live with their sisters and other female relatives of their own matrilineage, being only "visitors" in the houses of their wives. They may, as among the Trobriand Islanders, act as breadwinners not for their own wives and children but for their sisters and her children. And, also as in the Trobriands, they need not act as fathers for their children in the full social sense of having parental authority over them, even though biologically they helped produce them.

Wives in patrilineages are valued largely for their reproductive role. Among the Kachin, for example, a woman is thought to be merely a receptacle within which the child lives until it enters the world. However, the linkage of a woman to her husband's patrilineage is stronger than that of a man to his wife's matrilineage. This is because, despite the fact that children are members of the father's patrilineage, it is the women who nurture, mother, and fulfill the child's basic needs.

In general, then, because women nurture children, they are more bound to the patrilineage into which they marry than men are bound to the matrilineage into which they marry. Men too are influenced by the system of descent. In patrilineal systems men have authority within the lineage and in their own family; in matrilineal systems men may still have authority in the matrilineage but not within their own family.

As a corollary to the above, men are more bound to the matrilineages into which they are born than women are to the patrilineages in which they are born. This is because men dominate the political life of their matrilineage, whereas women do not dominate the political life of their patrilineage. The patrilineage draws in women from other patrilineages to serve as wives and mothers of the patrilineage's children. Women are freed of obligations to their patrilineages of birth rather easily since they have few legal or political responsibilities there anyway. Freed of their natal patrilineage they may become very attached to their husband's patrilineage owing to their nurturant bond with his children. Among the Igbo of Nigeria, for example, a woman may ask to be buried among the deceased members of her husband's patrilineage instead of among her own. In traditional China, a woman's purpose in life was to produce children, especially sons, for her husband's lineage. If she did so, she might eventually gain great influence within the family. If she did not, she might be sent back to her family in disgrace.

One implication of these social patterns is that marriage is less stable in a matrilineal society than in a patrilineal one. The life of a woman is more closely bound to her husband through bonds to his patrilineage than is a husband to his wife through bonds to her matrilineage. Divorce rates reflect this situation; they tend to be greater in matrilineal than in patrilineal societies.

Bilateral Descent

Most western countries such as the United States reckon descent bilaterally, i.e., emphasize descent through mother and father more or less equally. (This is not to deny such residues of patrilineal bias as passing the surname through the male line.) As with unilineal descent, bilateral descent also implies certain patterns. In contrast to unilineal descent systems, for example, bilateral descent does not encourage nonoverlapping and discrete descent groups such as lineages and clans. Reckoning descent unilineally means that each individual is clearly related to a particular set of kinsmen who trace their descent through a common matrilineal or patrilineal ancestor. The whole descent group shares exactly the same set of relatives and can thus act in concert if necessary. By contrast, in bilateral descent there is an infinite number of overlapping networks of kindred, each network existing uniquely through its orientation to a living individual. Only siblings share the same set of kinsmen in bilateral descent, and even the children of siblings differ in their kindreds. In American kinship, for example, brothers and sisters share the same kindred reckoned equally through both parents and ramifying out from them to distant kin. While the children of siblings share many kinsmen in common reckoned through one parent, they also differ in their kinsmen reckoned through the other parent (unless, by chance, the parents marry another close kinsman). Thus, first cousins would share one set of grandparents, but differ in the other set.

In bilateral descent systems there are also individuals who are related to you but not related to each other. That is, they may form a part of your kindred, but not of each others. For example, in American kinship your maternal kinsmen are not ordinarily related to your paternal relatives except through their common relationship to you. Hence, probably the only time they come together as a group is on some occasion or event relating to you, such as a birthday, graduation, wedding, or funeral.

There are a few exceptions to the general rule that bilateral kinship does not encourage discrete descent groups. When there is a substantial estate involved, for example, something resembling a descent group may be established even in a bilateral system. Very wealthy families like the Rockefellers, DuPonts, and Kennedys may form a corporate descent group which in some circumstances acts in concert even though membership in the group is determined bilaterally. On islands in Oceania where land is scarce but descent is reckoned bilaterally, there are descent groups called "ramages." Rights to land are held collectively by a descent group. To gain access to land, each individual must choose to identify with the landholding descent group to which he is related through either his father or his mother. Once the choice is made he is then identified with that particular ramage for landholding purposes, though he still acknowledges his relatedness to the other set of kindred. Finally, some groups who trace their relationship bilaterally to a famous person (e.g., Lincoln, Washington) form something similar to a unilineal clan.

In general, then, there is an infinite number of kindreds in a bilateral descent system because almost everyone's kindred group differs in membership from everyone else's. Everytime a first child is born into a family a new kindred is born. Conversely, a kindred goes out of existence when all its linkages, such as a set of siblings die. Although lineages and clans may be newly established or die out, they ordinarily persist over longer periods of time than one lifetime. The indeterminancy and impermanence of kindreds do not favor their serving as corporate groups in the same way that lineages and clans typically do.

Although one should avoid confusing cause with effect and arguing too simple a relationship, it is probably true that bilateral kinship reckoning has been one factor contributing to the dynamism and flux of modern Western societies. The identification of the individual with his kindred in a bilateral society is normally less binding than identity with lineage or clan in a unilineal society. The individual is freer to follow an individualistic life style and to enjoy geographic and social mobility. The other side of the coin is that because bilateral kinship does not require such close personal identification with his kin group, the individual may experience loneliness and alienation. Lineages and clans provide powerful and enduring social identity.

Sex and Marriage

Sexuality and kinship are in opposition. This pattern is best exemplified by the universal existence of some sort of incest taboo. The incest taboo proscribes marriage and usually any kind of mating between certain categories of relatives. Although the incest taboo normally precludes mating between members of the nuclear family (i.e., between fathers and daughters, mothers and sons, and siblings), it may also be extended to cover a wide range of extended kinsmen. Numerous explanations have been offered to account for the universality of the taboo on incest. One explanation of the nuclear family incest taboo emphasizes the importance of a secure and stable situation in which to raise the children who replenish society. The nuclear family incest taboo serves to shield close family relationships from the potentially disruptive effects of sex. Sex can breed passion, anger, and conflict, so if the members of the nuclear family are forbidden to relate sexually, they can perhaps relate more harmoniously.

The rule of exogamy extends this principle. Rules of exogamy require the individual to choose his mate from outside some specified group, such as his own lineage or clan. Sexual passions within the group might undermine the solidarity of this group in which the individual's social identity and livelihood are rooted. Exogamy siphons off the disruptive force.

Exogamy also has another positive aspect. Marrying out serves to link different descent groups. In tribal societies where there is no bureaucratic means for centralization, such marriage alliances between descent groups are crucial for societal integration. When a daughter of clan A marries a son of clan B, A and B are bound together in a ramified net of obligations, rituals, and privileges. When such exchanges are maintained for several generations the stable relationships help to cement the entire society.

This situation is exemplifed by a pattern manifested widely among such groups as the Australian aborigines (see chapter 5). Due to the harsh desert environment in which they live, aborigines are divided into small, isolated, and localized lineage segments. These practice exogamy. The preferred or prescribed marriage is between a particular type of cousin (a cross-cousin, either mother's brother's daughter or son [MBD or S] or father's sister's daughter or son [FZD or S]) while another type of cousin (a parallel cousin, either mother's sister's daughter or son[MZD or S] or father's brother's daughter or son [FBD or S]) is forbidden.[3] Such marriages between cousins living in different localized groups are maintained over several generations and form the skeleton for the complex aboriginal social organization. Under these circumstances one's parallel cousins will be members of one's own lineage or clan and thus forbidden by the incest taboo, whereas one's cross-cousins would not be members of one's descent group; therefore, cross-cousins would be appropriate spouses under the rule of exogamy. Among the aborigines, hundres of small localized lineage segments are linked together through such cross-cutting networks of marriage alliance. Kinship and marriage thus forms the skeleton of the aborigines' social system.

The prescription and proscription of marriage partners according to kinship criteria and the integrative role of such marriages underline an importeant point about kinship and marriage in most unilineal societies. That is, in these societies marriage is not a matter of individual choice in the sense that it is in most bilateral societies. Marriage is instead a means of alliance between groups, and the group has a vested interest in insuring that the appropriate alliances obtain regardless of the feelings of the individuals concerned. Of course, since kinship terminology in these societies is commonly classificatory (i.e., each term covers many persons) there are usually a number of potentially appropriate spouses available. Nevertheless, the degree of freedom of choice which individuals have in such societies is restricted and a broken marriage threatens not only the individual partners but the fabric of society itself.

Perhaps because of the potentially disruptive effects of the failure of a marriage as well as the restrictions on freedom of marriage there appear to be universal tensions if not open conflict between affines or in-laws. To avoid conflict, societies institute patterns of avoidance such that affines treat each other with exaggerated politeness to the point where in some societies they avoid any contact at all. Avoidance of mother-in-law by son-in-law is one such pattern. On the other hand, some affinal relationships are vested with a high degree of license. A woman may enjoy a special joking relationship with her husband's brothers, for example, so that they may tease each other obscenely or tell each other ribald jokes that are not otherwise condoned.

The seemingly universal tensions associated with relationships based on marriage reflect a simple principle: Units seen as opposite attract and repel whereas units seen as members of the same group incline toward a more solid relationship. Spouses are opposite not only because of the difference in sex but also the difference in descent group membership. Affines extend these differences in that one set of relatives is associated with the female, the other with the male. Persons deriving from the same descent group are seen as alike and solidary because they share common roots.

This principle generates a variety of patterns. In many societies, though kinsmen are thought to be of the same substance whereas persons related by marriage are not, it is persons related by marriage who are thought to have special influence over each other. Among the patrilineal Kachin of Burma, though the child is thought to be of the same substance ("bone") as the father; it is the mother whose looks ("face") come to the child. (Among the Kachin the term "face" not only includes physical appearance but also "reputation" as well, for a man's rank depends largely on the rank of the clan that has provided a wife for his father.) The matrilineal Trobrianders have the opposite belief. In these societies, it is affines who are thought to work sorcery on each other, to cause illness, bad luck, and death.

Despite the ambivalences and tensions that are manifested in affinal relationships, marriage, broadly defined, seems to be a universal institution. By marriage anthropologists mean a socially recognized and approved arrangement, which regularizes the sexual relationship and insures procreation. The edges of the definition are strained by the case of the Nayar who live in Malabar. Among the Nayar there is a ceremony arranged by members of a woman's matrilineage (the *tarvarad*), but the official husband does not then live or cohabit with his wife. Instead, after the marriage, the woman establishes a series of liasons from which the matrilineage acquires its new members.

Although some form of marriage is found universally, there are several typical variants. Monogamy is the pattern by which, at a given time, there is one spouse of each sex. This is the pattern found most commonly in Western society. When a marriage includes more than one spouse of either sex, that marriage is termed polygamy. Two varities of polygamy exist. Polyandry, one wife with more than one husband, is rare. More common is polygyny in which a husband is married simultaneously to several wives. Even in societies where polygyny is the ideal pattern, monogamous marriages are more frequent than polygynous. One reason is that usually the number of men more or less equals the number of women. Patterns that influence this ratio, e.g., female infanticide or the presence of celibate monks or priests, may encourage polygamy. A second reason is cost. In polygynous societies gaining a wife frequently requires a bride price payment, so few men can afford more than one wife. A final reason is tension. Several wives under a single roof typically breed competition and disharmony. Polygynous households seem to work best if the wives are drawn from the same descent group, particularly if they are sisters, so that solidarity of common origins overcomes the other problems. The same idea applies to polyandry which, when it is found, may (as among the Toda of India) have several brothers sharing one wife.

Disruptive, exciting, creative, sexuality is a force which kinship tries to control and bound; thus, by the incest taboo and by other rules, kinship controls whom one may (or may not) legitimately marry. In tribal societies, marriage is a matter of concern to kinship groups as much as to the individual. Accordingly, rules may dictate further marriages if the first is broken by the death of a spouse. One such rule, known as the levirate, was practiced by the ancient Jews and is mentioned in the Bible. The levirate dictates that the brother of a deceased husband will marry his widow. The sororate is a parallel practice that decrees that a widower will marry the sister of his deceased wife. Among other things such practices insure a continuity in affinal relations between groups once they are established. And, these practices also serve as a kind of "social security" system such that neither widows nor widowers will be left alone. Both practices epitomize the premise that members of the same descent group are fundamentally the same: Brothers and/or sisters are interchangeable.

Another instance of how kinship influences marriage is the set of prescriptions regarding where a couple will live after marriage. Such prescriptions are called residence rules. Residence rules of matrilocality and patrilocality are two common types. Under a rule of matrilocality, a couple should ideally live with or near the household of the bride's parents, whereas under a rule of patrilocality the couple should live in or near the household of the husband's parents. Commonly such rules are associated with matrilineal or patrilineal descent respectively. When there is a coincidence between descent and residence rules as among patrilocal Nuer and matrilocal Hopi, people will find themselves living in local groups which consist of lineage mates and with spouses derived from other lineages. But the correlation between residence and descent is not always perfect, and there are other variations on residence rules as well. For example, as was mentioned, the matrilineal Trobriand Islanders traditionally follow a residence rule termed avunculocal. At puberty a young man typically takes up residence in his mother's brother's village of residence which would be located on the land controlled by the matrilineage. On marriage a woman moves to the village of her husband. Thus, although rights to land are inherited by membership in a matrilineage, the women of the matrilineage never reside on the matrilineage's land.

In relatively modern and Western societies neolocality appears to be the norm. Neolocality means that there is no residence rule which determines postmarital residence on kinship grounds alone. With neolocality a couple may decide to live near the parents of either spouse, or may choose to set up housekeeping in some area without any relatives nearby. Indeed, Americans generally value the freedom of young couples to establish independent households and argue that tension will come from setting up housekeeping with the parents of either spouse.

In the preceding discussion we have emphasized social implications of kinship—the workings of kinship systems as social systems and the ramifications for tension and harmony in social relationships. Kinship, as anthropologists treat it, is also a *cultural* system. That is, kinship is a system of meaning which serves to classify, order, and give value to the world. Thus, as will be elaborated later, the Australian aborigines have the institution of totemism in which kinship groups and individuals are identified with various aspects of the natural environment, particularly animal species. Here a cultural system based on a conception of kinship serves to classify, order, and give value to existence by integrating human relations and the natural order.

A further example of the cultural aspect of kinship is unilineal kinship reckoning itself. According to Western biology, a child's genetic kinship derives equally from father and mother. Unilineal kinship is based on the premise that descent comes from the link with any one parent, *either* the father or the mother. A culturally constructed system is built up from this premise which, among many traditional societies, determines many spheres of life activity. Names, property rights, power, who one may or may not marry are dictated by the unilineal cultural system.

Kinship terminologies also exemplify the cultural dimensions of kinship. In classificatory kinship terminology a single kin term is applied to several kin statuses with the effect of lumping them into a single category. For example, in some of the types of cousin marriage mentioned earlier both matrilateral and patrilateral cross-cousins (MBD, FZD) may be terminologically lumped together and distinguished from the matrilateral and patrilateral parallel cousins (MZD, FBD) who may also be lumped under a single kin term. In other types of cousin marriage, such as the type called matrilateral cross-cousin marriage or "circulating connubium," the matrilateral cross-cousin (MBD) is distinguished from the patrilateral cross-cousin (FZD). Such classification of various kin types indicates that the reckoning of kin types is not determined simply by biological relatedness but by cultural factors.

Kinship is one of the most powerful and pervasive sociocultural systems. The power of kinship and family in human experience is shown by the extension of the idioms of kinship and the family into the wider world of nonkinship relations. The application of kinship and familial terminology to nonkinsmen is found in many contexts. In the widely found blood brotherhood rituals, a nonkinsman is transformed into a cultural kinsman who is pledged to a bond of lifelong mutual aid. Indeed, "fictive kinship" bonds may be felt to be stronger than actual kinship—holding to the point that one puts one's life in danger for the fictive kinsmen.

Myriad social service organizations, fraternities and sororities and the like use the symbology of brotherhood and sisterhood to create a sense of sameness and solidarity. Such is true of the Masons, as anyone knows who has read *War and Peace* or heard *The Magic Flute*. Even illegal organizations such as the Mafia are reported to be organized into "families" with membership rituals similar to blood brotherhood; the pattern is popularized as the "godfather complex." It is striking that similar criminal organizations in other societies, such as the *yakuza* of Japan, also use such familial symbology.

Kinship terms are frequently extended to nonkinsmen to symbolize age or status. For example, in Russia aged women may be called babushka (roughly, "grandmother") by those younger than they regardless of whether actually related or not. In Indonesia older women are often called *ibu* ("mother") and older men are called *bapak* ("father"). Indeed, in Indonesia the president of the country and other high officials may also be called "father." Here, kin terms express the respect one owes to people in authority, by equaling it with the respect one owes to one's older kinsmen.

In Western culture, kin terms have been generalized to many religious roles: A priest is "father," a monk "brother," a nun "sister." As we will see in chapter seven, the imagery of the Holy Family is a powerful one in the history of Western culture, providing a model of kinship relations for earthly families. In Spain and areas of the world where Spanish Catholic culture has been influential, such as Latin America and the Philippines, the relationship of a "godparent" to a "godchild" is especially important. Parents seek out a prominent or powerful nonkinsman who will aid the child in its future and serve as its godparent. The ritual of godparenthood establishes spiritual bonds between the godparent and godchild so intense that marriage between a person's child and his godchild is forbidden as incestuous.

In the modern world kin extensions are found among various groups which are promoting radical changes of various sorts. Revolutionary groups often use kinship idioms to refer to themselves and to their bonds with the masses. Black power groups term sympathetic blacks as "brothers" and "sisters" (and unprogressive blacks as "Uncle Toms" referring perhaps not only to Harriet Beecher Stowe's character but to the traditional practice of Southern whites to call older subservient blacks "uncle"). Women seeking liberation refer to other women as their "sisters." These usages show that kinship and family sentiments remain powerful even in the modern world.

Cultural Systems: Religion

When anthropologists study social systems they try to identify statuses and roles, networks and groupings. When anthropologists study cultural systems they concentrate on systems of meaning, symbols, values, and ideas. Meaning is provided by placing objects, events, actions, and persons, including the self, in some sort of overarching schema—a cultural system—which labels, classifies, and bestows value. Numerous forms perform these functions: language, arts, law, philosophies, and popular media, for example. In a sense, meaning imbues all spheres and levels of activity, from the most trivial and mundane to the most vital and sacred. To illustrate various facets of cultural systems as anthropologists study them, we will focus on those schemas which bestow relatively comprehensive—what some term "ultimate"—meaning. Religious systems and political ideologies—ranging from the great world religions and their theologies through the political ideologies of such mass movements as fascism or communism to localized traditions—exemplify such schemas.

Superordinate schemas such as religion or ideologies are always grounded in a nonempirical level of reality. That is, these cultural systems are built up from a set of axioms or primitive predicates about the nature and significance of the world and human life which cannot be verified by the senses. They are taken as "given" and their implications are elaborated and articulated to encompass the entirety of existence. In religious systems, for example, such entities as spirits, gods, heavens, hells, etc. may be postulated, believed in, and acted upon, though their material existence cannot be demonstrated. Their being depends on faith. Different religious systems root in different axioms. The Western religious tradition, for example, emphasizes the central importance of a great God who made and activated the universe and set out a code of laws to guide moral and ethical action. Rewards and punishments are based on whether the individual acts in conformity with God's will. In Buddhism, by contrast, the world is taken as given: Whether it was created by a god or "just happened" is religiously irrelevant. Religious rewards and punishments are meted out on the basis of the law of karma without the intervention of a deity or a set of divine commandments.

Ideology is illustrated by the United States as a new nation with a distinctive political values system. The founding fathers agreed on a number of assumptions about the nature of meaningful political society which they formalized in such "sacred" texts as the Declaration of Independence and the Constitution. They assumed, for example, that all men are endowed with certain inalienable rights and that just powers flow from the consent of the governed. The axioms and their derivations enshrined in these documents have guided and directed American political history. This is not to say that these political values were realized in every undertaking. Indeed, this vision of an ideal political order was tested on numerous occasions (the most clear-cut being the War between the States) and confirmed in others (such as the Supreme Court rulings on civil rights and "one man, one vote," which have enormous contemporary implication yet can be traced back to the founding axioms).

For most people most of the time, religious or ideological axioms provide a "ground of meaning" which is taken for granted and left unexamined. They represent the "way the world is." Indeed, since it seems that human beings require some system of superordinate values to make their lives meaningful, it is not surprising that they have a strong vested interest in maintaining the stability of that system into which they were born. If the axioms from which their lives derive meaning are destroyed, their lives become less meaningful. Therefore, if a superordinate meaning system is attacked, those who live by it may react in a violent and irrational way. In a word, believers regard their systems of meaning as "sacred."

Systems of meaning are not, of course, so rigid or monolithic that they are incapable of change. To endure, such systems must be adaptable. In fact, special roles are devoted to maintaining system stability while simultaneously inducing system reform. Such roles include those of theologians, philosophers, priests, judges, teachers, artists, critics, scientists, and even visionaries and mystics. Their task is to elaborate the axioms of a system of meaning so that it can encompass a world that inevitably includes change. Yet a system of meaning cannot always encompass changed conditions under traditional axioms. Under these circumstances the forms which once ordered life are questioned and thinkers search for a deeper and broader basis of order and meaning. Such a search is the preoccupation of theologians like Paul Tillich who formulated "the ground of being;" of mystics such as Meister Eckhart; of prophets such as Jesus, Buddha, or Mohammed; of reformers such as Luther and Calvin; of political visionaries such as those who founded the United States; and of charismatic political leaders of the Third World who seek a revolutionary new social order that goes beyond the traditional. The search for new and deeper grounds of being, for new axioms on which to build a cultural system, is not restricted to those who live in the contemporary world nor to those who live in relatively complex societies. As Paul Radin and others have shown, even in small, remote societies there live "philosophers" who carry on the search.

The study of religion has shared the same central place in anthropology as has the study of kinship. In part the reason for the centrality of religion is that in the traditional societies that have been the major focus of anthropology, religion pervades the cultural system as kinship pervades the social. Indeed, the two aspects are intimately intertwined in such societies, each giving a somewhat different glimpse of a common reality. Out of the study of kinship has come a picture of neat and orderly systems where one type of kinship rule leads to various functional consequences. The anthropological study of religion has not produced so clear a picture, perhaps because cultural systems have greater freedom and greater richness than social systems. Where the latter are limited by functional constraints, the former are limited primarily by constraints of logic and pattern of meaning. However that may be, most of the leading figures in anthropology at some point or other have addressed themselves to the problem of the role which religion plays in human life. Here we can only survey historically a few of the issues and themes that the anthropological study of religion has addressed.[4]

Early Anthropological Views of Religion

Nineteenth-century anthropology was once characterized as "Mr. Tylor's science." Certainly, Sir Edward Tylor made notable contributions to the anthropological study of religion though these were limited by the intellectual interests of the day. Like many nineteenth-century anthropologists, Tylor was an evolutionist interested in the development of culture from primitive origins to civilization. Tylor sought what might be called the simplest and therefore the earliest human belief that could be termed religious. He thought he had found this in the belief in spirits that he called "animism." Such a belief, Tylor felt, arose amongst primitives through mistaken deductions from such common experiences as death, dreams, visions, and trances. For example, on awakening, a person might recall a dream in which he had wandered to some distant spot or encountered someone who was deceased. His companions would tell him that he had not moved from the spot where he slept or that the deceased person had not actually been present. To explain this discrepancy, he would construct the notion of a spiritual entity or a "soul" independent of the body. From this simple belief in disembodied spirits, more complex and sophisticated beliefs, such as polytheism and monotheism, might evolve.

Tylor's contemporaries did not always share his views. One opposing view came from Pater Schmidt, the Jesuit founder of the German "culture-historical" (*kultur-kreise*) school who thought that the ideas of souls and spirits were too sophisticated for primitives to have invented by themselves. Drawing on known religious faith, Schmidt believed that the original state of religion was monotheistic with a high god. This original monotheism subsequently degenerated into the plethora of strange beliefs found amongst primitives though it has also been maintained intact throughout the stream of Western religious history.

R. R. Marett was a student of Tylor's and was his successor at Oxford. Marett thought that a "preanimistic" stage had preceded the animistic one. He called this stage "animatism"—a term denoting the idea of a disembodied and impersonal spiritual force which could attach itself not only to humans but also to other creatures and objects in the natural environment. Marett based his view on the presence among Melanesians of the notion of *mana* which was just such a force. Similar beliefs were also reported from American Indians. These beliefs struck Marett as logically simpler (hence chronologically prior) to the idea of a soul. Marett also believed that animatism derived not so much from mistaken inference as from emotional tension, which gained expression in magical beliefs and practices that foreshadowed full-blown religion.

Sir James Frazer was another nineteenth-century anthropologist who was interested in the relationships between magic and religion. Like Marett, Frazer thought a magical stage preceded a religious stage, which was then followed by science. Frazer argued in *The Golden Bough* that there were similarities between magic and science and differences between both of these and religion. Magic and science were similar in that both postulated a world subject to invariant laws. The difference was that the magician's laws were mistaken, the scientist's were, in Frazer's view, true. Religion differed from both magic and science in that it presumed the capricious intervention of spirits and deities. The attitude of the priest was one of fear and trembling that led him to supplicate, while the attitude of both magician and scientist was one of confidence that led to manipulation.

Classic Views of Religion

While the nineteenth-century evolutionists explored the roots of religion, the early twentieth century saw the emergence of an anthropology of religion that concentrated more on the fruits. That is to say, the evolutionists sought origins and stages of development while the classical approach was more concerned with the structure and function of religion in human society and culture. This structural-functional perspective, which is still basic in anthropology, derived especially from the theories of three figures: Emile Durkheim (1858–1917), Sigmund Freud (1856–1939), and Max Weber (1864–1920).

When Freud developed his psychoanalytic theories he was a psychiatrist devoting his life to the clinical treatment of middle- and upper-class neurotics in Vienna. Freudian psychoanalysis was based on the assumption that the psychodynamic processes are rooted in biologically determined instincts of human beings and are thus universally applicable. Accordingly, although Freud's theories grew out of his experience with Western neurotics he felt confident to generalize them cross-culturally, and in doing so he familiarized himself with the works of various anthropologists such as Frazer, Marett, and Robertson Smith. Like so many of his contemporaries Freud had an evolutionary perspective, though this was strongly influenced by various ideas derived from biological theories. Thus, Freud was influenced by Ernst Haeckel, a follower of Darwin, who held that "ontology recapitulates phylogeny." That is, the biological development of each individual of a species repeats the evolutionary development of the species as a whole. For example, at a certain stage of ontological development human fetuses display embryonic gills similar to those of fish. This suggested that in the biological evolution of the species human beings had gone through an aquatic stage. By the same logic, Freud saw a parallel between the psychic development of the individual and the evolution of human society.

In his *Totem and Taboo*, Freud hypothesized that human beings once lived in wandering hordes in which the dominant father-male monopolized all the women, denying younger males (his sons) sexual access to them. Frustrated, the sons banded together against the father and, in a primal act of parricide, killed him and ate him in a cannibalistic feast (a notion Freud derived from Robertson Smith). The sons were then overcome with feelings of guilt and remorse, so through a process of "displacement" they identified the father with a totemic species which they tabooed. Only on certain ceremonial occasions could the totemic species be eaten to commemorate and renew their collective and individual guilt. Freud supposed that some such primal act of parricide and its subsequent restrictions formed the basis for human social life. According to Freud, this act founded religion as well, for the father as totem was eventually transformed into a deity.

The motive force of human life for Freud was libidinal energy which was instinctual and closely tied to the sex drive. Following Haeckel's notion of ontology recapitulating phylogeny, Freud traced the libidinal development of the individual then generalized this pattern to the cultural-evolutionary development of human beings in general. According to Freud, the individual went through three major libidinal stages. The first is infancy. As an infant, the individual was unable to satisfy his needs directly, hence he experienced frequent frustration, which he expressed by crying and other infantile behavior. Freud postulates that at this stage the infant was characterized by "omnipotence of thought" (*allmacht der gedanken*). Coming to believe that he was the cause of his parent's efforts to relieve his frustrations, the infant felt himself to be the center of the universe and able to enforce his wishes on it. Freud equated this infantile stage of individual development with that of the magical-animistic stage of cultural development manifested by primitives. Like infants, primitives were deeply imbedded in instinct and affectivity. Primitives believed that their animistic rites and spells compelled the wished-for response just as infants believed their cries compelled alleviation of their frustrations.

As the infant matured it went through a second developmental stage as it internalized an ego ideal represented by the parents, particularly the father. The child learned that its wishes would be granted and its frustrations resolved if it acted in accordance with the wishes of the parents. Thus, the young child adopted the parent's wishes as its own, encouraging a state of dependency. At the same time the infantile wishes lived on, creating ambivalence in the child since its own wishes were constantly subordinated to those of the parent on which it was dependent. Freud identified this psychological stage of ambivalent dependence with the cultural stage which began religion. The parent's role was projected outward and magnified to take on the attributes of God whose wishes had to be fulfilled to gain salvation.

In the third and final stage, the individual became mature. Now he freed himself from both animistic superstition and the illusion of religion. He recognized and accepted reality and adapted himself to it. This psychological stage of maturity is analogous to the stage of science in cultural evolution.

Freud believed, then, that although religion is rooted in real childhood experiences, those experiences are misinterpreted. Religion is an

Weber's influence on the discipline has increased. Since we deal at some length with Weber's studies of religion in a later chapter we will make only a few comments here.

Like Durkheim, Weber saw religion as a universal characteristic of human life. Weber felt that religion was a uniquely human creative response to what he called the "problem of meaning." Unlike other creatures who were limited by their genetic makeup, biological evolution had made human beings capable of very generalized responses to the world in which they lived. In particular, the human capacity for symbolization permitted human beings to envelope mundane objects, activities, and events with meaning by connecting them to conceptions of an ultimate order of existence. For Weber religion was a "system of meaning" (*Sinnzusammenhange*) of vital significance for understanding human life.

Weber's concern for the religions of relatively complex society stemmed from his interest in the implication of systematic religious ethics for individual conduct and the social order. He rather disregarded primitive religions, seeing them as magical collections of taboos which prescribed or proscribed specific acts and met ad hoc terminal needs. The more advanced religions, by contrast, formulated systems of religious ethics which enforced modes of conduct in a coherent plan of life. As Weber saw them, systems of religious ethics led individuals to subsume their lives in a larger plan which simultaneously molded their personal dispositions and shaped the institutions of society.

Weber constructed a number of "ideal types" of religious orientations based on complex historical investigations of the religions of China, India, ancient Judaism, and various Protestant sects. Weber felt that these ideal types would allow him to compare the implications of each religious system for individual activity and for the development of the institutional order of society. Thus he compared Confucianism and Calvinism. Weber saw the Confucianism of traditional China as having little interest in the supernatural but rather providing a systematic ethical accommodation to the world. Confucianism was concerned with harmonizing the activities of individuals and groups with an underlying natural order of things (*tao*). Given Confucian values and beliefs, Weber thought the typical response of a Chinese would be to reinforce the given social order—thus to act as a Confucian scholar-official and seek to sustain the traditional bureaucracy. By contrast, Weber believed that certain forms of Protestantism, especially Calvinism, induced tension within its adherents which led them to order their lives in a rigorously ascetic manner which ran counter to the traditional medieval social order and to strive to change the world to conform with their image of a moral society. Hence, Weber felt that the Calvinist religious orientation was an essential ingredient in spurring the drive to change that undermined traditional western society and created the modern capitalist order.

Unlike many of his evolutionist contemporaries Weber was not concerned simply to outline evolutionary stages. He was concerned with the process of change, and especially with the dynamic role that religion plays in that evolutionary process. One of his key concepts was that of "rationalization." Weber's concept of rationalization was complex, but involved two notions: first, the systematizing and elaborating necessary to logically integrate the systems and all spheres of life; second, the linking of means and ends more efficiently. Weber believed that operating through history and underlying the cultural evolutionary process was a human disposition to rationalize the cultural and social orders and the lives of individuals. While rationalization might involve the systematization of a traditional cultural and social system, in some cases it involved a radical transformation of culture and society as well. According to Weber, the Protestant Reformation was one such transformation which had enormous historical implications.

Prophecy was another key element in Weber's understanding of the dynamic role of religion in society. He recognized that many prophets demanded that people conform to traditional moral order. Such prophecies might have the effect of rationalizing but not changing a traditional system. But some prophetic visions marked distinctive breaks with tradition and involved a breakthrough to a new system of meaning.

Overview

Rather like the linguist who strives to decode the patterning of a language, the sociocultural anthropologist strives to formulate the patterns of social and cultural systems. In so doing, he finds it convenient to divide such systems into subsystems. Two such subsystems central to the study of anthropology serve as the focus of this chapter. Kinship is the subsystem selected to exemplify the functional working of social systems. Religion is the subsystem selected to exemplify the logical expression of cultural systems. By working through these patterns, a sense is given of the way functional and logical analysis proceed.

Kinship systems are differentiated into unilineal and bilateral types, and it is shown how this difference implies a difference in the wider social life. Thus, unilineal systems encourage corporate kinship groups, while bilateral ways of reckoning descent discourage such groups. Unilineal systems can be further differentiated into matrilineal and patrilineal types, and these, too, differ in the functional patterns they imply. Cross-cutting the types of descent are types of residence, such as matrilocal, patrilocal, and neolocal. The former are favored in traditional societies, the latter in modern ones, and in other ways the pattern of residence is associated with the wider patterning of society. Sexuality stands in a certain opposition to all modes of kinship, and a certain amount of the patterning of kinship can be understood as an effort to control and order sexuality. Final attention is given to kinship as a cultural system, as a way of bestowing meaning and order on experience. Kinship continues to serve this need even in contemporary society, as is illustrated by the widespread phenomenon of extending kinship terminologies to label and classify relationships which are not, strictly speaking, based on biological kinship.

Religion is a cultural system which has received considerable study in anthropology. Despite the depth of knowledge of religious systems, the very richness of the subject has belied efforts to reduce it to orderly typologies. Accordingly, here no effort is made to organize the subject into such neat, if oversimplified, distinctions as is possible with the topic of kinship. Instead, the history of anthropology of religion is traced to the point when the ideas most seminal to current knowledge were formulated. Three major sources are identified: Freud, Durkheim, and Weber. Freud emphasized the psychological roots of religion, Durkheim its social roots, and Weber recognized most profoundly the character of religion as a cultural system. Weber understood religion as a system of symbols, beliefs, and values which orders existence and renders it meaningful.

Topic for Discussion

As a way of sensitizing oneself to the logic of patterns, one might attempt to construct some imaginary societies based on varying types of kinship systems (e.g., combinations of bilineal and unilineal, or without an incest taboo). Consider the way each system could operate or fall apart. One might then consider the issue of how the varying systems could be grounded in cultural meaning.

Suggested Readings

Kinship

Kinship and Marriage (paperback, 1967) by Robin Fox. Well-written exposition of current anthropological thought on kinship.

African Systems of Kinship and Marriage (paperback, 1950) edited by A. R. Radcliffe-Brown and Daryll Forde. A classic statement on the theory of kinship and marriage is found in the introduction.

Matrilineal Kinship (1961) edited by David M. Schneider and Kathleen Gough. General synthesis and theory on matrilineal kinship.

The Elementary Structures of Kinship (1969) by Claude Lévi-Strauss. A provocative synthesis.

Marriage, Authority, and Final Causes (1955) by George C. Homans and David M. Schneider. A vigorous attack on Lévi-Strauss's synthesis.

Structure and Sentiment (1962) by Rodney Needham. A vigorous defense of Lévi-Strauss by a rebutting of the attackers.

Social Structure (paperback, 1965) by George Peter Murdock. Statistically synthesizes a massive amount of data to produce a crude but seminal theory of kinship very different from Lévi-Strauss's.

The Human Animal (paperback, 1960) by Weston LaBarre. A suggestive and thoroughly readable psychoanalytically oriented theory of the biological, psychological, and cultural ramifications of the family pattern.

Psychological Anthropology: Approaches to Culture and Personality (1961) edited by Francis L. K. Hsu. Traces psychological implications of family patterning. See especially Hsu's and Whiting's articles.

World Revolution and Family Patterns (1963) by William J. Goode. Lucid and extensive analysis of kinship in relation to modernization.

"The Family" (1956) by Claude Lévi-Strauss.

"The Future of Kinship Studies" (1965) by Claude Lévi-Strauss.

"The Structure of Unilineal Descent Groups" (1953) by Meyer Fortes.

Schism and Continuity in an African Society (1957) by Victor Turner. One of the best analyses of a matrilineal society.

The Nuer (1940) by E. E. Evans-Pritchard. Classic analysis of a patrilineal society.

Kinship and Marriage Among the Nuer (1951) by E. E. Evans-Pritchard. Extends the classic analysis of patrilineal society.

The Javanese Family: A Study of Kinship and Socialization (1961) by Hildred Geertz. Analysis of the bilineal family in a complex modernizing society.

Honour, Family, and Patronage (1964) by John K. Campbell. A powerful and impressively written analysis of the bilineal family system of a tribal ethnic minority in contemporary Greece.

The Family Revolution in Modern China (paperback, 1968) by Marion J. Levy, Jr. Outstanding analysis of changes taking place in a family-centered, unilineal, large-scale society.

American Kinship: A Cultural Account (paperback, 1968) by David M. Schneider. A succinct but sophisticated exposition of the patterning of American kinship.

The Developmental Cycle in Domestic Groups (1958) edited by Jack Goody. A collection of articles analyzing the dynamics of family life in several societies.

Kinship. (1971) edited by Jack Goody. Well-rounded readings.

Manual for Kinship Analysis (1972) by Ernest L. Schusky. Useful guide to method.

Religion

Theories of Primitive Religion (1965) by E. E. Evans-Pritchard. A classic, lucid introduction.

Consciousness and Change: Symbolic Anthropology in Evolutionary Perspective (1975) by James Peacock. Surveys anthropology of religion in relation to developments in analysis of symbols.

Symbols: Public and Private (1973) by Raymond Firth. Wide survey.

Ecstatic Religion (1971) by I. Lewis.

SECTION
II

SOCIETY
AND CULTURE
IN EVOLUTIONARY
PERSPECTIVE

The objective of this section, which comprises chapters 4 through 10, is to utilize an evolutionary scheme in order to compare and analyze the patterning and dynamics of societies and cultures. Chapter 4 outlines this scheme. Chapters 5 through 9 encounter a range of societies and cultures, endeavoring to understand them in evolutionary terms. Chapter 10 utilizes the insights thus obtained to suggest future directions of sociocultural evolution.

In working through this analysis, the student should look not only for trends in history but also for patterning in society and culture. Such patterning is seen through change, for as one cluster of elements changes so must others; societies and cultures are systems. Only by appreciation of the systematic character of human patterning is proper insight achieved into the human direction.

chapter 4

The Evolution of Society and Culture

The nineteenth century was certainly Darwin's in the sense that the 1859 publication of his *On the Origin of Species* gave definitive form to an evolutionary perspective that dominated the thought of many scholars of the time. Students of society were not immune to the evolutionary virus. During the last half of the nineteenth century, social evolution was a major topic of anthropological speculation. Yet for the past half-century in Anglo-American anthropology the social evolutionism of Morgan and others has stood in almost total disrepute. Why this reversal? What was wrong with evolutionism? These are important questions, because underlying our presentation of anthropology is a theory that in many respects resembles those of the classical evolutionists.

"Morgan's fault," writes Godfrey Lienhardt, "like that of many would-be historians of institutions of his time, was to try to arrange all institutions in a universal time sequence. We must accept that there is not and can never be any historical evidence for one original form of marriage or the family, or indeed that any one original form ever existed."[1] One can certainly agree that the search for *an* archetypal form from which all subsequent society has sprung is fruitless; we simply have no way of knowing precisely what happened when humanity began. On the other hand, Lienhardt's criticism is unduly harsh and demanding, for, in principle, a social or cultural anthropologist should be able to follow a method parallel to that employed by the physical anthropologist. The physical anthropologist no longer searches for *the* fossil of *the* original human. Instead, from scattered finds of fossils, such as those of *Proconsul* (a primate that presumably existed in central Africa during the early Miocene period) or *Dryopithecus* (a primate that presumably ranged over north Africa, India, and Europe during the late Miocene or early Pliocene), he infers that the proto-hominoids who gave rise to both apes and men must have displayed one set of anatomical or physiological traits rather than another. The social anthropologist who paralleled this procedure would search not only for fossils, but also for tools and other artifacts. From these he would attempt to reconstruct the general features of the social life of man's ancestors. But, though there is nothing wrong with such a procedure in principle, in practice such reconstruction is extremely difficult because of the paucity of tangible evidence.

Another criticism leveled at the classical anthropological evolutionists is that they conceived of their postulated historical sequences as implacable natural laws: Every society had to pass through every stage of the proposed sequence; no stage could be skipped, nor could the order of the stages vary. This criticism, however, is based on a stereotyped misrepresentation of the evolutionists' views. As Marvin Harris[2] has shown, the evolutionists were, almost to a man, more flexible than this. Indeed, since different evolutionists proposed different sequences, it is hard to believe that each did not suffer some doubt as to whether his particular scheme was truly *the* revelation of universal natural laws binding on all societies.

Since it is tempting to think of any evolutionary scheme, including the sociocultural, as setting forth stages through which all societies must pass, we must emphasize the flexibility of sociocultural evolution. Societies are not like biological organisms. A society does not have a genetic program which insures that its maturation will proceed in order through stages *A, B, C*. While a society's government might propose a plan for such a sequence, the society can discard the plan (and the government), but an organism cannot reject its genetic program. The concept of sociocultural evolution also differs from the concept of biological maturation in that sociocultural evolution is largely a learning process. A society can always skip stages through which other societies have passed by learning from those societies how to avoid their mistakes. Japan, for instance, learned from the West, and so skipped some of the painful stages through which the West passed in its struggle to industrialize.

The nineteenth-century evolutionists have been castigated for their ethnocentrism. They did not hesitate to classify the societies or races of mankind into lower and higher levels, devising a scale from the apelike to the godlike, with Europeans at the top. The idea was that the higher societies were not only more advanced technologically but, with their monogamy, were also more righteous. Later scholars objected, asserting that technological sophistication does not necessarily imply higher morality. Lienhardt, for example, cites a study completed in 1915 by Hobhouse, Wheeler, and Ginsberg, which attempted to correlate moral traits with economic development. They were forced to conclude, however, that economic progress

> has no necessary connection with improvement in the relations between members of a society. It does not imply greater considerateness or a keener sense of justice, and may in some ways be held to be adverse to them. . . .[3]

Certainly we agree that economic or technological advance does not necessarily lead to moral improvement, but, conversely, economic stagnation does not necessarily lead to goodness. Some who idealize the natural savage or the spiritual Easterner appear to believe so, and such a notion would clearly appeal to those who hope that the meek and poor shall inherit the earth. We do not dismiss so easily the maxim voiced by others that "last guys aren't nice,"[4] that deprivation may engender frustration, resentment, and aggression. In any event, the proposition that economic progress fails to correlate with moral progress does not preclude the formulation of an evolutionary scheme. Whether moral progress is or is not correlated with economic progress, it is still both theoretically and practically possible to construct two scales, one measuring degree of moral progress according to some explicit criterion, the other measuring degree of economic progress. It is equally possible to classify societies according to how high they rank on each scale. If numerous societies rank high on one scale and low on the other, this simply suggests that scales more refined than the combined moral-economic ones used by the Victorians are required.

The defects of the Victorian evolutionary scales do not imply that all evolutionary scales are useless. The advantage of evolutionary scales, such as the modernization scale that we are about to present, is that they permit comparison, correlation, and classification of data which would otherwise remain in disarray.

The Dimensions of Modernization[5]

We distinguish five stages or levels of sociocultural evolution: primitive, archaic, historic, early modern, and modern.[6] The levels are conceptualized as distributed along a scale of relative modernity. This scale is composed of a number of dimensions which may be characterized as follows:

Social, Political, and Economic Organization

The more modern a society, *the more specialized are the units that compose it.* That is, societies at the upper levels of our modernization scale consist largely of units that specialize in the various social tasks— economic, political, religious, recreational. Conversely, societies at the lower levels of modernization consist largely of unspecialized units, each of which performs all or at least several of these tasks rather than just one.

Consider, for example, the task of education. Modern society contains a vast number of units that specialize in education. Not only are there primary, secondary, and advanced schools, but there are also dentistry, medical, and law schools, as well as schools for recently developed specialties, such as filmmaking and computer programming. Americans, who tend to take all of these specialized educational units for granted, may forget that throughout history education has predominantly occurred within a unit not specializing in education: the family. Where education has taken place outside the family, it has been in similarly unspecialized units, such as the temples or churches of historic Buddhist, Muslim, and Christian societies.

In other fields besides education, specialization also proceeds as societies modernize. In archaic Egypt, where the king was also a god, political and religious units tended to be unified, while in more modern societies, separation of church and state is generally the rule; some units specialize in government, others in religion.

The increasing distinction between units for work and units for play provides a final illustration of the trend toward specialization. The primitive both plays and works within his kin-based community, whereas modern man works in one unit, i.e., a factory or an office, while playing in another. Such clear separation of work units from play units encourages the vacations that are so important to modern man; vacations take place in play units that are clearly separate from work units, and for primitives who do not make such a clear separation *vacation* is a meaningless term.

In sum, as one moves up the scale toward modern society, one finds men dividing their time among an increasing number of increasingly specialized units. As one moves down the scale toward primitive society, fewer, less specialized units are found, and people function in all of them more or less simultaneously.

As modernization proceeds, not only do units become increasingly specialized, but *social relations become to an ever higher degree functionally specific, and to an ever lesser degree functionally diffuse.* That is to say that as we move up the scale toward modernity, we find that people increasingly define explicitly what is entailed in their social relationships. Conversely, as we move down the scale toward the primitive, we find that the rights and obligations entailed in social relationships are more often considered implicit to that relationship.

A comparison of traditional China with contemporary America furnishes a good illustration of the contrast between functionally specific and functionally diffuse relationships revolving around the institution of contract. Ideally, in America, the businessman-customer relationship is kept as functionally specific as possible. The relationship is often defined by a contract, and if the contract is vague it is considered a bad contract. Even where there is no written contract, as in simple retail transactions, the obligations involved in the American transaction are, ideally, precisely delimited. Thus, when a customer buys a soft drink, his only obligation is to pay the advertised price. If he hands over a sum less than the advertised price, the buyer is liable, and the seller can respossess the merchandise. The seller's obligation is to deliver the goods as advertised. If there is a rat in the bottle, the seller is liable for restitution of the price. Thus, simple business relations in America are more often than not functionally specific.

In traditional China, on the other hand, the ideal business relationship was kept functionally diffuse. The businessman was expected to feel a great sense of responsibility for his customer. He was expected to grant extra requests, to offer special prices, and—in extreme cases—to protect the customer even at the cost of his own financial ruin. All of this diffuseness derived from the kinship, friendship, or neighbor relationship that underlay the Chinese business relationship. When business in China was between strangers, rather than kinsmen, friends, or neighbors, a *caveat emptor* attitude obtained. Seller and buyer would work as fraudulently and as ruthlessly as possible, each to maximize his own gain.

Perhaps the common knowledge that business was basically immoral explains, in part, why in so many historic or archaic societies, such as traditional China or Japan, the status of merchant was ranked lowest of all by the great moral philosophies of the times, and why it was thus necessary to link the business relationship to some diffuse relationship, such as kinship, in order to establish trust. By contrast, business in America is governed to a striking degree by a code of fair play, backed by law and the courts. Therefore, strangers can do business with confidence and even with amiability. Perhaps, because business is comparatively moral, the businessman occupies a status in modern society, both morally and socially, that would be unheard of in nonmodern societies.

As societies modernize, *markets and media of exchange become increas-*

ingly generalized. The more modern the society, the wider the range of goods and services that each of its media of exchange (such as money) can buy, and the wider the range of choice of market partners with whom goods and services can be exchanged. Conversely, media used by more primitive societies can buy only a limited range of goods, and the markets available to these societies are rudimentary. The difference between highly generalized and highly restricted media and markets can be illustrated by Bronislaw Malinowski's description of the *kula* exchange among the primitive Trobriand islanders and the market exchange of modern society.[7]

Kula is an exchange of treasure objects and takes place largely between permanent partners. Each participant in *kula* can trade only with his permanent partners—five or six for a commoner, perhaps seventy or eighty for a chief. A man's *kula* partners come from islands other than his own, and what he gives to his partner or receives from him is prescribed by the location of the partner's island in relation to his. Thus, a man may give arm bands to his partners living on islands that lie in one direction, but he will give shell necklaces to partners living on islands in the opposite direction. Each time a Trobriander receives an object from his partner in the north, let us say, he passes it on to his partner in the south. The *kula* system, then, forms a huge ring several hundred miles in circumference. Necklaces traveling in one direction will pass arm bands coming from the opposite direction, and trading expeditions circulating around this huge ring provide great excitement and adventure for the Trobrianders.

Treasures used in the *kula* exchanges are not highly generalized media of exchange. A necklace can be exchanged only for an arm band, and an arm band only for a necklace. A necklace cannot even buy another necklace, much less food, housing, land, or labor. One is limited in what one can obtain with a *kula* object. By contrast, no matter how dreary it may seem when set beside the glitter and exoticism of the *kula* objects, modern money is a highly generalized medium of exchange. It is one of the great cultural achievements in that it is a symbol into which virtually everything can be translated and for which virtually everything can be exchanged. For this very reason, money can destroy a traditional culture: All traditional values are reduced to monetary value.

Just as money is a more generalized medium of exchange than *kula* objects, so the modern market organization is more generalized than the *kula* circle. The *kula* trader has only a few choices of trading partner, and the group from whom he chooses his partner was probably not his choice in the first place. He probably inherited it from a relative. And the type of object that the Trobriander wishes to trade strongly limits who his partner can be. If he has a bracelet in hand, he can trade with a partner who lives in only one direction; if it is a necklace, he must trade in the other direction. Thus, when the Trobriander sets out in his canoe with his necklaces or bracelets, he faces only a limited array of opportunities for exchange.

The trader in modern society, however, is free to choose as a partner anyone who will buy what he has to sell or who sells what he wants to buy. The field is open, he is not bound to a group of permanent partners, but only to his contractual obligations—which he enters voluntarily. Also, certain institutions in modern society insure that no man loses the freedom to seek new contractual partners. It is illegal for a man to sell himself into slavery, partly because as a slave his rights to enter new contracts voluntarily would be abrogated. Here lawful restraints insure continuing freedom of choice. It is the same, of course, with antitrust laws. As graduates of the Harvard Law School are admonished: "Administer these just restraints that you may make men free."

It is important to realize that generalized media other than money have emerged in modern society. For example, the vote, as employed in modern government, is a generalized medium. It can be exchanged for a wide range of goods and services. By "paying" his vote to the candidate of his choice, a citizen may hope to receive the kind of government he wants. Both the custom of "trading votes" and the institution of the "influence peddler" suggest other parallels between dollars and votes.

Centralization is another dimension of modernization. The more modern a society, the more centralized it is: the more tightly its parts become coordinated with one another under some central control. Such coordination and control is not just political. In the United States the ecumenical movement and the United Fund represent increasing centralization: Diverse churches and diverse charities become coordinated with one another under a central control. Similarly, centralization occurs when smaller unions are welded into one federation, and businesses merge to form larger corporations. The high stage of development of transportation and communication in the United States facilitates the centralization of its various institutions. Indeed, in all respects save the political, the United States is more highly centralized than the Soviet Union.

Obviously, in primitive societies like that of the Australian aborigines, where families are dispersed without intercommunication while wandering about seeking food, and where there is no chief or central government, the degree of centralization is low. Even in archaic societies, such as traditional China, which boasted a pony express capable of transporting the true relics of the Buddha from India to the Chinese capital in a few days over rough terrain, or in Rome with its imperial highways, centralization was not comparable to what it is today. Transportation and communications were simply too slow.

Anomalously, many contemporary primitive societies enjoy transportation and communication facilities (airplanes and radios) that are infinitely more efficient than those available to more modern societies of the past. Because of their airplanes and radios, these primitive societies are rapidly entering the sociopolitical network of the great powers, while the decisions of these powers (perhaps to form a guerrilla force backing one side in a war the native soldiers do not control) help to transform such societies into colonial appendages. In this sense, the primitive societies are not really skipping steps in their evolution toward modernity; they are simply being assimilated into a centralized system.

The speed with which bodies, goods, and messages move about the modern world not only changes sociopolitical patterns, but apparently leads to deep and important changes in the personalities of the people involved. According to studies carried out in the Near East (Turkey, Lebanon, Egypt, Syria, and Jordan), centralization encourages empathetic capacity.[8] As a society becomes centralized, its members learn to project themselves into the role of the stranger and to imagine themselves as participants in exotic situations. This increased empathetic skill is understandable, for in societies that are *not* centralized, most people live in small, self-sufficient villages. They deal mainly with people whom they know well and who are like themselves, and with situations which are familiar. There is little need, therefore, to develop skills of empathizing with the unfamiliar.

To test the ability of Near Eastern villagers to empathize with strange people and situations, researchers asked them such questions as: "If you were made the editor of a newspaper, what kind of paper would you run?" "If for some reason, you could not live in our native country, what other country would you choose to live in?" "Suppose you were made head of your country's government, what are some of the things you would do?" The researchers were only a little less astonished at the answers they received than were the villagers at the questions they were asked. In reply to "What would you do if you were president of your country?" a Turkish villager exclaimed: "My God! How can you ask such a thing? How can I . . . I cannot . . . president of Turkey . . . master of the whole world?" When a Shi'i shoemaker in Saida, Lebanon, was asked what he would do if he were editor of a newspaper, he first accused the interviewer of ridiculing him, then begged the interviewer to change the question. The interviewer consented, noting later that "the shoemaker" was making all kinds of frantic movements with his head and hands."

But a modern, centralized society such as America requires great empathetic skill for effective operation. In social contexts ranging from the most trivial to the most vital, Americans have burnished this skill to a high gloss. The slogans *Be a defensive driver* and *Think for the other guy* illustrate the need for empathy in our complex society—for our very survival. When an American votes, he chooses in large part on the basis of empathy with a stranger; it is extremely rare for the voter to know a candidate personally. But the most remarkable talent Americans display is for empathizing with the characters of television advertising whose breath is not sweet or whose hair is diseased. Yet on precisely such empathy do American advertising and the American economy depend.

As a society modernizes it becomes increasingly *bureaucratized.* Bureaucracy proliferates not only in government but also in firms, schools, and other institutions that organize functionally specific offices with well-defined lines of authority. Indeed, bureaucratization is so essential to modern society, and so ingrained, that even those who preach against it are forced to bureaucratize if they wish to propagate their message efficiently. Whether a modern society is communist, democratic, or socialist, it depends on bureaucracies. And at premodern stages of evolution, the shift toward bureaucratization is crucial. As we shall see, the change from *kin*ship to *king*ship as a basis for social organization marks the crucial emergence from the primitive pattern.

The great early archaic bureaucracies, although undeniably magnificent creations, were smaller and less effective than some people claim. The Chinese bureaucracy, one of the most intriguing of these early bureaucracies, never, by the most generous estimate, involved more than a half million persons. Nor did it ever really manage to overcome the interference of kinship ties. True, entry into the bureaucracy depended on performance in examinations on Chinese literature, and not on one's kinship bonds to officials; and there were other devices to insure that kinship favoritism did not interfere with the workings of bureaucracy. Nevertheless, when viewed carefully and comprehensively, the Chinese bureaucracy reveals itself to have been merely an island of functional specificity in a sea of functional diffuseness. Invariably, kinship bonds intruded. Nepotism and corruption, involving favoritism for one's kinfolk, always intefered with impersonal loyalties to the bureaucracy and the emperor. Perhaps this was one reason why eunuchs and celibates played important roles in so many archaic bureaucracies; not having children they could favor, the eunuchs and celibates were not so likely to insitute dynasties within the bureaucracy.

It is interesting to observe what happens when a "primitive" tribe, with a social structure based on kinship, is forced to deal with the bureaucracies of the nation in which it resides. In Greece, as J. K. Campbell[9] describes it, there is a tribe of shepherds, called the Sarakatsani, whose roving way of life frequently gets them into trouble with the Greek government. Since the Sarakatsani believes that he is too lowly to relate to so elevated a figure as a government official, he seeks an alliance with some influential person, usually a lawyer, who will act as a go-between. Since lawyers and bureaucrats meet in the hotels of Greek towns to drink coffee together, the Sarakatsani thinks that the lawyer might have influence with the bureaucrat. To bind the lawyer to himself the Sarakatsani commonly seeks to make him a spiritual kinsman. This he accomplishes by asking the lawyer to be his child's godfather, a request not easily refused. As the child's godfather, the lawyer must stand with the child at its baptism, which immediately follows the rite of confirmation, a critical rite for the Sarakatsani. During the confirmation rite the godfather, replacing the child's own parents, holds the child, names it, and at the close of the service hands the child back to its mother, saying, "I return the child to you in this life, but I shall ask it back from you in the next. Protect it well from fire, water, and all evil!" Ever after, throughout the child's life, the godfather's spiritual bond to the child is so like kinship that the child is forbidden to marry into his godfather's family, and, because of his spiritual kinship to his godchild, the godfather cannot refuse a favor asked by the parents in the child's name. The parent is now in a position to obtain favors from the lawyer—to ask him to intercede on his behalf with the bureaucracy. Thus, in Sarakatsani society, as in many similar societies, relations with the bureaucracy are conducted as much like kinship relations as possible.

Kinship and the Family Structure

What generalizations can be made about the effects of modernization on kinship? Evidence indicates that as society shifts from primitive to modern, the importance of the conjugal bond increases while that of the kinship bond decreases: More emphasis is laid on the bond between husband and wife, and less on that between child and parent. One sign of this conjugal emphasis in modern society is that a married couple resides neolocally: Husband and wife, more often than not, live apart from their parents. In contrast, primitive couples often reside patrilocally or matrilocally: either with the husband's parents and kinsmen or with the wife's parents and kinsmen.

A description of the way in which a Sarakatsani couple chooses a place to live illustrates the nonmodern society's tendency to emphasize kinship bonds rather than conjugal bonds.[10]

The first stage of the Sarakatsani domestic cycle occurs just after a man and woman marry. The wife comes to live with her husband in his parents' household: The couple begins its domestic life by residing patrilocally. At this point the husband's primary loyalty is to his kinsmen— especially to his parents and siblings. The husband acts as though he were ashamed of his wife: He insults her and sleeps with her only in secret.

The second stage of the cycle begins when the wife gives birth. The husband's behavior toward his wife changes. His insults cease. The back-breaking labor that the wife was forced to endure previously for the sake of her husband's family now diminishes. Why these changes? The wife is no longer simply a wife. She is also a mother. As such she is related more closely to her husband's family, through her blood relationship to her child, than she was before the child arrived. As a mother she is more highly regarded than she was as a wife, because it is the parent-child bond rather than the husband-wife bond that merits respect among the Sarakatsani.

Later when the wife finds herself and her child sharing the house of her husband's parents in company with the wives and children of her husband's brothers, the third stage begins. Even with only a few brothers, enough wives and children are on hand to fill the house with noise and quarrels. Each wife worries loudly about whether her child is getting a fair share of whatever the brothers jointly produce. Eventually this discord becomes so great that the loyalty the husband holds for his child takes precedence over his loyalty to brothers and parents. The husband takes his wife and children away from his parents' household, and establishes a household of his own. Clearly, this move is not for the wife's benefit; if he did not leave his parents in the early days of their marriage when she was unhappiest, why should he leave now? It is his child who is in difficulty—therefore he moves. Once more, as in most nonmodern societies, the child-parent bond carries the most weight.

In America the husband-wife bond counts more than among the Sarakatsani. Not only do American newlyweds usually set up housekeeping away from their parents for the sake of their marriage, but they also feel, in general, that if conflict arises between one's parents and one's spouse, one should take the spouse's side. In nonmodern societies, the reverse tends to be true.

Conjugal emphasis is at the core of the modern belief that marriage should be based on love, rather than on class or kinship. One ideal of the romantic love complex is that the individual should marry whomever he loves: that marriage is mainly the concern of the individuals involved. In most nonmodern societies, however, marriage is an alliance between kinship groups, such as clans or lineages. Since a healthy alliance between kinship groups is what matters most, elders from the two groups arrange the marriage. This situation is common in primitive societies, but even in historic societies, such as those of lowland Southeast Asia, parents frequently arrange their children's marriages. In Thailand and Java the young people yearn for the romantic marriages depicted in novels, films, and songs. For them opposition to parent-arranged marriage is still a burning issue, and choice of their own spouse still a highly charged fantasy.

Not surprisingly, romanticizing the husband-wife bond, and thus strengthening it, has weakened the parent-child bond. Not only does this imply that spouses will lose interest in their parents, but also that, as their interest in each other increases, they will lose interest in their children. At present, in societies such as Java, parents tend to be more interested in their children than in each other. A marriage is hardly considered sealed until it has produced children; this is indicated by symbols of fertility hung outside the wedding place and by the constant hopeful queries directed at a new wife to find out if she is pregnant. But in time the child focus should give way to a conjugal focus. Effective contraception methods will probably give impetus to this trend.

Let us again turn briefly to patterns of residence. We contrast nuclear-family households with extended-family households. The nuclear-family household, composed of parents and unmarried children, is dominant in modern society. The extended-family household, composed of parents, their children, and these children's spouses and children, was the mode among elite groups of the past. The ancient Icelandic tale, *Nyal's Saga,* tells of old Nyal's extended-family household in which lived not only Old Nyal and his wife Bergthron, but also their three sons and the sons' wives and children. Including servants, there were fifty people in this one household.

Among the advantages of such an extended living arrangement is that a father and his sons, who own a plot of land jointly, can live on that land and farm it together; but with the advent of modernization, fathers begin to care more about hiring efficient workers to farm their land, less about building and sustaining the bond with their sons. At the same time, sons lose interest in farming. Instead, they care more about making their own fortunes. The result is that extended-family households tend to give way to nuclear-family households established by the sons in cities or other locations away from home. Wherever modernization occurs, extended-family households may be seen giving way to nuclear-family households, and with this change the emphasis on kinship bonds diminishes, while the emphasis on conjugal bonds increases.

It cannot be too highly stressed that kinship, in all its aspects, thoroughly pervades nonmodern society. The Sarakatsani, for example, choose their friends mainly from among their kinsmen; in one survey, seven out of ten reported that they regard a "cousin" as their best friend. Nonkinsmen, on the other hand, are generally perceived as enemies, current or potential. A Sarakatsani traveling through hills inhabited even by his fellow tribesmen would not spend the night with "friends" who were not kinsmen. Not only friends but also coworkers are kinsmen or affines; "companies" of cooperating shepherds are composed of brothers and brothers-in-law, never of nonkinsmen. Generally, Sarakatsani mistrust nonkinsmen, and expect nonkinsmen to betray them. Conversely, kinsmen are expected to display total loyalty to one another. Campbell says of the Sarakatsani: "Where kinsmen betray one feels horror, as with treason in our own society."[11] The remark is revealing, since it suggests that for the Sarakatsani the family is the object of highest loyalty, just as the nation is for modern man. It is logical, then, that a Sarakatsani without family is as lacking in honor as a modern man without a country. Having no family and no honor, the bastard child is deemed hardly human, and is left on the mule path to die.

Social Differentiation, Mobility, and Change

In concluding these remarks on the characteristics of social modernization, let us outline three broad social factors. These factors, derived in part from those already mentioned, are *social differentiation, social mobility,* and *social change.*

Social differentiation (the separation of social units from one another) issues in part from the growing specialization of units that accompanies modernization. With modernization societies come to be composed of increasingly numerous units differentiated from one another by their specialties. At the early stages of modernization, this differentiation is mainly along class lines. From virtually classless primitive society emerges the archaic pattern which distinguishes the elite that specializes in religio-political functions and the masses who specialize in manual labor. The archaic stage is followed by the historic when religious elite and political elite form separate classes, both distinguished from the masses. We call the primitive pattern one-class, the archaic two-class, and the historic three-class. During later stages of modernization, society divides into a great number of political, occupational, religious, and other factions that cut across class lines. For this reason, with the advent of early modern society, we stop viewing social differentiation in such simple terms as class.

Social mobility is the movement of individuals between the strata of a society. Often a society's myths and ideology depict a higher rate of social mobility than actually exists. For instance, although the "American Dream" expresses the ideal that any man with the will can find a way up the social ladder, some commentators believe that the *actual* rate of movement between strata in America is declining. In any event, it is still a fact that with modernization both the idealized rate of mobility and the actual rate tend to rise: Not only do people think they can rise (or fall) faster in the social milieu but they actually can. One reason for increased mobility is that modernization weakens the bond between the individual and the group into which he was born; it becomes easier for him to move away from that group and up (or down) into a new group.

Finally, the more modern a society is, the more rapid is its overall rate of change. This point relates to the argument that fast-changing societies adapt best to a fast-changing environment and that among all types of societies, the modern is the fastest to change.

A major reason why modern men are more ready to change than nonmodern men is that modern men put less emphasis on tradition and more on rationality, *i.e.*, on efficient relation of means to ends. Modern men don't always act rationally, but they do feel a greater need to justify their actions on rational grounds. A Trobriand islander might farm quite rationally, efficiently exploiting available resources to produce bountiful yam harvests, but if asked to explain why he did what he did, he would likely reply: "Because this is the way we have always done it." On the other hand, the modern farmer, if asked to justify his method of fertilizing, might well reply: "Because this method produces a high yield per acre"—in other words, because method X is the most efficient, or rational, way to achieve the end he seeks. Since the modern farmer professes loyalty to the canons of rationality, he is bound to feel some pressure to keep searching for more efficient methods to achieve the desired goal of high productivity. Thus, even if he is a rural conservative, he is constantly goaded to change. The Trobriander justifies his practices by phrasing them as outgrowths of a tradition that, in his view, was laid down by his ancestors and has never changed. The Trobriander's ideology gives greater sanction to lack of change than the modern man's ideology, and on this ground alone we would expect the overall rate of change in modern society to be greater than in Trobriand society.

It can be said that all of the traits we have called modern speed social change. Take, for example, centralization. The more centralized the society, the more quickly change spreads through it. This is true not only of political, economic, and communications centralization, but also of what we might call "ethical centralization"—the development of a single ethic that applies to all situations. The relation between ethical centralization and the speed of social change can be illustrated by comparing the Judeo-Christian and Oriental religious traditions.

The monistic Judeo-Christian tradition decrees that its God and Law should be followed under all circumstances. To be Christian on Sunday, but not on Monday, is deemed morally exceptionable. To be Jewish at one hour, Buddhist at another, is not encouraged. Furthermore, most Jews or Christians would find it strange to be Catholic at home, Protestant in the office, and Jewish at play. Patterns like these are common in the Orient, however. Javanese do not feel uncomfortable professing Islam in some situations, animism in others, and a kind of

Buddhism in still others. Thai are not worried about acting, in various situations, as Buddhists, animists, or Brahmanists. Many anthropologists call such Southeast Asian patterns syncretic since they blend many traditions, but the traditions are not so much blended as distributed carefully and selectively among diverse situations. Situationalism rather than monism is the pattern not only in Southeast Asia, but also in East Asia. As noted earlier, the Japanese apparently does not experience the same discomfort the Westerner might feel if called upon to apply an ethic in situation *A* that contradicts the ethic appropriate to situation *B*. Perhaps in Japan this ethical situationalism encourages an unevenness of change. Japan has demonstrated a striking ability to industrialize rapidly while retaining customs alien to the industrial milieu, whereas in the monistic West, industrialization has brought sweeping changes in all spheres of life. It could be argued that the West's ethical monism fostered an attitude that change in any situation ought to be generalized to all situations, but that Japan's ethical compartmentalization helped to prevent change in one area of life from spreading into other areas.

Religion and Ideology

In the ideological and religious facets of modernization, we note the trend toward a *universalistic* ethic which decrees that men must be judged on the basis of merit or skill, rather than on the basis of some immutable status assigned to them at birth. Not kinship, race, sex, or caste, but deeds are what count in a universalistic ethic. Where such statuses count more than deeds, we speak of a *particularistic* ethic.

If we move from an archaic and particularistic society, like that of ancient China, to an early modern and relatively universalistic society, like that of nineteenth-century Britain, we observe a rise in the tendency to hire and fire on the basis of what a man can do, rather than on the basis of who he is in terms of kinship. In Britain and America the continuing trend toward universalism is reflected in the changing laws and attitudes regarding race, women's rights, and poverty. Another example of the trend toward universalism is provided by the developing nations. Many of these nations were formerly archaic or historic kingdoms, organized on the basis of particularism; the status into which one was born determined one's life. Colonialism, with its racist and elitist tendencies, helped perpetuate particularism, but at the same time it propagated the Western notion of universalism. Thus, colonialism sowed the seeds of its own decline.

Today, in many of the developing nations, the act of becoming modern is strongly bound up with the notion of universalism. An interesting symptom of the shift toward universalism in one develoing nation, Indonesia, is displayed in the themes of its folkplays or *ludruk*. In *ludruk* of earlier derivation, the villain could never lose if he came from a high class. The hero, if lowborn, could never win. In more recent *ludruk*, however, the characters are punished on the basis of what they do rather than who they are. This is only one of many signs of a growing Indonesian universalism.[12] But it should also be noted that, more often than not, the developing nations still cling to one form of particularism: Their nationalist ideologies will cause a man to be evaluated more favorably if he is of the home nationality than if he is foreign, even if the native and the foreigner are equal in merit and skill.

Ancient China furnishes an excellent illustration of a large-scale society that operated largely on a particularistic basis. According to Chinese ideal and expectation, kinship considerations always came first. Even an attempt to assassinate the emperor could be forgiven if the would-be assassin could prove that he did so to avenge a genuine wrong done to his father or another ancestor. Nepotism was no cause for embarrassment. In fact, if a traditional Chinese was caught *not* favoring his relatives for jobs, it was distinctly embarrassing. From the Chinese viewpoint, not to give preference to relatives was inhuman and bestial (in the China of today, cultural revolution on the mainland is eliminating many of the old particularistic ideals). While American politicians or businessmen are often nepotistic, they are commonly defensive about it and often criticized. Thus, although there are still particularistic practices in America, our ideals are generally universalistic.

There is a second broad ideological trend that accompanies modernization. The more modern the society, the less will its members believe that their society exercises control over their cosmos, or ideal system. The less modern the society, the more they will perceive or believe such control exists. With the advent of early-modern society, the cosmic came to be perceived not only as separate from the social, but also as taking control over the social.[13] This trend becomes clearer by examining, briefly for now, the following three stages:

1. *Primitive level: exemplified by the Australian aborgines.* The aborigines perceive little separation between the cosmic world, which they express by myth and ritual, and the actual world, in which they live. They imagine that their cosmic world, "The Dreaming," is populated by their own ancestral kin who live in "every-when." These kin merge the social present with the cosmic past, and the cosmic thus mixes intimately with the social.

2. *Historic level: exemplified by Thai Buddhists.* The Buddhists preceive a radical discrepancy between the ideal world and the real world. In fact, they claim that the real world is not real, but simply an illusion

from which men should flee. It is the Thai Buddhist attitude that the real world should be left behind by retreat into monastic seclusion. The monk, therefore, becomes a prestigious person and plays a central role in Thailand.

3. *Early-modern level: exemplified by the early Calvinists.* Like the Buddhists, the Calvinists perceived a radical discrepancy between the cosmic world, the "Kingdom of God," and the actual world, the "Kingdom of Man." But, unlike the Buddhists, they did not favor fleeing from the world to escape its imperfections. Rather, they were beset with a compulsion to reform the world in the image of the cosmic.

In this schematic overview, the shift from the primitive Australians to the historic Buddhists is accompanied by a rise in the perceived discrepancy between the actual social order and the imagined cosmic order. The Calvinists, like the Buddhists, perceived the discrepancy, but they also added another dimension—a compulsion to reform the actual to conform to the image of the cosmic. Hence, the Calvinists possessed a powerful stimulus to change society, a stimulus that the aborigines and Buddhists lack. Like *technological* modernization, *ideological* modernization helps society to change and adapt to altering environments.

Ecology and Technology

Sociocultural systems do not, of course, exist in a vacuum and they can not function without resources. Defined conventionally, the environment(s) in which sociocultural systems exist includes the surface of the earth, subsurface resources (water, minerals, etc.), climate, vegetation and fauna, and adjacent sociocultural systems. With respect to the physical environment human beings rely on a man-made technological order which enables them to exploit the environment and gain the necessary resources, such as food, shelter, raw materials, to sustain the sociocultural order. Humans are one of the few species that has been capable of sustaining life in virtually every ecological zone of the earth—indeed to go beyond the limits of the earth into outer space. Paleontological evidence now suggests that human biological evolution began in the relatively tropical regions of east African millions of years ago. Though the earth has gone through dramatic changes in climate, landform, and the like, human beings have spread across the face of the earth inhabiting even inhospitable deserts, mountains, and arctic zones.

Ecology is the study of the relations between living organisms and the environments in which they exist, including the flora and fauna as well as the physical features of the earth. Cultural ecology treats the relations between human groups, their sociocultural systems, and the environments in which they are found. Vantage points on these relationships range from that of the extreme "determinist" who argues that the nature of the environment—terrain, climate, and the like—totally determines the character of sociocultural systems, to the extreme "idealist" who sees sociocultural systems as autonomous and independent of environmental constraints—floating above the material world and developing by its own internal logic. Our own view is moderate: Environment and sociocultural systems can best be viewed as interacting in complex networks of causation similar to those of cybernetic systems. (A simple analogy is that of the relation between thermostat and furnace. The setting of the thermostat provides information which regulates or controls the operation of the furnace—"telling" the furnace to go on or off in relation to the preset temperature level. The furnace provides the energy which affects the thermostat—raising the temperature to the point where the thermostat no longer sends directions to the furnace. Thermostat and furnace are linked in a "feedback" relation, as are cultural systems [which give direction] and environments [which provide resources].)

Energy from the environment is essential for the maintenance of any sociocultural system, if only for the physical perpetuation of the group. In some measure the characteristics of the physical environment may impose limits on the sociocultural systems which exist in it. An arid desert or a precipitous mountain terrain pose different possibilities and impose different constraints than, say, a lush savannah or a temperate plain. But the contraints on sociocultural system imposed by physical environments are by no means absolute. Sociocultural systems also control the environments in which they are found. Thus, the American Indians used the Great Plains for hunting bison but were unable to tap its great fertility as a farming area. Only after the invention of the steel plow was the Great Plains' agricultural potential realized. Modern technology generally increases control of the environment. With air conditioning and heat pumps we can create artificial climates; we could, if we wished, grow bananas at the North Pole. But, although modern technology allows for greater control over the environment, it also increases our dependency on a wider range of resources drawn from all over the world. And with greater control and greater dependency also comes the potential for environmental destruction, pollution, and the exhaustion of nonrenewable resources.

Technology may be the most significant mediation between human groups and their environments, but sociocultural systems interact with and control environments in other ways too. For example, Australian aborigines attribute sacred qualities to various animal species which are identified with lineages and locations mythologically rooted in the ancestors. Being sacred, these species and locations are hedged with taboos which limit human usage. In traditional India all forms of life were deemed to have special value, but particularly the cow. As a result, many Hindus were vegetarians; and butchers and leather workers, thought to be polluting, were relegated to outcast positions. Even today large numbers of sacred cattle are allowed to wander freely and without hindrance. Many Westerners see the food which the sacred cow forage as using up resources which might better be used for alleviating human hunger, and they bemoan the loss of the protein which the cows represent. Yet, ecological anthropologists have argued that in fact India's sacred cows represent a positive rather than a negative ecological adaptation. Not only is their milk an important item in Indian diet, they graze on resources which humans could not recover, and their dung provides fuel and fertilizer.

Food taboos which may be religiously sanctioned represent another way in which cultural definitions may have an important impact on environmental adaptation. For example, certain broad classes of animals (most notably the pig, but a variety of other creatures as well) were defined as polluting and unclean for the ancient Jews in the Biblical abominations of Leviticus. Such proscriptions inevitably influenced the kinds of animals that were raised by the Jews for food. While sheep were carefully herded, pigs were raised neither by the Jews nor by the Muslims who followed the same Biblical proscriptions. In contrast to the abhorrence of pigs by Muslims and Jews, pork is the favorite item of food in many societies. In Melanesia, for example, raising pigs and providing their flesh in feasts can be the major avenue for gaining status. The Maring of New Guinea live in relatively small clan villages. Considerable enmity exists between the various villages though some are allied with others. Although the Maring cultivate yams, taro, and sweet potatoes, their favorite food is pork and they raise huge numbers of pigs. Every twelve years or so the Maring hold a feast at which large numbers of pigs are slaughtered and the meat is gorged by the villagers and their allies. This feast is the prelude to a period of active warfare between various villages, which is then followed by a period of prolonged truce. Rappaport has argued that the warfare cycle of the Maring is closely related to the raising of pigs. During the long truce periods the numbers of pigs increase dramatically to the point where it becomes too large relative to the amount of time and resources necessary to care for them. When the pig population becomes unsupportable the Maring kill most of them in the feast which ushers in the period of warfare. The pork eaten in the feast solidifies alliances between villages and also provides the Maring which high levels of protein which supports the extra efforts expended in warfare. The period of truce is used to build up the number of pigs in preparation for the next big feast which will trigger the cycle once more. Thus, according to Rappaport, the relationship of the Maring to their physical and social environment is a complex network of ecological and ritual factors.

Types of Ecological Adaptation

Although the relationships between sociocultural systems and the environments in which they exist are extremely complex, some generalizations can be made about the characteristics and implications of a number of well-known types of ecological adaptations. We will briefly discuss hunting and gathering, shifting (or swidden) agriculture, sedentary agriculture, pastoralism, and industrialism.

Hunting and Gathering.   It is widely held that the very earliest human groups followed a hunting and gathering mode of life, a pattern which still exists in isolated pockets. Recent examples are the Australian aborigines. Negritos of Malaya, and Bushmen of Kalahari. Hunters and gatherers typically live in small groups or bands made up of four or five family units usually related through kinship or marriage. Relying as they do on the natural availability of food and game in the environment hunters and gatherers follow a nomadic way of life. Each band has a territory through which it forages over an annual cycle. As the resources in one area are exhausted, the band moves on to another. Within the band there is a sexual division of labor with the men being responsible for hunting while the women, charged with caring for the young, gather edible plants located near the camp site. Despite the kinship relationships within the band group cohesiveness is not strong and family units are free to leave one band and attach themselves to another when food resources warrant or personal enimity develops. Although age is respected, there are no well-defined statuses of authority; leadership depends on skill as a provider and force of character. Indeed, among hunters and gatherers there is little specialization of roles, though there inevitably are differences in individual talent or skill. Because of the nomadic life style, each band must have a large territory available to support its small number of people. Hence, population densities among hunters and gatherers are quite low. (For example, it is estimated that hunters and gatherers of Malaysia have population density of only two to three persons per square mile.) For this reason and also because of the limited resource base, the level of social specialization, differentiation, and centralization that hunting and gathering can support is limited.

Pastoralism. The ecological adaptation of some sociocultural systems centers around the herding and husbandry of domesticated animals. The domestication of animals may extend even further back in history than the development of agriculture. Agriculturalists also maintain various domestic animals as draft animals and as food supplements, but pastoralists rely almost exclusively on their animals for food and trade as the economic base of their societies. Commonly pastoralists live in a symbiotic though tense relationship with sedentary cultivators with whom they trade their animals for agricultural products and other goods. Pastoralism is found primarily in Africa and Asia—on the deserts where the camel and horse run; in East Africa where cattle are kept by the Nuer, Dinka, Hereros and others; and on the vast steppes of Asia where the Kazaks, Tartars, Altai, Kalmuks, and Mongols maintain large herds of horses, sheep, and cattle. The Laps herd reindeer even in the Arctic regions, while Tibetans have Yaks in the mountains of the Himalayas.

Pastoralists follow a mode of life reminiscent of hunters and gatherers in that they wander in small groups where they can find grazing lands. Rights to graze are a major factor in the lives of Pastoralists and each group may be identified with a particular territory which it defends against encroachment by either other pastoralists or by sedentary farmers (cf. the movie portrayals of U.S. range wars between cattlemen versus sheepherders and/or farmers). Among sedentarists, pastoralists have a sometimes deserved reputation as being warlike and aggressive (cf. the Mongols' near conquest of Asia and Europe and the Arab conquests of the Near East and North Africa). Among the pastoral Bedouins the common unit is a band of patrilineally related kinsmen under the leadership of a senior male. These smaller units are organized into larger units called tribes and there is frequent feuding between tribes to gain grazing rights, access to water, and preeminence in terms of status. The migratory nature of pastoralism makes the integration of larger groups tenuous and difficult to maintain.

Agriculture. Agriculture as a mode of adapting human groups to their physical environment differs fundamentally from hunting and gathering, and carries different sociocultural implications as well. It appears that agriculture was independently invented at different times in several areas of the world. The first center of agricultural development seems to have been in the Near East, in the area known as the fertile Crescent in the drainage area of the Euphrates River. This development occurred about 10,000 b.c. and initially may have involved simply assisting naturally growing wild plants on hill sides and upland plateaus. Later agriculture moved to the more fertile river valleys. Various forms of wild wheat were among the first crops cultivated, leading to domesticated varieties which were then supplemented by such crops as peas and beans, linseed, and grapes. When agriculture spread from its nuclear area new crops were domesticated, e.g., rye and other cereals in Europe.

In Southeast Asia an agricultural complex depending on such root crops as taro and yams seems to have developed independently of the Near Eastern agricultural complex. This root crop agriculture spread from Southeast Asia throughout the islands of the Pacific where the coconut was added as an important crop. Recent archaeological evidence also suggests that rice may have been domesticated and grown in the Southeast Asian region prior to its cultivation in China.

The independent development of agriculture in the New World was considerably later than in the Old. Apparently about 700 B.C. maize was domesticated from a wild grass native to Mexico. The American agricultural complex included not only corn but also peas, beans, potatoes, gourds, peppers, cotton, and tobacco. By the time of the discovery of the New World in the fifteenth century, agriculture had spread widely throughout the Americas.

There exist numerous patterns of agriculture. Here we will discuss two types: shifting cultivation and sendentary agriculture. In terms of their social and cultural implications, both types contrast markedly with the hunting and gathering type of ecological adaptation.

Shifting cultivation is known by a number of names, including "swidden" and "slash and burn." This form of agriculture is spread widely throughout the world; it is practiced by such peoples as the hill peoples of Southeast Asia, the Indians of Amazonia, and the ancient Maya among many others. The form described here is characteristic of the Southeast Asian Hill peoples. Ordinarily a village group will clear an area of virgin forest, burn the felled trees and vegetation, and plant the burned-over area in millet, dry rice, gourds, and various types of legumes. Such a field may be planted for several years but then it loses its fertility, and the group moves on. Another area of virgin forest is cleared, burned, and planted while the original field is allowed to remain fallow to regenerate its plant cover. This cycle is followed over a period of many years so that eventually the farming group returns to the original field. Shifting cultivation, then, involves rotation of fields rather than rotation of crops. In contrast to hunters and gatherers who simply take advantage of the natural order without transforming it, shifting cultivators manipulate the natural order. Shifting cultivation is capable of producing stable and certain surpluses, hence larger populations can be supported by shifting cultivation than can be supported by hunting and gathering. (For example, southeast Asian shifting cultivators have a population density of 130 people per square mile.) The technical requirements of shifting cultivation do, however, limit the number of people which it can support. The effectiveness of the cultivation-fallowing cycle requires fairly large areas of land, some of which is productive, some of which is virgin forest, and some of which is fallowed. If there is not enough land available for extensive periods of fallowing the land quickly loses its fertility and may erode. Although shifting cultivators do live for long periods of time in relatively permanent villages, they are somewhat nomadic. After an area has been cultivated for awhile, families may split off from one village to affiliate with another which has more fertile land available. Eventually even whole villages may pick up and leave their old territory seeking new areas of virgin forest.

The surpluses and population densities produced by shifting cultivation render possible more centralized and differentiated complex social systems than are supported by hunting and gathering. Typically, villages of shifting cultivators are made up of nuclear family households drawn from a number of lineages. Although many such villages are autonomous political units in which there is little difference in status or wealth between householders, some villages may be united in a larger domain with autocratic chiefs who head clans, aristocratic lineages, commoners and even a class of "slaves." Such domains are integrated through a system of marriage alliances between ranked lineages and clans—e.g., the "cross-cousin marriage" and "circulating connubium" already discussed. Bridewealth payments, heirloom objects, and large ceremonial feasts serve to validate high rank and to redistribute the surpluses produced through cultivation. High status is partly rooted in a supposed special relationship between a chief and the spirits who are thought to control the fertility of his domain. Despite the status distinctions, there are few full-time specialists within shifting cultivator groups. Even the most powerful chief or high ranking aristocrat must work in his fields.

Sedentary agriculture, as its name suggests, requires a high degree of territorial fixity, not characteristic of either hunting and gathering or of shifting cultivation. Shifting cultivation relies almost exclusively on human energy supplemented by such simple tools as the digging stick. Sedentary or intensive agriculture typically involves the use of draft animals such as ox, horse, and water buffalo (or in its more developed forms machinery such as tractors), and such tools as the plow which allow for more effective use of subsoils. Although shifting cultivation involves manipulation of the physical environment, sedentary agriculture involves its transformation. Forests are permanently cleared, irrigation works constructed, boundaries of fields marked out physically, and permanent villages constructed. Sedentary agriculture produces greater surpluses than does shifting cultivation, and is able to support larger populations. (Population densities among the highest in the world, e.g., 1,000 people per square mile in Java, stem from sedentary agriculture.) Sedentary agriculture allows for greater societal complexity and is found associated with the development of writing, the emergence of civilizations, urbanism, and the formation of states.

In the society of sedentary agriculturalists there is a geographic division between a rural peasantry and an urban group charged with full-time responsibility for religious, political, and economic activities. The surplus production of the peasant farmer supports the nonfarming specialists through taxes collected in goods, labor, or money. Sedentary cultivation thus provides an economic base for political specialization and centralization, culminating in the state that encompasses large and socially diverse populations. The bureaucrats of the state administer all sectors of the society. Trade is not unknown among hunters and gatherers and shifting cultivators but it is a virtual necessity in societies based on sedentary cultivation. Traders and tax collectors serve to move the surplus production of the peasants to the urban centers. Since the urban dwellers enjoy a style of life different from the peasants, traders cater to the desires of the urban dwellers for foodstuffs and luxury goods that are beyond the means of the peasantry. The city is also the place where full-time artisans are found, producing goods for the city dweller and perhaps also for the peasants as well (e.g., agricultural implements, pots, utensils, etc.) though peasants tend to be far more self-sufficient than urban dwellers.

The surplus production of peasants also supports full-time specialists in such cultural pursuits as religion, law, teaching, and science. Their task is to standardize and elaborate the cultural base and articulate that to the existing social order and physical world. Thus, sedentary cultivation encourages not only more specialization, differentiation, and centralization, but also a higher degree of cultural standardization than that characteristic of hunters and gatherers and shifting cultivators.

Industrialism. Industrialism is, of course, the mode of ecological adaptation with which most westerners are familiar since it is characteristic of their own societies. Historically industrialism emerged from societies characterized by sedentary agriculture which provided the economic base and social complexity for the development of science, technology, and the large populations which are requisites for industrialism. A major contrast with sedentary agricultural regimes is the extent of reliance on nonhuman sources of power. Water power, fossil fuels, electricity, and nuclear energy provide the industrialized societies with the capacity to exploit the physical environment more extensively, intensively, efficiently (and perhaps destructively) than by any other known mode of ecological adaptation.

Industrialism makes it possible to support large and socially complex populations, and such populations are essential for its maintenance. Industrialization requires the coordination of a complex array of specialized skills. Industrialized societies are complex not only in diversity of skills but also in their hierarchical arrangements. Types of occupation are ranked, and within each type are gradations in terms of prestige, responsibility, authority, and skill. The need for a pool of diverse skills and a readiness to move and respond quickly to diverse opportunities makes the individual the unit of social life; kinship, which threatens mobility, declines and extended family ties are truncated. As agriculture becomes more technologized and efficient, the difference between rural and urban sectors of society become less significant. Small numbers of highly efficient farmers produce the food to support masses of workers. Cities become important as centers of research, production, and distribution and as the hubs in a complex transportation system necessary to coordinate and integrate a complex political-economic order. Most industrial societies have as their political form the nation-state in which all are equally citizens with generalized rights and responsibilities. But industrialism does not limit itself to conventional state boundaries. In its ceaseless search for raw materials and markets industrialism expands to include transnational structures to feed the ever expanding industrial order. Industrialism has allowed human beings to increasingly exploit the physical world but such exploitation brings threat as well as promise. The threat is that the exploitation of the environment may go too far, using up nonrenewable resources and polluting the world. The promise is that as a vehicle for mastering the challenges of the environment, industrialism might find within itself a solution to the threats it imposes.

Ecological and Sociocultural Types

Obviously there are relationships between the ecological types just described and the sociocultural types introduced in the preface and to be elaborated in the remainder of the book. Both sets of types derive from a roughly parallel schema of evolution. The hunting and gathering ecological adaptation is broadly associated with what we term the "primitive" level of sociocultural patterning. Sedentary agriculture is associated with archaic and historic sociocultural levels. Pastoralism and shifting cultivation support forms transitional between the primitive and archaic.

Industrialism is associated with the early modern and modern sociocultural types. No simple causal relationship is claimed, but clearly the ecological mode sets limits on the sociocultural patterning and vice versa. Thus, hunting and gathering has not supported an early modern sociocultural pattern, nor does industrialism flourish in primitive societies. This generalization does not deny mixture of extremes within some systems. Modern, industrial society permits a limited proportion of its energies to be devoted to a quasi-hunting and gathering life style as recreation or experiment. And discovery of oil has resulted in sudden industrialization of limited sectors of certain Arab societies while many features remain traditional. While some further note will be taken of ecology and technology, the emphasis of ensuing discussion will be on the evolving systems of society and culture.

The Dynamics of Modernization

More difficult than the task of formulating the dimensions of modernization is that of grasping its dynamics: What are the conditions that facilitate or inhibit modernization, what processes are involved, and what are the consequences? Considering these questions, we move from a typological to a more historical approach, formulating phases, trends, and movements.

Modernization, as we define it, has proceeded throughout human history, but the pace has quickened during the last three centuries. During this period an "early-modern" type of society had emerged, characterized by industrialization, capitalism, bureaucracy, and their various sociocultural correlates. While recognizing variability and overlap among the myriad societies which have moved toward the early-modern pattern, we distinguish three broad phases in this movement: (1) the early phase, during which societies located in Western Europe and the United States originated the early-modern pattern; (2) the middle phase, in which such societies as Japan, China, Turkey, and Eastern Europe, influenced by the Western model, began to modernize; and (3) the recent phase, in which modernization has proceeded in the formerly colonized and semicolonized nations of Africa, Asia, the Middle East, and Latin America. The first phase began as early as the sixteenth century and was well under way by the nineteenth. In the late nineteenth century the second phase began, and quickened during the period including World War I. The third phase has accelerated since World War II, and continues today, interrupted by upheavals and blockages.

Centering in England and its dominions, the United States, Scandinavia, and France, the early phase of modernization was spearheaded by Renaissance intellectuals, Protestant reformers, and individualistic entrepreneurs. Though many of the traditional monarchs and aristocrats were themselves sympathetic to modernizing trends, the vanguard bourgeoisie could proceed more smoothly because of such political and legal structures as Parliament and common law, which enabled them to act relatively independently of traditional authorities. In contrast to traditional societies, which centered around hereditary estates, these early-modern societies were organized in diversified and cross-cutting voluntary associations, ranging from religious sects to trade unions. Although activist agitators certainly existed in these societies, they tended to be absorbed into a system of political parties. Thus, their energies were channeled into orderly democratic processes rather than resulting in breakdown and disintegration. Though ethnic and regional divisiveness and conflict continued, these first modernizing societies generally succeeded in creating national identities and unities. They did this by linking political goals with the endeavor to industrialize and mechanize the manufacturing and farming processes. Ideological traditions such as Protestantism, English common law, French republicanism, and the Frontier Ethic played an important role in keeping the balance between economic dynamism, political expansion, and social order.

In Eastern Europe, for example in the German states and in Czarist Russia, bureaucracy was more important than legislative bodies, and it was dominated by regimes more conservative and more autocratic than those of Western Europe. In Germany, strongly nationalistic modernizing trends tended to oppose the traditional princely powers, resulting in both more agitation and suppression than in the West. The Eastern European intelligentsia was more politicized, both to the right and to the left, than that of the West, and ideological divisions were more absolute. Rationalist ideologies, such as those stemming from Calvinism, the English law, or French republicanism, were not so prominent in Eastern as in Western Europe. Germany industrialized rapidly and Czarist Russia made considerable progress, but the process was fraught with tension, sometimes expressed externally by military aggression and internally by political revolt.

Japan was the first non-Western society to successfully industrialize, a process that was initiated when the Japanese rulers, confronted by the industrialized Western nations, realized that modernization was essential if Japan were to maintain her sovereignty. Modernization in Japan was society-wide and extremely rapid. In Japan, modernizing agents such as entrepreneurs were supported by and strongly loyal to the ruling elite. Despite the demotion of the Japanese emperor after World War II, economic change in Japan is very much directed from above even today; change flows from the rulers through the bureaucracy and down to the employer, to whom employees maintain a particularistic, quasi-feudal bond that generates fanatically hard work and low mobility of labor.

By the nineteenth century, Latin America had thrown off direct colonial control, but the region was still dominated by a small elite who were culturally oriented toward Iberian Europe. Through each Latin American country has its own unique history, all are composed of three key strata: the European-oriented elite, the strongly elitist and largely urban mass, and the indigenous Indian rural populations. Each stratum in the hierarchy has tended to perceive its position as fixed, and therefore none have been particularly open to change. The elite are bound to the nonelite in a fuedal or patrimonial fashion, as *patron* to *peon*. Aside from the church, which supported the *patron-peon* structure, few if any symbols or values unify these quasi-colonial societies. Lacking Japan's unifying governmental framework and cultural tradition that are shared by both elite and mass, Latin America has industrialized and modernized erratically, with much upheaval, and the process has been dominated by neocolonialist societies to the north.

The revolutionary nationalist and Communist regimes, exemplified by Russia, China, Turkey, and more recently Cuba, have maintained tighter control over modernizing forces than have most regimes in Latin America. The leaders of these revolutionary societies have been eager for change within the bounds defined by their ideologies, but they have favored coercive rather than populist processes. Keeping incentives for modernization under state and party control, they have nevertheless opened new opportunities for upward mobility in such fields as education, science, and politics. The revolutionary societies have emphasized politics over economics, but have nevertheless kept such statuses as scientist and planner more dependent on technical and professional qualifications than on political cronyism—a differentiation that has incited conflict between advocates of technical expertise and advocates of ideological purity. Goaded by both technical and ideological concerns, the revolutionary regimes have engineered radical changes in societies which were in many respects quite traditional before the twentieth century.

In terms of the distinction between internally and externally generated modernization, the formerly colonized societies of Asia, Africa, and the Middle East stand at the opposite extreme from the colonizing societies of Western Europe and America. The colonialists created the modern pattern; the colonized had it imposed on them. The colonized societies reacted, particularly after World War II, by throwing off colonial rule and gaining independence; in some instances peacefully, in others through bitter struggle. Gaining independence, the new nations faced the problem of preserving their identities yet modernizing sufficiently to compete in the international arena and to meet the pressing problems of overpopulation, hunger, an underdeveloped economy, and an unstable political order.

During the colonial period, the Western colonialist powers generally tried to limit change in the native societies that composed their colonies while modernizing those aspects of the colonies' economy which would best serve the mother country. Thus, local laws and customs were sometimes preserved and even romanticized while those who followed them were transformed from subsistence peasants or tribesmen to wage laborers on European-run plantations. The endeavor to keep certain aspects of the colonial society constant while changing other aspects resulted in an unbalanced, "dualistic" society which exhibited great discrepancies between the traditional native sector and the modernizing European-controlled sector. Where the colonial regime succeeded in coopting members of the indigenous elite to serve the regime and to adopt European values, a gap was created between the people and their traditional leaders.

Though nationalist movements antedate the World War II era, it is only since the war that these movements have gained the momentum to break through the dualism created by the colonial period. The nationalist has sought not only independence for his nation, but also an expansion of modernity to all members of his society while creating at the same time a national identity. Since many of the new nations are composites created by colonialism, the struggle to create national identities has by no means been universally successful. Through their concern with political rather than economic or legal change, the new nations have created new dualisms. Expanding opportunities for political participation and for education while propagating utopian ideologies and slogans, the new nations have raised the expectations of the masses, but rarely have they engineered the institutional changes that permit realization of these expectations. The result has been underpaid intelligentsia and impoverished masses whose discontents and agitation have rendered economic development difficult, encouraging or forcing the leaders to adopt a one-party or military rule to counter political instability.

One theme running through this brief survey is that successful modernization requires a balance between a society's sources of change and its mechanisms of control. Sources of change include capitalism, colonialism, urbanization, protest movements, and religious reformation. Mechanisms of control center most obviously around governmental and legal structures, but also involve other structures, such as the educational, military, and religious. What seems to be true of the early modernizing societies of the West, as well as the more successful later ones, such as Japan, Russia, and China, is that the controlling structures allowed considerable play to the forces of change while channeling them into an orderly process directed toward goals. The earliest modernizing societies accomplished such channeling through a kind of "divide and rule" policy that differentiated the various forces either institutionally or temporally. Thus, these societies managed to develop strong yet flexible governmental systems prior to the major populist movements in education or politics. Also, they were able to separate the technical aspects of educational and governmental change from the ideological aspects. Such changes could therefore occur rather smoothly, but a danger inherent in such differentiation is that technical processes stripped of ideological meaning tend to seem sterile and meaningless to their participants. The later revolutionary modernizing societies, such as Russia and China, have attempted to avoid this danger through imbuing all processes with a heavily politicized symbolism rooted in the total society, but this has been done at the expense of individual freedom in thought and action.[14]

The discussion so far has been from what might be called a "liberal" viewpoint: Assuming modernization to be a good thing, what are the conditions and processes that bring it about? A more "radical" perspective raises questions about the human consequences of modernization: What does it do to people while it is being achieved and after it is established? The liberal would point to the advantages of modernity, such as the reduction of disease and hunger, the lengthening of life, the democratization of power and privilege, and the spread of literacy and knowledge. The radical joins with the reactionary in decrying the evil effects of modernity on the quality of human life.

Deploring industrial technology, the radical argues that it has induced conflict between grasping capitalists and sullen workers while shattering the organic unity of traditional society. Peasants who come under the influence of a capitalist market system have their lands expropriated or go into debt and have to sell them. The landless peasants become tenant farmers at the mercy of absentee landlords or join the urban proletariat who work in factories at dehumanizing jobs. Alienated from the nexus of obligations and bonds to kinsmen and neighbors that existed in the traditional community, the proletarian finds himself in a world of depersonalized social relationships controlled by trends of the market or whims of a capitalist elite maintaining its position through exploitation. Controlling social relations rather than being controlled by them, as in traditional society, the economy warps society into a distorted and unnatural form. Extending beyond the factory and firm, the capitalist-industrialist economy draws the government, the universities and schools, charitable organizations, the military, and even the family into its orbit. All institutions are transformed into handmaidens of the economy, resulting in such monsters as the "military-industrial complex."

From a radical perspective, not only institutions but also deeply held human values and attitudes are warped by modernity. With modernization, human existence is increasingly governed by the value of "rationality," which is to say, the efficient harnessing of means to ends. Time is conceived as a scarce good to be used efficiently rather than wasted. Work, play, and even sleep must be scheduled so that productivity is maximized, an attitude popularized through such maxims as "Early to bed and early to rise makes a man healthy, wealthy, and wise." Even sex, according to one viewpoint, is subordinated to the cult of productivity and efficiency with the result that the erotic impulse loses its spontaneity and joy. Education becomes less a quest for wisdom and knowledge than a means for producing efficient workers on the assembly line or in the office, and the educational system itself is judged according to the standards of mass manufacturing by administrators who apply "cost-effectiveness" analysis which emphasizes quantity rather than quality. The clan and the community, traditionally sources of social and psychological stability, disintegrate due to capitalistic market requirements that labor be mobile. The breadwinner, accompanied by his portable nuclear family of wife and children, must leave kinsmen and neighbors to go where opportunity calls. Separated from the wider network of kinsmen and neighbors, the nuclear family turns inward. Its members develop an extreme dependence on one another, which frequently results in an emotional intensity engendering revolt of children against parents.

Projected from the individual level to the collective, the cult of efficiency calls for the Plan and the Organization. To keep the Organization functioning smoothly and to insure that the Plan is achieved by a deadline, human impulses must be standardized and made predictable. Hence the individual's power to make decisions is removed or mechanized through such statistical procedures as the vote. The pure and in many ways admirable image of streamlined productivity is corroded by the technocrat who sacrifices humanity for efficiency or the power elite who greedily seek power for its own sake.

Revolting against imagined or real dehumanizing aspects of modernization, numerous modern groups seek a return to the kind of communalism and pastoral security that they associate with traditional society. Communes inspired by the *Whole Earth Catalogue* represent an interesting but still unstable attempt to return. Communes buttressed by religious loyalties, such as the Hutterite and Amish communities or the Israeli *kibbutz,* have been more stable and productive but are perhaps too coercive for modern youth and in any event probably require a modern society as a setting. Black Power and Red Power movements also exemplify a search for a lost identity that ideally could be distilled into communities immune from the worst abuses and alienation of modern society. Such religious movements as the resurgent Pentecostals or the Charismatics seek meaning at a different level. They search for a fundamental belief destroyed by the searing light of modern rationalism which renders faith anachronistic (since it is "useless"), and questions the ideological base on which traditional communities have rested.

Movements like these are not unique to modern society or the contemporary scene. They have occurred in societies disrupted by the forces of modernization throughout history. Though varying in form, the existence of such movements is so widespread that anthropologists have coined names for them, the most frequently used being "revitalization movements," a term supplied by Anthony F. C. Wallace.[15] Whether erupting in relatively primitive societies (as did the American Indian Ghost Dance of the Melanesian Cargo Cults), or in relatively modern ones (as did Methodism, Communism, or Black and Red Power), revitalization movements are typically incited by disruption of the traditional social order. The following are examples of these disruptions: when tribesmen are losing their loyalty to the clan, serfs are breaking fuedal ties and moving to town, peasants are selling their lands and becoming proletarians, or, in a modern context, when workers find their jobs meaningless, housewives find family life unfulfilling, and the young are radically disillusioned with the values of established society. The revitalization movement is distinct from those processes of change that occur unconsciously and without anticipation in that it involves a conscious and organized struggle to construct a new cultural pattern.

Capable of producing radical change of an entire society in a single generation, revitalization movements generally follow a certain sequence of phases. Initially, the society is at a relatively "steady state" in that its cultural design more or less fills its members' needs, and the society is more or less in equilibrium. The steady state may be interrupted by some internal contradiction (as seems to have been the case, for example, in the Reformation) or by external forces, such as colonization, conquest, or the intrusion of capitalism. The result in either case is that traditional human relations are disrupted, old customs lose their meaning, and venerated leaders cease to evoke respect.

These disruptions are followed by a phase of "cultural distortion." During this phase, tendencies toward psychic breakdown worsen. Some individuals may regress into extreme passivity or indolence, become depressed or extremely guilt-ridden, or turn to alcohol and drugs. The breakdown of traditional controls may result in increased violence or corruption. The people may become so disturbed by the state of society that they endeavor to extinguish it: by dying earlier and giving birth less often, by opening themselves to invasion and conquest, or by dispersing and thereby losing their common social identity.

Such dire events are often forestalled by the revitalization movement which simultaneously serves several functions: cultural, social, and psychological. The most important function is the formulation of a new cultural system—a framework or schema of ideas, symbols, and values—which promises some new form of existence that is more meaningful and legitimate, perhaps more heavenly and delightful, than the existence of either past or present. The formulation is often dramatic or abrupt, frequently conceived in a hallucinatory vision by a prophet. Such visions manifest a desire for a supernatural parent or guardian, an apocalyptic fantasy of the world's complete destruction, a feeling of personal guilt about one's own conduct or that of one's society, and a longing for the establishment of a new and utopian order. Whatever the vision's details, it is a symbolic entity constructed to overcome the very real feelings of disillusionment and meaninglessness that afflict the people, and therefore strikes a chord in them.

The vision differs from the ordinary night dream in that it is not merely a fantasy to release tension or fulfill unconscious desire, but a formulation of a coherent scheme that renders meaningful a chaotic situation. The prophet is not mad or out of touch with reality. He differs from the psychotic in that he does not ordinarily believe that he *is* the deity about whom he dreams, only that he enjoys some peculiarly intimate bond to that deity. He keeps his identity, unlike the psychotic who believes that he is Jesus, Napoleon, or God. Indeed, through his vision, the prophet may strengthen his sense of personal identity, become a more effective and integrated person, and even be cured of former maladies and addictions. Instead of being locked in a hospital, the prophet is driven to enter the public arena to shout his message, found a movement, and attract disciples and followers. Armed with his vision and his heightened sense of self, the prophet projects charisma and power, and he is able to convince the multitudes that they will benefit from the new order that he proposes to establish under the protection and patronage of the deity who appeared in his vision.

Revitalization movements typically encounter resistance, but they may be accepted by enough people that an organized program of action ensues. Radical cultural, social, political, and economic reforms may be enacted, and in time these reforms may be widely accepted even by those who reject the prophet's original message. The movement is then transformed into a respectable church responsible for the preservation of rituals and beliefs that are then considered established. Such a development marks the final stage of the revitalization movement: the new steady state. The new order is generally more modern than that which preceded it, and it is more meaningful and more legitimate to the people than the chaotic and distorted situation that resulted from the disruption of the traditional order, which was the initial steady state.

Most of the great world religions—for example, Buddhism, Christianity, and Islam—originated as revitalization movements that erupted in marginal areas.[16] Spreading widely, these religions have endured long. They have become the basis for powerful civilizations that have influenced the course of history to the present and they possess the potential to continue that influence into the future. Rivaling economic and political forces in the capacity to produce radical change, the revitalization movement erupts in situations that are chaotic and unstructured; hence they are open to the influence of the charismatic personality. Through such movements, the individual prophet gains a unique opportunity to formulate, propagate, and institute a personal vision and thus to influence the course of history for millennia.

Might the present period be ripe for a new revitalization movement, a new charismatic revolution of worldwide import? That this is the case is suggested by the florescence of Communism which, despite its atheistic ideology, might be viewed as the first new world religion since the emergence of Islam. Other suggestive trends, more intriguing though less organized than Communism, include the cults emerging throughout the West, ranging from Meher Baba and Hari Krishna to the Mediators and the New Left. All of these perceive a fundamental disintegration of the Western order despite its progression since the end of the Dark Ages. Such cults may signal that an important revitalization movement is already at hand; what form it will take is not clear. Most likely it will not focus around belief in an external, metaphysical deity or force as have the significant revitalization movements of the past. Modern thought has moved away from a symbolizing of meaning as concentrated in such external entities believed to exist in the universe and toward a search for meaning within the experiences of the self.

The Direction of World History

A society's environment includes not only its natural surroundings but also its man-made physical setting, its social surroundings formed by other societies, and its psycho-organic milieu (the bodies and personalities of its members). All these environments, especially the last three, are changing at an accelerating rate, and if a society is to make fullest use of them, its own rate of change must accelerate. Modern sociocultural patterns are associated with technology, organization, and values which provide potential to change rapidly in order to adapt to rapidly changing environments. It is true that modernity is maladaptive in many respects—from the creation of bureaucracies that breed corruption and disaffection to technologies that destroy environment and health. Yet, on balance, some version of the modern pattern appears the most viable yet envisioned to permit humanity to adapt and survive in its current situation of huge population and complex relationships.

Assuming the above is true, consider the principle of natural selection that has emerged from studies of biological evolution. This principle maintains that over time a population tends to display more and more the traits of its most adaptive members, since it is these who are most likely to survive and reproduce their traits. Since the less adaptive members tend not to survive and reproduce, their traits disappear over time. An analogous principle may operate for societies. The most highly adaptive societies at any period of history will be the ones that survive and reproduce—by disseminating their patterns. Therefore, these patterns become more and more widespread, while the patterns of the less adaptive societies become less common. In our own time, the early-modern and modern patterns are increasingly prominent, while during the past six or seven thousand years the trend has been away from the primitive pattern. According to one estimate, only six percent of the world's people still live in primitive societies. This trend reflects the greater adaptive capacity of the modern pattern and the lesser adaptive capacity of the primitive pattern.

Having made the analogy between natural selection in biological evolution and in sociocultural evolution, we must emphasize that this is only an analogy. Analogies are meant to suggest hypotheses, not to prove them.[17] The applicability of these statements to biological evolution is no proof that they are equally applicable to sociocultural evolution. Sociocultural statements must be judged on their own terms. Indeed, certain criteria employed by students of biological evolution would be inappropriate for the analysis of sociocultural evolution. For instance, the rate of biological survival and reproduction among members of a population can by no means be used to predict the rates of survival and reproduction of the sociocultural patterns which that population follows. The birthrate in nonindustrial societies today is much greater than the birthrate in industrial societies, yet the industrial pattern is the one that is surviving and spreading.

Sociocultural evolution appears to be moving in a different direction from biological evolution. Biological evolution is often likened to a branching tree, with more and more branches appearing as evolution proceeds. Thus, insects have branched out (undergone adaptive radiation) to such a degree that today some 600,000 insect species exist. By contrast, sociocultural evolution appears to be converging into a single "species." The trend seems to be one in which all societies will eventually assume some version of the early-modern or modern pattern.

A second difference between biological and sociocultural evolution is that men's motives and plans play a more important role in the sociocultural process than in the biological. Since the principle of natural selection was originated to explain the evolution of all animals, it does not consider motive and plan as possible causes. The principle of natural selection recognizes only that if by accident, mutation, or other process a more adaptive trait or pattern appears, that trait or pattern will tend to be perpetuated. No assumption is made about how the trait or pattern originated, and the biologist is particularly wary of talking as if the organism in which a given trait or pattern originated had planned it that way. The virtue of this position (which avoids the teleological fallacy) is plain, but at the same time we must take into account the observation by Redfield[18] and others that the more modern the society, the greater the capacity of its members to control their destinies—to move in the direction of consciously established goals. Hence, when an overwhelming number of today's developing societies say they yearn to modernize, we cannot ignore this yearning in predicting the direction in which the world's societies are likely to move. Of course, modernizing societies mourn the loss of their traditions, and they increasingly realize the maladaptive aspects of modernization. Nevertheless, they desire the material and perhaps sociocultural benefits of modernity.

Arguments such as this have inspired Marion J. Levy, Jr., in his *Modernization and the Structure of Societies,* to brand the modern pattern a "universal solvent." Levy claims that when a nonmodern society comes in contact with a modern society, the nonmodern society inevitably modernizes, whereas the modern society never "demodernizes." Levy believes that this occurs because every society, no matter how spiritual its values, contains some individuals who want the material advantages which modern patterns produce. The process of modernization need not occur all at once. Perhaps only part of a society is affected at first. But modernization is like a dye which, upon touching one thread, is slowly absorbed until it changes the color of the whole cloth. Adopting modern technology to gain material advantage soon results in changes in family structure, government, and other institutions. According to Levy, only romanticists could believe that part of a society can modernize while the rest remains entirely intact. Although societies such as Japan apparently do segregate modernizing sectors and traditional sectors for a time, it is doubtless true that such segregation cannot ensure forever.

Although this view of world history, according to which all societies will eventually conform to the modern pattern, may be crude, it seems better founded than the idea that there is no discernible direction to the transformations of today's societies. Modernization theory calls into question the belief that every society is developing along its own unique path according to its own unique genius.

Today's traditional societies might still be happily traditional in 3000 A.D. But with the onrush of modernization fewer and fewer backwaters in which to hide will remain. Modernization tends to integrate all regions of the world into one system. The few primitive societies found today remain primitive partly because they have been able to retreat into the jungles, deserts, or mountains and avoid the advance of modernity; but as modernity pushes further these havens too will be lost. Indeed, just as the pace of technological innovation has accelerated steadily since human history began,[19] so the process of sociocultural change itself has accelerated. As the world becomes more nearly a single system, changes in one sector instantly excite changes in the other sectors. Exotic societies, therefore, may be doomed.

Overview

Evolutionary theory tries to (1) formulate features common to all societies, and (2) study the differences among societies in terms of these features. Such dimensions of modernization as centralization and specialization achieve both these objects. They serve, on the one hand, to delineate and label processes common to all societies and, on the other, to define scales along which societies can be ranked and compared. All societies are to a degree undergoing processes of specialization and centralization. Because some societies have carried these processes further than others, we can ask how much greater is the degree to which one society has centralized or specialized in comparison with another.

Evolutionary theory also tries to (3) understand how each society functions, *i.e.,* to understand the principles in terms of which each operates. This objective is partly attained by delineating the functional relationships between processes such as centralization and specialization (for instance, we can state, as a generally valid principle, that the more specialized units a society has, the more centralized it must become in order to integrate its units). The objective can also be approached by classifying the world's societies into types, such as "primitive," "archaic," "historic," "early-modern," and "modern," and the correlated ecological patterns, and delineating the distinctive principles and patterns governing the operation of each type of society.

In its emphasis on formulating the principles according to which societies operate, evolutionary theory differs from conventional world history. From world history one learns the chronological sequence of the world's events, but not the principles governing the function of each type of society. For this reason, knowledge of conventional world history is not sufficient for making an accurate prediction of the future. Could one predict that an engine is about to explode merely by knowing the history of its use? Knowing its history would be helpful, but one would also need to analyze the engine's current condition and the principles of its operation. To predict a system's future, one must know not only the chronology of events that have resulted in its current condition, but its current condition and operating principles as well.

Evolutionary theory also tries to (4) plot the broad trends in the world's development. Thus, we have argued that all societies are moving toward modernization, a trend that involves many dimensions. A number of these dimensions might be summarized as different facets of a single broad trend, a trend toward a more complex and extensive society. With increased complexity (including increased differentiation and specialization of units and increased separation of cosmic and social orders), a society becomes more flexible in relating to its various environments. It is, therefore, able to adapt to a wider range of environments—conquering not only the land, the oceans, and space itself, but ultimately such environments as the human body and personality. The ability of complex societies to adapt to a wider range of environments encourages them to move into the environments of less complex societies. The result is either that the more complex societies assimilate (or destroy) their less complex neighbors or that the less complex societies assimilate the more complex patterns. Thus, all the world's societies are moving toward a uniform pattern of high complexity. Ultimately, all of these societies may unite to form a single complex and extensive society—a world society.

Topics for Discussion

An evolutionary approach to anthropology has a number of advantages. It enables the anthropologist to encompass the entire range of social and cultural diversity within a single coherent scheme, to recognize processes of change responsible for the diversity, past and present, of social and cultural forms, and to perceive relationships that might otherwise be overlooked. Unfortunately, the evolutionary approach also poses problems which the student should consider along with the advantages. It forces the anthropologist to measure and compare societies in terms of standards not necessarily held by any one of them. It thus violates the doctrine of cultural relativism: that a society should be evaluated only in terms of the standards held by that society. Many anthropologists favor relativism rather than evolutionism. Has the pace of change and centralization in the contemporary world affected the viability of a relativistic perspective? The student must consider the issues involved in choosing one point of view rather than the other.

Even if an evolutionary approach is adopted, the version which stresses modernization need not be. Environmental, medical, and sociocultural problems raised by modernization, both in the developing areas and in the highly urbanized industrial states, suggest that we should evolve toward some form other than the so-called modern one defined in this chapter. Yet many alternatives posed, such as retreat to a communal agrarian life style, seem inadequate to cope with the world's huge populace and complex problems. What viable alternative directions can be envisioned?

Suggested Readings

Recent Social and Cultural Evolutionists

Man Makes Himself (paperback, 1956) by V. Gordon Childe, a seminal archaeologist.

What Happened in History (paperback, 1946) by V. Gordon Childe.

Social Evolution (paperback, 1951) by V. Gordon Childe.

The Primitive World and Its Transformations (paperback, 1953) by Robert Redfield.

Primitive Social Organization (paperback, 1962) by Elman R. Service.

The Theory of Culture Change: The Methodology of Multilineal Evolution (1955) by Julian H. Steward.

The Evolution of Culture (paperback, 1959) by Leslie A. White.

Societies: Evolutionary and Comparative Perspectives (paperback, 1966) by Talcott Parsons.

Human Societies: A New Introduction to Sociology (1970) by Gerhard Lenski.

The Evolution of Political Society (1967) by Morton H. Fried.

Origins of the State and Civilization (1975) by Elman R. Service.

American Sociological Review (June, 1964). This issue contains several seminal articles on social evolution, including the source for the scheme of the present book, Robert N. Bellah's "Religious Evolution."

Diffusionist Theory

Writings of the *diffusionists*, who frequently argued against the evolutionists, usefully supplement evolutionary writings. Rather than formulate stages of development applicable to all societies of the world, the diffusionists sought to show how cultural patterns and inventions that emerged in one society spread to others.

Anthropology (1948) by Alfred L. Kroeber. Provides fascinating and readable examples in chapters 11 and 12.

The History of Ethnological Theory (1937) by Robert H. Lowie. Furnishes summaries of diffusionist theories.

Configurations of Culture Growth (1944) by Alfred L. Kroeber. Offers semidiffusionist portrayal on the grand scale, of the rise of civilization.

Theory of Modernization

Modernization and the Structure of Societies: A Setting for the Study of International Affairs (paperback, 1969) by Marion J. Levy, Jr. Volume I, part I, chapter 1. Summarizes much of Levy's theory of modernization, to which the present authors are strongly indebted.

The Homeless Mind (1973) by Peter Berger. Reflects a European view of modernization as alienation, which usefully supplements Levy's more American viewpoint.

Economics

Economic Anthropology (paperback, 1965) by Melville J. Herskovits. An extensive if naive treatment of the role of culture in primitive economic life.

Primitive Polynesian Economics (1939) by Raymond Firth. A classic of economic anthropology.

Peasant Marketing in Java (1962) by Alice G. Dewey. An informative study of small-town economics.

Peddlers and Princes: Social Change and Economic Modernization in Two Indonesian Towns (paperback, 1963) by Clifford Geertz. Compares the role of Javanese Muslim traders and Balinese Hindu nobles in Indonesian economic modernization.

The Gift: Forms and Functions of Exchange in Archaic Societies (paperback, 1967) by Marcel Mauss. A classic analysis of the cultural implications of exchange among primitive and archaic peoples.

Perspectives in Marxist Anthropology (1977) by Maurice Godelier. Provocative analysis.

"Economic Anthropology: Problems in Theory, Method and Analysis," (1973) by Scott Cook.

"Ethics, Economics, and Society in Evolutionary Perspective" (1976) James Peacock. Links economics to *The Human Direction.*

Politics and Government

African Political Systems (1940) edited by M. Fortes and E. E. Evans-Pritchard. The classic British social-anthropological view of tribes without rulers. See especially the introduction.

Tribes Without Rulers (1958) edited by John Middleton and David Tait. Treats six African "stateless" societies.

Bantu Bureaucracy (paperback, 1965) by Lloyd Fallers. Applies some of Max Weber's categories in a careful analysis of a nonmodern governmental system.

Political Systems of Highland Burma (paperback, 1965) by Edmund Leach. Brilliant analysis of the dynamics of political and social change.

The Politics of Modernization (paperback, 1965) by David Apter. A turgidly written—yet brilliantly argued—analysis of the major changes occurring as tribal and other nonmodern societies modernize. It builds on more restricted anthropological studies of tribal politics.

Political Anthropology (1970) by Georges Balandier. A difficult but intriguing introduction.

Law

The Law of Primitive Man: A Study in Comparative Legal Dynamics (paperback, 1968) by E. Adamson Hoebel, Provides a general theory of law in primitive society.

Justice and Judgement Among the Tiv (1957) by Paul J. Bohannan.

The Judicial Process Among the Barotse of Northern Rhodesia (1955) by Max Gluckman.

The Ideas in Barotse Jurisprudence (1965) by Max Gluckman.

The Cheyenne Way: Conflict and Case Law in Primitive Jurisprudence (1941) by Karl N. Llewellyn and E. Adamson Hoebel.

Technology and Ecology

Power and Privilege: A Theory of Social Stratification (1966) by Gerhard Lenski. Broad correlations of technological changes with sociocultural changes extending from primitive to industrial society.

The Theory of Culture Change: The Methodology of Multilineal Evolution (1955) by Julian H. Steward. Correlation of technological and sociocultural change primarily at the primitive level.

Medieval Technology and Social Change (paperback, 1962) by Lynn White, Jr. Fascinating analysis of a historic case.

The Rise of Anthropological Theory (1968) by Marvin Harris. Lists numerous works that correlate sociocultural evolution with techno-environmental development and presents extensive and lively argument in favor of emphasizing the latter factor.

"Nature, Culture, and Ecological Anthropology," (1971) by Roy Rappaport, in *Man, Culture, and Society,* edited by Harry L. Shapiro. A sophisticated introduction to cultural ecology.

"An Ecological Approach in Cultural Anthropology," by Andrew Vayda, in *Explorations in Anthropology,* edited by Morton Fried (1973). A simple introduction.

Human Ecology, An Environmental Approach (1976) edited by Peter Richerson and J. McEvoy.

Culture and Practical Reason (1976) by Marshall Sahlins. Provocative argument in favor of a cultural as opposed to materialist perspective.

Revitalization Movements

Pursuit of the Millenium (1961) by Norman Cohn. Detailed and vivid description of messianic movements in medieval and Reformation Europe.

The Trumpet Shall Sound (1957) by Peter Worsley. Sophisticated analysis of Melanesian revitalization movements.

"Revitalization Movements" (1956) by Anthony F. C. Wallace. A synthesis.

The Ghost Dance (1972) by Weston LaBarre. A provocative psychological analysis.

Utopia and Its Enemies (1972) by S. Kateb. A sophisticated introduction to the important social principles behind movements.

Films

Although modernization is too broad a process to film *in toto,* several films dramatize specific confrontations that flow from modernization.

The Exiles. Portrays the night life of three young Indian men who have left the reservation to live in Los Angeles.

Fincho. Depicts the penetration of Western technology and capitalism into a remote Nigerian village.

Trobriand Islanders. Might be of interest since the Trobrianders are used as illustration in this chapter.

Trobriand Cricket: An Ingenious Response to Colonialism. Brilliantly and wittily depicts a case of culture change.

chapter 5

Primitive Society and Culture

Examples of primitive society and culture, the Australian aborigines were branded by early anthropologists as the most backward of peoples.* Although they are only hunters and gatherers possessing a simple set of tools—basically, the digging stick, the boomerang, the spear, the spear thrower, the stone axe, the fire-making stick, the wooden or stone chisel, and the stone knife—the aborigines have managed to survive in a desert that has strained the endurance of well-equipped European expeditions. The aborigine's sensitivity to natural signs and seasons is the basis of his survival ability. The aborigine does not place equipment between himself and nature; he approaches his

*Although many contemporary aborigines have settled near missions and ranches as hired sheepherders, or have taken other jobs (a recent bantamweight boxing champion of the world, Lionel Rose, is an aborigine), some still follow a mode of life similar to that of the past, and we shall write as if all did. That is, we shall follow the anthropological convention of writing in the ethnographic present.

Aboriginal culture is of course much more complex than we portray it here. Considering both the complexity of the society and the diversity of anthropological interpretations, we have chosen mainly to follow the generalized synthesis of A. P. Elkin, *The Australian Aborigines.*

surroundings in a direct manner that yields him a precise and intimate knowledge of nature. He is a man to whom the rising of Orion early on a June morning reveals that dingo pups are being born in secluded places and may be sought for food, to whom the yellow flowers of the wattle tree signify that magpie geese will be flying along certain routes where they can be stunned by thrown sticks. He can track wallabies, scrub turkeys, or men with an uncanny skill.

Despite his knowledge of nature, however, the aborigine has never practiced agriculture or animal husbandry. Because of primitive technology and the absence of agriculture, the aboriginal population has never been great—even though aborigines have probably roamed the Australian continent for more than ten thousand years.

"Primitive" is used not as a pejorative, but rather as a technical term denoting a distinctive pattern of society, culture, and ecology. Those who object to the term "primitive" doubtless assume that it connotes negative values such as "backwardness," and they understandably desire to avoid a slur. On the other hand, "primitive" connotes positive values such as authenticity and solidarity when contrasted to the alienation which some see as characteristic of modernity. We have not found a suitable value-free term, but the reader is free to substitute any term he wishes in order to denote the pattern of society, culture, and technology we describe. It has been estimated that when the first British colonists appeared in 1788, fewer than 300,000 aborigines (divided into about 500 separate tribes) existed. A recent census counted only about 50,000 full-blood and 40,000 mixed-blood aborigines. On the basis of technology it is certainly legitimate to classify the aborigines as primitive. It is equally legitimate on the basis of their social organization, although aboriginal social patterns are quite complex and ingenious.

Social Organization

Anthropologists have commonly classified the aborigines into tribes ranging from 100 to 1,500 members. Each tribe usually has its own language or dialect, its own territory, its own customs, and its own name. Not every tribe possessed a name, however, and some tribes, such as the Murngin of northeast Arnhem Land, are vague about their territorial boundaries. A reason for this vagueness, which is characteristic not only of the aborigines but also of other primitive groups, is a low degree of bureaucratization and centralization. Indeed, the aborigines lack a king or even a chief. Authority among them is vested in elders of patrilocal groups. A tribe—which seldom if ever functions in concert except on ceremonial occasions—is basically a confederation of these patrilocal groups, and the bonds that unite the groups are those of myth of ceremony and of kinship or marriage.

Aboriginal notions of owning a territory differ fundamentally from modern concepts of ownership. In contemporary Western societies land can be bought, rented, or sold. Land is *alienable*—it is an object to be disposed of by the owner in whatever fashion best suits his purpose. By contrast, the aborigine is not so much master of his land as his land is master of him. Aboriginal tribal territory "owns" the tribe as much as the tribe owns the territory. So strong is the bond between a tribesman and his tribal territory that it can never be severed. Its power issues from the mythical significance of the land itself. A tribe's territory is rich with memories of heroes and ancestors who dwelt in the mythical "Dreamtime." Tribal mythology associates each detail of the landscape with some adventure or some creation of its heroes and ancestors: At this pile of stones an ancestor rested while on a journey, at that waterhole a hero created a new rite of fertility. Each site and each hero possesses and is possessed by a particular tribe. Since the aborigine is born into his tribe and thus cannot sever his bond to it, neither can he sever his bond to the land and its myths. Because tribe, person, myth, and land are joined in one enduring relationship, wars of territorial conquest have no meaning in aboriginal society.

Intertribal relations, too, are sanctioned by mythology. An aboriginal coalition of tribes is not a nation, for it possesses no central government or leader. Meetings among tribes, when they occur, are arranged and managed by the elders of the various tribes. (The kind of centralization in which there is an intertribal chief is found in archaic societies such as those of the Near East, Africa, Asia, and Polynesia.) Intertribal meetings among the aborigines are important, for it is at these gatherings that customs are exchanged and myths jointly celebrated. Thus, a number of tribes in northeastern South Australia convene to celebrate the adventures of mythical heroes known as *mura mura*, in whom they collectively believe; by such celebration the well-being of each tribe will be assured. But no single tribe can "own" the whole mythical cycle; each tribe can be responsible for only a particular portion or phase. One myth, for example, is reported to be "700 miles long"—a tale of heroic adventures ranging over a territory 700 miles in length. The telling of such a myth requires the cooperation of all the tribes residing within this area. Since each tribe "owns" part of the 700-mile adventure, the whole story can be told only if all tribes are present.

More important to the aborigine than his tribe is his patrilocal group, for in this group he spends most of his time. The group is also patrilineal, tracing its ancestry through males descended from particular ancestors who lived within a particular locale; an aborigine's grandfather, father, brother, son, and grandson—all would be proper members of his patrilocal, patrilineal group.

Comparing the role of kinship in aboriginal society with its role in American society will demonstrate the great importance of kinship to the aborigine. Most Americans do not bother to trace their kinship network beyond the most immediate family, perhaps including first or second cousins. Among aborigines—where the patrilineal, patrilocal group is the main unit of social life—relationships will be carefully traced throughout the community and even beyond the borders of the tribe. All social relations among aborigines must be kinship relations; an aborigine does not know how to act toward a stranger until he has discovered how the other is kin to him. It has been said that if such kinship could not be discovered—or fabricated, as when a European is adopted as brother— the stranger would have to be killed. There is simply no way for an aborigine to deal with a nonkinsman.

In modern society, individuals tend to relate to one another *universalistically* (on the basis of what each can do), rather than *particularistically* (on the basis of kinship). Most modern relationships are governed by such considerations as "This person is selling what I want to buy," or "This person can flunk me," or "This person must be treated politely because all people should be treated politely." Most primitive relationships, such as those among the aborigines, are guided by a single consideration: "This person is kin to me in a particular way, therefore, I must treat him in a particular way."

The principle that each kinship relationship is associated with a particular set of rules specifying how the kinsmen should interact is revealed in avoidance customs. Aborigines taking food at a mission station will face in all directions, instead of sitting face to face and chatting as Americans might do under similar circumstances. Some will sit back to back, neither speaking to nor looking at one another. Or sometimes the group will split into two segments with no conversational exchange. These arrangements conform with precise rules stating that persons related in certain ways must avoid one another. This avoidance does not signify hatred or dislike, but rather the great respect one kinsman holds for the other. Thus, the aboriginal man must avoid his mother-in-law because "She is the greatest friend I have, for she has provided me with a wife." Similarly, a man must demonstrate respect for his wife's mother's brother by avoiding him, because, by custom, it is he who helps arrange the marriage of the man's niece. Nor are such avoidances restricted to in-laws. In some tribes, brothers and sisters, once childhood has passed, must face in opposite directions when they converse—a custom linked to the taboo against incest.

Although these avoidance customs spring from diverse conditions and serve varied functions, all of them work chiefly to preserve the intricate aboriginal kinship network. In the modern community, where people are usually unrelated, a fight between kinsmen will not throw the entire community into turmoil; but in the primitive community, where kinship is pervasive, a fight among kin could be disastrous. By decreeing that relatives with a high potential for tension between them must avoid each other, these customs help stabilize the primitive community.

Just as aborginal kinship determines avoidances, it also determines alliances, especially by marriage. Moderns tend to view marriage as a matter of individual choice based on romantic love; but for aborigines, it is kinship more than affection that determines the marriage partner, and thus determines which families become bound together as in-laws or affines. The marrying couple have little to say about their own marriage. Kinship rules often specify the kinship the two mates should or must hold to one another; hence a mate selection is limited to persons who fall within the proper kinship category. The marriage will probably be arranged by senior kinsmen of the couple's local groups. Infant betrothal is common. One set of relatives may promise a daughter to the son of another set even before the two spouses-to-be are born; under these circumstances the wishes of the spouses count less than the kinship bonds between the two in-law groups. Since the groups are already kin, the marriage is a handy way of perpetuating and strengthening the existing bond. In some respects aboriginal marriage resembles a system common to European royalty: The son of one king marries the daughter of another king who is already a relative of the first, thereby strengthening the ties between the two royal houses and between the nations they rule. However, not all Europeans marry in this way, while traditionally *all* aborigines do.

It has recently been suggested that the many complex types of aborigine marriage systems should be understood as variations of a basic pattern of sister exchange between groups. From this perspective, marriage among the aborigines is interpreted as an attempt by men of two or more groups to marry each other's sisters. (Of course, since aborigines use classificatory kinship terminology, any woman born into a man's local group might be classed as his "sister.") After two groups have exchanged sisters for several generations, men from one group actually are marrying their cousins from the other group. A man marries his father's sister's daughter or his mother's brother's daughter, and these might be precisely the same person. Such cousins are called cross cousins, that is, children of siblings of the opposite sex (mother's brother's daughter and father's sister's son) to distinguish them from parallel cousins, who are children of siblings of the same sex (father's brother's daughter and mother's sister's son). Among the aborigines, where descent is reckoned patrilineally, parallel cousins would be members of the same patrilineal group. Because of the incest taboo which prohibits members of the same patrilineal, patrilocal group from marrying, marriage among parallel cousins is forbidden. The system just described is known as the Kariera System, after the aboriginal tribe of that name which furnishes the best known example of its practice.

The Kariera System can also be viewed as involving two large unilineal descent groups, or clans, whose members are divided into various local groups. Each local group is a smaller unilineal descent group, or *lineage*. Let us label the two clans A and B. The lineages composing each clan are A_1, A_2, A_3, A_4, and B_1, B_2, B_3, B_4, B_5. All the males of clan A remain in place, whereas all the females of clan A ("sisters" of the A men) are given to males of clan B as wives. Similarly, the female B's are given to the male A's as wives, while the clan B males stay in place. Any clan A male can take his wife from any one of the several B's (B_1, B_2, B_3, B_4, or B_5), and any clan B male can take his wife from any one of the several A's. A set of such marriage exchanges might, then, take the form shown in the diagram.[1] So long as these exchanges of women continue, and so long as no A men marry A women or B men marry B women, a man will always marry a woman who is his cross cousin, or of the same kinship type as his cross cousin. His female parallel cousins are members of his own clan and are, therefore, unavailable.

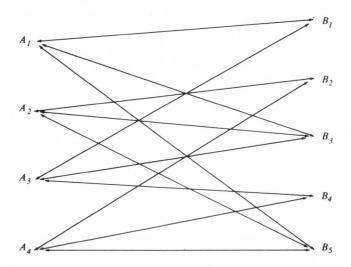

Any number of mind-bending elaborations on this system can be found among the aborigines. As these systems become more complicated, more and more distinctions are recognized, with the result that the category of kinsman whom one can or cannot marry becomes more and more clearly defined. The essential point, however, is that all of these systems subordinate the sentiments of the individual to the kinship rules of the group. Individual freedom is small, and choice is dictated by particularistic fiat.

The local group is, as we have noted, composed of persons related to one another patrilineally, so the ordinary aborigine belongs to and lives in one group with his father, his father's father, his sons, and his sons' sons. Since aborigines deny the male's physiological contribution to procreation, they cite a nongenealogical reason for a person's local group membership. They believe that a person's spirit exists in a given locale long before the person—or even the person's father—is born. Should the father happen to be in that locale, and should he dream that the person's spirit enters his wife's womb, she will conceive and the person will be born—the spirit is incarnated as a child. The child is then bound to the locale where the dream occurred, for it is in that locale that the child's spirit preexisted, and since the dream usually occurs in the territory of the father's local group—the territory where he spends his time—it usually happens that the child is bound to the same territory as his father.

The aborigines believe, too, that a person must return before death to the place where his spirit preexisted. Should he die in a different place, his spirit would become lost, and, wandering in anger and despair, might inflict pain on the living. The aborigine, therefore, tries to remain near the place where his spirit preexisted. Obviously this hampers his spatial mobility. Contrast this to the Christian belief in Heaven. Heaven is located above the earth, not on any particular earthly spot. Accordingly, the Christian's soul can enter Heaven no matter where he is when he dies, and his spatial mobility is not limited by his belief—a situation that works to encourage the spread of modern, Christian patterns, as opposed to the primitive, aboriginal ones.

The aborigine is also affiliated with a nonlocal descent group. This group is matrilineal. One is allied to such a matrilineal group through one's bond to one's mother, mother's mother, and other kin traced through one's mother. Since women move out of the patrilocal groups into which they were born in order to live with their husbands (who stay fixed to the patrilocal groups into which they were born), it is likely that persons related through a common matrilineal bond will live in different places. Thus, the matrilineal clan is not localized. Although matrilineal kinsmen may be scattered, they consider themselves spiritually connected; the bond that unites them is symbolized by their totem.

Totemism and Totemic Cults

Members of an aboriginal group profess kinship not simply to one another, but also to one or more animal or vegetable species—the kangaroo or emu, or the lowly witchety grub—known as the group's totem. A patrilineal or matrilineal group's totem is called its flesh or meat, as well as its guardian, friend, or kinsman. When an aborigine states that the woolly-butt tree, his totem, is his uncle, he refuses to draw the modern distinction between men and nature; he counts the tree in the same class as a human. An aborigine should not kill, injure, or eat his group's totem, and since all who share the same totem share the same flesh, they must not intermarry. Union of the same flesh is incest.

Although both patrilocal groups and matrilineal groups among the aborigines have totems, it is in the patrilocal groups, where the totemic bond is reinforced by coresidence based on the notion of preexisting spirits, that totemic cult life is most intense. Each local group maintains a cult "lodge," composed of the fully initiated male members of the group. This "lodge" serves to preserve the group's portion of the tribal totemic myth, to celebrate its rituals, to guard its sacred totemic sites, and to perform rites that will encourage fecundity in the group's totem species.

Located along paths that cross the territory of each local group are special sites where mythical heroes accomplished the feats celebrated in tribal mythology. As birds and animals, humans bearing animal and bird names, or animals and birds who talk like humans, these mythical figures are totems as well as heroes. Members of the local cult lodges adorn themselves with painted designs denoting attributes of their totem-hero; and in order to instill his image in the minds of the younger men, they ritually dramatize his adventures.

Not only do ceremonies performed at sites sanctified by the totem-heroes seek to stimulate the totem species to multiply, but they are also meant to assure that nature will sustain her proper order. Certain natural phenomena are associated with each totem—with the crow, lightning, thunder, rain, clouds, hail, and winter; with the cockatoo, the moon and stars. Each group must order its own part of the cosmos by performing ceremonies so that the entire universe will maintain harmony.

A totemic system thus forms a classification scheme in which each entity has its place. The cosmos is conceived as a set of categories each of which is composed of a particular cluster of animals, plants, and celestial bodies, all linked to a particular group and its territory. Should new elements appear, they can simply be inserted into one of these categories. When European sailors came to Australia, they were categorized along with other totems as belonging to a particular totemic cluster. The appearance of new elements does not require rearrangement of the scheme; it is loose enough already so that anything new can be incorporated into it. Looseness is in fact one feature distinguishing the totemic scheme from scientific theory—unlike scientific theory, the totemic scheme cannot be refuted by the appearance of new evidence. The totemic scheme is also distinct from a theology. No group "owns" the whole scheme, and no group regards its part as monopolizing truth. The concept of religious conversion therefore makes little sense to the aborigine. In the totemic view, it makes more sense for all groups to cooperate—through ceremony and rite—in a joint effort to order the cosmos.

The Dreaming and the Secret Life[2]

Totemism cannot be understood without some comprehension of a remarkable concept, which the aborigines call "The Dreaming." The Dreaming is a sacred, heroic time of long ago, when man and nature came to be as they are today. But neither time nor history in the Western sense is implied by The Dreaming. The aborigines possess no word for time as an abstract idea, and The Dreaming does not denote a golden age located in some definite past epoch. One cannot fix The Dreaming in time and history—instead, "It was, and is, everywhen."[3]

Just as an aborigine's dreams by night affect his life by day, as when a father's dream causes a child's birth, so does The Dreaming mix with the aborigine's life. Indeed, dreaming—in our sense of the word—is important during aboriginal rites, for in these dreams the natives imagine themselves to be heroes of The Dreaming. Thus they merge within their own personalities the Dream-time and the here-and-now.

The Dreaming is a cosmogony—an account of the creation of the universe—and it is also a cosmology—a theory of how what was created became an orderly system. Great marvels are revealed and portrayed in accounts of The Dreaming: how fire and water were stolen and recaptured; how men erred and now their descendants must die for it; how certain customs and taboos were instituted; how tribes and clans were divided up; how marriage, exogamy, and sister exchange came to be. The aborigines believe that as life was created in The Dream-time, so it must exist today and through eternity. The Dreaming still exists, life still conforms to the eternal mold, life is therefore a "one possibility thing."[4]

Unlike the Christian's Kingdom of God and Kingdom of Man, The Dreaming and life are considered one. The Dreaming is no celestial realm that floats above life; it is like a fluid that seeps into life. Nor are heroes of The Dreaming, such as Biame and Darumlum, gods separated from the daily world by their superhuman powers and positions. They are simply heroes—manlike, not godlike, bound by bonds of kinship to the tribes and local groups which perpetuate them by rites and myths of The Dreaming.

Perceiving no clear distinction between the ideal world of The Dreaming and the actual world of real life, the aborigine feels no need for saints or illuminati to mediate between the ideal and the actual. Nor is there a need for prophets, an Isaiah or an Amos, to castigate men when they deviate from the ideal. For when ideal and actual are one, there can be no deviation. In the absence of a separate ideal world against which to compare, judge, and censure the actual world, there can be no mood of criticism, pessimism, dynamism, no craving for reform. The Dreaming has happened, and everyday life *is* The Dreaming. The mold for life is set.

In the West, much creative energy pours into the formulation of ideal worlds—theologies, ideologies, theories. But the aborigines, undistracted by ideal philosophical orders, concentrate on the living social order. Instead of abstract theories, the aborigines produce systems of social permutation and combination, with highly complex rules to decree who shall marry whom. These impressive products of the savage intellect inspired Claude Lévi-Strauss to write:

> ... few civilizations seem to equal the Australians in their taste for erudition and speculation and what sometimes looks like intellectual dandyism, odd as this expression may appear when it is applied to people with so rudimentary a level of material life. But lest there be any mistake about it: these shaggy and corpulent savages whose physical resemblance to adipose bureaucrats or veterans of the Empire makes their nudity yet more incongruous ... were [intellectual] snobs. ...[5]

Within their complex systems of kinship the aborigines have arranged facets of nature which, to modern man, are independent of the social order and have no place in it. It would be as if we were to believe that the chordates are mystically linked to the upper classes of society, the athropods to the middle classes, and the coelenterates to the lower; or that Protestants could be identified with worms, snails, and clams, Catholics with reptiles, fish, and mammals, and the Jews with birds, spiders, and squids. Obviously, the zoological schemes of the West bear no direct connection to social divisions as they do in an aboriginal totemic zoology—no species is the kin or the property of any social group. Similarly, there is a great difference in the concept of time. For the West, time is an abstraction, detached from any group or social phase, yet a framework in which all groups and social phases can be classified. For the aborigine time is generational and social—a staircase proceeding through a genealogical family tree.

In sum, the aborigines illustrate clearly the primitive fusion of ideal and actual, of cosmic and social, and because of this fusion there can be no saints, no prophets, no God, and no Heaven. Nor is there a secular equivalent of Heaven, a Great Society, or a socialist utopia, for the ideal is the actual and the cosmic is the social. Surely it is no accident that through study of the aborigines, Emile Durkheim was led to conclude that religion and society are one.

Although the aborigines have fused the sacred and the secular to a great extent, they have not done so completely. Although The Dreaming permeates all life, it is most concentrated in the "secret life"—and the secret life, in turn, focuses on the initiation of youth into manhood.

Now and again, at special times, a group separates itself from the world of hunting and gathering and goes in search of the secret life. It makes a camp, where the women remain, while the men proceed to a remote and concealed site. There, in touch with the heroes and ancestors of The Dreaming, the men remain for hours, days, weeks, even months, singing and performing rites that are considered potent in their effects not only on the surroundings but on the participants as well. Indeed, the youths who share in these rites display profound changes of personality. Missionaries lament that even those who were raised in the missions are so altered by tribal initiation that they abandon the church entirely. They are lost from Christianity to the secret life which leads toward The Dreaming.

During the course of the rites a youth passes through several phases. In one region (the Broome-Sunday Island district) the youth must complete eight phases, few of which he regards as unalloyed pleasure. He begins as Leminem; then, at the end of the week, when several of his teeth have been knocked out, he is known as Lainyar. A few days later he is circumcised and becomes Palil. With this he is made privy to a few tribal secrets. Later he is taken through an important blood ceremony. He is now Djainanga and is fit to receive deeper revelations. Some weeks or months later, when his blood is drunk by elders from a vein opened in his arm, he is Gambel. And still later, when a bird wing is inserted in his head band, he is Rungor. With the placing of a pearl-shell pendant around his neck, he becomes Bungin. Finally, when he is admitted to the ranks of married men, he is ceremonially painted and becomes known as Mambangan. He is now a man and he comprehends some of the mysteries of The Dreaming.

All aborigine initiation rites proceed from a point when the novice is removed from camp, the women screaming and pretending to resist his abduction, on through the period of bodily operations to a time of seclusion, and finally into a stage when the secrets are revealed. During the latter period the neophyte learns the myths of The Dreaming heroes and is taught of their holiness. He is shown sacred objects such as the bull-roarer—a large wooden cylinder which, when swung by a cord, produces a roar frightening to the uninitiated: the "voice" of the sky-heroes and the totemic ancestors. Such consecrated objects, kept in secret storehouses and handled only with the permission of the elders, live close to the Dream-time. By touching and caressing them, the newly initiated youth is automatically transported back into the time of The Dreaming. He becomes part of the hallowed life of the heroes. In some tribes he is given his own object to bind him to his own alter ego or "secret sharer," in Joseph Conrad's sense—a Dream-period hero with whom the youth spends much time in the venerated storehouse. A new name, possibly that of the secret sharer, is bestowed on the youth, a name to revered and so private that it is never uttered except as a whisper in the sacred area. "It is indeed a password into the eternal, unseen world of ancestral and totemic heroes."[6]

Another rite weaving the here-and-now into the eternal Dreaming is the increase rite, meant to insure that the totemic species will multiply. Myths of The Dreaming tell how a hero created ceremonies to cause some species to multiply. Perhaps the hero left behind him, as a storehouse for the life and spirit of the species, a stone. Thus a spiritual power can be released even today by a rite performed near that stone, a sacrament of The Dreaming. At the site of the stone one commands: "Let there be plenty of kangaroos, here and there," or one takes powdered stone from the sacred place, mixes it with blood, and deposits it wherever he wants, or expects, the multiplication to occur. By such incantations and acts, the natives intend to excite a transfer of spiritual power from the stone to the land. The kangaroo spirits or images, imprisoned in the stone, are thereby set free and come forth incarnated as live animals.

Not control of nature by magic but cooperation with nature is the intent of the increase rites. They guide, direct, and inspire nature at just those seasons when an increase of the species is most propitious. Ritual actors do not see themselves as the operative cause of an increase in species; instead it is through the rite that they express their wish for it to happen and provide the animating force of the species with an opportunity to take flesh. Such a conception reflects a close mesh between seen and unseen; man's role is to unleash the unseen, The Dreaming, in his own space and his own time, here and now.

This presentation of aboriginal existence has perhaps exaggerated the dominance of kinship and the unity of cosmic and social, but it is precisely these features that contrast most strikingly with modern ones, and our concern is with such contrasts. One final contrast, implied all along, can be summarized in the notion expressed by Lévi-Strauss, that aboriginal society is "cold" and modern society is "hot."[7] Aboriginal mythology ignores change, while modern "mythology" is eager— perhaps overeager—to recognize change. Among the aborigines, men die and children are born, patterns of settlement alter, modes of food-getting shift; but such changes in life are perceived as constancy because life is The Dreaming and The Dreaming is constant. Life is perceived as static—"cold." According to modern Western concepts of history, on the other hand, life is in flux; we greet even a hint of change in politics, business, or society as "news." Life is perceived as active—"hot." But to say that aboriginal life is perceived as cold, modern life perceived as hot, is not to say that aboriginal life is changeless. However, the aborigine's "cold" mythology probably makes him less ready than the modern man to exploit change when it does occur.

Southeast Asian Hill Tribes

Although most of the traits peculiar to primitive society are exemplified by the Australian aborigines, some are more vividly displayed by—or have been more carefully studied in—other primitive societies. Certain facets of marriage, incest taboos, and cosmology are better illustrated by numerous Southeast Asian hill tribes.

In this case the designation *primitive* is applied to societies technologically further advanced than the hunting-and-gathering aborigines. The hill tribes practice a form of agriculture known as "slash and burn;" that is, unlike the aborigines, the hill tribes are food-producing, rather than food-gathering. Aboriginal increase rites might be regarded as an attempt at food-producing, but it is plain that the hill tribes' techniques of slashing, burning, and planting are more efficient. Not only technologically but also socially the hill tribes' patterning is more complex than that of the aborigines. The hill tribes distinguish clearly between aristocrats and commoners, and they have chiefs.

Circulating Connubium

In chapter 2 we discussed the Trobriand *kula* ring, where goods of one kind (necklaces) were exchanged for goods of another kind (bracelets), the necklaces moving in one direction around the circle, the bracelets in the opposite direction. The hill tribes also engage in a circular system of exchange, but besides goods they exchange women. This system is called *circulating connubium.* It can be depicted, if somewhat simplistically, in the following way.*

Imagine three unilineal descent groups (which in actuality may be localized subdivisions of clans, but which we shall call simply clans), labeled *A, B,* and *C.* The clan *A* males remain where they are (the clan is patrilocal), and the females marry out of the clan's village to males of clan *B.* Since *B* males remain it their own locale, the *A* females must move in with them at marriage. Then, females born into clan *B* marry males from clan *C,* who of course remain where they are to receive them. Finally, females from clan *C* marry males from clan *A,* and the circle of movement through *A, B,* and *C* is completed. In practice there are often more than three clans (or subclans), but there cannot be fewer. Circulating connubium is thus more complex than the sister exchange of the aborigines, which involves only two groups.

Counterbalancing the movement of women in one direction is a movement of goods in both directions. Whenever a clan receives a wife it acknowledges its "inferiority" to the wife-giving clan by presenting goods and services to that clan. The wife-receiving clan may pay a bride-price of meats or chickens, knives or guns, rice beer, and gongs. In return for these "masculine" goods, it receives "feminine" goods such as cloth, a loom, brass plates, and baskets—gifts that accompany the bride to her new home.

The hill tribes coin words to distinguish wife-giving clans and wife-receiving clans from one's own clan. Thus, among the Purum, an "old Kuki" tribe of Manipur living on the eastern border of India, the clan from which one's own clan receives wives is known as *pu,* whereas the clan to which wives are given is known as *tu.* Among the Kachin of Burma,[8] the equivalent of *pu* is *mayu,* and that of *tu* is *dama.* (The Kachin also recognize another set of groups, the *lawulahta*—kinsmen who are potentially but not presently either *mayu* or *dama.*)

How does one distinguish his *pu* from his *tu?* The rule of thumb is that a man should take his bride from the group to which his mother belongs. That group is his *pu.* A man's daugher should be given as a bride to the same group that took his sister as a bride. That group is his *tu.* A clan's alliance to its *pu* or *tu* persists for several generations, and in

---

*This analysis follows that of Rodney Needham, *Structure and Sentiment,* pp. 74–100. Although Needham's analysis has been harshly criticized (see Marvin Harris, *The Rise of Anthropological Theory,* pp. 506–12, for a summary of and references to the major critiques), its problems do not seriously affect the schematic picture we present here. The thrust of most criticism has been to show that numerous Purum marriages do not follow the circulating connubium pattern. It remains true, however, that circulating connubium is a highly valued ideal pattern for the Purum and that significant ceremonies, symbols, and important members of the society do conform to this pattern.

time it works out that a man's wife is always his mother's brother's daughter or a woman classified in the same category as his mother's brother's daughter. Because a man is thus required to wed a woman fitting the category of cross-cousin on his mother's side, and is forbidden to wed his cross-cousin on his father's side, the marriage system found among the hill tribes (as well as in other regions, such as Siberia or Bolivia) is called *matrilateral cross-cousin marriage.* In such a system, to marry one's patrilateral cross-cousin would be to take a wife from a clan to which one's clan is obligated to give wives—to reverse the direction of circulation of women and goods, a taboo action regarded as sorcery or incest.

Why matrilateral cross-cousin marriage is encouraged and patrilateral cross-cousin marriage is forbidden has excited much ingenious analysis,[9] but the point we wish to emphasize is that matrilateral cross-cousin marriage, like aboriginal sister exchange, illustrates the importance of kinship in primitive society. Again, it is kinship that prescribes whom one should marry. Kinship controls marriage just as it controls so many other aspects of primitive life.

Incest Taboo

Prescriptions of whom one should marry in a system of circulating connubium are balanced by proscriptions on whom one should not marry. One proscription is the incest taboo. The incest taboo among the hill tribes forbids one to marry within one's local kinship group. One must go outside the group for a spouse, a requirement that is useful for hill tribe society. The Southeast Asian hills are sparsely populated, and with no central government to unite the scattered groups, far-flung alliances of kinship and marriage encouraged by the taboo against marrying within the local group are useful integrating bonds. The incest taboo helps integrate the scattered local groups into a more or less unified society.

The incest taboo has long been regarded as a distinctly human custom. If animals may be designated as *natural,* and if men may be called *cultured,* then the incest taboo may be defined as a cultural rule created by men to curtail their natural urges to copulate with anyone of the opposite sex whether he be kinsman or not—urges which animals do not curtail. The cultural basis of the incest taboo is not always recognized by modern men; more often it is seen in a biological or genetic light as a way to avoid inbreeding and thus to minimize the incidence of feeble-minded children. Of course this particular interpretation cannot account for the hill tribes taboo against marriage to one's patrilateral cross-cousin. After all, the rule does not prohibit marriage to one's matrilateral cross-cousin, and this is as much a form of biological inbreeding as is the other. Folklore often recognizes the cultural basis of the incest taboo. In a Moroccan story a man turns into a monkey because he has had incestuous relations with his sister and has indulged in other anticultural activities such as copulating during the Muslim fast month, urinating in milk, and wiping himself with bread after defecating.[10] Here folk wisdom emphasizes that incest taboo is a trait of cultured humans rather than of natural animals.

The taboo on incest within the immediate family is one of the few known cultural universals. There is no society that allows fathers to mate with daughters, mothers with sons, or brothers with sisters unless, being of royalty, they enjoy the prerequisites of a nearly godlike status. But in addition to the universal taboo on incest within the immediate family, there often exists in primitive societies (but rarely in modern societies) an incest taboo that extends far beyond the immediate family to distant cousins, as in the hill tribes' taboo on patrilateral cross-cousin marriage.

Perhaps the universal taboo on incest within the immediate family and the primitive taboo on incest among distant kin serve different functions. The wider taboo aids the integration of primitive societies such as the Purum, but the narrower taboo, found in modern as well as in primitive society, serves a nurturing function rather than a political function. If fathers openly lusted after their daughters or mothers after their sons, they would be distracted from the nurturing duties of parenthood. The incest taboo prevents such distraction, and thus helps the modern family to fulfill practically the only function it still retains: raising its children.

Not only is the incest taboo more extensive in primitive society than in modern society, primitives and moderns also differ in their attitudes toward it. First, primitives appear more preoccupied with incest if we judge from their mythology. Primitive mythology is permeated by the incest motif; in modern literature it is rare. Second, primitives seem to view incest in a more institutional fashion; among moderns it is viewed more psychologically. A theme common in primitive mythology is the founding of a tribe by a brother and a sister who married each other. When modern literature treats the topic of incest, it dwells more on sexual and emotional attraction and less on such institutional outcomes as the establishment of a family or society. In *The Sound and the Fury,* although brother and sister are attracted to each other, they never marry. Faulkner's concern was not with institutional consequences of incestuous feelings, but with the feelings themselves.

The contrast between these two treatments of incest may also reflect general differences between primitive and modern societies. In modern society, incest is part of the Freudian Oedipus complex; involving intimate, unconscious emotions that flourish within the privacy of the nuclear household, it is ordinarily expressed only in fiction or confessed to the psychiatrist. In primitive society, incest is of public concern—it is a crime that threatens the integration of society itself. The emotions that surround it are codified into myths, known to all, that commemorate the founding of the society. Like other institutions, the patterns of incest and incest taboo reflect the minor role that kinship plays in modern society, by contrast with its major role in primitive society.

Cosmology

Incest, marriage, and religion are for the hill tribes a single complex. Consider the case of the Purum. Among the Purum, when a man wishes to arrange a marriage between his son and a maiden whose clan occupies the appropriate *pu* status, he takes a gift of rice beer to the girl's father. At the wedding he again gives the *pu* father rice beer along with meat. In both instances the *tu* man's gift to the *pu* father symbolizes the latter's superiority of status; by his actions toward *pu, tu* recapitulates the veneration expected of an inferior mortal to the superior spirits. Should *pu* accept the beer and meat—thus acknowledging the inferiority of *tu*—he gives *tu* his daughter as a bride, together with her feminine goods. Thus, the superior group receives masculine goods (beer and meat) and gives feminine goods to the inferior group.

This exchange is only one of many that symbolize the contrast between *pu* and *tu* categories. Other categories holding similar contrastive significance are the following:

tu is associated with	*pu* is associated with
wife-taker	wife-giver
inferior	superior
mortals	gods
below	above
female	male
earth	sky
west	east
left	right
back	front
death	life
even	odd
profane	sacred
forest (jungle)	village
famine	prosperity

From this list emerges an image of the Purum conception of the cosmos. *Pu* is associated with one section of the cosmos, *tu* with another, and together they represent the total cosmos. Therefore, if *pu* and *tu* properly order their relations to each other, the cosmos will be ordered; and if the *pu/tu* alliance is sustained for generations, it will come to represent the enduring alliance of the two halves of the cosmos. Obviously in such a society incest is serious. When a man obtains a wife from his *tu* instead of from his *pu*, he does not merely commit a sexual transgression or violate a social institution. His crime, as Needham puts it, is an "onslaught on the entire complex of identically ordered relationships which are the society, and on the symbolic classifications which are its ideological life."[12] Incest not only mixes inappropriate mates and groups, but it also mixes cosmic compartments—all the elements in the *pu* category are jostled into the *tu* category, the *tu* elements into the *pu* category. In the primitive pattern, the cosmic and the social are interlocked.

The Ndembu of Rhodesia: A Primitive Drama

The previous discussion may give the erroneous impression that primitive society is a seamless fabric of socioreligious bonds, woven so tightly as to resist tearing. Under strain the social fabric of primitive society can become frayed. One source of such strain is the aberrant personality. Indeed, this type of person is a more direct threat to the primitive community than to the modern community. Modern society has specialists and specialized agencies either to "cure" or to conceal deviants: doctors and hospitals, policemen and jails. The primitive community must cope with the deviant directly and collectively.

Kamahasanyi's Neurosis

Kamahasanyi was a male inhabitant of a Ndembu village in Northern Rhodesia, a member of a society in which descent is reckoned matrilineally, but residence is virilocal. Upon marrying, the Ndembu man is expected to leave his father's village, where he was raised, and to move with his wife to the village where his matrilineal kinsmen, including his mother's brother, reside. According to anthropologist Victor Turner,[13] Kamahasanyi did not live up to this expectation. He could not bring himself to emigrate from his father's village until several years after his father's death when Kamahasanyi had already reached the age of forty and had been married several times. Because Kamahasanyi continued to live with his father's kin and did not move to join his mother's kin, he was stigmatized as a man who could not face responsibility. With the Ndembu, as with many matrilineal societies, it is among his matrilineal kin that a man acts like a man. It is here that he assumes adult rank and duties in matters of ritual, trade, and law; but among his father's kinsmen, a man is without status and function. Irritated by Kamahasanyi's presence, his father's kinsmen eventually insisted that he leave.

In addition to Kamahasanyi's problems with his patri-kin, he was personally a bit odd. While Kamahasanyi's father had been recognized as a man of great force and authority, Kamahasanyi was considered effeminate. He plaited his hair in a feminine style known as *lumba,* and spent his time gossiping in kitchens. Although he had married four times, he had failed to beget children. For his fourth wife, he had chosen a domineering woman upon whom he was dependent. Indeed, when through ineptitude he had fallen into debt, Maria had rescued him by selling cassava. Not only was Maria domineering, but she was also Kamahasanyi's cousin on his mother's side, so that when Kamahasanyi finally came to live with his mother's kin, he had returned to Maria's kin as well, to the village where she had been reared.

In this village lurked trouble for the unfortunate Kamahasanyi. Prior to her marriage, Maria had taken as a lover a man named Jackson, and upon her return to her natal village the affair was resumed. Liaisons are not uncommon among the Ndembu, but this one was conducted openly. When he encountered Maria's mother, Ndono, Jackson would rush away—as if Ndono were his mother-in-law. The Ndembu practice mother-in-law avoidance, so in this manner Jackson insinuated that Maria was his wife. To Kamahasanyi the insult was brazen and galling.

Probably as a result of his troubles, Kamahasanyi began to suffer from impotence, heart palpitations, and mild paranoia. Even if people were not actually maligning him covertly, Kamahasanyi imagined they were. Finally he withdrew to his hut, and the curer Ihembi, master of the Ihamba cult, was summoned.

The Cure

Ihembi, a resident of the area, was aware of the conflicts and hostilities that afflicted Kamahasanyi—indeed, that afflicted all his kinsmen. Ihembi believed that to cure Kamahasanyi he must in effect cure the entire community, and to do so he prescribed seven ceremonies.

Ihembi elected to hold one of them at the site where Kamahasanyi had once dreamt that, out of anger with Kamahasanyi for quarreling with his father's kin, his father's spirit had bitten him. The spirit was obviously the immediate source of Kamahasanyi's pain, and Ihembi decided to begin at the source.

In diagnosing Kamahasanyi's illness, Ihembi suggested two

causes—the faithless Maria and her mother, Ndono. Both were witches, Ihembi intimated. They yearned to "kill Kamahasanyi for his meat," and to obtain Jackson for husband and son-in-law, respectively. To dispose of Kamahasanyi they had magically sent little men who beat Kamahasanyi with hoe handles. This was one cause of Kamahasanyi's pain.

Not only the ill wishes of Maria and Ndono caused Kamahasanyi's suffering, said Ihembi, but also those of his neighbors and kinsmen. The dream of the biting spirit was a product of all of them and, for this reason, curing the bad feelings would also cure the biting spirit and insure its departure. Ihembi's ceremony was designed to dramatize both happenings.

The ceremony proceeded fitfully. Horn cups through which the biting spirit was to leave were affixed to Kamahasanyi's body, and there ensued a phase of drumming and singing, with Maria, Ndono, Jackson, and all the villagers participating. This continued until Kamahasanyi fell into a fit of trembling. When a horn shook loose, Ihembi would order the drums to stop. After inspecting the horn and discovering that the spirit had not yet emerged, Ihembi would offer an explanation which included an account of Kamahasanyi's troubles and an invitation to the villagers to step forward and confess their own malice. Ihembi would then reaffix the horn cup, the drumming and singing would recommence, and soon Kamahasanyi would resume trembling. Thus the sequence was repeated again and again, until as the night wore on the group began to feel a unanimous craving for the spirit to emerge.

Finally, at Ihembi's command, Maria herself took action. She entered the bush and returned with leaves from the *mudyi* tree, which because of its milklike secretions is an Ndembu symbol of motherhood, matrilineality, and womanhood. Turner reports that Maria then chewed the *mudyi* leaves and spat the juice on her husband's temples, feet, and hands—the centers of his thought and action—to "give him strength." By these gifts of spittle she reaffirmed her wifely obligations to Kamahasanyi and the good will she bore him, at the same time denying the alleged witchery.

It was now Kamahasanyi's turn. He complained bitterly that his matrilineal kinsmen were remiss in their duties to him and had not helped to ease his suffering—he had had to send for the curer himself. But now, since telling of his grudge, he felt all would be well. His hard thoughts no longer blocked the cure.

With that, Kamahasanyi began quivering violently. The cup on his temple fell off, dropping what appeared to be a small chunk of flesh. The congregation felt certain, Turner writes, that the hidden animosities of kinsmen and neighbors were being drawn out of the patient. Ihembi, who had been sitting quietly, now fitted a long horn over the little finger of his right hand, pointing it at another cup attached to the patient. As Turner recounts:

> The whole congregation rose to their feet as one man, and Ihembi fastened on the twitching Kamahasanyi, who fell on his side, writhing convulsively. Kamahasanyi cried out and sobbed when Ihembi removed the blood-dripping horn in a large skin-purse. Mundoyi and Kachilewa [two men who assisted Ihembi in the ceremony] threw large quantities of medicine over the patient. Ihembi rushed to the small calabash (containing medicine and blood from previous cuppings) and threw the cupping horn now concealed by the purse into it. He then spat powdered white clay on the really ugly bulge on Kamahasanyi's neck where the horn had been, "to cool and purify it." Kachilewa now held his hand poised over the leaf-concealed calabash while all of us waited intently. He removed the leaves and dredged with his hand in the bloody mixture. After awhile he shook his head and said "Mwosi" ("nothing in here"). We were all disappointed. But Ihembi with a gentle smile took over. He plunged his fingers into the gruesome fluid and when he brought them up I saw a flash of white. Then he rushed with what was in his fingers out of the avid circle of on-lookers. From the edge of the village, he beckoned to the elders and to me . . . we went one by one to Ihembi. It was indeed a human tooth, we had to say. It was no bush-pig's tooth, nor a monkey's. Jubilantly we told the women, who all trilled with joy.[14]

Turner goes on to say that, with the ceremony completed, and the spirit's tooth extracted, people who had been cool toward each other now beamed and warmly shook hands. Even hours later, "a mode of quiet satisfaction still seemed to emanate from the villagers."

A year later Turner revisited the village to find Kamahasanyi well and Maria still his wife. Jackson had left for employment in town, and Kamahasanyi had worked himself into the community. In fact, by persuading his younger brother and sister to join him in living with their maternal kinsmen, he had extended his personal entourage and had gained considerable stature. Kamahasanyi was snaring game and also in other ways acting like a responsible adult male.

Implications

The difference between tensions found in primitive society and those common to modern or early-modern society is revealed by comparing Ihembi's psychotherapy (for in effect this is what it was) with the psychotherapy of Sigmund Freud. Freudian psychotherapy was evolved to cope with the tensions peculiar to modern and early-modern life: to cure *intra*psychic tensions—tensions between id, ego, and superego. Ndembu therapy is designed to heal *inter*psychic tensions—tensions between members of a community. By treating the community neurosis, Ihembi was also treating Kamahasanyi's. Nor is Ndembu therapy quite like the group therapy that has been developed since Freud. Group therapy is not aimed at healing the tensions of the group; it is simply a means of relieving tensions suffered by individuals within the group. Group therapy sessions encourage these individuals to talk about their problems, thus to gain insight into them; but once the therapy is concluded and the job of curing its individual members is done, the group disbands—its members might never see each other again. Individuals in the Ndembu community group, on the other hand, may expect to live together for years. Harmonizing the relationships between individuals is necessarily as much an aim of Ndembu therapy as is the cure of their personal neuroses.

Freudian therapy and group therapy strive to prepare the patient to perform various roles successfully in groups away from the hospital or couch. But among the Ndembu the therapy group and the group in which the patient will play his life roles are the same. The contrast simply reflects once again the fact that in modern society units are more specialized. Hospital and clinic are separate from firm, family, and church, whereas in Ndembu society, the patient's therapy group is his kinship group, his economic group, and his religious group. The merging of groups, however, can also heighten the impact of intragroup conflicts on the individual psyche, for the better as well as for the worse. If Kamahasanyi's group could so strongly disturb his psyche, it could also cure it. Ihembi's therapeutic drama worked wonders, despite its brevity, while Freudian psychotherapy, to achieve the same result, takes years.

Curative power, such as that displayed by Ihembi, flows not only from the merging of a group, but also from the group's strength of faith. By manipulating symbols and beliefs that were already deeply ingrained in the Ndembu community life, Ihembi was actually exploiting a preestablished faith in the drama's curative efficacy. Modern psychiatrists cannot rely upon such popular faith in their curative techniques; laymen are not reared from birth to believe in a religion called "psychiatry" that underlies all facets of community life. Once more it becomes evident that in primitive society units are not specialized—religion, therapy, and community life are undifferentiated.

Overview

In primitive society, life is carried on in groups that are relatively unspecialized, with emphasis on kinship groups. Among the Ndembu, for instance, it is the matrilineal kinship group within which a man seeks political stature, debates legal issues, grows food, worships, falls ill, and becomes cured. Similarly, among the aborigines and the hill tribes a man lives largely within the confines of his patrilocal, patrilineal group. By contrast, in modern society a man typically divides his time, efforts, and concerns among several specialized groups such as family, factory, church, and hospital.

Primitive society is more particularistic than modern society; that is, primitive society places greater emphasis than does modern society on kinship status. The primitive man's kinship status determines to a great extent whom he marries, which totem he venerates, what manners he displays, and what political stature he achieves. Although the modern man's kinship status does have some effect on his life, he is much freer than the primitive man in his choice of mate, job, and religion.

Anthropologists have debated at length the issue of whether marriage or kinship bonds are more important in primitive society. Generally, anthropologists who did their research in Africa (e.g., Fortes and Gluckman) consider kinship bonds more important, while those whose interests lie in Southeast Asia (e.g., Leach and Lévi-Strauss) consider marriage bonds more important. From a wider viewpoint one could state that kinship bonds are more important in primitive societies and marriage bonds are more important in modern societies. Kinship controls marriage in primitive society since the aborigine or hill tribesman must choose his mate from a group that is kin to his own group in a specific way. Romantic love, which strongly influences the choice of a mate in modern society, is less influential than kinship rules in determining whom the primitive marries.

In unspecialized units such as primitive kinship groups, social relationships tend toward functional diffuseness—each relationship tends to be multidimensional. The primitive man is a kinsman, neighbor, coworker, coworshiper, and many other things simultaneously to *each member* of his local group, while the modern man's social relations tend to be one-dimensional: He plays but a single role to each member of his society. Therefore, disruption of the typical modern social relationship is less serious to the society and the individuals involved than is disruption of the typical primitive social relationship. If the modern man is merely a customer to his newspaper boy, the boy's forgetting to leave the paper one morning is hardly likely to provoke emotional damage or community uproar. Yet disruption of a single primitive relationship may have just these effects, and more serious ones as well. Defaulting on a primitive relationship not only can produce emotional disturbance and community disorder, but it can also play havoc with the entire universe— since individual, community, and universe are intimately connected in primitive culture. For this reason, primitives create rituals that are designed both to resolve psychic and social conflicts and to repair the associated cosmic disruptions. Rituals of this type, which Max Gluckman has labeled "rituals of social relations,"[15] require the participants to play the same ritual roles vis-à-vis one another within the rite as they play in daily life. (Kamahasanyi and Maria related to each other as man and wife inside the rite *and* outside it.) Ritualizing these relations, thus giving them order, will through a mystical, suprasensory process transfer the same order to society, nature, and the cosmos.

Rituals of social relations tend to emerge wherever the members of a group interrelate diffusely. Diffuse, multidimensional enclaves even within modern society can inspire such ties; thus, communal hippy groups celebrate rites calculated to unleash "flower power," a force believed mystically to alter the universe. Most modern men depend not on rituals of social relations, however, but on specialized societal agencies such as courts to rectify disputes within their commonly one-dimensional relationships. Courts are expected to uphold contracts, but not to bring into line the natural and the supernatural, and if one wants further proof of the spread of functional specificity among moderns, he need only note that kinship, diffuse in primitive society, is in modern society a specialty of domestic relations courts.

Little has been said about primitive economics, but it is clear that none of the primitive societies discussed earlier depends strongly on a generalized medium of exchange, such as modern money, or on specialized economic systems, such as modern markets. Like so many aspects of primitive life, the exchange of goods and services is carried out in the context of kinship and ritual. The exchange of women, goods, and ritual services among the hill people of Southeast Asia is typical and illustrates that the media used by primitives are restricted rather than generalized. Male goods can be exchanged only for women and female goods.

Nor is any of these groups highly centralized or bureaucratized. The aborigines have no chief. The Ndembu and the hill tribes do, but their chiefs usually control only a small domain, perhaps a village or two, and they sanction their rule on the basis of kinship. As a relevant contrast, in archaic society there are kings and bureaucracies that rule through other fiat—by popular will, recognized authority, or force.

The primitive society has no king, nor does it have a kingly class that is distinct from, and not kin to, a commoner class. Primitive society is a one-class society in which all the members are kinsmen. Yet among primitives is found an interesting example of a borderline two-class system, the Kachin of Burma. As incisively analyzed by Leach,[16] Kachin society is composed of two types of groups: democratic (*gumlao*) and autocratic (*gumsa*). The Kachin democratic group fits the description of

primitive one-class society: All persons within the group hold equal social status and place great emphasis on their kinship bonds to one
another. In the Kachin autocratic group, however, nobles are clearly
distinguished from commoners. According to Leach, these autocratic
groups have borrowed a model of what we would call archaic two-class
society from their valley-dwelling, king-ruled neighbors, the Buddhist
Shan. Unfortunately, the hill-dwelling Kachin possess primitive features
(a slash and burn agriculture, circulating connubium, a religion based on
animism and on feasts of merit) that do not support this archaic pattern.
Therefore, Kachin groups which set themselves up as autocracies are
constantly breaking down and assuming the one-class democratic form.
Yet with the autocratic ideal before them, the democratic groups constantly strive to be autocratic. Kachin society continuously oscillates between the two patterns, and the Kachin have never achieved a stable and
enduring kingdom or anything close to it. We would say that the Kachin
are moving toward the boundary between primitive and archaic, but
have not yet managed to cross it.

Since primitive society is a one-class society and there are, therefore, no classes to move between, there is obviously less social mobility
than in a multiclass society. Furthermore, since primitive society is not
highly centralized, another type of mobility is impossible: mobility from
periphery to center. There is no capital city to which the rustic from the
provinces can move, one village is much like another, and so a primitive
who changes villages does not radically change his life style—the sort of
change implied by the notion of social mobility.* Although the mobility
of the primitive individual is restricted, the primitive community is often
highly mobile geographically. Many primitives relish a nomadic life. The
Australian aborigines move about within a given territory, hunting game
and gathering plants, and the Southeast Asian hill tribes move about
slashing, burning, and planting. Primitive communities can wander easily because they travel light. Their tools are easy to transport, as are their
ceremonial objects. A primitive bullroarer is much lighter than an archaic temple.

Again, it should be emphasized that the spiritual and mundane
aspects of primitive life merge into one complex. The Dreaming is
"everywhen," as much a part of the here and now as of the distant past,
and religion premeates everything. Incest threatens the cosmic order.
Rituals to mend the social fabric are thought also to redress disturbances
in nature and supernature. Cosmic figures, such as the heroes of The
Dreaming, are not gods—they are too involved in the world to stand
above and control it. Nor are they worshipped as gods. Men identify with

---

*Primitives today can change their life style by moving to modern settlements,
towns, and cities, but this is not mobility *within* primitive society.

them in rites of the secret life when "everywhen" becomes now, and men in their dreams become these heroes.

In primitive society, just as the cosmic is welded to the social, so the religious institution is part of the overall social organization. There is no church clearly distinct in location, function, and membership from other groups. The basic religious group among the aborigines is the patrilocal group, which is also the basic economic, political, residential, and kinship group. Among the Ndembu or Kachin, kinship groups form the basic religious groups as well. Primitives hew to no doctrine separating church and family.

How great is a primitive society's capacity for change? This is a difficult question to answer, partly because no anthropologist can live for several lifetimes in a primitive society—an opportunity that would allow direct observation of primitive history. Moreover, the problem of measuring the rate and the capacity for change is an immense one. Even so, if one were to plot on a graph the rate of technological change at various periods in human history, one would find that during the modern era technology has changed at an overwhelmingly higher rate than during periods prior to 7000 B.C.[17] Since all societies were primitive prior to 7000 B.C., one can say that the rate of technological change in a world largely populated by modern societies is greater than that in a world populated by primitive societies. Because sociocultural changes accompany technological change, one could generalize further and say that the rate of sociocultural change in a world largely populated by modern societies is greater than that in a world populated by primitive societies. We conclude, therefore, that primitive societies left to themselves—in a world without modern societies—change slowly. This implies that primitive societies do not contain within themselves a strong impetus to change.

Various "brakes" on change can be discovered in primitive religion. Since primitive religions are "cold," primitive peoples, instead of eagerly seizing as new each opportunity that the world presents, classify the new as simply another manifestation of the old. Similarly, since primitive religion pervades all spheres of life, every sphere is rendered sacred, hence difficult to change—for to change the sacred is to throw the whole of existence into turmoil.

But these arguments simply point to a conservative bias in primitive patterning, a bias that should not be exaggerated since upon contacting modern men some primitive societies have changed radically and quickly. What is at issue here is whether primitive societies have an *internal* impetus to change—whether, if left alone, they would spontaneously initiate changes. Here we return to the formulation proposed earlier. The primitive's ideal order is blended with his social order; hence the primitive possesses no transcendent, distinct, differentiated ideal order against which to compare and criticize his present social order. A major internal impetus for reform and change is therefore lacking.

Topics for Discussion

Two approaches for applying the study of primitive society to the study of modern society can be distinguished: the Durkheimian, which is followed by most French and British social anthropologists, and the Weberian (after Max Weber), which is followed by this book. Durkheimians emphasize the similarities between primitive and modern patterns. They often attribute to modern rites, symbols, or customs, dynamics and functions that apparently underlie primitive rites, symbols, or customs. Weberians, on the other hand, emphasize the differences between primitive and modern patterns. They attempt to define the dimensions according to which modern patterns have evolved beyond the primitive patterns. Both these approaches can illuminate our understanding of modern man, or of man in general, through their perspectives are different. The student might profitably consider the advantages and disadvantages of each of the two approaches.

Our discussion of Kamahasanyi's neurosis is derived from the intensive studies of Ndembu life by Victor Turner. Turner has pioneered in the analysis of what he calls "social drama," and his accounts of primitive life often differ strikingly from those of traditional social anthropologists. Social drama commonly focuses on the events in the life of a particular individual and abstracts a narrative of events with climax and resolution. By contrast, traditional social anthropology, exemplified by our treatment of the aborigines, seeks to delineate broad sociocultural patterns as expressed in the lives of many individuals and in group life. These two modes of abstraction, one emphasizing a narrative of events, the other emphasizing sociocultural patterns, could usefully be compared.

In his provocative analysis of Southeast Asian hill tribes, Leach has posed yet another methodological problem with respect to primitive society. Among the hill tribes, a group's cultural (e.g., language) boundaries are rarely the same as its social (interactional) boundaries. This observation raises some important questions about the relationships between cultural systems and social systems and precisely how we are to determine a society's boundaries.

Suggested Readings

The Australian Aborigine

The Australian Aborigines (paperback, 1966) by A. P. Elkin. A comprehensive, authoritative, and readable survey by one of the leading scholars on the Australian aborigines.

The Tiwi of North Australia (paperback, 1960) by C. W. M. Hart and Arnold R. Piling. A short book on a somewhat deviant aboriginal tribe. Suitable for the beginning student, and to elaborate and vary the picture presented in this text.

Black Civilization (1964) by W. Lloyd Warner. A classic study of the Murngin tribe. Too detailed for the average beginner, but excellent in its careful delineation of a single group.

"The Dreaming" (1965) by W. E. H. Stanner. A beautiful and profound portrait of aboriginal thought and religion.

Totemism (paperback, 1963) by Claude Lévi-Strauss. An analysis providing much insight into totemism in aboriginal thought and society.

The Savage Mind (1966) by Claude Lévi-Strauss. Provocative, if speculative, analysis of aboriginal thought and society.

The Elementary Forms of the Religious Life (originally, 1912; paperback, 1965) by Emile Durkheim. The classic analysis of aboriginal religion; still well worth reading for its theoretical as well as empirical insight.

The Jigalong Mob: Aboriginal Victors of the Desert Crusade (1974) by Robert Tonkinson. A portrait of some aboriginese adapting to change.

Southeast Asian Hill Tribes

The Elementary Structures of Kinship (1969) by Claude Lévi-Strauss. Classic analysis of circulating connubium, particularly among southeast Asian hill tribes.

Structure and Sentiment (1962) by Rodney Needham. Deals with the theory of circulating connubium and matrilateral cross-cousin marriage.

"The Structural Implications of Matrilateral Cross-Cousin Marriage" (1966) by Edmund Leach. Seminal analysis of marriage patterns, including that of circulating connubium in Southeast Asia and elsewhere.

Political Systems of Highland Burma (paperback, 1965) by Edmund Leach.

The Structure of Chin Society (paperback, 1963) by F. K. Lehman.

The Economics of the Central Chin Tribes (1943) by H. N. C. Stevenson.

The Social Organization and Customary Law of the Toba-Batak of Northern Sumatra (1964) by J. C. Vergouwen.

Feasting and Social Oscillation (1973) by A. Thomas Kirsch. A synthetic treatment of the hill tribes in mainland Southeast Asia.

The Ndembu

Schism and Continuity in an African Society (1957) by Victor Turner.

The Forest of Symbols: Aspects of Ndembu Ritual (1967) by Victor Turner.

The Drums of Affliction: A Study of Religious Processes Among the Ndembu of Zambia (1968) by Victor Turner.

Primitive Religion in African and American Tribes

Nuer Religion (1956) by E. E. Evans-Pritchard. Classic treatment.

Divinity and Experience: The Religion of the Dinka (1961) by Godfrey Lienhardt. Outstanding.

African Worlds: Studies in the Cosmological Ideas and Social Values of African Peoples (paperback, 1954) edited by Daryll Forde.

Introduction to Zuni Ceremonialism (1932) by Ruth Bunzel. An American contribution to the study of religion.

Ceremonial Patterns in the Greater Southwest (1948) by Ruth M. Underhill. Outside the British social-anthropological tradition.

Primitive Religion—General Works*

Religion in Primitive Society (1961) by Edward Norbeck.

Primitive Classification (paperback, 1963) by Emile Durkheim and Marcel Mauss.

Religion Among the Primitives (paperback, 1964) by William J. Goode.

"Myth in Primitive Psychology," in *Magic, Science and Religion and Other Essays* (paperback, 1954) by Bronislaw Malinowski.

"Les Rites de Passage," in *Essays on the Ritual of Social Relations* (1962) edited by Max Gluckman.

Purity and Danger: An Analysis of Concepts of Pollution and Taboo (1966) by Mary Douglas.

"Colour Classification in Ndembu Ritual: A Problem in Primitive Classification," and "Betwixt and Between: The Liminal Period in Rites de Passage," in *The Forest of Symbols: Aspects of Ndembu Ritual* (1967) by Victor Turner.

"Religion as a Cultural System" by Clifford Geertz in *Anthropological Approaches to the Study of Religion* (1966) edited by Michael Banton.

Religion: An Anthropological View (1966) by Anthony F. C. Wallace.

Sacrifice: Its Nature and Function (1964) by Henri Hubert and Marcel Mauss.

The Birth of the Gods: The Origin of Primitive Belief (paperback, 1960) by Guy E. Swanson.

Reader in Comparative Religion (1965) edited by William A. Lessa and Evon Z. Vogt. Includes mainstream articles and an extensive bibliography.

Modern Religion

The Religious Factor: A Sociological Study of Religion's Impact on Politics, Economics and Family Life (paperback, 1961) by Gerhard Lenski.

Protestant, Catholic, Jew (paperback, 1955) by Will Herberg.

The Secular City (paperback, 1965) by Harvey Cox.

These works treat modern religious patterns and provide a useful contrast to primitive patterns.

*For readings on primitive kinship, see references listed after chapter 3.

Films

Primitive People. Depicts the life of the Australian aborigines.

Djalambu. Depicts a mourning ceremony of the aboriginal Emu clan.

The Great Unfenced. Portrays the desert environment of the aborigines.

Tiuringa: The Story of Stone Age Man. Portrays aboriginal ritual and the quest after food.

Walkabout: A Journey with the Aborigines.

6

chapter

Archaic Society and Culture

The Swazi

The Swazi are a Bantu-speaking people living in Swaziland, a country about the size of Hawaii, surrounded on three sides by the Union of South Africa and on the fourth by Mozambique. In the early 1940s when research on the Swazi was completed,[1] they numbered about 184,750. At that time Swaziland was a British territory, ruled by King Sobhuza II. Today, still under the rule of King Sobhuza II, Swaziland is prospering (Swazi exports almost tripled during the period 1965–1968). On September 6, 1968, Swaziland obtained independence.

Swaziland's scenery, climate, and soil vary widely—ranging from the high veld of the West, broken, wild, and often veiled in mist and drizzle, to the warmer and drier middle veld and lowlands of thick bush, squat thorn trees, and short, sparse grass. In these regions the Swazi plant grain, tend cattle, and hunt game, thus exhibiting a form of food-getting more advanced than that of the Australian aborigines. The tempo of these endeavors is set by the rhythm of the seasons as they change from hot to cold, from rainy to dry. On these cycles depend the

166

ripening of crops, the conditions of the herds, and the availability of game. Partly because the Swazi's life is so closely bound to the seasonal cycles, the cycles carry a ritual significance for them. The great Incwala, a ceremony held at the height of summer when the first crops have ripened, is one example.

Swazi Kingship and Society

Swazi commoners live in homesteads that are scattered about the countryside and are occupied not just by the immediate family, but often by additional kinsmen, such as brothers of the homestead head and their families. The eldest male acts as the head, or patriarch. More than seven people reside in the homestead of the average Swazi commoner, while more than twenty may live with a chief or prince. Although the polygynous homestead—in which each of a man's several wives lives with her own children in a separate hut—is considered ideal, in practice the average Swazi can rarely afford more than one wife. (The rich, powerful aristocrat, however, may have several wives.) Aside from the extra huts for the additional wives, every homestead includes a "great hut," decorated with the skulls of animals sacrificed to patrilineal ancestors. The great hut is under the charge of a woman called the patriarch's "mother," who may actually be his first wife. No ordinary wife may enter this hut—only the mother.

The Swazi king lives in a homestead in many respects similar to that of the commoner. The king's homestead, however, includes many non-kinsmen and is much larger than the commoner's—in fact, it might be better defined as a village. In 1934 King Sobhuza II had 265 persons living in his capital homstead, Lombamba. The king's village, like the commoner's homestead, is built around a great hut, but the king's great hut is really a compound of huts called the Great Abode, an exceedingly sacred area. The Swazi maintain that if an inappropriate person, such as one who has recently had contact with menstrual blood or participated in sexual relations, should enter the Great Abode, he would bring madness on himself and disaster to the land.

The queen mother, a central figure in Swazi society equal in importance to the king himself, resides in a village apart from that of the adult king. As a child the king lives in his mother's village, but upon reaching manhood he moves away to establish his own village, the nation's capital. The king's village serves as the nation's administrative and military headquarters; the queen mother's village serves as the ceremonial center and the home of the national ritual objects.

The king's capital village, the queen mother's village, and the villages occupied by the king's wives are all major sites of national activity. Here courtiers compete for royal favors, leading legal cases are discussed, festivities are celebrated, and large labor forces are organized. The sophistication and excitement of court life is highly coveted by the ordinary Swazi, who speak of the deeper wisdom, the finer polish of those who mature in the villages of the "great," rather than in the common households "away from the people."

The territory of Swaziland is divided into principalities and districts ruled by the princely relatives of the king, by royal governors, and by hereditary chiefs. All of these officials are either the king's direct appointees or have had their authority ratified by him. The districts over which they rule range in size from about four square miles to more than twenty, and vary in population from 100 to 2,000 persons. Since the boundaries of these districts are established partly by traditional hereditary rights and partly by national decisions of the king, they are often vaguely defined and remain so until a dispute occurs, which is settled by the king or by one of his governmental deputies. The Swazi appear to be more concerned about the precision of land boundaries than are the Australian aborigines. To Swazi agriculturalists, who own fields and pastures, boundaries mean more than they do to the nomadic aboriginal hunter-gatherers. And because Swazi territory is alienable—it can be bought and sold—the opportunity for title disputes is greater. A centralized ruler and a bureaucracy are empowered to resolve such disputes and to set precise boundaries. The aborigines, lacking such agents, could not delimit precise boundaries even if they wished to do so.

By decree of national ideology, the ownership of all national territory is vested in the king, not in local groups or in citizen landowners. The king allots land to his people through his noble magnanimity. To the Swazi mind, he is not selling land but "serving" it; in analogous fashion, certain foods are never sold, but are served to strangers and hungry neighbors. In practice, however, the king finds upon acceding to the throne that his kingdom is already divided into districts and, within these, into plots of land to which individual Swazi have staked hereditary claim. The king, therefore, simply ratifies a preestablished arrangement. If a commoner believes he has been treated unfairly or evicted unjustly by a local leader, or if he cannot obtain land equal to his needs, he may appeal to the king or the queen mother. The king has the power to depose a leader or to dictate a leader's heir, and in this way he can control malfeasance on the local level.

Each Swazi clan is fragmented into numerous segments scattered among the various districts. Since any local settlement is likely to include homesteads belonging to several clans, therefore, a dispute among such homesteads cannot be settled by any single clan's authorities. To resolve their disputes, the homesteads must consult "cold people," district authorities who govern all homesteads in their districts and who are not necessarily kin to any. Clan authority, then, has given way to governmental authority.

This situation did not always exist among the Swazi. At one time Swazi society comprised a number of small, localized clans of approximately equal status and power. Through a gradual process of assimilation and conquest, one clan, the Dlamini, became the royal clan and assumed rulership over the entire nation. Hence, at least since the reign of King Mbandzeni in the late nineteenth century, Swazi society has been a pyramidal hierarchy of clans and lineages, with the Dlamini clan at the apex. Many common clans no longer maintain their own territorial identity, but distinguish themselves from other clans solely by their contributions to the royal Dlamini clan. The Matsebula and Motsa clans, for example, contribute specialists in ritual to certain royal ceremonies, and the Hlophe clan furnishes tutors for princes. Myths which in the past glorified individual clans have been supplanted by national sagas. Thus, Swazi society has become increasingly centralized—a society in which clans have surrendered their local territorial sovereignties and have become arms of the central government and king.

The breakdown of Swazi clan organization was further encouraged by the emergence of age-graded warrior regiments. Formerly, men of all ages fought together for their own clan against rival clans. Now, each Swazi male owes military service directly to the head of the Dlamini clan, the king, and each man is classified into an age-graded regiment. Every five or seven years the king forms a new regiment. All males falling into the age range established for that regiment leave their homesteads and take up group residence in all-male barracks composed of huts quartering four to six men each. The men are organized into squads (*siceme*) consisting of eight to twenty men who drill and dance together ceremonially. Several squads make up a platoon, which is often commanded by a son of the king or of a district chief. Platoons are combined into local regiments, which in turn are combined into the entire age-class regiment.

Each regiment follows its own leader, flourishes its own emblem, shouts its own cry, and forms a conspicuous unit on national occasions when age mates from scattered districts gather together in a single enclosure in the royal capital to take part in national ceremonies. Living together, eating together, smoking hemp together, age mates develop a strong camaraderie. At the same time, the age-grading system serves to detach father from son, older brother from younger brother, and to substitute for these familial loyalties a new loyalty—to age group. Furthermore, since loyalty to the age group means loyalty to the regiment, it means also loyalty to the supreme commander of all regiments, the king. In fact, certain regiments are stationed in the royal capital to serve the king, much as marine units attend the White House. Any man of the proper age class can join these elite regiments, and no father, guardian, or district chief can prohibit a man from "working for the king, father of the nation." A father is eager, as a rule, to have at least one son remain several years in the capital to be educated as an elite soldier. These young men aspire to deeds of bravery for the regiment and the king, and in the days of active warfare, death on the battlefield was the one death that no kinsman could mourn since it was for the sake of the nation.

Since the Swazi reckon descent patrilineally, the king inherits his position from his father. Only the son of a king may become king, but since a king has many wives and thus many sons, an heir must frequently be chosen. Wars of accession are averted by ranking the king's wives and thus eliminating at least some of the children from contention for kingship. Usually the king's heir is the eldest son of the king's highest ranking wife, and since the royal Dlamini clan is permitted to marry within itself (although the king and his wife may not have kinship ties closer than a common great-grandfather), the heir is considered to have "the blood of kingship" from both maternal and paternal sides.

Because it is the king's mother who by her rank confers royal status on the king, she is a figure of prestige and influence. Called "Lady Elephant," she sustains a delicate balance of power between herself and her son, the king "Lion." It is believed that conflict between the king and the queen mother will menace the entire nation with civil war, drought, or flood. Harmony between king and queen is essential, and to the Swazi it is more likely to exist between mother and son than between husband and wife.

The king relies heavily on his closest royal kinsmen, especially his half brothers and his uncles. Not only are these senior princes consulted on all important issues of state, they are also appointed by the king as governors of vacant district posts, insuring the loyalty both of kinsmen and of district residents. The royal kinsmen, with other councillors drawn from less noble clans, act also as the king's teachers and as his critics. They may be summoned to help determine the heirship of a noble line, to arbitrate a property dispute, or to name a successor after the king's death.

Even more closely identified with the king than his kinsmen, however, are two men who are not kin, called the *tinsila*. Although they represent common stock, they undergo a ritual transference of blood, elevating them to a mental and physical status that in many ways connects them more intimately to the king than any status sanctioned by kinship. The rite turns the *tinsila* into ritual doubles of the king. The

Swazi believe that if sorcery or evil is directed at the king, it will be deflected onto his doubles; it is therefore considered advantageous if these ritual alter egos are sickly, for by these symptoms it is apparent that they are doing their job well. Besides being interceptors of evil, the *tinsila* mediate disputes and, above all, endeavor to keep peace among the people. To aid in this task, they have administrative authority equal to that of the highest prince.

Other nonkinsmen who also assist the king are the *tindvuna,* or councillors of the royal villages. These too are drawn from commoner clans, and are selected by the king in consultation with his advisers. The *tindvuna* try legal cases, render judgments, and advise the king on the mood of the people. They are also accorded powers and privileges equivalent to those of the royal kinsmen themselves, and they may actually be conferred membership in the royal clan. If they are granted membership in the royal clan, they will be permitted to eat from the dishes used by the royal princes, will be forbidden to marry a close relative of the king (symbolically that would be incest), and upon death may expect to be buried with royal ritual. But no matter how great their talents or how numerous their responsibilities, these councillors still lack royal blood, hence they are never eligible for the kingship itself.

Kingship in Swaziland is, in part, the reign of the royal clan, which is extended throughout the nation through bonds of blood and marriage. As the Swazi say, "A wise king recognizes the value of kinship." Yet by comparison with primitive societies, many of the most significant bonds that unite the Swazi nation are not those of kinship but those of loyalty to the concept of Swazi kingship and to the king as the embodiment of that concept. The age-graded regiments and the services of the ritual doubles and the royal councillors contribute to this pattern. A third institution, that of vassalage (*kukhonta*), makes a further contribution. Chiefs offer homage to the king, commoners to their local chief, youths without property to some wealthy homestead headman. In each case the underling begs of his superior the right to be his "boy" or "dog." Especially at the lower levels of society, this system of *kukhonta* establishes between nonkinsmen a quasi-kinship bond. Thus, a vassal who has been assisted by his superior in obtaining a wife may establish his family in the superior's household, rather than in the household of one of his own kinsmen. It is a great honor to be sought as a lord by a would-be vassal. By helping the poor or unfortunate, the lord demonstrates his generosity and his nobility.

Notions of status and hierarchy pervade Swazi society. Although chiefs and leaders are trained to "feel with" their subjects, no subject dares to stand upright in the presence of a chief, instead, he "shuffles forward with bended knee and utters exaggerated praise."[2] Even more exalted than chiefs are the king and the queen mother, in relation to whom all other Swazi are ranked. The king is "The Lion," "The Sun," "The Bull of the Nation," "The Milky Way;" the queen mother is "The Lady Elephant," "The Earth," "The Beautiful," "Mother of the Country;" the highest officials, by contrast, are "tiny stars" or "little ant heaps;" and the average man is a "dog," a "stick," a "nothing."

Despite these bold metaphors distinguishing the lowest from the highest, differences in Swazi rank are not correlated with wide variations in wealth or standard of living. Swazi technology, although more developed than that of the aborigines, is still crude. It cannot support, for any length of time, those who do not directly contribute to the basic needs of survival, such as food and shelter. Even royalty works—queens toil in the fields, princes erect their own houses—but, it is true, they do not work as hard as commoners. Some older princes "allow their nails to grow into long talons to show that they need not exert themselves."[3]

As in many other African societies, cattle are the key symbol of wealth and power in Swaziland. Men devote considerable energy to building up great herds of cattle—for ritual purposes more than for nourishment. Cattle symbolism is common throughout Swazi culture. For example, in the days of intertribal wars, a strategic military formation required the army to advance in a semicircle, which represented the curved horns of a bull; also the king is considered the bull of the nation. For reasons of ritual as much as of survival, the king and the aristocrats maintain large herds of cattle, and are able to do so because, having many wives, they can produce many daughters—primary currency to exchange for cattle.

The line separating royalty and commoners is obviously more sharply defined for the archaic Swazi than it is for the primitive Kachin. The Kachin tend to distinguish the elite from the lowly on the basis of birth, but their overall social system is so unstable that this tendency has never become crystallized into a kingdom. Kachin aristocratic (*gumsa*) groups always break down into democratic (*gumlao*) groups. It is not known whether this ever took place among the Swazi, but clearly the shift from a one-class to a two-class society is accompanied by strain. Some of this strain is reflected in Swazi royal ritual.

Swazi Kingship and Ritual

The Swazi king is the symbolic focal point of the nation—the man who is "more than man," who is the "father" and also the "son" of the people. Because king and nation are so closely identified in Swazi thought, the king's health and strength are equated with the health and strength of his subjects, and further with the fertility of nature. The king's illness brings dread, his death disaster. Therefore, one role of ritual is to protect the monarch, and thereby the nation, from such threats.

Since the king, in a very real sense, is "akin to" the nation, as he matures the nation matures, and each stage of his and the nation's maturation is marked by a national rite. When the king attains full manhood, the nation provides him with his first two wives, ritual queens traditionally chosen from two special clans. The first is his "righthand queen," Matsebula; the second his "lefthand queen," Motsa. Matsebula, called also "a man, a ruler," accompanies the king to the royal harem. Here, in a ritual hut, her blood is mixed with the king's; and, to symbolize his manhood, the king spits medicines of fertility through holes cut in the walls. Henceforth, the righthand queen is regarded as part of the king and is addressed as "mother." A few weeks later the king marries the lefthand queen, Motsa, in a similar ritual. Only after the king has married his two ritual queens may other wives or concubines enter his harem.

So removed must the king be kept from death for fear that the nation will be contaminated that he may not partake in more than a few days of mourning for anyone; as the Swazi say, "When the king is in blackness, the whole nation is without strength." Understandably, the death of the king himself represents a grave threat to his people, and thus the event is kept secret until a successor has been ritually installed. Only the queen mother, the governors of the royal villages, the *tinsila*, specialists in the royal death ritual, and two intimate attendants are aware of it. Day and night the king's body is guarded with reverence and ceremony. Though the people may suspect the truth, they dare not speak their thoughts lest they be accused of "wishing to kill the country." Secretly, in the dark of night, the king's body is moved to the ritual hut in the harem where he celebrated his marriage to the first ritual queen, Matsebula. Only after his heir is announced does burial take place. The Swazi believe that at this point the king's spirit joins the other royal ancestors in an afterlife that is hierarchically constructed in the same way as the world he leaves behind. The dead king is mourned for three years, with sacrifices offered in his name as well as in the name of the nation. The dead king becomes the link between the living nation and the dead royalty, and by these ceremonies the bond is strengthened between the nation and its entire ancestry.

The central ceremony of kingship is the annual Incwala ceremony, the "heavy play of all the people." The leading actor of the Incwala is the king. When the king is still young, the ceremonies are kept simple, but as the king and his capital mature, the ceremonies increase in complexity and potency. When the king reaches the age of twenty-one, the first full Incwala is held; and when he is in his prime, the Incwala—now fully formed, rich and elaborate in symbolism and nuance—is also at its peak. Since the last five kings have died in their prime (by sorcery, the Swazi believe, for no death is from a natural cause), the Incwala ceremony has not recently been allowed to decline in richness as the king declines in vigor.

Special national priests are in charge of the Incwala ceremonies; one group is known as the *bemanti* ("people of the water"), the other as the *belwandle* ("people of the sea"). The *bemanti* fetch river water and the *belwandle* fetch sea water to strengthen the king. They participate in no other ceremonies, but duty in the Incwala alone is enough to confer national stature; the head priest of each group ranks as a leading chief. Although the head priests are not members of the Dlamini royal clan, they are among the most prominent citizens of Swaziland. When one of them dies he is buried with the full honors of a Dlamini prince.

Joining the main participants—the king, the priests, the *tinsila,* and the royal regiments—the rank and file of the Swazi nation come in local contingents, each led by a chief or his deputy. Although not all the Swazi take part in the Incwala, practically every male Swazi does so at least once in his life.

Before the official ceremony begins, a black ox—which plays a key role in the Incwala—is stolen from the herd of a loyal subject who is not of the royal clan. The anger and pride felt by the owner when he discovers the theft is thought to "help the medicine" of the Incwala.

Also before the ceremony begins, the water priests (the *bemanti* and the *belwandle*) gather in the cattle enclosure of the capital, ready to undertake their exodus to the river and the sea. While an official "praiser" shouts praises of the great journey to come, the priests squat to inhale snuff provided by the queen mother. They then set off on their mission, quietly and in single file. Once they have left the capital, the priests' posture of humility changes to one of arrogance. They pillage the countryside, drink beer, and levy fines on the citizenry, as they move toward their destinations. They return with the sacred waters—still pillaging, strutting, and drinking as they go—and wait at a royal village near the capital until they are summoned to bring their water "medicines" (serving ritual rather than health purposes) for use in the first part of the Incwala, the little Incwala.

On the opening day of the little Incwala, messengers summon to the capital the water priests, who bear the sacred strengthening waters. The honor of opening the Incwala falls to the regiment from the village of the king's grandmother. Members of this regiment between the ages of fifty and sixty-five clothe themselves in leopard skin loincloths and black plumes and sing the first of the sacred sons:

> *Uye uye oyeha—you hate the child king mu u u oyeha,*
> *you hate the child king (repeated).*
> *I would depart with my Father (the King),*
> *I fear we would be recalled.*
> *mm m u oyeha—they put him on the stone:*
> *mm m u oyeha he—sleeps with his sister:*
> *mm m u u u he—sleeps with Lozithupa (Princess):*
> *uye uye oyeha—you hate the child king.*[4]

The song celebrates the people's hatred of the king and recognizes the royal clan's right to marry incestuously. During the song, the men and women of the capital and the members of the regiment of the king's grandmother's village whoop and dance into the cattle enclosure. After a time a second chant is started, the men shaking sticks and the women holding wands quivering in rhythm:

> *shi shi ishi—you hate him*
> *ishi ishi ishi—mother, the enemies are the people. . . .*[5]

Other chants follow, while the king is treated with the priests' medicines. As the sun sets, the king enters the sacred enclosure. The dancers vary the pattern of their dance—imitating the shape of the moon as it goes through its phases—and again and again the people sing the *simemo*, a litany for all the important occasions of the king's life, such as his first marriage and his burial:

> *Jjiya oh o o King, alas for your fate*
> > *(refrain)*
> *Jjiya oh o o King, they reject thee*
> *Jjiya oh o o King, they hate thee.*[6]

Abruptly the song ends. A priest in the enclosure with the king cries "Out, foreigners!" and non-Swazi and all those of the royal Dlamini clan, including women made pregnant by men of the Dlamini clan, must leave. When the king is surrounded by only his most loyal (unrelated) supporters and subjects, the priest shouts, "Eh! Eh! He stabs it with both horns. Our bull!" In this way are the people informed that the king, by splitting the medicine, has "broken" the old year to prepare for the new. The people shout, "He stabs it!" The king has produced what all desired; as the medicines strengthened him, so has he strengthened the earth. He has nudged the sun out of its "hut" to begin its journey through a new year. The day's climax has been reached, a concluding anthem in praise of the king is sung, and as the regiments and women disperse, the king enters his harem for sleep.

At dawn the people awake, once more to hurl insults at their ruler: "Come, Lion, awake, the sun is leaving you!" The *simemo* is sung, the king again spits to the east and to the west, and again everyone rejoices and shouts, "He has bitten the passing year!" The warriors "work for the kingship" by weeding the queen mother's garden, and in return the queen mother provides beer. There is feasting. The people then return to their houses until the moon is full. The little Incwala is over—in a few days will come the great Incwala.

Each day of the great Incwala bears the name of its main event. The first day, devoted to fetching the "sacred tree," a species of acacia, is called *lusekwane*. Just as in medieval legend only "knights without stain" might set forth in quest of the grail, so only pure Swazi youths may fetch the sacred tree. Early in the morning they are enjoined, "Go out! With all powers! At once!" "As you say," they respond, and, flourishing sticks, they rush into the cattle enclosure. There, joined by the king, they dance for hours under the midsummer sun, then depart on a journey of twenty-two miles—practically without food—to the sacred tree. Reaching the tree as the moon rises, they hack down branches with knives or spears, journey to a resting place where they tarry briefly, and then return with their branches to the capital at dawn.

As the sun rises on the second day of the great Incwala, the king, fetched from his harem, meets the returned pilgrims and leads them into the sacred enclosure. Lustily singing about how their branches will comfort the king, the youths drop them in a heap and begin another dance, again in the blazing sun. The youths, who have gone virtually without food or sleep for thirty-six hours, are then dismissed and permitted to rest.

The third day is the day of "leaves" and of the bull. The sacred enclosure is covered with foliage, with an aperture left open at one end. Through this the "bull" (actually the ox stolen earlier from a commoner, but now made potent by the medicines) rushes toward the naked and ceremonially purified youths. When one of them manages to take hold of the madly charging beast, the rest, singing vigorously, pummel the animal until it is near death. The ox is killed by the *belwandle,* and pieces of it are then cut off to serve as medicine for the king.

Another black ox is driven into the enclosure. The king straddles it, naked, while his hands are bathed in a foamy, medicated water meant to confer potency. The *simemo* ritual is enacted again, then the men go to the river to wash while the water priests prepare for the next day's climactic ceremonies.

On this day, called the "great day," the people are awake, singing and dancing for the king, before dawn. He emerges from his sanctuary clad only in a white ivory penis cap. His potent nudity evokes weeping from his subjects, and the queen mother says, "It is pain to see him a king. My child goes alone through the people." The king spits some "medicine" (unstrained beer, in this instance) through the holes of the hut in which he was wed to his first ritual queen (a place deemed mystically bound to the national well-being). A councillor cries, "Eh! Eh! He stabs it!" By this act of spitting, it is believed that the king's strength and potency will penetrate "right through and awake his people." At this stage the king is strong enough to "bite" (i.e., eat) the most potent of the new season's crops, and after this the people spend the morning performing their own "first fruits" ritual. The midday and early afternoon are devoted to a display of finery by the people; then, late in the afternoon, the Incwala enters a new phase. The king reenters, with his royal regiment and the royal clan surging behind him, and a new song is sung:

> *We shall leave them with their country,*
> *Whose travellers are like distant thunder,*
> *Do you hear, Dlambula, do you hear?*

The women sing:

> *Do you hear?*
> *Let us go, let us go.*

According to Kuper:

> The words and the tune are wild and sad like the sea "when the sea is angry and the birds of the sea are tossed on the waves." The royal women move backwards and forwards in small, desperate groups uttering their cry. Many weep. The men's feet stamp the ground vigorously and slowly, the black plumes wave and flutter, the princes come closer, driving the king in their midst. Nearer and nearer they bring him to his sanctuary. The crowd grows frenzied, the singing louder, the bodies sway and press against the sides of the enclosure, and the king is forced within. The priests follow; the princes draw back a little; an old man in full Incwala finery jigulates in the doorway, spurring on the dancers, keeping them from seeing what is happening to their king.[7]

Some of the Swazi claim that the king's royal relatives are symbolically urging the king to join them and to migrate away from nonkinsmen strangers, whom king and kinsmen have befriended and ruled, but whom they still distrust. Kuper feels, however, that the explanation offered by other informants is more accurate:

> The Malangeni [royal group] show their hatred of the king.
> They denounce him and force him from their midst.[8]

This seems to be confirmed by what follows. As the song again changes, the royal princes attempt to lure the king from his hut, inviting him by song to come forth:

> There emerges a figure weird as the monster of legends. He is *Silo*, a nameless creature. On his head is a cap of black plumes that cover his face and blow about his shoulders, and underneath the feathers is glimpsed a head-band of a lion's skin. His body is covered in bright green grass and evergreen shoots that trail on the ground. In his left hand he holds a shield smeared with fat of the sacred herd, the *mfukwane*. His right hand is empty and as it moves it gleams with the lines of dark medicine. . . .
> In this powerful costume the king appears reluctant to return to the nation. He executes a crazy, elusive dance with knees flexed and swaying body. The movements are an intuitive response to the rhythm and situation, a dance that no ordinary man knows and that the king was never taught . . . his eyes shine through the feathers as he tosses his head, his face is dark with black medicine, dripping down his legs and arms are black streaks—he is terrifying, and as the knife-edged grass of his costume cuts into his skin he tosses his body furiously in pain and rage.[9]

Warriors who had earlier helped capture the "bull" appear with large black shields like those used in ancient warfare.They dance and sing, the king approaches, retreats, approaches, and retreats again, all the time holding a long black wand. Finally, the king appears with empty hands—the signal for aliens and royalty to leave. When he next appears he is bearing a vivid green gourd, a sacred calabash he has kept in his possession since the Incwala of the previous year. It is the *Luselwa Lwembo*—the wild gourd from Embo, the region from which the Dlamini clan first emigrated to Swaziland. Amidst the wild stamping of feet, frantic hissing, and the excited thumping of shields, the king throws the gourd onto the shield of one of the warriors, which is held horizontal. The king is then led away, his bizarre costume, except for the medicine painted on his body, is removed, and he enters the hut of the righthand queen for the night.

During the fifth day, the king remains unapproachable because he is "painted in blackness." Only his two ritual wives are believed strong enough to withstand the demonic power possessing him at this time. The

people, too, are in seclusion and in a taboo state—with sexual inter-
course, late sleeping, merrymaking, and other pleasures suspended. Finally, on the sixth day, the king, the queen mother, and the entire nation
are reinvigorated and are prepared to face the coming year. The sixth
day, and the Incwala itself, end in feasting and revelry.

Considerable attention has been devoted to the Incwala, not only
because it is important for the Swazi, but also because it illuminates an
archaic concept of kingship. As Kuper[10] points out, the words of the
Incwala songs may surprise the European, who is accustomed "to hear
royalty blatantly extolled, the virtues of the nation magnified, and the
country glorified" at national celebrations. The Incwala songs do not
extoll the Swazi king; instead, they express hatred and rejection. The
king is reviled and insulted more than he is glorified and eulogized.
Despite this ritual display of hostility, Kuper believes the total effect of
the Incwala is to strengthen the institution of Swazi kingship, and with it,
the entire Swazi nation.

This line of reasoning has been developed most fully by the British
anthropologist Max Gluckman,[11] who terms such ceremonies as the Incwala "rituals of rebellion." The Incwala allows Swazi citizens to display
openly their ambivalent feelings toward the king's authority, which
Gluckman feels ultimately strengthens the kingship. "Ritual rebellion" is
in effect a catharsis, a purge of emotional grievances, and a way to avert
political rebellion. Indeed, it is a substitute for rebellion, but it is also
more than that. Gluckman maintains that the Incwala helps to remind
the Swazi that their kingship is so solidly entrenched in their society that
ritual rebellion can occur without endangering the kingship. Such ritual
rebellion could not occur in the historic kingdoms of Europe, because if
they did occur the basic form of government would be questioned or
even undermined. Ritual rebellion can only exist, therefore, in traditional, or archaic, societies where kingship is firmly and unquestiona-
bly ingrained—societies in which kingship and society are one.

The American anthropologist Thomas Beidelman[12] challenges
Gluckman's view. Beidelman feels that the *simemo* and the other activities
of Incwala that vilify the king are not primarily expressions of hostility or
ambivalence. Rather, they are delicate ritual devices that serve to separate the king symbolically from the various groups making overlapping,
and potentially conflicting, claims upon him. Thus, certain phases of the
Incwala separate the king from his own royal kinsmen, those who might
seduce him from his national obligations; by freeing him from factional
demands, the Incwala strengthens the king for the burdens of kingship
and national priesthood.

Beidelman observes that in the first portion of the Incwala, the

king's magical potency is gradually heightened until he is able to influence the supernatural forces that animate the world. At the climax of the
ceremony, when the king appears as an otherworldly monster apparently transcending normal society by means of the strength and disorder
of the demonic forces coalesced within him, these forces are set loose.
When the king emerges naked except for his penis cap, the queen
mother moans that it is a pain to see her child go "alone through the
people;" the ritual queens say, "We pity him;" and the others agree that
"the work of the king is indeed heavy." Beidelman suggests that the
Swazi, through this ritual, recognize the king's "lonely, denuded status
outside any single social category"[13] which enables him to gather within
himself the extraordinary forces of the cosmos. When the king hurls the
sacred gourd onto a warrior's shield, Beidelman terms the act a symbol
of the king's return to the nation and to the world of men. He places his
dangerous and unruly power back within the confines of the social order. The last phase of the Incwala, therefore, is a gradual deintensification of the potent, dangerous forces that had accumulated around the
king during the first phase.

Although Beidelman's analysis of the distinctive and rich meanings
of Incwala symbolism may be more subtle than Gluckman's, the two
analyses are not mutually exclusive. Since rituals are highly condensed
symbolic acts with meanings at *many* levels, the Incwala could serve
simultaneously as emotional catharsis and as symbolic intensification-
deintensification.

As Beidelman's analysis suggests, the Incwala could also be viewed
as illuminating the theme of social evolution. When the Swazi first entered the region known as Swaziland, the institutions of clan and kinship
affected their society in a manner similar, perhaps, to the way in which
these institutions affected the Southeast Asian hill tribes. Somehow—
precisely how is not known—the Swazi were able to add a new dimension
of complexity to their society by transforming themselves into a nation
based on a set of loyalties superseding those owed to kinship. However,
because kinship bonds still remained strong and important, strains developed not only among the people, but also within the king's psychological makeup. The king had to find a way to balance his loyalties to royal
kinsmen evenly against those to nonkinsmen, that is, to his nation. Since
the populace is not easily persuaded of the king's impartiality, the Incwala serves to segregate the opposing loyalties, and, by excluding the
royal clansmen from the ceremony at climactic points, it helps to reaf-
firm the king's fundamental commitment to his nation, above and beyond his clan. Perhaps, in this way, the Incwala both relieves popular
suspicion and displays to the nation the king's unique power of transcending clan loyalties in a way commoners cannot. In this manner, king,
kingship, and nation are all buttressed.

Ancient Egypt and Mesopotamia

Religiously endowed kingship is central to archaic society. The most elaborately developed god-king complex in history is found in ancient Egypt.

Although ancient Egypt exemplified during the course of her history several societal types, an archaic society existed from roughly 2700 to 1465 B.C.—the era designated as the Old Kingdom and the Middle Kingdom (which includes the Intermediate Period). During this span of time came the development and consolidation of the elaborate notion of divine kingship—a belief and a way of life that deeply penetrated Egyptian culture.

Archaeologists working in the area near the Nile have been able to trace the gradual transition (which took place over thousands of years) of a society with a social pattern based on hunting and gathering to one with a more settled style of life based on farming along the banks of the Nile. In the early phases of this transition, Egyptian society was isolated from neighboring societies and so developed more or less in its own way. Some evidence indicates, however, that just prior to the establishment of the first Egyptian dynasty, Mesopotamian culture did provide impetus for Egypt's development by introducing the cylinder seal, the building material of sun-dried bricks, and the idea of writing (the hieroglyphs, which came later, were the Egyptians' own invention). In spite of these early Mesopotamian influences, Egyptian society developed a sociocultural style that differed radically from Mesopotamia's and from those of other neighboring societies.

Scholars generally agree that Egypt's unusually favorable geographical features contributed greatly to the development of her particular sociocultural patterns, characterized in part by a distinctive societal unity. Two features were especially important: first, Egypt's relative isolation from her neighbors by the mountains to the south, the massive deserts to the east and west, and the Mediterranean Sea to the north; second, the existence of the Nile River. The land of Egypt, for all practical purposes, was the area adjacent to the Nile. The Nile's seasonal inundation, which supplied life-giving fertility to this area, encouraged all who lived there to stay there. In addition, the Nile provided a channel of unifying communication.

Although some of Egypt's geographical features encouraged national unity, others encouraged regional divisions. Upper Egypt (the southern part of the country) was a narrow trough, a valley four to twenty miles wide, lying between the river and the cliffs that directed the river's course. The cliffs of Upper Egypt were never out of sight, effectively isolating the valley residents up to the point where the Nile's upper (southern) reaches disappeared into the equatorial wilderness. Lower (or northern) Egypt was, by contrast, a vast riverine delta, offering wide arable expanses and more contact with civilizations of the Mediterranean and the Near East. The attitudes and behavior of the people living in the north were thus more commercial and cosmopolitan than those of the people living in the south; and out of these differences between Upper and Lower Egypt crystallized differences of dialect and temperament that endured throughout ancient Egyptian history.

Egypt's earliest societies, of the hunting-gathering type, could support only small populations. With the emergence of agriculture, however, population increased and, with it, social complexity. Over many centuries and in many regions, petty princedoms presumably arose, but none was able to dominate and endure. The birth of Egyptian greatness came with the union of Upper and Lower Egypt under a single leader. This probably occurred in the third millenium B.C., with the founding of the first Egyptian dynastic rule.

Divine Kingship in Egypt

The rulers of predynastic princedoms might have claimed divine qualities, but the full and popularly accepted merging of ruler and divinity into one being did not come until the time of Egypt's unification under the first pharaoh. Indeed, divine kingship was probably essential to the act of Egypt's unification, for if the gods existed above all regions of the land, the king who could identify himself successfully with the gods became liberated from any one region. The regions of Upper and Lower Egypt merged under the protection of a single divine ruler, a unity symbolized in several ways. Although there were two crowns, the White Crown of Upper Egypt and the Red Crown of Lower Egypt, they were united in the pharaoh's rather ungainly Double Crown. The pharaoh also proclaimed himself. "The Two Ladies," signifying a combination of the two goddesses who stood respectively for Upper and Lower Egypt. As his pharaohdom was consolidated, the pharaoh's divinity was proclaimed ever more elaborately. By the fifth dynasty he was identified as the son of Re, the sun god, and often the Supreme God; or as son of Hathor, the mother goddess; or as Horus, the falcon god. Upon his death the pharaoh became Osiris, god of the dead and father of Horus—in the minds of his subjects he was transformed into his own father.

Although national divinity overarched the entire land, different locales became centers for the worship of different deities, each vying with the other to enthrone its own god prominently in the national pantheon. Thoth, scribe of the gods during the early dynastic period, was proclaimed creator of the world by his supporters in the city of Hermapolis. Heliopolis was, during the same era, a center for the worship of the sun god Ra-Atum, whose supporters proclaimed him creator of the world. The city of Memphis, which became the royal seat of the Old Kingdom, was a center for the worship of Ptah, who was regarded as an ancestor of Ra-Atum. It is not surprising that the political success of a god's supporters could affect the god's rank in the pantheon. Thus, when a dynasty ruling in the Middle Kingdom shifted its royal seat to the city of Thebes and patronized the obscure Amon—the hidden god of air and atmosphere—Amon soon rose to prominence as Amon-Ra, becoming identified with the sun god himself.

Partly because the Egyptians habitually ascribed to several gods the attributes of one and to one the attributes of several, the Egyptian pantheon became extremely complex and tangled. The Egyptians tolerated as reasonable what appear to us paradoxical and contradictory claims about the character of a god. Thus, in life the pharaoh was Horus, son of Osiris, but upon dying the pharaoh became Osiris himself, an expression of one incest theme latent in the Egyptian divine-royal mythos.

Incest played a role in the actual conduct of Egyptian kingship. Although the pharaoh had wives and concubines in his harem, as did the Swazi king, and although these wives and concubines could be expected to bear him children, the heir to his throne would be the child who possessed the purest royal blood. To guarantee an offspring of the required purity, the pharaoh would ritually mate with a close female relative—a sister, a half sister, or a close cousin. He drew religious sanction for this act from myths that described similar matings between the gods—for example, Osiris and his sister, Isis. Although incest was prohibited among nonroyalty, its practice by royalty served an important administrative function. Just as the pharaoh freed himself from the risk of close territorial or kinship interests by identifying with overarching national deities, so he freed himself through incest from obligations to in-laws, obligations that would have been inevitable had he produced his successor by mating with a nonroyal wife. Incest made the pharaoh self-sufficient and omnipotent. Furthermore, the royal line, by perpetuating itself through incest, displayed divine traits and thus reinforced its own claim to being of divine origin.

To the Egyptian, pharaoh and society were the same. His vocabulary lacked any word for "government," "state," or "nation" as institutions or sociopolitical systems. Society and state were simply extensions of the pharaoh's divine personality. During the early period of dynastic consolidation, the pharaoh was involved personally in all key decisions of government, but in time the kingdom became too complex for him to supervise directly. His duties then became more those of ritual—to insure the proper ordering of the gods, the seasons, and the world—and the task of day-to-day administration fell instead to a complex bureaucracy. Since government derived from divinity, temples and priests played as great a part in the bureaucratic system as offices and officials; but in spite of the kingdom's bureaucratization, its officials remained simply extensions of the pharaoh's person, ranked in importance by their proximity to the divine ruler. This concept is reflected in the Old Kingdom custom of placing the tombs of officials near the pharaoh's tomb, apparently so that the officials might follow the pharaoh easily into the next world and there continue as his "arms."

Vast cities of temples and palaces, irrigation projects, mines, soaring pyramids to serve as the eternal home of the pharaoh, the 365-day calendar (which was evolved from years of observing the Nile floods) were all accomplishments of the early Egyptian bureaucracy and were made possible in part by the willingness of the people to accept the pharaoh's divinity. Work for the pharaoh was considered a religious as well as a civic duty and that notion, aided by the sting of the lash, allowed the bureaucracy to mobilize a huge labor force—a significant advance in terms of efficiency and yield over the primitive headman's reliance on his kinsmen or affines.

Many of the most impressive architectural feats of ancient Egypt, such as the building of the giant pyramids, were achieved during the Old Kingdom period. Perhaps the transformation of Egypt from a primitive to an archaic system, fostered by the creation of divine kingship, stimulated a sudden vitality. The unification of Egypt brought peace, which in turn brought economic and welfare assurances in the form of the reclamation of swampland, the construction of irrigation works and storehouses for surplus grain, and the development of new medical techniques. As a result, perhaps, of these and other advances, the rate of population growth increased, prompting a rise in labor manpower and a consequent surge in public construction. In fact, one could speculate that any shift from a primitive to an archaic societal pattern will encourage a population increase, hence a rise in cultural achievement.

The pharaoh as god-king became the link between society and divinity. In some respects, the bond between the social and the cosmic found in archaic Egyptian society is like the fusing of these same orders in the aboriginal Dreaming. But for the Egyptian, the cosmos was far more objective and systematized than for the aborigine. Gods of the Egyptian pantheon were more clearly identified and arranged and more carefully distinguished from ordinary men than the aboriginal heroes of The Dreaming. By their ability to record the cosmology in writing, the Egyptian priests could achieve more precision, systematization, and permanence of characterization than the aboriginal laymen, who can only recount their myths orally from memory. The setting down of thoughts in writing also tends to abstract them, to objectify them, and to make them more distant from the writer. The systematized cosmology of the Egyptians, objectified beyond the self and the flux of daily life, tended to appear above self and life and in control of them. The Egyptians saw the cosmos and cosmology as an eternal, constant order directing the fluid movement of daily existence (again in contrast to views held by the aborigines, who perceive daily existence as fixed and static).

This eternal, constant order, called *Ma'at,* is described by Wilson as

> the cosmic force of harmony, order, stability, and security, coming down from the first creation as the organizing quality of created phenomena and re-affirmed at the accession of each god-king of Egypt. In the temple scenes the pharaoh exhibited *ma'at* to the other gods every day, as the visible evidence that he was carrying out his divine function of rule on their behalf. Thus, there was something of the unchanging, eternal, and cosmic about *ma'at* ... it was the order of created things ... it was the just and proper realtionship of cosmic phenomena, including the relationship of rulers to the ruled. . . . *Ma'at,* then, was a created and inherited rightness, which tradition built up into a concept of orderly stability, in order to confirm and consolidate the status quo, particularly the continuing rule of the pharaoh.[15]

According to Wilson, the Egyptian perceived transitory phenomena of life as expressions of the timeless and eternal order of *Ma'at.* For the Egyptian

> the phenomena and activities of his little world were asserted to be momentary flashes of the everlasting, rocklike order of the gods. So this little pharaoh who sat upon the throne of Egypt was no transitory human but was the same "good god" that he had been from the Beginning and would be for all time. So the relationship of beings was not something which had to be worked out painfully in an evolution toward even better conditions but was magnificently free from change, experiment, or evolution, since it had been fully good from the Beginning and needed only to be reaffirmed in its unchanging rightness. Aspects of the divine kingship and of *ma'at* might be subject to temporary misfortune or challenge, but the generalities of these two concepts came to be fundamental in acceptance because they gave timid man freedom from doubt through the operation of the immutable.[16]

The pharaoh himself was both the personification and the ultimate interpreter of *Ma'at,* and its distinctive capacity to categorize the temporal as expressive of the eternal is exemplified in the succession of

pharaohs. The death of a pharaoh and the enthronement of his successor implied, in a very real sense, the creation of a new world. The old
Horus became Osiris and created a new Horus. Yet the new Horus and
the old Horus were believed to be the same, one, eternal Horus. Change
in the political order and the progression of historical events were
classified as an expression of the immutable cosmic order: Dynasties rose
and fell, but Egyptians construed their world as without change.

The pyramid can be seen as a symbol of the rigidly hierarchical
Egyptian society. At the pinnacle, the apex of cosmos and society, stood
the pharaoh. Directly below him were his "servants," the elite—nobles,
high officials, priests, and major landowners—who drew influence in
proportion to their spiritual and political proximity and similarity to the
pharaoh, fount of all power. At the base of the pyramid were the toiling
peasants and artisans. Egyptian society was basically a two-class society,
with a very sharp cleavage between the elite and the masses. While kinship and marriage bound noble to noble, peasant to peasant, and artisan
to artisan, the bond between the elite and the masses was essentially
forged not out of kinship and marriage, but out of worship and authority.

Mediating Kingship in Mesopotamia

"Horizontal" Mesopotamia presents an interesting contrast to "ver-
tical," or hierarchical, Egypt. If the structure of Egyptian society could
be compared to a giant pyramid, the structure of Mesopotamian society
can be compared to a series of small mounds, each fairly independent.
There was no single, overriding figure, such as the pharaoh, to unify the
cities; therefore they functioned as semiautonomous city-states.

Extending from the central part of the Mediterranean Sea,
through the islands, peninsulas, and coasts, eastward to the valleys of the
Tigris and Euphrates rivers—the heartland of ancient Near Eastern
society—Mesopotamia, unlike unified but isolated Egypt, was in constant
contact with other cultures. With its vast open lands, Mesopotamia was
vulnerable to unpredictable storms that would sweep across the open
spaces and was, therefore, denied gentle, steady, and fructifying seasonal rhythms like those enriching the Nile valley. Partly as a result of
these geographical features, Mesopotamia tended to be fragmented, factional, unstable, and dynamic.

To the Mesopotamian view, the lands owned by the city-states were
really the property of the city-state's gods—hence, under the control of
the temple priests and officials, the gods' human agents. Each city-state
was a confederation of land-holding and labor-mobilizing temples. In

each city only one god reigned supreme; the other gods were members of the supreme god's family or were considered his neighbors in the cosmic community. The citizens of each city were the people of that city's god, and the chief priest of the god's temple served as governor of the city-state. Not only did the priest-ruler superintend worship of the supreme god, but he also administered the city's irrigation system and negotiated with other cities in matters of diplomacy and trade. Unlike modern communities, in which separate functions are well defined, the Mesopotamian city-state was an independent religio-politico-economic community, in which it was difficult to separate one function from the others.

The elite of Mesopotamia normally inherited their positions and, as with Egypt and Swaziland, kinship was important in structuring Mesopotamian government. However, the bond between the elite and the masses was again not of kinship and marriage, but of politics and religion. The god of the city-state made known his wishes to the governor, who then gave orders and directives to the people. In carrying out the god's commands, in effect by worshipping him, the people insured the proper ordering of the portion of the cosmos identified with that god.[17] The city-state, then, was populated by worshippers of a particular deity, of a god who occupied a place among the other gods, who collectively represented the total cosmos and its association with all Mesopotamia. Among the foremost deities were the cosmic gods: Anu, god of the heavenly regions; Enlil, god of the atmosphere and of storms; Enki, god of earth; Utu or Shamash, god of the sun; Nannar or Sin, god of the moon; and Inanna or Ishtar, god of the morning star. To this pantheon of gods, with their influence over the total cosmos and society, the god of each of the city-states served as a bridge.

By an extension of this reasoning, the relations among the city-states were thought to reflect the relations among the gods of the various cities. The leaders of a city were expected to champion the position of their god in the intercity pantheon, thereby strengthening the city's position politically. The result of this rivalry was warfare. The goal was not to convert worshippers from one god to another, but to force the enemy to acknowledge that his god was inferior to one's own. To demonstrate how inferior, one city-state might conquer another city-state and then tear down its walls, wreck its irrigation works, and exact financial tribute. This pattern, which really involved putting one's deity above others in the spiritual order through distinctly unspiritual force, is reflected in the rise and fall of several empires—Sumerian, Babylonian, Assyrian—each dominated by a particular city worshipping a particular god. As a city became dominant, its scribes would see to it that the myths of the surrounding area were rewritten so as to celebrate and elevate the dominant city's god. Thus, feats attributed in Sumerian mythology to Enlil were ascribed by the later Babylonians to their own god, Marduk, who was superseded in turn by the god of the conquering Assyrians, Assur.[18]

Eventually, however, there emerged in Mesopotamia a form of kingship that proved successful in uniting the various city-states. Military men were appointed by the city's leaders to cope with occasional emergencies, but since the state of emergency persisted, the temporary generals evolved into permanent kings. Unlike the Egyptian pharaoh, who merged society with the cosmos, the Mesopotamian king mediated between society and the cosmos. God and man were more distinct than they were in Egypt, a difference in conception that gave rise to other differences as well.

Since the Egyptian pharaoh was a god, one needed only to talk with him to learn the wishes of the gods. In Mesopotamia, where the king was not a god, the gods' wishes were less easily communicated. Mesopotamians needed different channels. Thus, since the important gods were celestial, they turned to the heavens for signs of their gods' bidding, an orientation that both stimulated and exploited notable developments in astronomy—not as a science (as we know it) but as a technique for decoding the cosmic cipher. A way of speaking to the gods was also needed. The rite of sacrifice filled this need. By sacrificing animals to the gods, people curried the favor of the gods and made the gods receptive to the people's wishes. The gods, in turn, could communicate their commands to the king by dreams, omens, and portentous natural events, and the king would interpret these for the people. If the king had understood the gods properly, and if the people had properly obeyed the king, the gods rewarded the people with prosperity and happiness. Failure to comprehend or to implement the commands of the gods resulted in drought, famine, flood, and defeat in war. The king's authority depended, therefore, on his ability to mediate between the gods and the people in such a way as to achieve harmony and to fend off disaster.

Separation of the cosmos and society also promoted in Mesopotamia the development of law. In Egypt, law was the pharaoh's word, an expression of the eternal unity of the cosmos and the eternal verity of *Ma'at*. There was no law transcending the pharaoh's personal decree, nor could there be. In Mesopotamia, where gods transcended the king, their decrees necessarily transcended his own. The gods made the laws, and the king himself was bound by them; indeed, it was his duty to codify the gods' laws. Thus, there emerged a number of law codes, the most famous being the Code of Hammurabi (ca. 1700 B.C.), from which sprang the concept of the free citizen of city-state or empire, who was guaranteed the right to hold land and property, to enter into contracts of trade and marriage, and to obtain legal redress. The rights of the

Egyptian, by contrast, were defined only by custom and the pharaoh: Whether one was treated justly or unjustly depended on one's kinship connections or on one's influence in high places. Compared to Egyptian justice, Mesopotamian justice was universalistic. However, Mesopotamian law did not accord all men equal rights. It systematically allowed greater privilege to aristocrats than to commoners; it decreed harsher punishments for crimes committed by common men than for those committed by the elite. And, as might be expected, slaves were denied all rights. In general, however, the Mesopotamian citizen could expect to be treated according to a codified set of standards; he was less subject to whim, favoritism, or accidents of kinship.

Another consequence of the Mesopotamian legal system was the encouragement of trade. In Egypt, commerce was relatively undeveloped. Rudimentary money (a piece of metal that served as a measure of value) was employed, but most transactions involved barter. In Mesopotamia, not only was money common within the city-states, it was also negotiable among them. Traders ranged widely, spreading Mesopotamian currency through the Delta and the Persian Gulf, overland to Persia, Egypt, and the Mediterranean coast, possibly as far west as Crete and even into the Aegean Sea and Greece. Money transactions implied the notions of contract, an institution particularly well developed in Mesopotamian law, and of lending, which was done at interest. The man who inscribed the terms of a contract on clay tablets could depend on the law and the courts to validate and uphold the contract. To the Mesopotamian trader, this was a boon; supported by laws binding upon all citizens, he could negotiate confidently with all citizens, rather than merely with kinsmen, neighbors, or those to whom he had particularistic ties. He had greater freedom than the Egyptian; furthermore, since he could depend on the stability of codified law to define his rights and obligations, he could calculate his risks with greater certainty.

Although Egypt and Mesopotamia represent basically the same general type of society—the archaic—Mesopotamia advanced further toward modernization than did Egypt. There is another society, likewise a variant of the archaic, that should be noted—the lowland Southeast Asian society.

Early Lowland Southeast Asian States[19]

Early in the first millennium A.D., a number of empires, such as those of the ancient Khmer and Javanese, emerged in the lowland areas of mainland and archipelago Southeast Asia. These lowland Southeast

Asian states illustrate the interrelationship of several factors in the emergence of archaic society. First, we observe the role of divine kingship, as in Egypt, and of the temple-dominated city-states, as in Mesopotamia. These Southeast Asian societies may also serve to illustrate how the transition from a primitive to an archaic pattern can be stimulated by contact with alien societies rather than primarily by indigenous processes as was the case among the Swazi, the Egyptians, and in Mesopotamia. And, finally, the lowland states illustrate the contribution of technological advance, such as irrigated agriculture, to the development of archaic society. This last point is best supported by contrasting the lowland Southeast Asian states with the Southeast Asian hill tribes discussed earlier.

On the mountain slopes they inhabit, the Southeast Asian highland tribes practice a slash and burn form of agriculture; that is, they cut down and burn trees to prepare the land for crops of dry rice, millet, or Job's tears. Irrigation is not required because these crops are watered sufficiently by the annual monsoonal rainfall. The fertility of the fields, however, is quickly exhausted, and the tribesmen are thus forced to relocate frequently. Every year or every few years, a community will clear new land, leaving the old to regain its fertility for reuse in perhaps a decade. Since each group must circulate among many fields, these mountain areas can be only sparsely settled. It is estimated that each family of five requires twenty-five acres of land per year, so that the maximum population density can be only 130 persons per square mile.

Quite different is life on the lowland plains. For two thousand years the lowland farmers have cultivated rice in irrigated fields; accordingly, lowland population densities are much greater than in the highlands. The same irrigated field can be used year after year, less land is needed per person, and the density of population ranks with the world's highest. In rural areas of central Java, for example, there are more than 1,000 persons per square mile.

These contrasts in agriculture and demography are correlated throughout Southeast Asia with differences in society and culture. The highland society of the mainland remains a patchwork of incredibly individualistic and fragmented tribes, with even close neighbors often unable to understand each other's languages. Many of the hill tribes were constantly at war prior to the *pax colonialis* imposed by British and French colonialists, yet despite their bellicosity, or perhaps because of it, they were never able to weld themselves into strong centralized states that could muster large armies to conquer lowland areas. As was discussed in chapter 3, the tribes were united only by systems of kinship and marriage, not by an overarching government; and as the analysis of the Kachin illustrates, attempts to centralize by creating kingdoms always failed. The lack of centralization was encouraged by the hill tribes' pattern of agriculture: Slash and burn farming cannot support a large concentration of people in one spot, such as the capital city of a centralized empire.

The irrigated rice agriculture and high population density of lowland Southeast Asia have, by contrast, encouraged extensive political centralization in the form of cities, kingdoms, and empires. What is known of their prehistory suggests that the lowland dwellers moved gradually from a hunting and gathering mode of life toward a settled one based on irrigated agriculture, and that a major surge of population growth and political centralization possibly occurred about the time of Christ. Archaeological finds (such as large and elaborately decorated stone temples bearing records of the deeds of emperors, priests, and gods) made throughout the lowland plains indicate that during this period there emerged complex, archaic societies, perhaps not unlike those of Mesopotamia. These emerging civilizations were influenced by India, many hundreds of miles to the west. Lowland chiefs had "witnessed from afar the splendor of India,"[20] and had adapted Indian myths and religion, alphabets and writing systems, stone techniques, and symbols of royalty in their own advance toward centralization and civilization.

Precisely how or why the contact between India and Southeast Asia came about is not clear. The lowlanders probably met Indian merchants and adopted some of the latter's patterns simply because it was politically advantageous to do so. For instance, the Indian concept of the god-king (*deva-raja*) allowed the Southeast Asian kings to be regarded as incarnations of such gods as Siva or Vishnu. With such exalted status, they were able to mobilize great armies and kingdoms. To the people a divine fragrance diffused from the god-king's body throughout the surrounding countryside, coating it with prosperity, happiness, and security. In return for these benefits, the people gave the god-king their loyalty, their crops, and their labors to build intricate irrigation networks, roads, hospitals, and magnificent temples such as Angkor Wat in Cambodia and Borobodur in Java.

The Indian-derived god-king institution of Southeast Asia resembles that of ancient Egypt, and the associated temple-cities are reminiscent of ancient Mesopotamia. Each temple-city dominated an agricultural hinterland and was ruled by a god-king, who was believed to be the incarnation of the god to whose worship that city's temples were devoted. As in Mesopotamia, each temple-city schemed and struggled to establish the ascendancy of its god over the gods of the rival cities; hence, the history of the early Southeast Asian empires is one of power shifts among cities and dynasties.

During its archaic phase, lowland Southeast Asia was a two-class society composed of a religio-political elite—including the god-king and his officials, priests, kinsmen, and in-laws—and a toiling peasant mass who supported the elite by worshipping and paying tribute to them. Although this archaic patterning was inspired by India, certain local differences were significant. For example, the priests who attended the temples were always subordinate to the divine king, a deviation from the Indian pattern, where the priest (*Brahman*) is deemed superior to the warrior or king (*Ksatriya*). Incorporated into Southeast Asian societies were the Indian notions of the god-king, of hierarchical society, and of the capital city as a core of temporal society and of the universe itself. Even without the stimulus of these Indian elements, archaic society and culture might have emerged in Southeast Asia, but because Indian patterns were available, the transition was facilitated.

Overview

A simple way to identify and distinguish between archaic and primitive societies would be to say that archaic society is based on kingship, primitive society on kinship. Moving from the Australian aborigines, the Ndembu, and the Southeast Asian hill tribes to the Swazi, Egyptians or Mesopotamians, and Southeast Asian states, we shift from one-class societies composed of kinsmen, all of whom are roughly equal in status, to two-class societies composed of commoners and an elite—kings, priests, and aristocrats—with the two classes bound by ties of authority and worship rather than kinship.

Primitive societies do make a distinction between leaders and followers, but never are these leaders set above the people so markedly as they are in archaic societies. As can be seen from the Kachin, when chiefs act like kings in a primitive society, their followers revolt and set up separate communities based on the *gumlao* (egalitarian) ideology.

One cannot assert that kinship and marriage bonds are unimportant in archaic society since elite (or nonelite) status is inherited. Among the Swazi, for example, the king is considered the "father" of his people; but in archaic society such terms are used metaphorically. No ordinary Swazi would claim the king as his genealogical father, or even as a kinsman; indeed, in archaic society customs frequently exist to insure that the king will not be related to the masses or even to other members of the elite. Thus, only the Swazi royal clan has the right to marry within itself; and in Egypt, only the pharaoh could marry his sister.

In archaic societies, the elite class—especially the king—is deemed superior in every field. The king is either divine (as in Egypt), or has special access to the gods (as in Mesopotamia), or is the cosmos itself (as in Swaziland). His political power and his wealth are also great. The elite, other than the king, function as priests, officials, and business managers. In sharp contrast to primitive society, the masses in archaic society are as disadvantaged religiously, politically, and economically as the elite are privileged. For example, among the aborigines all males are not only approximately equal politically and economically, but they also participate directly in ordering the universe through their identification with the heroic figures of The Dreaming. In other words, they are equal religiously, with each man functioning as a priest.

The social cleavage between the elite and the masses implies a degree of specialization in archaic societies exceeding that found in primitive societies. In primitive society there is some specialization of labor—for example, the role of the headmen among the Australian aborigines or of the curers among the Ndembu—but almost all men in a primitive society perform essentially the same tasks. In archaic society, the specialization of labor is dramatic and is based on the premise that some men are innately better qualified than others to pursue certain callings. The elite specialize in mediating between gods and men, or in similar functions; the masses, in manual labor.

It might be argued that archaic society is more universalistic than primitive society—that the archaic man's status is more strongly based on his deeds, the primitive's man's on his descent. It is true that kinship is a major factor in determining the archaic man's status, but if he did not perform effectively in that status, he could be removed from it. The ineffective pharaoh or king could be deposed in a palace coup; it would be harder to indict the aborigine if a rite failed to produce results. In primitive society, many persons or factors, often the entire community, can be blamed. In archaic society, however, one can point to the specialist. Thus, with the increase in specialization emerges the notion of individual responsibility, setting the stage for a new image of the person.

Consider, in this regard, Mesopotamian law. In Mesopotamia roles implied by the contractual-commercial relationship were separated by law from those implied by the kinship-personal relationship, suggesting that archaic man possessed some freedom to enter a contractual-commercial relationship without kinship-imposed restrictions. To some degree, a man from kinship group X could choose among commercial-contractual relations $A, B, C \ldots$; he need feel no obligation to deal only with a fellow X. Each member of group X could choose among a variety of trade contacts, and members of group X were likely to vary widely in the number and kind of their contacts. In the extreme approached by primitive society, by contrast, each member of kinship group Y could relate only to his fellow Y's, and therefore the members of group Y

would vary hardly at all in the number and kind of their contacts. A member of archaic society, therefore, would be more likely to be regarded as a unique configuration of social roles—that is, as a *distinct self*—than a member of primitive society.

Although relationships in archaic society—such as those between masses and elite which involve mixed political, religious, and economic obligations—are diffuse by comparison with those in modern society, they are less diffuse in archaic society than they are in primitive society. Since archaic man spreads his desires and duties among nonkinsmen as well as kinsmen, he never experiences the primitive man's concentration of all facets of social life within a single extremely diffuse relationship, the kinship relationship.

Archaic societies are more centralized than primitive societies. In archaic societies populations are concentrated and coordinated into cities, kingdoms, nations, and empires; and with the increase of centralization, there inevitably emerges a high degree of bureaucratization. Because of centralization and bureaucratization, archaic kings achieved a control over the populace that allowed them to exploit the people as a labor force in the construction of gigantic projects such as the pyramids of Egypt and the temples of Southeast Asia. Primitive man excels in coping with his environment, archaic man surpasses him in exploiting it.

It was certainly not by chance that archaic societies such as Egypt, Mesopotamia, and early lowland Southeast Asia developed extensive irrigation works. In Southeast Asia, primitive and archaic societies can be neatly discriminated according to the presence or absence of irrigation. In the Near East and Far East, scholars such as Karl Wittfogel[21] have perceived similar correlations. Archaeologists have also observed connections between irrigation and archaic patterning in Meso-America and Peru.[22] What is not clear, however, is whether the irrigation systems had to be developed before archaic society and culture could flourish. The Meso-American, Peruvian, and Mesopotamian cases suggest not, since in these societies great irrigation systems seem to have emerged only after archaic society was well under way. Taking into account these findings as well as others (the Swazi, for example, have archaic patterns but no irrigation system), we can conclude that irrigation is not a necessary condition for the emergence of archaic society and culture; however, a society must develop some system of food production, as opposed to food-gathering, before it can advance to the archaic stage.

In archaic society, the cosmic and the social world are distinct and different; in primitive society, the cosmic and social world are fused. Among the Australian aborigines, sacred order and social order are considered the same. Sacred figures are identified with ordinary men. And when men *become* their gods, the aborigines suffer little doubt about their gods' intentions; they need only ask their god-selves what they think or what they desire. Archaic gods, on the other hand, are separate and distinct from men. Men cannot identify with them easily. Yet the thoughts and desires of the gods must still be ascertained. The gods must also be dealt with, for they live in the midst of men—not in a heaven, as in historic religion, but in a forest, on a mountain, or as a god-king in a capital city.

How, then, does archaic man communicate with these gods who live with him and control him, yet who are so distant from him spiritually that he does not know their wishes? One important way is by sacrifice, an institution more prominent in archaic society than in primitive society. Sacrifice, especially in Mesopotamia, allowed gods to keep their distance from men. Since archaic men did not identify with their gods during sacrificial ritual any more than they did in daily life—and certainly never to the extent of the aborigine in his "secret life"—they were forced to interpose between themselves and the gods a sacrificial animal or plant, perhaps even a priest. If the mediating element successfully bridged the gap between men and the gods, men would know the gods' commands, and the gods in turn would learn men's needs. Sacrifice involved more uncertainty than did the aboriginal secret life. The archaic man could not control how the god would respond to his offering, whereas by fusing himself with the heroes of The Dreaming, the aborigine to some extent could. Thus, sacrifice was an agent and a reflection of the general increase in freedom that accompanied the shift from primitive to archaic society.

The archaic society's separation of cosmos and society is reflected in its division between classes. Archaic elite claim a special kinship to the cosmic, either by serving as intercessors between it and the people or by identifying themselves with it. Although the elite claim special sanctity, other elements of archaic existence are sacred as well. Not only is the state the object of worship and cult, so too are household and lineage, health and illness, life and death, crafts and agriculture. Since all life is sacred, any change in it might anger the gods; hence archaic life is warped in some measure toward conformity and conservatism.

A question appropriate to each evolutionary level would be: How much more likely to move in the direction of modernization is a society at the level under consideration than a society one level below it? In comparing archaic society with primitive society, one could suggest that because the separation between the cosmic and the social world in archaic society is greater, there is greater potential for change. Archaic man could imagine modeling the social world after the cosmic, for the two are clearly differentiated and defined. Primitive man would find such a process almost inconceivable, because for him the cosmic and the ordinary are fused. On the other hand, archaic society has its own inhibitant to change: when the king is god, it is difficult to revolt against him in the name of god.

Topics for Discussion

In our discussion of the Swazi Incwala ritual we noted that Beidelman ("Swazi Royal Ritual") and Gluckman ("Rituals of Rebellion in Southeast Africa") offer alternative interpretations of the same event. This phenomenon is common in anthropology. Given the frequency of alternative interpretation, the student might consider the methodological question: Can alternative interpretations be allowed by a true science?

The student might also have observed that two types of data furnish a basis for the sociocultural portraits presented in this chapter and in the related readings: archaeological and ethnographic. The portraits of the ancient Egyptian, Mesopotamian, Southeast Asian, and North and Middle American civilizations were reconstructed mainly from artifacts discovered by archaeologists. The portrait of the contemporary Swazi kingdom was reconstructed from an ethnographer's observations of living people. An interesting exercise would be to compare the two methods of reconstruction.

Suggested Readings

The Swazi

An African Aristocracy: Rank Among the Swazi (1965) by Hilda Kuper. The standard
work on the Swazi.

The Swazi: A South African Kingdom (paperback, 1963) by Hilda Kuper in the
"Case Studies in Cultural Anthropology" paperback series. An excellent
summary, designed for the beginning student.

Bunyoro: An African Kingdom (paperback, 1960) by John Beattie. Also in the "Case
Studies" series. The Bunyoro can be usefully compared with the Swazi.

"Rituals of Rebellion in Southeast Africa" (1963) by Max Gluckman. An interpretation of Swazi ritual.

"Swazi Royal Ritual" (1966) by T. O. Beidelman. An alternative interpretation of
Swazi ritual.

Egypt and Mesopotamia

The Culture of Ancient Egypt (paperback, 1956) by John A. Wilson. An outstanding
general account of Egyptian society and culture suitable for beginning
students.

Everyday Life in Ancient Egypt (paperback, 1967) by Jon E. M. White. A useful if elementary introduction.

Kingship and the Gods (1948) by Henri Frankfort. On Egypt and Mesopotamia.

Before Philosophy: The Intellectual Adventure of Ancient Man (paperback, 1967) by Henri Frankfort et al.

The Face of the Ancient Orient (paperback, 1962) by Sabatino Moscati.

The Greatness That Was Babylon (paperback, 1968) by H. W. F. Saggs.

Oriental Despotism (paperback, 1957) by Karl A. Wittfogel. Provides an interesting argument on the connection between technology and culture in the ancient Near East and elsewhere.

Lowland Southeast Asian States

Hill Farms and Padi Fields: Life in Mainland Southeast Asia (paperback, 1965) by Robbins Burling. A sound introductory treatment. See especially chapter 5.

The Making of Southeast Asia (1966) by George Coedès. A stimulating synthesis.

Angkor: An Introduction (1963) by George Coedès.

Conceptions of State and Kingship in Southeast Asia (1956) by Robert Heine-Geldern. A classic work. Still useful, although it does not refer exclusively to the archaic pattern.

Southeast Asia: Crossroad of Religions (1949) by Kenneth Landon.

North and South America

Mexico (paperback, 1962) by Michael D. Coe.

Ancient Mexico (paperback, 1959) by Frederick Peterson.

Prehistoric Mesoamerica (1977) by Richard E. W. Adams. A clearly written, well illustrated synthesis.

Peru Before the Incas (paperback, 1967) by Edward P. Lanning.

An Introduction to American Archaeology, I: *North and Middle America* (1966) and II: *South America* (1973) by Gordon R. Willey.

These works treat aspects of the archaic pattern as it developed in North, South, and Middle America.

Films

The Ancient Egyptian. A brief but visually rich film.

Ancient Mesopotamia. Attempts to reconstruct Mesopotamian society.

Excavations at La Venta. Depicts archaeological uncovering of an archaic Middle American society.

7

Historic Society and Culture

The cultural foundations for historic societies were laid down by the great historic religions: Buddhism, Christianity, and Islam. By conceiving a wide gulf between this world and the otherworld and then devaluing this world, historic religious made salvation the focal problem of life. Historic man's attempts to solve that problem drove him toward new social advances.

Buddhism and Thailand

Speakers of Thai dialects are scattered throughout the contemporary states of Southeast Asia, but most Thai speakers live in Thailand. Bounded on the west by Burma, on the east by Laos and Cambodia, and to the south by Malaysia, Thailand covers an area of about 200,000 square miles. Most of its 26 million people cluster in the fertile valley of the Caw Phra Jaa River.

Thai history begins in the thirteenth century with a kingdom called Sukhothai, located in a northern province and composed of a number of semiautonomous city-states. The earliest inscriptions from Sukhothai indicate that its inhabitants were followers of Theravada Buddhism, a religion they had adopted from their Mon and Burmese neighbors. While practicing Buddhism, the Thai continued to cling to animistic beliefs in spirits and magic and to follow certain Hindu rituals. As a result, Thai religion was an amalgam. Today, although this is still true. Buddhism dominates and is the state religion.

Thai Buddhism

Buddhism developed around 500 B.C. in India, and subsequently divided into two great schools that are still recognized today. The northern school, commonly called Mahayana, spread from India into Tibet, China, Japan, and from China into Vietnam. The southern school, called Theravada (or Hinayana) spread into Ceylon, Burma, Thailand, Laos, and Cambodia. Many scholars regard the Theravada tradition as being closer than the Mahayana to original Buddhism.

Although Christianity and Islam conceive of an otherworld infinitely more glorious than this world, Buddhism goes even further in devaluing this world. In its extreme philosophical position, Buddhism holds that the visible, physical world is sheer illusion. Only the otherworld, represented by religious symbolism, is real. Fundamental to this "real" world are the doctrines of *karma* (in Thai, *kaam*) and of multiple rebirths.

The doctrine of karma holds that every action is deserving of merit (*bun*) or demerit (*bab*). Every person is the product of the sum of his meritorious acts balanced against the sum of his unmeritorious ones, of his *bun* balanced against his *bab*. A kind of cosmic computer (not a god) keeps track of these sums automatically, so that each person at all times is treated by the cosmos in accordance with the amount of merit he has accumulated.

The doctrine of multiple rebirths holds that an individual's religious life extends through a series of several lifetimes. The individual is repeatedly reborn, and the status he occupies in each new life reflects the meritoriousness of his deeds in the life before; the more merit he accumulated in his last life, the better his status in this life. Ultimately, the Buddhist may even make so much merit that he is freed from the treadmill of birth and rebirth. Then he has attained Nirvana.

The creatures of the universe are, in Theravada Buddhism, ranked according to the amount of merit they have accumulated. At the top of the scale sit the gods (*thewada*), such as Siva and Indra, who live in the heavens. Below the gods stand men (*manut*). Below men crawl the animals (*sad*). At the bottom skulk the spirits (*phi*) and demons (*preet*). At each level there are subdivisions; thus at the level of men, monks are of exalted status. Thai Buddhists believe that deep and basic differences separate the various ranks, that all men are ranked relative to one another, and that no social relationship is between equals—in short that all existence is structured *hierarchically*.

Although Buddhism emerged from Hinduism and still retains many Hindu concepts, it has imbued these with distinctively Buddhist meanings. Generally Buddhism provides a more individualistic emphasis. In Hinduism the individual's moral status is irrevocably fixed by the status of the caste into which he is born. By faithfully obeying the commands and taboos, the *dharma* of one's caste, one may be born into a higher caste in the next life, but one has no hope of rising socially in this life. In Buddhism, however, a person's moral and social status is thought to depend more on his own actions and qualities than on the group into which he is born.

Buddhism also differs from Hinduism in its universalism. For the Hindu, it was as much a sacrilege to adhere to the rules of a caste other than one's own as it was to disobey the rules of one's own caste; but for the Buddhist, certain rules apply to every man, whatever his caste. All Buddhists are expected to follow the five precepts; to refrain from stealing, fornicating, killing, lying, and drinking alcohol. Pious laymen may on special occasions, such as the Buddhist Sabbath, undertake to obey three other precepts: to refrain from eating solids after noon, from indulging in entertainment and adornment, and from sitting or lying on a high or wide mattress filled with cotton. Furthermore, any man who is especially eager to accumulate merit may become a monk and assume the burden of following a total of 227 rules. The Buddhist who wishes to do so may follow any or all of these rules, whereas the Hindu may follow only the rules of his own caste.

The Monk in Thai Society

The Buddhist monk's shaved head, orange robe, and secluded temple quarters separate him from the layman, as do the 227 rules. He may not marry or even receive objects from a woman's bare hand. Unlike the Christian monk, the Buddhist monk is not allowed to grow his own food because while plowing the land he might inadvertently take the life of some animal, and thus violate one of the rules. The monk earns the respect of all Thais by submitting to a life of restraint. By his discipline he demonstrates that he is morally superior.

To affirm the monk's superiority ritually, laymen sit at a lower level and address monks in honorific speech. In fact, in the Thai language the gulf between monks and ordinary men is constantly stressed, since speech to and about monks employs the modifier *ong,* meaning "mana-filled object" and used in regard to gods, king, and the Buddha, as well as monks. Ordinary people are referred to simply as *khon,* meaning "person."

Since the rules the monks follow do not allow them to work, the laity must support them. Each morning monks pass along the paths and roads, silently accepting the food offerings placed in their alms bowls by the laity. Westerners see this as an expression of the monk's dependence on the layman, but the Thai take the opposite view. By accepting the layman's offerings, the monk furnishes the former with an opportunity to accumulate merit. Although charity and generosity are always good, directing them toward a monk is particularly meritorious, for it demonstrates a willingness to part with worldly goods for the sake of the otherworld represented by the monk.

The monks are organized into the Sangha, Order of Buddhist Monks. The primary concern of the Sangha is to provide a secluded realm, a retreat in which the monk can follow the 227 rules. The Sangha also plays a missionary role, spreading Buddha's teachings so as to perpetuate the Buddhist order. In the past the temple schools of the monks provided the only education in Thailand—religious education, to be sure, but also schooling in reading, writing, healing, and crafts. The young men who composed the bulk of the student population (for women were allowed little contact with monks) often studied to prepare for bureaucratic careers. They needed not only literacy, but also indoctrination in Buddhist belief so that they might acquire moral qualities proper for careers in a Buddhist state.

Unlike the vows of the Christian monk, the Buddhist monastic vows are not binding for life. A monk can leave the order any time he desires. Ideally, every Thai male should spend a brief period as a monk, and as many as one man out of fifty does so during a typical year. The shortest time that a man may spend is one "lenten season," the three months during the rainy season when farm work is light. The ideal that all men should serve as monks reflects the Thai feeling that monks exemplify a virtue proper for all men—the capacity to maintain an impassive, retiring demeanor in the face of danger and the vicissitudes of life.

Monastic discipline epitomizes the basic Buddhist belief that one acquires merit by renouncing the world. Part of the monk's ordination rite is the renunciation of his kinsmen and friends. The young monk's parents also give him up, and by so doing they gain merit for themselves; this is particularly true of the mother, who is considered especially attached to her son. Some youths actually become monks in order that their mothers may gain merit, for women do not enjoy many merit-making opportunities.

The Sangha penetrates more deeply into Thai society than does the state, for the state administers no unit below the level of the district, whereas the Sangha enters directly into the life of the village. It must be kept in mind, too, that Buddhism, personified by the Sangha, is a more important object of moral commitments than the state. Indeed, the state draws much of its legitimacy from its relationship with the Buddhist Sangha.

Bureaucracy and the Thai King

Relationships between the Sangha and the state have always been intimate. In traditional belief, which held sway until the 1932 coup, the king was regarded as a Chakravartin, or Buddhist World Emperor. He ruled not only because of his power and status, but also because of his unique religious qualities. He was to a degree divine. In the coronation ceremony priests consecrated the king as a Hindu-Buddhist god; he was endowed with the same *ong*, or mana, as the monks.

The king acknowledged his subordination to the Buddhist order, and pledged to serve as protector and defender of the Buddhist faith. He was expected to hold monastic lands in trust, to supervise examinations for promotion within the Sangha, to wage war on neighboring nations who might threaten Buddhism, and to stage ostentatious and exemplary merit-making ceremonies. The king's fundamental duty was to insure that his kingdom was one in which Buddhism could flourish. He was to preserve harmony and peace, and also prosperity, so that the laity would have the material means to support the monks. If the people could thereby gain merit, the Buddhist order would eternally endure.

Because of his status as a Chakravartin, the king's life was hedged by numerous complex rules. An elaborate court etiquette prescribed in detail the king's daily schedule, and a corps of court Brahmans (priests) labored as astrologers to determine auspicious occasions. Moral codes such as the Dharmashastras, a Buddhist version of the Hindu Code of Manu, defined the general ethics of kingship. Occasionally in Thai history, a king attempted to claim more power than he was given under the rules designed to constrain him, but he was always thwarted. Thus, the eighteenth-century king known to the West as Taksin claimed to be the living Buddha. He was deposed as a madman and eventually executed.

Thai kingship and bureaucracy were patterned after the Hindu-Buddhist conception of the cosmos. The cosmos was conceived of as a set of concentric circles at the center of which was located Mount Meru, home of the gods. Similarly, the kingdom was conceived of as a set of concentric circles at the center of which was located the capital city, with an artificial mountain in its midst representing Mount Meru. The innermost circle of the capital was the treasury, under the control of the Department of the Center (Klang). The next circle was the Department of the Royal Palace (Wang), which administered the affairs of the court and palace. Surrounding this circle was the Department of the Capital (Myang), which took charge of affairs inside the capital but outside the palace. The outermost circle was the Department of Lands (Na, literally "rice fields"), which supervised the countryside and performed many of the duties that would today be expected of a department of agriculture and public works.

The activities of these departments were as much ritual as administrative. Thus, the Department of Lands not only maintained the irrigation works, but also supervised the annual rites that insured the order of the seasons and the prosperity of the nation. Even in modern Thailand, vestiges of this pattern remain, for the people still consider the performance of rites to insure national prosperity the responsibility of the government, and court priests still schedule the annual rituals.

Since Hindu-Buddhist theory placed the king at the center of the cosmos and nation, every Thai was assigned a status relative to the king. Even remote villagers were attached to one of the king's bureaucratic departments. Every lowly person was a "client" to some more prestigious "patron," who in turn was some still more exalted patron's client. Eventually such chains of patron-client relationships converged on the person of an official who headed a department; and ultimately, of course, all of these officials, with their attached chains, were clients to the supreme patron, the king.

In the fifteenth century, King Trailok promulgated the Law of Civil Hierarchy whereby every Thai was assigned a number indicating his rank in society—which is to say, in bureaucracy, since Thai society was composed of human chains converging on the royal departments. These ranks, called *sakthina* ("power of the fields") assigned the number 25 to an ordinary farmer, 50,000 to the brother of the king, 2,400 to an outstanding monk. Periodically, royal officials traveled around the countryside, registering the people, recording their allegiances to the royal departments, and assigning them their proper numbers. A royal department could mobilize its allied chains, even down to the level of peasants, for war or for several months of annual service.

The Thai pattern of interlocking and converging patron-client chains differs strikingly from the feudal pattern familiar to students of medieval European history. Feudal manors provided lords with localized bases of power from which they could oppose the king. But in Thailand there could be no independent landlords since the king owned all the land, and all power revolved around the capital and the king. Under the patron-client system, the closer an official was to the capital and king, the greater was his power. Regional officials could, of course, build a local following, but since they owed their position to the king, they rarely opposed him. Thai kings were more often overthrown by palace coups than by provincial revolts.

Who would succeed the king on his death was always unclear, for there were no definitive rules of succession. As a step toward narrowing the slate of eligible competitors, the Thai instituted a rule of declining descent whereby with the accession of a new king all of the old king's relatives became one degree less eligible for the kingship; after five generations, they dropped from the ranks of royalty altogether and became commoners. Another device was the appointment of a "second king," or Uparat, who would be strongly favored to succeed the king. Despite these arrangements, however, the throne was in effect available to anyone; a prince, an official, or even a commoner might succeed in usurping the throne by intrigue, assassination, or glorious military deeds. Whoever seized the throne automatically demonstrated the moral qualities necessary for rule.

Thai Villagers

Under Western impact, the hierarchical structure that linked the Thai peasant to the capital through chains of patron-client relations was eliminated in the late nineteenth century. Thai villages are now part of a Western-style administrative system consisting of provinces (*cangwat*) and districts (*amphur*) staffed by officials appointed by the central government; the villages themselves (*mu baan*) are guided by locally elected headmen. Channeling orders from the central government to the villagers, these local leaders gain power through their charm and forcefulness rather than through their official position in the administrative network.

Approximately 85 percent of the contemporary Thai live in the rural villages, which are devoted to irrigated rice agriculture. In the central region of Thailand, the villages straggle along the banks of rivers and canals which supply water for rice cultivation as well as provide avenues for travel. In more arid areas of the country the villages tend to be concentrated in clusters. In all villages, a local Buddhist temple is the center. The monks live in the temple and wander through the village each morning to gather food offerings from the people, whose generosity is rewarded with merit. Aside from its religious functions, the village temple historically served as the local schoolhouse and the local meeting hall at which village affairs could be discussed.

Large villages and villages close to cities may have a store or two (often run by a Chinese merchant), but the main units are the households. The typical household is inhabited by a nuclear family whose members cooperate in the cultivation of land. Because rice farming is not only the village's major source of subsistence but also the economic base of the household group, access to rice lands is extremely important and is linked to the developmental cycle of the household and to marriage patterns.

In Thailand, where descent is reckoned bilaterally and such kinship units as clans are unimportant, such taboos as that of incest are confined to very close relatives, and choice of mate depends very much on personal inclination. As children mature, they meet maturing children from their own or a nearby village, and boys and girls who "fall in love" agree to marry. But before the marriage is arranged, the young couple should seek an astrologer to insure that their astrological qualities are compatible (if the boy is "wood" and the girl "fire" they are badly matched since the girl would consume the boy with her ardor, though the reverse combination is acceptable). The final arrangement is made by a go-between, usually a respected elder, who obtains the agreement of both sets of parents and establishes what goods each will provide to help the couple set up housekeeping.

After the wedding, the young couple commonly lives in the household of the bride's parents, remaining there until the first child is born. During this period, the newlyweds adjust to their relationship, and the young husband should show his in-laws that he is hard-working and dependable. Thai marriages are most fragile at this time, which is when most separations occur. The husband may simply move out of his own accord, or he may return home one day to find his goods piled outside the house, and take the hint. For most couples all goes well.

Young couples are eager to set up housekeeping on their own. With the assistance of goods provided by both sets of parents, they typically build a house near one set of parents, and they gradually acquire independent rights to cultivate some of the parents' rice land. Thus, as their children grow up and marry, parents parcel out their land to them. The youngest daughter of a household, together with her husband and children, frequently remains in her parents' household and eventually inherits the remaining lands. As the parents grow older, they gradually retire from active life and devote themselves to merit-making in preparation for death.

Thai culture strongly devalues overt expression of hostility and aggression, and anthropologists living in Thai villages have been impressed with the friendly courtesy of the villagers and the apparent harmony of village life. Though villagers maintain much personal autonomy, they unfailingly express their mutual respect through polite actions and speech. However, the forms of politeness practiced by Thai villagers have been likened to a "social cosmetic" which masks stresses and tensions with a harmonious surface. Observing the surface serenity of the Thai villagers, one discovers that hostility and aggression need rarely emerge overtly because subtle patterns of interpersonal avoidance serve to isolate potential protagonists.

Thai villagers could be portrayed as the stereotyped "pastoral peasant," but Thai villagers are not, and never have been, isolated from the wider world. Today more than formerly, these villagers are strongly oriented toward the larger Thai society—the nation and its capital, Bangkok—and in this attitude they are encouraged by Buddhism.

Hinduism and Traditional India[2]

Considerable archaeological evidence reveals that a complex civilization existed in the Indus River Valley prior to 3000 B.C. Great cities such as Mohenjo-daro and Harappa were made possible by the channeling and the exploitation of the flood waters of the Indus. Enduring for a thousand years, the Indus civilization developed a system of public sanitation, various projects of urban planning, and a government on the order of that of the Mesopotamian city-states. Eventually the Indus civilization disappeared, perhaps in part because of gradual processes such as population pressure and deforestation, but largely because of sudden and cataclysmic forces. It may have been conquered and destroyed by fierce invaders, the Aryans.

The nomadic Aryans began to penetrate India around 1500 B.C. They introduced a new language, Sanskrit, and a new religion centered on the Vedic gods. They imposed their Indo-European culture, along with their authority, on the Dravidian peoples whom they encountered upon their arrival.

The Aryan conquerors were said to be lighter in color than the Dravidian natives. Whether this indicates a racial difference between the two groups or simply reflects a cosmology that attributed light colors to the ruling class is unclear. In any case, Vedic religion divided society into three groups called *varnas* ("colors"), which were distinguished according to vocational specialty: The Brahmans were the priestly caste, the Ksatriya were the warriors and nobles, and the Vaicyas were the landowners and merchants. Membership was reckoned patrilineally, and intermarriage was taboo. These three *varnas* comprised the "twice-born," those who were symbolically reborn through initiation rites, hence were religiously privileged. Below them were the Sudras, tillers of the soil and servants of the twice-born. Eventually, the Sudras divided into two groups, the untouchables and the touchables. The untouchables performed such ritually polluting tasks as butchering cattle, and even a glimpse of an untouchable's shadow was sufficient to pollute a member of the twice-born.

The ranking of the *varnas* was based in part on the degree of ritual purity versus pollution. The Brahmans were the purest. A Brahman's willingness to perform ritual for a group determined that group's purity (Brahmans were unwilling to perform any rituals for the untouchables). Since Brahmans did not pollute, they often served as cooks; food prepared by them was pure. Indeed, because of their purity alone, the Brahmans—who lacked great wealth and power—were ranked as the top caste. Purity was sufficient to sustain the Brahman's high position even though they never constituted an organized religious elite, as did Buddhist monks or Christian priests.

Although some of the Brahmans worked (e.g., as cooks), their primary occupation lay in the priesthood, and their primary achievement was a speculative philosophy that rendered their ceremonies metaphysically meaningful. From such speculation emerged the Hindu concepts of *karma* and of transmigration. The cycle of births and rebirths was regarded as a mere surface manifestation of the deeper reality called Atman. The visible world was simply illusion, and the goal of religion was to escape from the *karmic* cycle and to merge with the eternal Atman.

Although Hinduism rejected the visible world in favor of a deeper reality, Hindu philosophy, because of the doctrine of *varnas* and castes, had the ultimate effect of bestowing sanctity on the visible world. Unlike Buddhism, which decreed that salvation could be attained by any man, Hinduism stated that a man's moral stature was set at birth according to the caste into which he was born; only the twice-born were qualified to seek salvation. Furthermore, each Hindu was enjoined to obey the *dharma* of the caste into which he was born—not to strive or rebel, for that might result in his rebirth as a lower creature, even an animal. Hinduism thus had the effect of sacralizing and conserving the established order.

India, then, was not a very universalistic society. Hinduism encouraged a marked inequality and separation of groups, and this has rendered India difficult to centralize. It is striking that in precolonial India, only one Hindu empire, the Gupta dynasty of the fourth century B.C., was of any size or duration. Fragmentation made India vulnerable to foreign conquest, such as the Muslim invasion resulting in the Mogul Empire, and, finally, the colonization by Great Britain.

Islam and the Islamic Empires[3]

In the sixth century A.D. the Arabian peninsula was a no man's land wedged between two contending empires, the Byzantine and the Persian. It boasted important trading towns, such as Mecca, but no large-scale governments, other than the puppet states serving the great empires as buffers and outposts. Its inhabitants were largely wild and nomadic tribesmen who belonged to patrilineal descent groups that were not united under a central authority. Much conflict existed among the various tribes, subtribes, and lineages; blood feuds were common. The fragmentation into diverse tribes, subtribes, and lineages was reflected in the native religion, which was a potpourri of practices associated with the diverse groups and places.[4]

Through Islam, these scattered units were welded into a single entity, "God's elect." Under Islam the united Arabs were inspired to spread Allah's kingdom throughout the world, creating the great Islamic empires that held sway from Spain to Southeast Asia, from the sixth century to the twentieth. Although the message of Muhammad, Allah's prophet, was initially directed at the fragmented Arab society, Allah was deemed Lord of all creation, his message true for all men. Hence, the Muslims were driven to missionize, expand, and centralize.

Muhammad viewed himself as the end of a long line of prophets that began with Abraham and continued through Jesus. As the final vehicle of God's revelation, Muhammad professed to clarify what earlier prophets had obscured. The notion of a line of prophets parallels a linear notion of history in general. Like the Christian, the Muslim conceives of history not as a cyclical process of births and rebirths, but as a continuous line extending from the Creation through various revelations, prophesies, and errors to a final Judgment Day. Not only the history of mankind, but the history of each man is viewed linearly. Each man lives a life that proceeds from birth to death, with no instant repeated. Each man is given only one life in which to accept or reject the message of Allah. The wrong choice means infinite suffering in hell, the right choice offers infinite joy in a heaven of sensuous delights. Life, therefore, is a tense struggle to assure one's salvation before it is too late. There is no second chance. Without doubt, this view of time and history intensified the urgency with which the early Muslims pursued and spread their faith.

The Qur'an (often written "Koran") codified Muslim ethics and law. Although this codification did not produce a complete legal system, it was an advance over the earlier Arabic practice of simply listing past legal decisions to guide future ones. Arabic tradition, however, heavily influenced the substance of Muslim ethics and law. Thus, Muslim laws of inheritance favor the "naturally superior" male. Polygyny is allowed, though the limit is set at four legal wives (plus an unlimited number of slave concubines). Divorce is easy for a man. A husband, without being required to state his reason, can simply say three times to his wife, "I divorce you," and the deed is done. On the other hand, certain attitudes of Islam improved the position of women. For example, Muhammad's wish to include women in the spiritual life of the community was contrary to Arabic tradition.

Muhammad set forth a system of rituals which the faithful are compelled to enact. The believer must state his uncompromising acceptance of Allah as the one true God and of Muhammad as Allah's true and final prophet. He must pray five times per day while facing Mecca, fast during the holy month of Ramadan, abstain from intoxicants and the flesh of swine, give to the poor by paying a tax, and make the pilgrimage to the holy city, Mecca. What is striking is how little communion between believer and Allah is offered by these rituals. Even the five daily prayers are less a personal communion with God than a ritual display of commitment to God. Although in later Muslim history, Sufi mysticism gained popularity, orthodox Islam regarded Allah as distant and remote, not to be reached by prayer or meditation.

Islam inspired egalitarianism. Muhammad attacked the foundations of the old Arabic order by preaching that Allah scorned noble ancestry and that all believers were equal. Muslims regarded class distinctions as of little religious significance (by contrast to the Hindus with their caste system). It should not be concluded, however, that Islam achieved a fully egalitarian community. In fact, after Muhammad's death, the trend toward equality was reversed; a new and religiously legitimate basis for social distinction emerged with the notion that a descendant of the prophet was "more equal" than other Muslims.

Islam spurred urbanization. Wherever the Muslim conquerors went, they founded cities. In cities, all the conditions of proper Islamic social and ritual life—a market, a public bath, and a central mosque— could best be instituted. Furthermore, a city, Mecca, was the symbolic focus of Islam. Toward this urban shrine the believer had to turn daily in prayer, and to it he had to make his pilgrimage. Certainly these rituals, serving as foci of the daily life and the total lifetime of the believer, helped inculcate urban-oriented attitudes.

Islam encouraged the commercialism for which Muslims in some countries are famed. Regarding the Islamic view of business, von Grunebaum writes:

> Only the ascetic, the mystic, the scholar, and the public official are exempt from the duty of earning their bread by the work of their hands or commerce. From their conduct of business the character of the people will be known and their religion and piety be tested. The good merchant will conceive of his trade as a social obligation, for with the cessation of trade the community would perish.[5]

Particularly for Muslim merchants, sometimes as far from Mecca as India or Southeast Asia, the cost of the pilgrimage itself must have stimulated the desire for profit and the pursuit of commerce.

The medieval Islamic community was political and social as well as religious. It was a theocracy, a commonwealth that Allah controlled, but that his deputy, Muhammad, administered. The community's political and religious boundaries were the same. The ruler and all citizens were believers. The People of the Book, *i.e.*, Christians and Jews, were allowed to live within the community as *dhimmi*, persons protected by a special treaty; they were not, however, regarded as citizens equal to the Muslim believers and were accorded only safety of person and property. For pagans and idolaters, there was, in theory, only the choice between conversion and death.

To Arab tribesmen, warfare had served to establish ranks, to avenge slights, to gain booty; but Islam gave warfare new purpose. Allah was an awesome, transcendent, and uncompromising figure. By comparison to Him, the devout were regarded as sinful and inadequate. They could not compel His forgiveness, they could only worship and obey, and in a heedless moment they might nullify a lifetime of piety, dooming themselves to eternal suffering. Yet if the faithful were persuaded of their own puniness and sinfulness in the eyes of Allah, how much more flawed did they consider the infidels and idolaters who flouted His rule. The inner guilt and desperation of the faithful was projected outward toward the wretched infidels. These should be compelled to convert, or die. The world was divided into two domains, *dar al Islam*, the region of God's elect, and *dar al harb*, the region of war. There being no neutral ground, the Muslim was obliged to combat the infidel. The pressure to conquer, and if possible to convert, never ceased, with holy war (*jihad*) bringing religious merit. Through warfare, Allah's dominion was extended and his faith expanded, all with incredible speed.

The spread of Islam generated dilemmas such as the practical one that conquest was often too fast to allow conversion of the conquered, the result being a political state without a religious base. But a more fundamental problem was rooted in theology. Islam assumed that all of life should conform to the divine, and that since there was only one God, there could be only one acceptable way of life. Yet with the spread of Islam into new areas, new situations arose that were not treated by the orthodox and immutable doctrines. What should the believer do in situations not covered by the Qur'an? This dilemma encouraged a tendency toward formalism and legalism. "Customs" *(sunna)* and "sayings" *(hadit)* were collected to fill gaps left by the Qur'an. No central board of experts was empowered to distinguish heresy from orthodoxy and decree which sayings should be included and which omitted. Islamic tradition thus became an infinitely expandable collection of items, with diverse schools focused on the various subcollections. Which school was heretical, which orthodox, depended largely on which boasted the greatest power and following.

An associated problem centered on leadership. During the life of Muhammad, he was the unquestioned political and religious leader of the Muslim community, the *umma.* Upon his death, however, there arose two schools of thought regarding succession. The Sunnis championed as leader the *caliph,* one empowered by the community to serve as its defender and ruler, but religiously the equal of all other believers. The Shiites, on the other hand, thought that the community's leader should be an *imam,* a religious teacher who possessed unusual spiritual powers. The Shiites believed in a special line of prophets endowed by God with a divine spark; the *imam* would inherit this spark from Muhammad. What is of interest is not so much the particular disputes between the Sunnis and the Shiites or other schools, but the effects of these disputes on Muslim society. The conflicts obviously hampered unification of the *umma* (community), rendering unattainable Muhammad's vision of a politically united Muslim world.

Unification of the *umma* was also blocked by the awesomeness of Allah and the formalism of Muslim ritual. The failure of the ritual to provide personal communion with God apparently left an emotional gap that the believer was tempted to fill by mysticism or by animistic practices derived from folk traditions. Certainly it is more true of Islam than of Christianity, especially Protestant Christianity, that belief in magic and spirits is retained even by the pious. An encouragement to such belief is that formalistic Islamic ritual requires primarily *outward* expression of faith, perhaps leaving intact inner attitudes flowing from traditional religions.

To summarize, Islam encouraged primitive Arab society to advance to the historic level. It undercut particularistic and diffuse social relationships, such as those of kinship, and it inspires an aggressive centralization resulting in empires far exceeding in size and power any achieved by archaic society. The centralization was in part stimulated by Islam's transcendent God, in whose name the unworthy were energetically to be transformed. At the same time, divisive and formalistic qualities of Islam limited the development toward centralization and modernity.

Overview

The single outstanding characteristic of historic religions is their dualism. Archaic religions conceive of a wider gap between the cosmos and society than primitive religions, yet archaic man still believes in a single world inhabited by both gods and men. Historic man rejects such monism in favor of a dualism that conceives of a radical gap between the real world and the religiously defined order, between this world and the otherworld.

Not only is the otherworld separate from this world, it is infinitely better. The Buddhists are most radical in this view, for they consider this world mere illusion. Both Muslims and medieval Christians* idealized life after death; the latter, especially, regarded this life as simply a dreary interlude before salvation. Nirvana, Heaven, or Paradise are infinitely preferable to anything this world has to offer.

Historic man, accordingly, was obsessed with the need to be saved to achieve the eternal bliss of the afterlife. Among other things, the quest for salvation fostered universalism. In primitive religion, a man's fate depends on his kin status, in archaic religion, on his class status. In historic religion, on the other hand, it depends on his actions toward salvation. How much merit does he accumulate? Does he pray five times a day and make the pilgrimage to Mecca? Historic religion undercuts particularism by regarding even the humblest man as capable of salvation—through proper action.

Historic religion fosters a new sense of selfhood. In archaic society an individual atones for a particular error with a particular sacrifice, but in historic society man worships by begging forgiveness for a deep sinfulness within his total self. Whether through inheritance of some "original sin" or simply through deeds the Christian, Buddhist, or Muslim comes to possess a sinful personality. Because it is the total personality that is sinful, sacrificial correction of one or a number of wrongdoings

*This overview will concern itself not only with Buddhist, Hindu, and Muslim religion, but also with historic Christianity, which will be discussed further in connection with Protestantism in chapter 8.

is insufficient. Salvation is attained only by commitment of the total self to the ultimate, to Allah, God, or Atman. This concept presupposes and encourages a sense of selfhood, a notion of personality as integrating and transcending discrete acts. It also poses a great risk for the total self, and a great opportunity—promises the total self possible participation in the ultimate, yet threatens it with the danger of hell-fire, perpetual rebirth, or other horrible alternatives to salvation.

Here a difference between the Buddhist and the Muslim or Christian is worthy of note. The Muslim and the Christian conceive of each individual as having only a single life in which to work out his salvation; hence, each individual is under great pressure. The Buddhist, on the other hand, expects to be reborn again and again; hence, if he fails to achieve salvation in this life he may try again in the next.

Despite this difference, all historic religions, Buddhism included proclaim that much is at stake for the individual. Facing the choice between damnation and salvation of the total self, he has much to gain if he is saved, much to lose if he is not. It is logical for him to devote all his time to the search for salvation, and it is appropriate for the Buddhist and Christian monks to withdraw from life in order to devote themselves to worship. Islam has no monks but instead conceives of the entire *umma* as a pure body withdrawn from the sinful world in order to seek salvation.

The existence of a monkhood institutes a new social pattern. Archaic society is two-class with a religio-political elite separated from the common people. Historic society is a three-class society, with the elite dividing into religious and political groups that are separated from each other and from the masses.* The religious elite, for example, the monkhood, claim a monopoly on the channels to salvation. The political elite, the kings and ministers, are more strictly political and no longer claim to control the religious elite. This situation is clearly illustrated in Thailand, where Sangha and government, though intimately related, are separate. The relationship between the medieval Christian church and the state was similar. The Muslim theocracy does not so clearly separate the religious and political leadership in theory, but in practice considerable separation does occur.

*It could be argued that historic society tends toward a four-class arrangement, with a differentiation among the masses that parallels that among the elite. With increased urbanism, the urban masses became more clearly distinct from the rural, and not uncommonly the rural folk were regarded as second-class citizens religiously by comparison with the more devout urbanites. Thus, there were religious and secular elite and religious and secular masses making up the four classes. We believe that in historic societies the division within the masses is less distinct and universal than within the elite, hence we refer to historic society as composed of three classes, but we have no strong preference for the three-class as against the four-class designation.

The division between political and religious elite in historic society furnished new potential for confrontation. Whether conflict was between Buddhist monk and king, Muslim teacher and *caliph,* or christian Pope and emperor, the new assumption was that politics could be confronted by religious standards that transcended the political, that religious commitment could justify political rebellion and reform. Now one *could* oppose the king in the name of God. At the same time, political interests could oppose religious ones, as in Henry VIII's bout with the church.

Aside from particular issues dividing religious and political interests, one general difference is important. In historic society religion tends to be more universalistic than government. Buddhism, Christianity, and Islam made entry into religious elite open theoretically to all men, whereas entry into the political elite continued to depend on inherited status. This situation might have served to sustain the status quo, since the lowly, who were excluded from the high circles of politics, could compensate by religious achievement. On the other hand, the religious universalism provided a vision of a condition beyond political particularism, and stimulated a drive to change the political in the direction of that vision. The challenge to hereditary Arab aristocracy mounted by Muhammad's equalitarianism provides an example.

In historic society, culture and learning also underwent great changes stimulated by religion. Christians and Muslims achieved significant advances in medicine, engineering, mathematics, and science. Buddhists, on the other hand, turned their speculations inward and discovered some of the secrets of psychology. All of the historic religions encouraged literacy by their emphasis on scripture and sacred language. Vast libraries of revealed truth were recorded in Pali or Sanskrit for Buddhists, in Latin for Christians, and in Arabic for Muslims.

One consequence of these sacred langauges, all of which because of their sacredness, were set apart from daily speech, may have been to symbolize and accentuate the separate and transcendental character of the sacred or the otherworldly, thereby reinforcing the dualism of historic religion. Historic religion achieved a cultural unity that was more extensive than any political unity achieved by historic society. A comparison of the Catholic community with the Holy Roman Empire, of the Muslim community with any Muslim empire, of the Buddhist community with any Asian empire, is sufficient to show that historic political empires were neither so broad nor so permanent as were historic religious communities. Historic empires were, however, more extensive than archaic empires.

The case of India, which we have treated as an example of archaic society, is instructive for the understanding of historic society. Hinduism, which contained many historic ideas, emerged in India. From

Hinduism came Buddhism, clearly an historic religion. India was not, however, receptive to Buddhism, and Buddhism was thrust out. Nor did the historic ideas of Hinduism spread widely in India. They were restricted to the Brahmans. The Hindu ideas that did spread, such as *dharma,* served to reinforce an archaic and particularistic caste structure. Thus, the mere presence of historic ideas was not enough to alter a well-established archaic social pattern.

A similar situation is apparent in China. Despite the vast expanse of the classic Chinese empire and its remarkably universalistic bureaucracy and philosophy, we consider it archaic because it was organized around a kinship unit, the patrilineal clan. Yet historic religions and ideas existed in China. For a time Mahayana Buddhism was potent there, but through persecution and other means Confucians, who supported the patrilineal pattern, managed to isolate Buddhism from the majority of the people, and China remained essentially archaic until this century. Perhaps China, like India, had advanced so far in archaic organization that historic ideas did not promise enough further progress to encourage the incorporation of these historic ideas into the structure of society. Today, both China and India confront not historic but modern or early-modern ideas, and many of the archaic patterns that withstood the historic onslaught are now dissolving.

This brief discussion of China and India is not meant to minimize the power of religion to provoke social change. The spread of historic society could never have occurred without the spread of historic religions and ideas. Nevertheless, the cases of China and India suggest that the mere introduction of new religions or new ideas is no guarantee that social change will occur.

Topics for Discussion

This chapter has focused on the major dimensions of historic society as they have emerged through the spread of historic religions. Historic religions have been perpetuated, elaborated, and spread by a literate urban elite. Peasant society is a topic usefully introduced in connection with historic society, for the urban-centered "great traditions" are commonly balanced by the rural-centered "little traditions" of the peasant masses who make up the bulk of the population of historic societies. Anthropologists have placed considerable emphasis on the study of peasantry, but study from an evolutionary point of view indicates that in all historic societies peasants are continually changing in the direction of the more modern patterns displayed by the religious traditions and national culture centered in the major cities. Accordingly, it seems that if an anthropologist wishes to understand the direction in which society is moving, he should place less emphasis on the peasantry and more on the "great traditions" emanating from the cities. Yet the question remains worth exploring: In what ways does the study of peasant life contribute to an understanding of historic societies.

Given the basic foundation of historic culture, how would one expect it to confront rapid social change? An especially important case is that of Islam. Owing to the enormous wealth of the oil-producing Islamic counties, they are experiencing extremely rapid change in some spheres. What will be the relation between this process and Islam?

Suggested Readings

Burma, Thailand, and Buddhism

Hill Farms and Padi Fields: Life in Mainland Southeast Asia (paperback, 1965) by Robbins Burling. For contrast read chapter 7 on the Thai and chapter 6 on the Burmese.

The Golden Road to Modernity (1965) by Manning Nash. An excellent comparison of two Burmese villages.

Burmese Supernaturalism (paperback, 1967) by Melford E. Spiro. An illuminating analysis of Burmese religion.

Anthropological Studies in Theravada Buddhism (1966) edited by Manning Nash. A collection of essays.

Ancient Siamese Government and Administration (1965) by H. G. Quatritch Wales. On ancient Thai society.

Thai Peasant Personality (1965) by Herbert Phillips. A suggestive psychological view of the Thai.

Hinduism

The Religion of India (paperback, 1958) by Max Weber. A basic source.

Philosophies of India (1956) by Heinrich Zimmer. Discusses philosophical and religious aspects of Hinduism.

When a Great Tradition Modernizes (1972) by Milton Singer.

India: The Social Anthropology of a Civilization (1971) by Bernard S. Cohn.

Mind, Body, and Wealth (1973) by David Pocock. An excellent introduction to India through one field site.

Islam

Medieval Islam (1961) by Gustave E. von Grunebaum. A basic source.

History of the Islamic Peoples (paperback, 1960) by Carl Brockelmann. A good discussion of early Arab history.

Mohammedanism: An Historical Survey (paperback, 1962) by H. A. R. Gibb. An excellent and readable historical account.

The Social Structure of Islam (paperback, 1962) by Reuben Levy. A basic sociological source.

Islam Observed: Religious Development in Morocco and Indonesia (1968) by Clifford Geertz. A vivid comparison of Islam in the Near East and Southeast Asia.

The Venture of Islam (1974, 3 vols.) by Marshall Hodgson. A monumental introduction.

China

The Religion of China (paperback, 1951) by Max Weber. A basic work, complex and detailed.

Chinese Civilization (paperback, 1958) by Marcel Granet.

Under the Ancestor's Shadow (paperback, 1948), by Francis L. K. Hsu.

Peasant Life in China: A Field Study of Country Life in the Yangtze Valley (1946) by Fei Hsiao-t'ung.

The Family Revolution in Modern China (paperback, 1968) by Marion J. Levy, Jr.

Peasant Society

Peasants (paperback, 1966) by Eric Wolf. General treatment.

The Primitive World and Its Transformations (paperback, 1953) by Robert Redfield. A classic statement.

Peasant Society: A Reader (paperback, 1967) edited by J. M. Potter, M. N. Diaz, and G. M. Foster. Contains useful articles and extensive bibliography of classic monographs on peasant life in various parts of the world.

Films

Apu Triology by Satyajit Ray. Includes *Pather Panchalli, Aparajito,* and *The World of Apu.* Available in 16 mm.

North Indian Village. A more orthodox ethnographic film, depicting a village and various social institutions of India.

Journey to Mecca. Shows pilgrims from Turkestan, India, Yugoslavia, and as far away as Malaya and the Philippines making the pilgrimage to Mecca.

Moulay Idriss. Depicts the holy week during which pilgrims converge on Mecca.

Mecca, the Forbidden City.

chapter 8

Early-Modern Society and Culture

To illustrate a particular level of sociocultural evolution, each previous chapter chose several societies from among the many primitive, archaic, and historic ones that exist or have existed in world history. Since the primitive era, the trend of history has been toward larger and larger societies. Finally, in the early-modern era, all societies are merging into a single system, the world society, which, strictly speaking, should constitute our illustrative case for this chapter. Rather than make the entire world the subject of our analysis, however, we shall follow the less ambitious approach of treating the origin of this early-modern pattern. The region of origin is Europe, and our focus will be on European history. In order to sketch something of the diffusion of the early-modern pattern to non-European areas of the world, we shall analyze Japan as an example of a highly successful latecomer to modernization and Indonesia as an example of a problematical new nation.

The question of the origin and spread of the early-modern pattern will be treated from the theoretical perspective known as the Protestant Ethic Thesis and commonly identified with the German social theorist Max Weber. In spite of the controversial character of Weber's views, his theories are comparative and evolutionary, hence can contribute much to social and cultural anthropology. Furthermore, Weber's Protestant Ethic Thesis provides a general framework for a discussion of the interplay of cultural, social, and psychological forces of evolution.

The Rise of Historic Christianity

Christianity emerged from Judaism. The Jews regarded themselves as the "chosen people" of a transcendent and monotheistic God, Jehovah (or Yahwe), with whom they had established a covenant; in return for obeying the commandments of Jehovah and worshipping Him above all gods, the Jewish people would be exalted above all others. Ancient Judaism was thus more archaic and less universalistic than Christianity in that the Jewish God was the God of the Jewish people, whereas the Christian God was concerned with all men, regardless of their nationality.

In broadening its appeal and widening its mission to include all men, Christianity eliminated certain practices that were conspicuously tied to the society of its origin (for example, the Jewish customary laws concerning circumcision and food taboos) and that were distasteful to some peoples of the Greek and Roman world. It is not certain whether Christian proselytizing was given its force and power through the universalization of Christian custom or the distinctive theological message of Christian preaching—that the millennium was imminent and the need for conversion was great. Whatever the reason, Christianity succeeded in spreading throughout the Roman Empire.

At first, Christianity was greeted with hostility by the Roman elite because it threatened the archaic religions that sanctified imperial power. However, the conversion of Emperor Constantine in the early part of the fourth century gave Christians a favored place in the official religious complex. Christian bishops proved willing to cooperate with a Christian emperor, considering him chosen by God for his high office. The alliance between Christianity and the imperial establishment reached its logical conclusions at the end of the fourth century when Emperor Theodosius proclaimed Christianity the state religion and prohibited all rival faiths.* Christianity thus became the exclusive official religion of the Roman Empire, and thereby of the entire "civilized" Western world.

---

*This alliance was the forerunner of the "divine right" of kings—an institution that became established in the West at a later date—and was very different from the archaic "divine kingship" in that the king himself was not considered a god, but was legitimized by God and church.

Once Christianity was firmly established, its influence extended even beyond the limits of the Roman Empire by the successful conversion of the foreign and primitive barbarian hordes that swept through Rome on expeditions of sacking and looting. Christianity introduced universalistic ideas that undermined the barbarians' tribal organization and encouraged them to establish feudal kingdoms, such as those of the Goths, the Visigoths, and the Franks.

Christian Imagery and Medieval Society

Like the other historic religions, Christianity saw a radical gap between the divine order and the social order in which men lived—a view that contrasted with those of archaic religions of the day. Thus, the archaic Greeks localized their pantheon on Mount Olympus, but the Heaven of the Christians was above the world of men and was not associated with any earthly spot; the Greek could see his Olympian Mountain of the Gods in a way no Christian could see his Heaven.

Besides creating a chasm between the divine and the everyday, Christianity placed infinite value on the divine, little value on the everyday—an attitude, once again, that contrasted with those of archaic religions of the day. Thus, in archaic Judaism the question of life after death was secondary to the task of preparing for the messiah so that the Jews, as God's chosen people, would collectively enjoy exalted status in the world. In Christianity, by contrast, the primary question was that of the individual's salvation, that he might enjoy a life after death. Because salvation was so important for the Christian, the Christian ideal was withdrawal from this world, as in monastic life, in order to concentrate on gaining salvation in the otherworld; if one could not withdraw from this world, it was good to emulate Saint Paul and "be in the world, but not of it."

As Christianity spread through the Roman Empire and beyond, and the expected millennium that was to create God's Kingdom on earth did not materialize, symbolic and social hierarchies were built to connect this world and Heaven. The gap between Heaven and Hell was bridged by such intermediate stations as purgatory and Limbo. Heaven itself was hierarchical, with God at the pinnacle, then ranked orders of angels, a pantheon of saints (some of whom were probably ancient pagan heroes and spirits incorporated into the Christian hierarchy after their worshippers were converted), and the souls of the departed faithful. The sacraments and rituals of the church and the church's hierarchy of bishops, priests, monks, and nuns furnished additional steps to God.

These symbolic and social hierarchies were philosophically grounded in the notion of positions stretching from God down to the most insignificant creature. Each creature had its place on this continuum, each formed one link in the Great Chain. Each was expected to submit to God's plan, stay in its place, and thereby contribute to the harmony and order of the universe. Save for withdrawal into a monastery or convent, movement from one's inherited place was a flaunting of God's will.

Particularly in Western Europe, the church was able to establish a more stable and inclusive social system than was achieved by any secular empire. The acceptance of the Pope's position as the Bishop of Rome, the successor of Saint Peter, and the undisputed leader of the Western church provided a single locus of authority.* Unification of the church hierarchy was also aided by the adoption of Latin as a common language for all men of learning and all churchmen. Lacking these unifying forces, the secular society was fragmented into numerous kingdoms and diverse languages and dialects.

Nevertheless, medieval society displayed a uniform feudal pattern, partly because most medieval men were Christian. Preoccupied with Christian teachings that promised to save their souls, medieval men were taught to think in feudal terms. The Great Chain of Being implied a hierarchy of positions fixed by birth—in other words, a feudal hierarchy. The medieval conception of society as a vast organism, created and animated by God, carried similar feudal implications. Secular society was the body politic, and the church was the visible body of Christ. Like a body, society was composed of members interdependent, but not interchangeable. In a body, a foot could not replace a hand; in society, one member could not perform another's special task. This Organic Analogy, like the Great Chain of Being, taught that every man should stay in his place.

The Organic Analogy carried a monarchical bias since it implied that society, like the body, should have a single head to which all other members were unalterably subordinate. Furthermore, the Organic Analogy discouraged change. The healthy body was harmonious and regular in its functions, and any radical modification of its normal shape was a sign of deformity and disease. Treatment was aimed at restoring the status quo. Innovation, like a tumor, was best excised as soon as possible so that the body could return to its former condition.

History, viewed in terms of the Organic Analogy, was cyclical, paralleling the body's cycle of birth, maturation, and death. Christian

---

*These remarks apply more to the Western portions of the Roman Empire than to the Eastern portions. In the West, the church achieved considerable unity under the Pope, although the political hierarchy was unstable. In the East, the reverse was true: No single authority dominated the Greek-speaking church, since authority resided in the council of bishops and each bishop was nominally the equal of the others. Nevertheless, the political hieararchy was united under the Byzantine emperor residing in Constantinople.

notions of Genesis and Judgement Day may have favored a view of history as a line, stretching from a beginning to an end of the world, but the Organic Analogy encouraged medieval Christians to view history as recurrent cycles of rise and decline. Biblical tales as well as the history of classical civilizations such as Greece and Rome could readily be understood from this viewpoint, for the societies of antiquity had risen, matured, declined, and disappeared.

The family was another image dominant in medieval thought. God, the Father, superintended the deeds of men, his children. The church was the Holy Mother, the priest was father to his flock, monks and nuns were brothers and sisters. Just as religion drew its imagery from the family, so the family gained sanctity from religion. The family was an integral part of nature established by God, but even more significantly, the family was sanctified by the sacrament of Matrimony, instituted by Christ, which proclaimed family bonds indissoluble. Children were believed to be granted to parents by God, and the authority of parents was strengthened by God's explicit command. The parent-child relationship was one of tender authority and innocent submission, solidly rooted in the natural and sacred orders.

The medieval family was not the nuclear family of modern society. Family relations extended lineally back through time and laterally out into space to include both ancestral and local bonds, so that each family was part of a ramified kinship network. Based on the hierarchical parent-child relationship, this extended family network became a model for all society; the relationships of subject to king, vassal to lord, and apprentice to master were imbued with the hierarchical and authoritarian aura of the parent-child bond. Like the family, the quasi-familial feudal hierarchy was sanctioned by the church.

In sum, Christianity lent religious sanctity to feudal society. Feudeal institutions of inherited status, hierarchy, and degrees of privilege drew meaning and force from the Christian concepts of the Great Chain of Being, the Organic Analogy, and the sacred family. These concepts endowed medieval society with a rigidity of shape and style that persisted for centuries, until the concepts were challenged and radically changed by the Protestant Reformation.

Calvinist Imagery and New Social Forms*

The feudal pattern, in spite of its common core, varied from region to region, and so did the Protestant Reformation. But everywhere the

---

*Our analysis of medieval imagery and of the changes in it wrought by Calvinism leans heavily on Michael Walzer, *The Revolution of the Saints*, especially chapter 5. Medieval

Reformation was accompanied by the decline or collapse of the medieval hierarchical structure, a breakdown especially pronounced with the Calvinistic branches of Protestantism, which we, following Weber and others, take as prototypic of early-modern religion.

The Calvinists, like most Protestants, retained the medieval Christian notion of a radical gap between God and man, but they rejected outright the hierarchical structure that had served as a ladder to God and repudiated the very idea that such mediation between God and man could exist. The result was a yawning gap between man and God. Calvinism transcendentalized God, made him more distant, more omnipotent, and totally inscrutable. In the absence of mediating devices, confrontation between this God and puny man could be terrifying.

As God became a more distant and elevated monopolist of good, man became a more lonely and despicable vessel of evil. Satan, the embodiment of evil, was frighteningly close at hand, enticing men to follow their naturally evil inclinations. The Calvinist was forced, therefore, to guard continuously against natural impulses by exercising a rigid self-discipline. Paradoxically, although Calvinists had repudiated the monastic style of life, the Calvinist came to live as ascetically as the monk, but in the world instead of in seclusion.

By sweeping away the mediating hierarchical structure and transcendentalizing God, the Calvinists undermined the concept of the Great Chain of Being. If God monopolized power, man and nature could not share that power; instead of a continuum of power between man and God, there was a gulf. From God's lofty vantage point, all men were weak. Authority, power, and inequality among men were meaningless in the eyes of God; therefore the social order lost its sanctity, indeed it ceased to be an *order*. The world was a playground for sin and evil, and man was inherently wicked, hence the natural state of society was chaos. Only the implacable will of God and the unceasing struggle of His servants could impose a minimal order on the unheeding world.

Rejecting the medieval church's distinction between monks and laity, the Calvinist substituted the distinction between the elect, who were predestined by God for salvation, and the damned—the vast majority of men, in the Calvinist view—who were predestined for eternal perdition. The elect were the chosen few who would carry out God's plans, just as the monks had been God's special servants. But unlike the monks, the elect would do God's will in the wide world and would dress and live like ordinary men. No one knew for sure who the elect were: They were not set apart by appearance, nor were they exclusively the highborn, for God

imagery did not disappear with the rise of modern society, as our discussion may seem to suggest, but it did cease to guide the total field of social behavior, becoming instead restricted to certain limited contexts.

did not regard a man's social rank. To Him a man's serviceability counted more than his status.

A crucial task for the Calvinist was ascertaining precisely what God called him to do. His inherited status was not a reliable sign, and he recognized no religiously superior priests who could provide authoritative advice. One recourse open to him was to seek direct revelation from God; another recourse was the Bible. Although the Calvinists had rejected the ceremonies and rituals of the church, they retained the Holy Scriptures, the literal, revealed truth of God. Since the Bible was for the Calvinist the sole remaining visible and codified statement of God's word, it assumed for him an overpowering importance. In order that every man might be able to read God's word, the Calvinists rejected the Latin Bible in favor of Bibles written in the vernacular, and they encouraged literacy and education.

From the Bible, the Calvinists derived the notion of a covenant between God and man. In return for worshipping and obeying Jehovah, declared the Bible, the Jews became the chosen people. This account accorded with the Calvinist notion of a covenant between God and the elect. The covenant was like a contract, although it was hardly between equal parties, and Calvinists could not coerce God to keep his agreements, as the ancient Jews had tried to do. God was seen as the creditor of all mankind, but only His elect, His saints, were, by His grace, enabled through their obedience partially to repay man's debt. "The covenant was a way of activating men, not of controlling God."[1]

The Calvinist covenant was not between God and a group, as in the case of Jehovah and the Jews, but rather between God and each individual. God in His grace sought an individual who was predestined for salvation, and by His grace allowed him to enter a covenant with Him. The individual then became a saint and an instrument of God's purpose. Since the saint could if necessary transcend social constraints to carry out God's will and plan, the concepts of covenant and calling gave religious sanctity to individual striving and accomplishment.

Calvinism also sanctified the devout voluntary group that stood apart from the traditional social order—the sect. The sect, like the saint, was God's instrument within the wicked world. A sect was led only by God and the Bible. Even the minister merely taught the Scriptures, which could be read by all. Membership in the sect was voluntary, dependent on the individual's active consent.

The voluntarism and individualism of Calvinism clashed with medieval images of polity. Calvinists found the image "ship of state" more congenial than the old one of "body politic." The leader of the state should, like the ship's captain, hold his post because of skill rather than inherited status; if the captain proved unskillful, the crew could legitimately mutiny. It is no accident that where Calvinism found deep roots, the rule of kings and nobles was undercut or overthrown. The political murder, as opposed to assassination, of Charles I by the Puritans is only the most glaring example of Calvinist politics.

The Organic Analogy of medieval times inspired a cyclical view of history—history followed no plan, moved in no direction. Calvinism, on the other hand, viewed history as guided by God's purpose. God employed ordinary mortals as instruments of that purpose, even when they were unaware of it; and the rise, decline, and fall of societies were according to God's plan, even when mere mortals could not comprehend it. The image of a ship of state reflected the Calvinist sense of purpose: Society, steered by a captain, is on a voyage.

Family imagery was not repudiated by the Calvinists, but it was modified to fit the Calvinist world view. Calvinism rejected the medieval Christian idea that the authority of parents was rooted in the natural order, which was sanctified by God. For the Calvinist, the natural order was wicked. Parental authority was, therefore, not "natural," but was derived specifically from God's commandments as stated in the Scriptures. The individual who accepted the calling of parenthood was obligated to mold his children into God-fearing Christians, a task that demanded careful guidance as well as constant evaluation of the child's achievements and godliness. Parental concern was thus focused inward, toward the child and immediate family, rather than outward, toward extended kin. Calvinistic notions of parenthood encouraged the nucleation of kinship.

Calvinist rejection of the medieval sacraments also affected family organization. The medieval sacrament of matrimony sanctioned enduring and irrevocable bonds between husband and wife and, by extension, between other kinsmen as well. Calvinists, however, viewed marriage as a civil contract between two consenting parties, rather than as a sacramental bond. And if marriage was simply a legal contract, it did not irrevocably bind extended kinsmen who did not directly consent to the marriage. The contractual view of marriage thus further encouraged the nucleation of kinship and the breakdown of extended kinship networks.

In sum, Calvinism postulated an order in the universe different from that envisioned by historic Christianity. This altered vision was expressed not only in such specific doctrines as predestination, the majesty of God, and unmediated salvation, but also in Calvinist imagery. Images could be more potent than doctrines in that they were not explicitly religious, hence might attract those who opposed particular Calvinist doctrines. Such persons might discover that the new images rendered their lives more meaningful than did the old Catholic images. Of course, many Calvinist images were neither new nor exclusively Calvinist. The Reformation leaders themselves claimed to return to a pristine and primitive Christianity that the church had debased and corrupted, and they chose images to symbolize the ancient order. But these images were incorporated into configurations fit for a world drastically different from the world of antiquity within which early Christianity had existed. This new world was feudal-historic, and Calvinism bore its stamp even as it sought to destroy it. Thus, Calvinism assimilated the Catholic notion of monkhood, conceiving of all men as voluntary ascetics in the service of God: "every man a monk and the whole world a monastery."

Calvinist notions did not always have immediate impact, like sledgehammers loudly smashing medieval structures. Yet the long reach of Calvinist patterning is apparent even today. Feudal systems have been replaced by early-modern systems. These make themselves felt not so much in class hierarchies as in competing and contending factions, such as political parties, labor unions, business firms, religious denominations, professional associations, and academic organizations, each of which is joined voluntarily. America, the "nation of joiners," is perhaps the most notable example of such a society. Precisely how Calvinism contributed to the emergence of early-modern society is an exceedingly complicated question, but it is clear that Calvinism supported the concept of the voluntary group. The Calvinist congregation was a model voluntary group in that each member joined of his own free will, in effect signing a contract that obligated him to assume certain responsibilities in return for the advantages of membership. The religiously sanctioned model of the voluntary group doubtless helped inspire voluntary and contractual modes of organization that could replace the declining feudal system.

The social fragmentation that is encouraged by the proliferation of voluntary groups is countered in early-modern society by the clustering of the groups into giant organizations—political, educational, scientific, economic, religious, medical. Whereas in medieval society only the church could stand against the state, in early-modern society any of these giant organizations can do so. Naturally, they can also team with the state to form such entities as the "military-industrial complex."

Early-modern society is in constant flux, partly because of its competing interest groups and partly because the idea of social reform became a guiding value of early-modern society, built into its ideologies, laws, constitutions, and governments. This pattern was at least partly inspired by Calvinism. Calvinism departed from the traditions of historic religion by emphasizing that *because* the Kingdom of God was radically better than the Kingdom of Man, man should incessantly reform the latter in the image of the former. The world was wicked, not sacred, and therefore any reform of it could only glorify God; certainly it would not violate His will, as the historic Catholic believed. Quite the contrary—the Calvinist felt guilty when he was not feverishly engaged in reform, an attitude that pervades America to this day.

The Western industrial society, with its Calvinist origins, is the prime example of the early-modern type—a society characterized by self-reforming political-legal institutions, voluntary associations, mass literacy, nuclear families, contractual relations. The classic theory of the Calvinist origins of early-modern Western society was advanced by Max Weber in his voluminous *Religion-Soziologie;* and although we have already anticipated many of Weber's points, we will summarize his argument and discuss some criticisms of it.

The Protestant Ethic Thesis[2]

Weber agreed with Marx that capitalism was a unique phenomenon, which was nonexistent before the advent of the modern world. By "capitalism," Weber meant a bureaucratically organized, rational, ascetic system for the pursuit of profit. Capitalism is bureaucratically organized in that it is carried on within a complex organization of firms, factories, and associated governmental, legal, and social agencies, all of which are oriented toward economic profit. It is rational in that it is systematic and methodical rather than sporadic and adventurous. It is ascetic in that its profits are regarded as a measure of the success of the enterprise and a means for its perpetuation rather than as a reward to be hedonistically enjoyed.

Weber took great pains to show that bureaucratically organized, rational, ascetic capitalism did not flow from human nature. Far from being common to all men, it was unique to men in early-modern society. From where, if not human nature, did this "unnatural" development derive? And how did it survive once it appeared? Weber observed that the capitalist threatened the traditional order with his rationally exploitative procedures that made "tallow out of cattle and money out of men."[3] The early capitalist was, therefore, frequently persecuted and ostracized in premodern Europe. Weber believed that some extraordinarily powerful force was required to keep the early capitalist functioning and, more important, to transform the values of traditional Europe into those vehemently capitalistic ones that have inspired the gigantic capitalistic complexes dominating the West today. Weber concluded that this force was Calvinism.

Calvinism called men to work in the world as a devotional program to glorify God. Life was a God-assigned task that required continuous and methodical striving. Wasting time was the deadliest of sins, for it distracted men from that task. Hard, continuous physical and mental labor glorified God and purified the soul, while "idleness is the Devil's workshop." Regular work was the most desirable, irregular or casual work was, at best, a necessary evil. No sport was justified except when it increased work capacity and moral purity. Theater, idle talk, sex, or self-adornment were sinful. Sober utility ranked far above beauty, since the beautiful object was contemplated for itself rather than employed as a means toward God's purpose. A Faustian or Renaissance yearning to do and be everything was condemned in favor of specialized and disciplined work, which was necessary in order that one's special task be completed.

Why should men assume such a burdensome calling? For Weber, the answer lay in Calvinist theology. God had predestined that some men be saved and others be eternally damned. Neither ritual, nor faith, nor good works could change God's decision. No one but God knew whether a man was to be saved or damned. Desperately clutching at clues to God's will, Calvinists eventually accepted an individual's work and achievement in an earthly calling as a sign of his chances for salvation. The individual was therefore driven to work and achieve in a disciplined and ascetic style in order to prove that he was one of the elect who would be saved. No other method—neither magic, ceremony, priest, sacrament, nor special group—could either bring about or signify salvation.

Medieval Christianity did not force each believer to organize his life according to a systematic plan. Indeed, the sacramental system permitted a man to live for the moment—to sin when he felt like it, repent when the mood demanded, then sin again, knowing that the sacrament would provide forgiveness. Ethically, the ordinary medieval Christian could live "from hand to mouth."[4] But the Calvinist, who had rejected the sacraments, yet feared damnation, felt compelled to gear his entire life systematically toward achieving inner conviction of his salvation. Weber argued that this plan-ahead attitude was useful for operating in a bureaucratically organized, rational, ascetic capitalist system. Thus, Calvinism inadvertently taught attitudes and values useful for capitalism.

Weber's argument is more complex than this presentation of it might make it seem. It entwines numerous lines of thought, some of which he elaborated more than others. For example, he emphasized the debt of Calvinism to Judaism; Judaism also taught belief in a transcendent God who called men to carry out His commands on earth. Weber treated Calvinism and capitalism as part of the broad trend away from traditionalism and reliance on kinship ties that had been gaining momentum in the West since the time of the Roman Empire.[5] Obviously, Weber did not claim that Calvinism was the only stimulus to the rise of capitalism. Nor did he ignore the role of economic factors; after all, he was an economic historian. But Weber's argument was in part directed against Karl Marx's interpretation of capitalism, which in Weber's view overemphasized economic factors. Weber believed that a complex configuration of cultural, social, and psychological, as well as economic factors had to be considered in order to comprehend the by no means inevitable rise of capitalism.

Weber followed two methods of argument, the comparative and the structural. Arguing structurally, Weber delineated the *Geist* ("spirit") of capitalism, the set of mental attitudes that guided it, and then went on to show that these attitudes were logically or "structurally" congruent with those encouraged by Calvinism. Since the points of agreement were so strong, it seemed that Calvinism and the spirit of capitalism must have sprung from a common condition or have mutually influenced each other. But Weber further claimed that Calvinism had influenced capitalism more than capitalism had influenced Calvinism. Through a study of Calvinist writings, Weber was able to show a transition from an early anticapitalist theology to a later theology encouraging capitalism. Weber argued that the transition came about not as a response to socioeconomic changes, but as a logical working out of theological dilemmas. Once the new Calvinism emerged, the stage was set for the generation of attitudes favorable to the rise of capitalism, which then began in earnest. This argument opposed the simplistic and popular one that Calvinism was simply an ideology created by already practicing capitalists to justify and excuse their material ambitions.

Weber studied and compared a wide range of actual situations to demonstrate that where the Protestant Ethic flourished, capitalism and the spirit of capitalism flourished as well, whereas the absence of the Protestant Ethic tended to be correlated with a limited development of capitalism. Focusing on the West, Weber made use of statistics showing that German Protestants, for example, tended to choose a technical, scientific, or business education, whereas German Catholics tended to choose a humanistic education. Weber suggested that Protestant education was oriented more toward capitalism than was Catholic education, and that this orientation was reflected in the relatively larger number of Protestants than Catholics who owned and managed capitalist enterprises in Germany. The accuracy of Weber's statistics has been questioned, but the criticisms are not fundamentally damaging to his argument.

Extending his analysis beyond Europe, Weber compared the West to China and India. At certain points in Chinese and Indian history, Weber suggested, natural and social conditions favored the rise of capitalism even more, perhaps, than they had in the West, yet capitalism did not flourish in China and India. What was lacking, Weber believed, was a religious ethic like that of Calvinism.

In ancient China, for example, commerce and a bureaucratic merit examination system encouraged markedly greater social mobility than existed in the feudal West; and this relative mobility should have encouraged capitalism.* Also favorable to capitalism should have been China's peace and stability during long periods, as well as its remarkably centralized, rational, and universalistic bureaucracy. In spite of these favorable conditions, however, nothing remotely approaching Western capitalism emerged in China.

Weber maintained that Chinese religion was the culprit. Yet at first glance even Chinese religion would seem to favor capitalism. Confucianism, the core of Chinese religion, was worldly and rational. Displaying little concern with the otherworld, the Confucianist war primarily interested in the practical world of government and society. His demeanor was not intemperate or erratic, but disciplined and orderly, for Confucianism, precisely because of its worldliness, failed to inspire a drive toward changing the world. The Confucian gentleman, unlike the Calvinist reformer, did not envision a transcendent Kingdom of God in the image of which he must constantly remold the world. Therefore, the Confucianist was content to harmonize with the world as given—to accept its magic, its clans, its traditions. Confucianism encouraged conservatism rather than the radically innovative spirit of capitalism.

Weber did not claim that Calvinism was necessary to sustain contemporary capitalism, only that Calvinist ideas had encouraged the origin of capitalism. Nevertheless, he did point to contemporary patterns that display the imprint of Calvinism, even though such patterns are fully divorced from particular Calvinist doctrines or organizations. Comparing the reserved Englishman or mechanically friendly American with the sentimental, emotional, *gemütlich* (South) Germans, Weber speculated that the contrast reflects the impact of Calvinist Puritanism on England and America versus the Catholic and Lutheran influence on Germany. In Benjamin Franklin he detected another example of the

---

*Note, however, Levy's "Contrasting Factors in the Modernization of China and Japan," pages 169–70, which shows that the marked mobility in China did not necessarily encourage capitalism there. Because Chinese values ranked the landed gentleman-scholar-bureaucrat at the apex of society and the merchant at the bottom, merchants who acquired wealth used it to buy land and join the landed class. Thus, the very openness of the traditional Chinese class structure encouraged constant flight of the most able merchants out of the merchant class. Presumably, this inhibited China's capitalistic development.

effect of Calvinism. He was well aware that Franklin was no practicing Calvinist, yet he saw in Franklin's frugality and rationality a reflection of a milieu strongly influenced by its Calvinist origins. Besides Franklin, of course, numerous other American prototypes of the Protestant Ethic character could be described; Sinclair Lewis's portrait of a captain of industry, Dodsworth, can serve as an example:

> He always wore large grave suits, brown or gray or plain blue, expensively tailored and not very interesting, with decorous and uninteresting ties of dull silk and no jewelry save a watch chain. . . .
> He made his toilet like a man who never wasted motion—and who, incidentally, had a perfectly organized household to depend upon. His hand went surely to the tall pile of shirts (Fran ordered them from Jermyn Street) in the huge Flemish armoire, and to the glacial nest of collars, always inspected by the parlor maid and discarded for the slightest fraying. He tied his tie, not swiftly but with the unwasteful and extremely unadventurous precision of a man who has introduced as much "scientific efficiency" into daily domesticity as into his factory.
> . . . He would certainly (so the observer assumed) produce excellent motor cars; he would make impressive speeches to the salesmen; but he would never love passionately, lose tragically, nor sit in contented idleness upon tropic shores.[6]

Weber's Protestant Ethic Thesis has been criticized on a variety of grounds. Although we agree that certain problems plague Weber's arguments, we also believe that many of the common criticisms[7] miss his point, distort his views, and obscure the usefulness of his thesis.

"Weber is wrong since many contemporary capitalists are not Calvinists or even practicing Protestants" is a frequently heard criticism. Weber's thesis, however, was not that Calvinism is necessary for capitalism today, only that Calvinism was the creative force behind the first capitalistic societies. Therefore, his thesis is not refuted by citing the numerous examples of non-Calvinist, non-Protestant capitalists of today. Besides, statistics show that in general Protestant nations are even today significantly more successful at capitalism than non-Protestant (e.g., Catholic, Buddhist, Muslim) nations* and that within at least one major

---

*David C. McClelland, *The Achieving Society,* pp. 50–52; Gerhard Lenski, *Human Socities,* chapter 10, table 25. The table in Lenski's book shows that the present median per capita income of predominantly Protestant nations is approximately six times the median for non-Protestant nations (including not only Eastern Orthodox and Roman Catholic, but also Buddhist, Muslim, and other nations). The median of Protestant nations is approximately three times the median of Eastern Orthodox and Roman Catholic nations.

city of Protestant America, Protestant groups tend to be more capitalistic than Catholic groups.†

Students of history sometimes argue that Weber's thesis is incorrect because in pre-Reformation and post-Reformation periods there were many successful non-Calvinist capitalists.‡ But Weber's central point was not that Calvinism was required to spur each individual or family to capitalistic feats, but that Calvinism was the driving force behind whole societies as they became organized capitalistically. In Weber's view, the difference between traditional and capitalistic societies was qualitative rather than quantitative. Capitalistic society did not result merely from the presence of numerous capitalists, but also from the organization of a complex of legal, governmental, educational, scientific, and economic institutions in such fashion as to facilitate capitalistic enterprise. Traditional societies were organized in such a way as to hamper capitalism; thus even if numerous capitalists were present, these had to work against the grain of society.

Some scholars suggest that capitalist societies existed before Calvinism—as in medieval Italy and Flanders. However, were these so-called pre-Calvinist capitalistic societies capitalist in Weber's sense of the word? Did they consist of a complex of governmental, educational, scientific, and economic institutions that were oriented toward facilitating the conduct of rational, ascetic, bureaucratic capitalism? Or were they simply traditional societies containing numerous capitalists? Anti-Weberians often claim that capitalism was presented before Calvinism, but their definition of capitalism differs from Weber's. Obviously, to show that capitalism of type X is present when the Protestant Ethic is absent is not to prove that Weber's capitalism of type Y could flourish without the Protestant Ethic. To show that X occurs without Z is not to disprove the correlation between Y and Z.

A final criticism is that Calvinist leaders (e.g., Calvin, Baxter, Wesley, Penn) explicitly preached against the accumulation of wealth; hence, say the critics, Calvinism discouraged rather than encouraged capitalism.[8] Actually, Weber himself went to some pains to show that Calvinist leaders such as Calvin and Baxter preached against the accumulation of wealth, particularly the accumulation of wealth for its own sake. Weber was fully aware that Calvinist theologians did not intend to

†Gerhard Lenski, *The Religious Factor* (1963). Although Lenski's study covers only one city, Detroit, there is evidence that it could be generalized to numerous other American cities.

‡Brentano, one critic who raised this issue, comes from a family that produced successful Catholic capitalists about the time of the Reformation. Misconstruing Weber's thesis as saying that only Calvinists could be good capitalists, he took it as a maligning of his ancestors (Samuelson, 1961, p. 12).

encourage capitalism. But their attitude certainly does not disprove Calvinism's unintentional encouragement of capitalism. Weber argued that, regardless of the *intent* of Calvinist preachers, the pattern of Calvinist belief was such as to foster a drive toward salvation that found expression in capitalist action and institutions.

We should note in passing that Weber's critics have usually dealt exclusively with his analysis of Calvinism and capitalism in the West, although this is only a fragment of his work. His full analysis deals with Asia as well as Europe; it inquires not only why capitalism flourished in the West, but also why it did *not* flourish in the East. His approach to China in these terms has already been mentioned; we will shortly consider post-Weberian studies that extend the question to Japan.

Defense of Weber should not obscure legitimate questions that can be raised concerning his views. We shall propose a few questions we regard as legitimate because they derive from and build on Weber's penetrating insights and are amenable to empirical research.

Weber regarded England and the United States as the best examples of the modern capitalistic pattern, and Calvinism was certainly an important force in molding the institutions and values of both. Calvinism, however, was only a part of the Reformation, and England and America are only two capitalist societies among many. Can so limited a phenomenon as Calvinism account for so general a phenomenon as capitalism? Did Weber overlook important contributions to capitalism and modernism flowing from the total Reformation movement? After all, the entire Reformation, not Calvinism alone, transformed old social images, overturned the old feudal order, and rejected the church hierarchy. Perhaps the widespread, Reformation-inspired rejection of a single, legitimate, hierarchical authority opened the door for a pluralism and dissent of modern society, which insistently refuses any single authority the right to decree the truth.

In the face of competing systems of belief and value—those of traditional Christianity and of non-Calvinistic Protestantism—how could the beliefs and values of Calvinism prevail and become the basis of a new society? Were the Calvinistic ideas intrinsically more compelling and forceful than the competing ones? Did they frighten even non-Calvinist Christians into adopting Calvinist methods for salvation? At a more secular level, did Calvinistic institutions, such as the contract, inspire such successful business transactions that competitors were forced to adopt at least the institutions, if not the underlying doctrines? Confrontations like these between Calvinism and the non-Calvinist world may have stimulated the spread of Calvinist values without necessarily transforming the world's peoples into card-carrying Calvinists. Indeed, such confrontations might even have encouraged the secularization of Calvinist ideas:

Individuals who began acting like Calvinists, but who, religiously, remained non-Calvinist, would tend to deny the religious base of their actions and values.

Broad historic questions emerge from the Weberian studies. Although Weber focused primarily on the economic impact of Calvinism, later scholars have traced the effects of Calvinism on politics and on science. Much remains to be done in analyzing the impact of Calvinism on philosophy, but it is clear that Calvinistic notions seeped into the minds of Locke, Hobbes, and Adam Smith, to mention only a few.

A further elaboration of Weberian analysis is of pressing contemporary concern. What can the Weber thesis say about the prospects of modernization of the non-Western nations of today? Let us turn to Japan first, then to Indonesia, to illuminate this question.

The Protestant Ethic Thesis and the Industrialization of Japan

The development of early-modern society in the West was, of course, a gradual and lengthy process, but eventually the capitalistic, industrial early-modern pattern did spread throughout Western Europe and European settlements, such as America. It has proved remarkably difficult to export the pattern to non-Western societies. The efforts of missionaries, colonists, and, more recently, development agencies have hardly met with dazzling success. Although contact with the West has always elicited some modernization, almost no society has successfully modernized. Japan, one of the few that has, to a degree, been successful in modernizing is therefore of special interest.

In a remarkably short time, Japan managed to transform itself from a basically feudal-agrarian society into one of the most industrial societies of the world. That feat was the more striking because it was accomplished without great natural and economic resources. In terms of raw material, surplus population to employ in industry, and availability of capital to entrepreneurs, Japan was less favored than some of the other non-Western societies, such as neighboring China. Yet

> with an almost complete absence of internal blood-letting, the Japanese altered their governmental system, maintained their national independence, formed effective capital at an astonishing rate and virtually without foreign loans, and by the fourth decade of this century had become one of the five or six most "highly modernized" and powerful nations in the world.[9]

How was Japan able to achieve so much so fast? For one thing, Japan could profit from the experience of the West—emulate its successes, avoid its mistakes. With no model before it, the West, by contrast, had struggled toward capitalism through painful trial and error, guided by religious ideologies, the economic implications of which were unclear even to their believers.

But this advantage was open to all non-Western societies. The model of the West was there for all to see. Why, then, was it Japan, and not the others, who successfully industrialized? Could it be something special about Japan's sociocultural patterning? We might ask, with Robert Bellah, "Was there a functional analogue to the Protestant Ethic in Japanese religion" that contributed significantly to Japan's unique success in industrialization?[10]

Prior to its industrialization, Japan experienced almost unprecedented stability and peace for over two hundred and fifty years, during the Tokugawa period (1600–1868). Tokugawa society was composed of semi-independent feudal fiefs united under the *shogun* ("military ruler"), who wielded his power in the name of the emperor. The emperor himself, lacking power, lived neglected and ignored at his court in Kyoto, while the actual operations of government were centered at the shogun's court in Edo (present-day Tokyo).

Tokugawa society was rigidly stratified into a hierarchy of classes. At the apex were the emperor, the shogun, and the feudal lords who ruled the great fiefs. Immediately below these were the samurai, or Bushi, who were nominally warriors but who also served as officials and administrators of the fiefs. Separated from these elite by a wide gulf were the masses who, like the elite, were stratified. Peasant-farmers were at the top because they furnished food to the elite; artisans ranked next because they provided objects of beauty and utility for the elite; merchants were near the bottom because they were unproductive—they were mere middlemen distributing goods produced by others. At the bottom slunk the outcaste groups, the Eta and the light-skinned hairy Ainu. Although mobility within each class was common, mobility between classes was difficult if not impossible.

Although Japan had borrowed much from China (e.g., Mahayana Buddhism, Confucianism, and a writing system), its values were its own. The Japanese placed overwhelming emphasis on political values—values pertaining to the attainment of collective goals. Membership in a collectivity was essential since all blessings (*on*) were thought to flow from the various collectivities to which the individual was attached. For example, a person's parents and family provided life and identity, and his fief and lord gave status and protection. For blessings (*on*) received, the individual was expected to return blessings (*hoon*), particularly his loyalty, to the group.

Yet loyalty alone was not enough. The Japanese demanded performance as well. Only continuous performance in the service of group goals validated one's position. Even the group's head was accountable for his performance; the emperor himself had to report periodically to his ancestors and the gods on his performance while in office. The strong emphasis on performance did not allow passive devotion or docile subordination; it demanded active service.

Given the central values of loyalty and performance, it is not surprising that the military (samurai), who strikingly manifested these values, were very prestigious. Even during the long period of Tokugawa peace, the samurai managed to retain their prestige. Indeed, Bushido ("the way of the warrior") came to symbolize the ideal life style for Japanese of all classes. All Japanese were influenced by the military notion of self-sacrifice in the interest of the overlord.

Of course, economic activities could serve social goals, and when they did they were regarded as legitimate and essential. All classes were urged to maximize production and, at the same time, to minimize consumption—to live frugally so that resources could be diverted toward collective ends. When work did not serve collective ends, it was not valued. Hence, the farmer and the warrior were praised because they produced for fief and lord, but the merchant was suspected of working for his own interests and was consequently ranked low in the hierarchy.

Education was highly regarded, but not, as in China, for its own sake. Learning was valued primarily for its social contribution. The learned man had to be first and foremost a loyal man, exploiting his knowledge for the good of the group. Education thus contributed to conformity, rather than providing independent standards that might lead to critical comparison and perhaps rebellion.

Nor did a person's private emotions escape society's emphasis on loyalty and performance. Yearnings for romantic love were not satisfied by marriage since the elders, who expected the young to subordinate their feelings to the needs of the family, arranged their children's marriages. That such sacrifice was not always easy is demonstrated by the Japanese tradition of love suicides, prominent in literature, art, and even in life. Lovers could not simply elope; only through death could they violate loyalty to the group.

Japanese values were inspired and sanctified by Tokugawa religion, a composite of Confucianism, Mahayana Buddhism, and Shinto. These religions postulated a bond between man and the supernatural that paralleled the ideal bond between man and the group whereby the group conferred blessings (*on*) and man reciprocated with loyalty and performance (*hoon*). Shinto stressed the *on-hoon* relationship between the people and the national gods who oversaw their fate. Since the emperor represented the gods, loyalty to the emperor was loyalty to the gods. To repay the gods for blessings they bestowed, one performed for the emperor. Japanese Confucianism also emphasized loyalty to ruler and polity; but, in contrast to Chinese Confucianism, loyalty to ruler and polity ranked even higher than loyalty to the family. Mahayana Buddhism obliquely reinforced the same theme in that it preached the believer's dependency on a particular Buddha figure (*bhoddhisattva*) through whose grace one could attain heavenly reward; this figure could be a political superior. All religions, then, placed major emphasis on service and loyalty to the group and the leader. If the individual's service were sufficiently disciplined and ascetic, he could purify himself of his evil impulses and desires.

This Japanese attitude paralleled the ascetic-activist attitude of the Protestant Ethic, and probably served Japan as the Protestant Ethic had served the West: to inspire continuous, methodical, diligent work within a capitalistic economy. But whereas the Western Protestant Ethic encouraged achievement for God and self, Tokugawa religion encouraged achievement for emperor and state. It was this motive which Japan harnessed in the service of industrialization.

By the late nineteenth century the Tokugawa regime was at an end and the post-Tokugawa leaders, drawn mainly from the old samurai, faced the threat of the West. They clearly saw that, because of the West's superior technology, Japan would be crushed in a military contest, that colonialism threatened and that Japanese tradition could be eroded by Western capitalism. To maintain its autonomy and identity, Japan would have to transform itself into an industrial state capable of competing with the industrial nations of the West. The first order of business was to abolish the old feudal system and create a national state. The leaders accomplished this with the aid of the Shinto concept *Kokutai* ("national polity"), which sanctified the state by identifying service to the emperor with service to the gods. Disseminating the concept of *Kokutai* through the schools and shrines, the leaders successfully elevated loyalty to emperor and state above all else and mobilized all loyalties and efforts to implement national goals, among which was the establishment of an industrial economy similar to that of the West.

Japan's industrialization differed from that of the West not only in being faster and more government-directed, but also in proceeding from a different cultural base. The Japanese managed to erect an early-modern technoeconomic system on an essentially archaic sociocultural foundation: The Japanese emperor, like the Egyptian pharaoh, was identified with divinity. But a more general difference between

Japan and the West was that in the West economic and political revolution followed religious reformation, whereas in Japan a similar economic and political revolution utilized ancient religious patterns, revitalizing them to fit new demands.

The New Nations: Political Religion in Indonesia

Since the end of World War II, which marked the end of the colonial empires, many new nations have been established. These nations are presently struggling to achieve some measure of parity with the long-established industrial nations, and, as part of that struggle, they aim to incorporate into their diverse traditions certain facets of the early-modern pattern.

In the West a radical cultural transformation, the Protestant Reformation, was a prelude to the emergence of early-modern society. In quite a different manner, Japan was able to incorporate many early-modern features without radically transforming her basic cultural patterns. But in both Japan and the West, cultural systems—systems of values and ideas—played a central role in socioeconomic modernization. These did more than render socioeconomic modernization meaningful: They made it seem as though such modernization flowed inevitably from the nature of existence.

Socioeconomic change in the new nations has not proceeded as smoothly as it did in Japan. Admittedly, the economic and political conditions confronted by the new nations differ from those confronted by Japan in the nineteenth century. A fundamental problem is the lack, among most new nations, of cultural systems that are readily harnessed to modernization. The new nations must undergo deep-seated cultural changes similar to those of the European Reformation before modernization can proceed at a significant rate. Perhaps they can learn even more from the European experience than from the Japanese one.

It is noteworthy that the leaders of many new nations are charismatic figures who, like Reformation preachers, proclaim a vision of a new society. With their millenarian quality, these visions lend urgency to exhortations aimed at inflaming the masses. Leaders like Gandhi, Mao, Sukarno, Kenyatta, U Nu, Nkrumah, Nehru, and Sihanouk have preached what may be called a new species of religion—"political religion,"[11] a system of values, ideas, and symbols often divorced from and hostile to the supernatural beliefs of conventional religion. Yet like conventional religion, the new ideologies offer hope of salvation and immortality for the believer by promising a secure future in a life not yet experienced by mortal man.

Political religion also promises new identity through the union of the individual with a system larger and more powerful than any he has experienced. This system, be it the nation or something wider and deeper, draws the citizen away from traditional attachments to kinship, ethnic, or local groups. Youth is especially vulnerable to such appeals, for the young crave identity and are more ready than their elders to forsake the securities of traditional loyalties.

Exciting new goals are created by political religion. Citizens are urged to work and struggle to actualize in five-year plans the vision of the charismatic leader. By "retooling" themselves as instruments for the fulfillment of that pure vision, the citizens are supposed to feel cleansed and purified. A political religion can foster a political puritanism paralleling Calvinistic puritanism.

The problems the new nations encounter as they seek to transform their old societies are unbelievably complex. Americans, deeply grounded in their own culture with its peculiar Calvinist-capitalist-democratic warp, are necessarily biased in their perception of these problems. Typically, the American view is that if the new nations would simply repair their economies, stable political and social orders would automatically follow. Many of the new leaders—who are presumably sensitive to the needs of their societies—view the situation differently. They not only treat economic reform as a secondary problem, but even brutally manhandle their economies. Perhaps they sense that a stable economic, political, and social order cannot be achieved without first establishing a cultural order that wins inner as well as outer commitment of the citizenry. Democracy emerged from the Reformation, and Americans should entertain the possibility at least that from the current ferment may emerge cultural systems that inspire governmental systems different from any we now imagine.

A sketch of the rise of political religion in one new nation— Indonesia—may render these general remarks more meaningful. The sketch will cover the period from 1949, when Indonesia became an independent nation, to 1965, when Sukarno's fall signalled the collapse of political religion in Indonesia.[12]

When Indonesia gained its independence in 1949, Hatta, who was prime minister, was more powerful than Sukarno, who was president. The next few years bore the stamp of Hatta's rational but humdrum rule. The press was free; a constitutional democracy, with a parliament, operated with reasonable effectiveness; courts were not overly entrapped in politics; rice production soared and exports increased; and education expanded enormously at every level.

Unfortunately Hatta's regime could not sustain the loyalty of the people and the political parties. The uncharismatic Hatta, who could not bear the touch of the crowd and who scorned ideology and symbolism, failed to satisfy those who "had come to expect government and politics to provide their personal lives with meaning."[13] For this and other reasons, Hatta lost support, and in 1953 the last pro-Hatta cabinet fell and was replaced by a pro-Sukarno cabinet. Then began an era of revolutionary Indonesian political religion centering on such mythical symbols as Sukarno's Pantjasila, the charter of the Indonesian nation. Unlike Hatta, Sukarno and his colleagues were willing to sacrifice economic prosperity for nationalist-revolutionary spirit and meaning. Thus, to encourage deeper sentiments of national unity, Sukarno "Indonesianized" the economy by replacing important Dutch enterprises with Indonesian ones, a step that caused incredible inflation and serious decline in production.

Economic disruption and political turbulence marked the years from 1953 to 1956. Ideological conflicts, stimulated by intense and bitter electioneering that drew the energy of the parties away from socioeconomic reform, divided the nation. The basic schism was between the Muslims and the Nationalist-Communists. The Muslims, represented by the Masjumi and Nahdatul Ulama parties, were favored by businessmen and by the people of the outer islands (such as Hatta's Sumatra). The Nationalist-Communist faction, represented by the Indonesian Nationalist Party (PNI) and the Indonesian Communist Party (PKI), was favored especially by bureaucrats, workers, and the people of the central island, Java (Sukarno's homeland).

As conflicts worsened and civil war threatened, Sukarno proposed a solution to strife: his concept (*konsepsi*) of Guided Democracy. Guided Democracy, unveiled in 1957, called for the formation of a single cabinet, in which all major parties would cooperate harmoniously, and a national council that would unite the various functional groups— workers, peasants, and national businessmen—through consensus rather than the vote. Sukarno's idea was to abandon the free-for-all democracy of the West, which had led to conflict, and to replace it with a system patterned after the government-by-consensus supposedly practiced in ancient and idyllic Indonesian villages. With the nation in danger of shaking apart, Sukarno's Guided Democracy loomed as the one hope for unity and order. In the late 1950s Sukarno and the army acted to institute Guided Democracy.

Sukarno dissolved the elected parliament and the cabinet responsible to the parliament—agencies that restrained his power—and instituted a 616-member People's Consultive Assembly (which seldom met), appointed a parliament, and set up a cabinet responsible to him alone. He also created a 75-member National Planning Council, a 45-member Supreme Advisory Council, and a National Front Organization enrolling

200 political parties, mass organizations, and functional groups, and encompassing, by 1962, a membership of thirty-three million.

By mid-1958 political parties were "no longer leading actors on the Indonesian stage."[14] By its "guiding actions" the army had banned Communist political meetings, labor union activities, and activities of parties opposing Sukarno. The decline of parties and parliamentary apparatus was accompanied by a marked diminution of civil liberties: Strikes and newspapers were banned and legal guarantees were brushed aside.

Once Guided Democracy was under way, Sukarno turned his attention to political religion as the means of sanctifying the new social order. He made clear that he was not just a politician: He was a prophet attempting to improve "values and standards," to bring about "spiritual changes," and to set in motion a "mental momentum" that would culminate in "spiritual revolution." He claimed to pattern his speeches after the narrations spoken by the *dalang,* priest narrator of the sacred Javanese puppet play, the *wajang.* He developed street-cleaning rites to signify retooling for the future. He portrayed the Constitution of 1945 as a "magically-sentimentally-nationally-loaded" creature that occupies a "throne" and has a "soul and spirit." He verbally transformed mosquito-ridden West New Guinea into a land of paradise to be wrested from Dutch imperialists by lady paratroopers emulating the mythical heroine Srikandi. And he appointed a poet to formulate a plan for economic development, which, when completed, consisted of eight major sections, each composed of seventeen subsections, to symbolize the August 17 birthdate of Indonesia. Sukarno enthusiastically praised the plan for its "symbolic richness."

The central ideology of Guided Democracy was Manipol-Usdek. Manipol-Usdek, an acronymn coined by Sukarno and his associates, stood for several exalted objectives: to attain, the Sukarno's phrases, the "Just and Prosperous" society organized under "Socialism à la Indonesia," financed by "Guided Economy," in keeping with "The Indonesian Personality." Taught in schools, preached by newspapers, and propagated by song and dance, billboards, shanty-town gates, and movie commercials, Manipol-Usdek was supposed to elicit absolute loyalty. Editors, professors, and other intellectuals were made to swear allegiance to it. Civil servants who did not display sufficient allegiance were "retooled," i.e., demoted or dismissed, and their successors were made aware that their positions depended on active loyalty to the current political leadership and to Manipol-Usdek.

The symbolism of political religion always appeals to youth, and in Indonesia youth was both the target and the source of such symbolism. Sukarno preached that Indonesia began with a nationalist declaration by the Congress of Indonesian Youth in 1928, and that the Indonesian nation itself was a youth. Passing through a "transition period" like that of "puberty," Indonesia was trying to show the "whole world that . . . we are a nation of men with the spirit of a bull" and at the same time that it had to "search for and attain our own identity."[15] Like Indonesia, Sukarno himself took on the imagery of youth; he often preferred to be called not "father" (*bapak*), in accordance with traditional custom, but rather "peer" (*bung*), in accordance with his role of symbolic youth within the gang of actual and symbolic youths of which he was the leader. Nor was youth imagery restricted to Sukarno's speeches and labels. Important streets and buildings bore the names "Youth Street" and "Youth Hall," and youths were prominent in congresses, cleanups, and other public actions. Indeed, the youth possessed real power since each major political party had its youth wing—that of the Communist party being the only Communist appendage directly financed by the central committee.

Although Indonesian political religion did inspire dynamism and creativity, it was carried to such a point that it interfered with practical economics and government. Government money was diverted from practical tasks into the purchase and construction of such prestige symbols as bombers, destroyers, missiles, nuclear generators, giant stadiums, luxury hotels, and the National Monument. More important, political religion sanctified the rule of symbol wielders, such as Sukarno, rather than rational administrators, such as Hatta. At all levels of Indonesian government, positions were awarded in recognition of charisma and fervor rather than of technical qualifications. Even those rational administrators who retained their positions found it difficult to bring about practical reforms because practical reforms possessed little merit under the ideologies of the day.

With the decline in rational administration came hardship and corruption. As prices tripled yearly and government salaries did not rise to match, bureaucrats saw themselves obliged to make ends meet by stealing and accepting bribes. Even though salaries within the bureaucracy decreased in buying power, the political power of the bureaucracy rose sharply owing to the decline in power of business groups. The banning of the Muslim "business" party removed the one major nonbureaucratic group that heretofore had counterbalanced the authority of the bureaucracy. By the 1960s, bureaucracy had become a law unto itself, and politics had become simply bureaucracy bolstered by political religion.

Certain parallels can be seen between Indonesian political religion and European-American Protestantism, that is, between Sukarnoism and Calvinism. Both undercut hierarchy. Calvinism erased the hierarchies that extended from man to God. Sukarnoism collapsed those that, in traditional lowland Southeast Asia, had extended from peasant to god-king. Sukarno's assumption of the role of peer (*bung*) instead of father (*bapak*) symbolized this transformation, as did the replacement of the Javanese language with a new national language, Indonesian, which was egalitarian in that it dispensed with the Javanese rule of employing special vocabularies when speaking to persons of high rank. Indeed, although Sukarno's Guided Democracy accented "guidance" more than "democracy," even this development signified a rejection of the hierarchical order in favor of a vision of communal equality. Guided Democracy conceived of Indonesian society not as an archaic hierarchy but as an incredibly complex system of cross-cutting voluntary groups— congresses, parliaments, parties, movements—united by loose consensus. Guided Democracy differed from early-modern democracies of the West in that the various groups had only limited power to challenge the state. The Indonesian bureaucracy, encompassing all interest groups, was a law unto itself rather than an instrument of commerce, science, education, or the pursuit of happiness.

Calvinism inspired free enterprise, in many senses: Business for business's sake, science for science's sake, and art for art's sake were encouraged by Calvinism and early-modern society. Work of any kind was good, production of any kind was good. "What's worth doing is worth doing well" was a guiding motto, and "What can be done well is worth doing" was a basic value. To the pious Calvinists, such work was directed toward God's glory; few felt strongly that it should be harnessed to the glory of the state. Sukarnoism, on the other hand, nourished the attitude that business for business's sake or science for science's sake was not sufficient. It behooved the businessman or scientist to demonstrate at all times that his enterprise served Sukarno, and frequently such a demonstration of loyalty took precedence over or interfered with the enterprise itself. Perhaps the danger of interference with accomplishment is greater when the object of ultimate loyalty is a real person than when it is a spiritual symbol, whose requirements, according to some points of view, can be tailored by the believers to fit their desires. In Calvinism demonstration of spiritual loyalties could be scheduled at the convenience of the worker, whereas in a political religion such demonstration is decreed by an earthly leader.

A system such as Sukarno's Guided Democracy is obviously more immanent in the state and the world than is God's Kingdom. Therefore, political and economic chaos, corruption and stagnation, could and did tarnish the image of Guided Democracy, and Indonesians became disillusioned not only with the worldly reality but with the utopian image as well. By contrast, the image of God's Kingdom retained its purity however terrible earthly conditions became, and wickedness in the state and in the world only intensified the Calvinist's resolve to fulfill his calling and build God's Kingdom on earth. Nor could any man prove that God's Kingdom was impure, for no man had been there and returned to report. Calvinism thus possessed certain psychological advantages over Sukarnoism. Undoubtedly, some of the problems of Indonesia and Sukarnoism are rooted in the psychological contradictions that are intrinsic to political religion.

Overview

Archaic religion was monistic, historic religion dualistic. Archaic man conceived of one world, inhabited by both gods and men. Historic man envisioned two worlds: an otherworldly realm of the gods (or other ultimate entites) and a this-worldly realm of men. Linking the historic otherword and the real world were symbolic-social hierarchies, which, because of their sacred aura, historic man was disposed neither to view objectively nor to change.

Calvinism, the prototype of early-modern religion, swept away the hierarchies. With Calvinism, the real world and the otherworld were linked only through the faith and commitment of individuals. The real world, wicked and devoid of sanctity, was regarded as a chaotic jungle through which moved committed individuals guided by purposes and plans issued from the otherworld. No longer sacred, the real world could be viewed and criticized from the perspective of these divine purposes and plans. Should The Divine call for worldly change, the world would be *changed*. Since Calvinism denied the efficacy of ritual, such change could come about only through the rational action of active work and reform.

Historic society was significantly more universalistic than primitive or archaic societies, for in historic society at least most *religious* statuses could be achieved by all men, regardless of their status at birth. But in nonreligious sectors, even in historic society, particularism was still the rule. Thus, the feudal system of Europe, rooted in such images as the Great Chain of Being and the Organic Analogy, decreed that every man should stay in his inherited place. The destruction of feudal particularism was in part the work of Calvinism, which denied any earthly power or authority the right to dictate what status an individual should occupy. For Calvinists, the individual's rank was determined solely through his covenant with God.

Calvinism regarded the relationship between God and the individual as a contract voluntarily made by each party. This contractual pattern spread from the religious to the secular realm and became dominant in early-modern life. No longer did the individual accept without question his inherited and fixed bond to another; he was expected actively to seek contractual relations. Even marriage became a contract. The kinsmen of the marrying couple, who were not party to the contract, were not bound to each other by the marriage. The extended network of kinship was weakened, therefore, and concern shifted from extended kinship to the nuclear family and to the marriage tie itself.

Early-modern society is composed of myriad voluntary groups to which each individual relates contractually. Each person's relation to a group is functionally specific rather than diffuse. Each group asks its members to perform roles which, being specialized, exploit only a part of each member's personality; that is, each member spreads his personality among a number of specialized roles. Conflict among such roles inevitably arises. Being a worker gets in the way of being a father, being a Democrat interferes with being an industrialist, being a Quaker with being a soldier. The task of integrating conflicting, specialized roles into an organized self is greater for the early-modern personality than for the archaic or primitive personalities.

Primitive society was one-class, archaic society two-class, and historic society was structured around a hierarchy of three classes. Calvinism undermined this class structure. Where Calvinism became dominant, kingship, aristocracy, and class hierarchy were either eroded or destroyed and replaced by a flexible, multicentered pattern of cross-cutting voluntary groups. In early-modern society, firms, factories, unions, parties, and associations all compete for a share of power, and no single authority, such as church or state, monopolizes all power. Bureaucratization, mass media, and giant national parties are among the mechanisms that have emerged to centralize the diversified voluntary groups of early-modern society.

The very complexity of early-modern society stimulates change, for conflicts and strains among diversified interest groups inevitably result in change. A thrust toward change is also part of early-modern *culture*. Early-modern culture, derived from Calvinism, denied the sacredness of the world and affirms the need to reform the world in order that it may approach the transcendent model of the Kingdom of God. Because the discrepancy between the model and the reality is unceasing, the individual feels incessantly driven to change the reality. Although the majority of early-modern men no longer recognize the specifically religious substance of this pattern, its secular manifestations remain strong. Built into the very core of ideologies governing early-modern law, government, education, science, business, social welfare, and community life is the notion that reforming reality to match transcendental models is necessary and desirable. The resulting drive to change makes early-modern society a self-revising system. Regardless of outside stimulation, its inner dynamic sustains an incessant process of change. In this, it is more "modern" than primitive, archaic, or historic society.

Since we have treated early-modern society and culture as products of the Protestant Reformation and especially of Calvinism, it is not surprising that America and Western Europe should be viewed as prototypes of early-modern society and culture. Tendencies toward early-modern society have appeared sporadically in Buddhist and Muslim cultures; only in the West, however, was the early-modern pattern successfully instituted in a total society.

Japan, which has established certain early-modern socioeconomic institutions while at the same time managing to retain an archaic cultural base, contrasts instructively with India. In elite spheres of Hinduism, India displayed a movement toward historic religion (some might even say, toward modern religion), but these ideas did not penetrate deeply and widely enough to transform India from an essentially archaic society. Japan, on the other hand, exploited its archaic god-king religion in such a way as to industrialize and nationalize with great speed, but these changes in the socioeconomic order did not suffice to transform Japanese culture from its archaic form.

Indonesia and other new nations face problems that are, in one respect, more like those of the medieval West than they are like those of Japan. Just as the West underwent a radical religious reformation before it successfully modernized its society and economy, so the new nations are undergoing radical cultural transformations, which are apparently necessary for successful socioeconomic modernization to occur. Cultural reformations in the new nations are led by charismatic prophets, such as Sukarno, who strive to create political religions. Political religion seeks to capture the loyalty of its citizens, to free them from traditional identities, and to provide a new sense of purpose. It aims to provide a moral basis for transforming and modernizing a nonmodern society in order to create a system better adapted to the contemporary world. Although political religions are of fundamental importance in the struggle of the new nations, they do create contradictions and problems. As was suggested in the analysis of Indonesia, political religions tend to create disillusionment to a greater degree than conventional religions such as Calvinism. Nevertheless, they have an increasingly valuable function, for with the decline of supernaturalism throughout the world, conventional religion is becoming less and less capable of serving as a framework for modernization. Political religion is the first postsupernaturalist attempt at sanctifying and rendering meaningful the process of modernization.

Topics for Discussion

This chapter has suggested a number of areas for further exploration of the Weber thesis. For example, the student might consider more fully the impact of the total Reformation movement on the development of early-modern Western society. The root causes of the Reformation itself might be considered. Did some radical disjunction between the way medieval men conceived of their society and their actual experience of that society goad them to change their religious views and ultimately their society? The success of Japan in grafting early-modern patterns on a basically archaic foundation poses further questions. Was the success of Japan a unique occurrence, the result of its peculiar value system? Or can the Japanese accomplishment provide a model for other societies undergoing modernization? In contemporary Japan the rise of a number of new religions is causing considerable religious ferment. Are these new religions modifying the Japanese value system to accord better with the conditions of an industrialized society? More generally, why are religious or quasi-religious movements (the political religions are an example) so common during periods of great social upheaval and change? Exploring this question, the student may discover significant facts about human existence and character.

It is also interesting to consider the relative advantages and disadvantages of the Protestant Ethic pattern and of other sociocultural patterns that man has evolved. For example, how do primitive religion and some of the early-modern substitutes for conventional religion, such as political religion, compare with the Protestant Ethic in their consequences for human stability, productivity, creativity, and happiness? The student might try to design a substitute for the Protestant Ethic which would satisfy the conditions of today, yet provide the same psychological and social benefits that the Protestant Ethic apparently provided in the past.

Suggested Readings

The Protestant Ethic

The Protestant Ethic and the Spirit of Capitalism (paperback, 1958) by Max Weber. The basic source for this chapter.

The Structure of Social Action (paperback, 1968) by Talcott Parsons. Part III provides an excellent summary and evaluation of the Weber thesis.

Max Weber: An Intellectual Portrait (paperback, 1962) by Reinhard Bendix. Part II supplies a first-rate summary and evaluation of the Weber thesis.

Religion and the Rise of Capitalism: A Historical Study (paperback, 1961) by Richard Tawney. Expands the historical basis of the Weber thesis.

The Protestant Ethic and Modernization: A Comparative View (paperback, 1968) edited by S. N. Eisenstadt. Extends Weberian analysis into new areas outside the West.

The Religious Factor: A Sociological Study of Religion's Impact on Politics, Economics, and Family Life (paperback, 1963) by Gerhard Lenski. A careful test and extension of the Weber thesis in an American city.

Protestantism and Capitalism: The Weber Thesis and Its Critics (paperback, 1959) edited by Robert Green.

Religion and Economic Action: A Critique of Max Weber (paperback, 1961) by Kurt Samuelsson. A suggestive if misguided critique.

"Puritanism, Pietism, and Science" in *Social Theory and Social Structure* (1957) by Robert Merton. Shows the implications of Calvinism for science.

The Revolution of the Saints: A Study in the Origins of Radical Politics (paperback, 1968) by Michael Walzer. Shows the implications of Calvinism for politics. Chapter 5 provides a more detailed discussion of medieval imagery from the perspective of the Weber thesis than is given in our text.

"Mystics and Merchants in Fourteenth Century Germany" (1969) by James L. Peacock. Amplification of our discussion of medieval imagery from the perspective of the Weber thesis.

Modernization in China and Japan

Tokugawa Religion: The Values of Pre-Industrial Japan (1957) by Robert Bellah. On the cultural basis of the industrialization of Japan.

"Contrasting Factors in the Modernization of China and Japan" (1953) by Marion J. Levy, Jr.

"Some Aspects of 'Individualism' and the Problem of Modernization in China and Japan" (1962) by Marion J. Levy, Jr.

"Reflections on the Protestant Ethic Analogy in Asia" (1963) by Robert Bellah.

Political Religion and the New Nations

The Politics of Modernization (paperback, 1965) by David Apter.

Old Societies and New States (1963) edited by Clifford Geertz.

The Ideologies of the Developing Nations (paperback, 1963) by Paul E. Sigmund.

"The Ideologies of Delayed Industrialization: Some Tensions and Ambiguities" (1962) by Mary Matossian.

Indonesia

"The Dynamics of Guided Democracy" (1963) by Herbert Feith. On Indonesia as a new nation embracing political religion.

Indonesia (1963) edited by Ruth T. McVey. Provides general background on Indonesia. Chapters are available separately in paperback.

The Religion of Java (paperback, 1964) by Clifford Geertz. A basic book on Java, the largest ethnic group in Indonesia and the dominant source of its political religion.

Rites of Modernization: Symbolic and Social Aspects of Indonesian Proletarian Drama (1968) by James L. Peacock. An analysis of Indonesian modernization as experienced via certain symbols by a particular group.

chapter 9

America: An Emerging Modern Society and Culture

Carrying forward the thrust of the argument in the last chapter, this chapter will sketch the penetration of early-modern patterns into American life and the movement beyond the early-modern, which America is now experiencing. The focus on America is certainly not meant to imply that the latest sociocultural advances are to be found only, or even primarily, in America. Full analysis would certainly include the total world system, of which American trends are a part. Nevertheless, since American trends are among those influential in the world, understanding of America will contribute significantly to understanding of other parts of the world. More important, for the purposes of this book America is the proper system on which to center the *American* reader's attention at the end of a far-ranging survey. Now that he has progressed through various alien patterns, with opportunities for comparison, he should be prepared to perceive America in a more distant and objective fashion.

Extension of the anthropological perspective to include the anthropologist's own society is neither new nor unusual. Anthropologists have dissected American communities (e.g., Hortense Powdermaker, *After Freedom: A Cultural Study in the Deep South*); they have emulated sociologists in analyzing American class structure and popular culture (e.g., Lloyd Warner, *American Life: Dream and Reality*); they have developed distinctive perspectives on certain American subcultures (e.g., James Spradley, *You Owe Yourself a Drunk*); and they have even attempted sweeping assessments of the American character (e.g., Margaret Mead, *And Keep Your Powder Dry;* and Geoffrey Gorer, *The American People: A Study in National Character*). Of course, the anthropologist is not the only one who has trained his sights on American society. The anthropologist who analyzes America can consult the writings of journalists, essayists, social critics, social scientists, and others concerned with the contemporary scene. Indeed, since the focus of this chapter is on emerging trends rather than on the enduring patterns that have most attracted anthropological attention, we shall rely more on those social prophets who undertake to fathom emerging trends than on the anthropologists themselves.

Shaping a New Society

A new society emerged from the religious reformation and political revolution of sixteenth- and seventeenth-century Europe. Freed from explicit ties to conventional religion, this new society could, despite its origins in religious reformation, be characterized as *secular*. Politically it might be deemed *nationalistic,* for it was based on the nation-state that had replaced the narrower feudal forms. Thanks to its great technological and economic advance, it was *industrial*. Because its population had shifted to the cities, and its cities had become the center of affairs, it was *urban*. And since its various segments and processes were bound together by large-scale, rationally and universalistically based organizations, it was certainly *bureaucratic*.

In Europe the shaping of the new society was influenced by the existing old forms. Monarchical traditions, institutions of nobility, craft and guild organizations, and local rivalries remained to alter and mask the emerging structure. In America, on the other hand, the new patterns emerged with special clarity because the old forms were absent and because many of those who helped found America were radical dissenters from the old European society who had deliberately repudiated the traditional order and who consciously sought to establish a new society in a new land.

From the beginning, American society deviated from the feudal and postfeudal pattern of Europe. Although aristocratic ideas crossed the Atlantic to the South and to portions of New England, values emphasizing equality of opportunity and of rights were more widely held. Hereditary elite groups, whether religious, political, or economic, were viewed with suspicion. This egalitarianism did not, of course, deny that there were significant differences in social status among men, but it denied that those awarded by birth and inheritance were binding and immutable. Each man had the opportunity to demonstrate by deeds his claims to status and power.

The idea that the right to govern depended on the voluntary consent of the governed, a concept similar to the Puritan notion of the covenant, had a strong influence on American politics. An obvious extension of this idea was the belief that the will of the majority should prevail. These democratic convictions opened effective channels for changing the government without destroying it, thereby encouraging a politics of persuasion and consensus instead of force and tyranny. The Puritan base of democratic concepts is clearest in New England, where such democratic institutions as the town meeting flourished. The town meeting, which fostered a sense of individual participation and of collective morality, was in many respects a secular form of the Puritan congregation.

As the nation expanded westward and the population grew, government too expanded at every level. Its function, however, remained restricted. Government was regarded as merely a facilitating service to smooth the functioning of community, school, and court in a but recent wilderness. In marked contrast to Europe, few in America expected or desired government to penetrate deeply into daily life or dictate the direction of social development. Only after the industrialization of America had progressed quite far was government seen not only as a facilitating service, but also as a protector of a collective public interest which might overrule certain private interests.

Despite the eventual commercial importance of a few ports such as Boston, New York, and New Orleans, the early American economy was even more predominantly agricultural than was the European economy. Initially, then, Europe, with its extensive commercial network and a nascent industrial system originating in medieval times, had a more complex economy than did early America. America, however, did not have the disadvantages of traditional structures to inhibit the development of new and progressive industries, and in agriculture, too, innovation was easier in America than in Europe. In Europe, the development of large-scale commercial agriculture was hampered by the necessity of destroying feudal enclosures or relocating tenants in order to consolidate lands. In America, especially in the South, great plantations could be carved out of a virgin wilderness. The result was that large-scale farming, geared to production of commercial crops and raw materials for European industries, flourished in America.

Subsistence, as well as commercial, agriculture took on a distinctly American pattern. In Europe, farmers lived clustered together in villages, going forth each day to cultivate the surrounding fields. Although they were no longer serfs, they *were* peasants, bound to their land and locale. Each generation succeeded the previous one, with little expectation of either geographic or social mobility. In America, however, the farmer typically lived in an isolated farmhouse set in the midst of wide fields—a pattern of living which both reflected and encouraged American individualism. The American farmer did not feel bound to a particular locale. The pioneer could not have pulled up stakes and gone West to tame vast frontiers had he been hobbled by the traditional values of the European peasant. The mastery of successive frontiers became itself a potent influence on American culture and character, and the "frontier ethos" came to pervade all realms of American life.

Although America remained predominantly agricultural during the taming of the frontier, the expanding needs of the spreading populace also stimulated extensive industrial growth. Textile mills, wagon factories, and other industries sprang up, aided by the emergence of centers of commerce and trade routes along strategic rivers and roads as well as on the coasts. To a degree, the regions specialized—the South in production of agricultural raw materials for Northeastern industries, the West in food production and mining. With the growth of regional specialization and the expansion of commercial, communications, and transportation networks linking the various areas, the tendency to centralization increased, with resultant economic ramifications. The building of railroads, for example, encouraged the development of heavy industries and mining to supply rolling stock, rails, and coal. And since the railroads were left in the hands of private entrepreneurs, these entrepreneurs were forced to abandon the traditional family firm and partnership modes of organization and create corporations in order to cope with the complexities of coast-to-coast transportation systems. Thus, big business grew, and big government was encouraged to grow as well to serve as counterbalance and mediator.

The remarkable growth in American productivity is indicated by measures of *work output*. In 1850, work output per person per year was an estimated 435 horsepower hours—a figure not much in excess of that of the average agrarian-historic society. By 1950, the figure was an estimated 4,470 horsepower hours, with the increase coming primarily from innovations in technology which tapped new sources of energy. In 1850, 65 percent of the energy consumed by work in the United States was supplied by men and animals, another 28 percent by wind, water, and wood. A century later, these traditional agrarian-historic sources of energy supplied only 1.5 percent of the energy; the remainder came from the fossil fuels (e.g., coal, oil) and hydroelectric power. The new sources of energy increased productivity in the established industries and stimulated the creation of new industries, such as mining and petrochemicals.[1] In a recent phase, ecologically destructive effects of such industrialization have been recognized, and the ecologically-minded have sought energy sources and productive techniques that are less destructive of the environment.

A general cultural theme that helps account for the statistics is the American readiness to *innovate* in technology. It is striking that, unlike Europe, America chose for its folk heroes inventors as frequently as it did political or military leaders. Eli Whitney, Cyrus McCormick, Thomas Edison, George Washington Carver, and Henry Ford are some of the better known examples. The American values emphasizing individual achievement and constant change are apparent in this phenomenon.

With economic growth and industrialization came, of course, population growth (attributable, in part, to the massive influx of migrants, whose assimilation was facilitated by American universalism and emphasis on individual achievement). Even more dramatic, however, was the shift in the distribution of population. Early America conformed to the typical agrarian-historic pattern, with 90 percent of the populace living in the country and only 10 percent in the cities. By 1960, however, only 30 percent of the American population lived in rural areas. The shift was made possible through the growth of urban industry and the mechanization of farming. With greatly increased agricultural productivity, a few farmers could produce enough for hordes of urbanites. By 1962, only 9 percent of the American labor force was engaged in agriculture, yet great surpluses were still produced. With the mechanization of agriculture, the family farm tended to be replaced by the large commercial farm—the rural counterpart of the urban factory. The demise of the family farm and the movement of rural people (often the farmer's children) to the cities meant that "the whole fabric of rural and small town social organization was disappearing throughout the rural Midwest, West, and South."[2]

Most of the early urban population growth was in the city proper. In recent years, however, much urban growth has really been suburban. Bedroom suburbs on the outskirts of the city have flourished, and with these, the commuter syndrome. In fact, many have left the largest, most problem-plagued cities altogether, fleeing to smaller cities or even to the land. In the city itself, formerly respectable downtown neighborhoods have deteriorated into dingy ghettos as rural migrants and ethnic or racial minorities came to dominate the city's core. The great downtown mansions have been transformed into museums, offices, and headquarters for foundations.

The flight from the center city to residential suburbs has been paralleled by a movement of business to industrial exurbs. Even the *Wall Street Journal,* whose very name indicates its urban affiliation, has moved its major offices to the New Jersey countryside. Major arteries encircling the city or leading directly to its heart are now preferred locations for industries wishing to avoid urban congestion (for example, Route 128 in Boston is a favored site for electronics and other light industries). Still more exurban are the industrial park complexes that attract industries into the virtual wilderness (an example is the Research Triangle of Raleigh-Durham-Chapel Hill, North Carolina).

The movement of population and business away from the center city might suggest at first that America is becoming decentralized, rather than increasingly centralized as the modernization theory would predict. Actually, the movement outward from the center, instead of allowing the former urbanites to escape from centralization, is serving to integrate the countryside into the centralized society. Indeed, the ruralization of business and living has required and stimulated the development of complex systems of transportation and communication. Increasingly complex highways, telephone systems, radio, television, high-speed trains, airports, traffic planning and control have made possible the shift to the country, and at the same time have widened the network linking the country to the urban centers.

America's shift from agrarian-rural to industrial-urban (suburban) patterning produced significant changes in the patterning of social relations, especially relations of family and kinship. In the days of the family farm, the family was typically an economic as well as a kinship and residential unit. The rural family was like a small corporation, a family firm, whose task was to run the farm. The family was large and often consisted of several generations, with still more relations living nearby. Producing its own food, it was self-sufficient and ruggedly independent, yet it could rely on nearby relatives and neighbors for special occasions: harvest time, a house-raising, a birth or death, a financial crisis. Local affairs dominated its attention, and except during elections or wars, the nation and the world were far removed from the family farm.

With increasing industrialization, the members of the rural family were drawn away from the farm to work for industries in the cities. In the industrial-urban family, the father's role became sharply segregated into occupational and familial components—the former associated with the factory or office, the latter with the home—in contrast to the family-farm pattern, where the two components are fused. The industrial-urban family is smaller, its generational depth shallower, since parents, grandparents, uncles, aunts, and other kinsmen are left behind or scattered far and wide. It is cut off from the nexus of neighbors and relatives on whom the farm family can depend in time of crisis. Although such nexus are to a degree replaced by ethnic neighborhoods and urban kinfolk, the general trend is that the urban family turns to impersonal, large-scale, bureaucratic organization—public welfare agencies, finance companies, hospitals, and banks. Because these bureaucratic agencies are closely bound to supralocal affairs, the family's interests naturally move away from the local toward the national and international.

The farm child of early America could expect to live a life rather similar to that of his parents; like his father, the son would also be a farmer, and he would live in the same or a similar rural locale. Parents could, therefore, serve as direct models of what the children would grow up to be. At an early age, children began learning to be like their parents, by milking the cow, feeding the chickens, and plowing the fields. Formal schooling was often limited to the learning of the three R's in traditional one-room schoolhouse. Parents had few doubts on how to raise their children to fit them for adult life. They were raised "naturally" to emulate their parents.

Very different is the situation in industrial society. Since the father is away at his job and the child is away at school, the father is not immediately available as a model for emulation. Both the occupational and the educational systems thus decrease the opportunity for parents to serve as role models for their children. Parental role models become less relevant anyway, since industrial society changes so rapidly that children are unlikely to follow in their parents' footsteps, hence find it unprofitable to emulate their parents. With the decline in the role-model function of parents, schools and other bureaucratic organizations become increasingly important in preparing children for adult roles.

As their child-rearing responsibilities decrease, parents, paradoxically, become increasingly anxious about whatever responsibilities they do have. In the absence of traditional guides to child-rearing, they turn to Doctor Spock and to faddish "scientific" programs for instruction in proper "socialization." Since parents can teach the child little of vocational importance, they concentrate on that area where they can still have impact—the formation of the child's personality. Attempting to treat this delicate and subtle process scientifically, however, transforms the character of the parent-child bond. The child's progress is measured against norms established statistically by researchers. Instead of the myths of Santa Claus and the Easter bunny, the child must be taught scientific "facts" to prepare him for "real life." Now the parent is advised not to say simply, "Do this," and expect the child to do it, but to provide technical (rather than formal or traditional) explanations so that the child understands why he should do as he is told.*

American society has become increasingly centralized owing to the development of large-scale bureaucratic organizations, which serve to coordinate the increasingly differentiated and specialized units that compose the society. American Telephone and Telegraph employs more than the half million people employed in the imperial bureaucracy of archaic China, and it is simply one gigantic example of the organizations essential for the operation of a complex industrial society. In government, the Department of Health, Education and Welfare reportedly spends daily half a billion dollars—certainly equal to the annual budget of many traditional societies. Mass organization and bureaucratization exist and are apparently necessary in virtually all spheres of industrial society—politics, religion, education, medicine, science, and the arts.

Bureaucracies are able to integrate and coordinate great populations and differentiated activities by clearly delineating specialized duties and specific lines of authority. It is this mode of organization, designed to insure efficient functioning, that endows bureaucracies with a distinctive structure. Bureaucracies are composed of three strata: a small elite of professional managers; a larger group of white-collar workers and middle managers; and the mass of skilled, semiskilled, and unskilled workers. Although the standards of recruitment and reward vary, they tend to be universalistic for all strata of bureaucracy, reflecting the American emphasis on individual achievement. Thus, new recruits are expected to show evidence of either training or proved or potential competence for their specific duties, while promotion depends on output, creativity, dependability, and, of course, gamesmanship.

The development of bureaucracy is not, of course, unique to America or even to industrial-modern society. What *is* unique to America is the degree to which bureaucracy has penetrated all levels and spheres of life. America has also uniquely contributed to a particular form of bureaucracy—the industrial form. The distinctly American development of mass-production industrial organization, linked with the name Henry Ford,† is essentially the application of bureaucratic principles to the productive process.

*One reflection of this technical approach to child rearing is the "conditional love" pattern reported by various American analysts (e.g., Geoffrey Gorer, *The American People*, p. 174). Instead of loving their children unconditionally (formally, particularistically)—that is, simply because they are their children—American parents tend to love them conditionally (technically, universalistically)—responding affectionately to them only when they achieve designated goals.

†Ford's achievement, of course, built on earlier American developments, such as Eli Whitney's remarkable advances in creating interchangeable and standardized parts for machinery (see Jeannette Mirsky and Allan Nevins, *The World of Eli Whitney*).

Another distinctively American bureaucratic form is the labor union exclusively concerned with the material condition of the worker. Unlike European workers, American workers have never become a separate political faction; there is no labor party in the United States, and although union leaders commonly endorse one party or another, the ability of union leaders to deliver the votes has never been demonstrated. In striving for the worker's economic betterment, however, the American unions have had notable results. The American worker's wages rose more than fourfold between 1871 and 1944, and 300 percent between 1939 and 1959 despite shortened work weeks.

With bureaucratization, formal education has become increasingly important in America. Modern bureaucracy calls for literacy: Workers must be able to read the instructions, manuals, and memos that serve as the instruments of bureaucratic functioning. Bureaucratic specialization of tasks calls for highly specialized training, whether on the production line or in research and design. Personnel offices, faced with huge numbers of applicants for jobs, depend on such standardized ways of assessing competence as diplomas or degrees. Thus, schools and other educational agencies have been called upon to fill the distinctive needs of a complex, industrialized, bureaucratic society. And American education has flourished. More than 90 percent of all American children, aged seven to thirteen, attend school; and 18 percent of college-age youths attend college. (America produces a higher percentage of college graduates than any other nation.) American universities, however, now face serious problems derived from the very trends that encouraged their development. Like other institutions of American life, American universities have become increasingly bureaucratized in order to accomplish the increasingly complex tasks that the bureaucratized society has demanded of them. This bureaucratization has bred an impersonality that contributes to students' feelings of alienation and discontent. Coupled with employment difficulties and accelerating costs of college, this bureaucratization renders problematical traditional models of liberal arts education.

Schools provide more than training in specialized technical skills and knowledge. The school is a microcosm of the larger society, and it helps to instill in the young the larger society's central values, attitudes, and orientations. Thus, the American school inculcates values underlying bureaucratic, industrial America. The school separates the child from the family unit, just as the American factory or office does the adult. Like other bureaucracies, the school is organized along clear-cut lines of authority and responsibility. The school divides time and work into differentiated and specialized periods and courses. It teaches that the individual is responsible for his own work and that achievement is differentially rewarded according to universalistic standards. In these and other ways, the school teaches values of universalism, specialization, and achievement that the modern American must assimilate in order to function successfully in virtually all of his society's statuses and jobs.

The increasing bureaucratization of America has aroused concern among many observers. One of the most provocative of these remains C. Wright Mills, who expresses the view that the major leaders of American bureaucracy, i.e., big businessmen, politicians, and the military, have united to form a single, tyrannical "power elite."[3] From their strategic "command posts," the power elite make the crucial decisions that determine the direction of American life, and remain uninfluenced by the mass democratic process. Indeed, the democratic games of the masses, such as elections, serve the interests of the power elite: They keep the people at play in the yard while the decisions are made upstairs.

Although the power elite exercise their control through bureaucracy, Mills feels that they gained that control through ownership of wealth and property. They are the very rich Americans whose wealth has grown disproportionately by comparison with the earnings of their countrymen. Mills is alarmed by this situation because he believes that the great wealth of the elite effectively frees them from legal or governmental constraints. They are free to act irresponsibly in pursuing power.

Mills associates the rise of the power elite with the decline of an independent middle class whose economic and political security were anchored in small, local businesses and properties. He estimates that small businessmen and entrepreneurs today form only 40 percent of the entire American middle class (20 percent of the labor force as a whole). They have been replaced by the Organization Man, the white-collar bureaucrat, who, unfortunately, enjoys no independence from the bureaucracies controlled by the power elite because he is employed by them and, therefore, cannot effectively oppose their policies. According to Mills, the faithful remnant of the independent entrepreneurial-business group is carrying on constant battle against the ever-increasing centralization and control of the bureaucracies and the power elite, but their efforts are vain.

Mills's theory is of special interest because it resembles those of left-wing and right-wing radicals, both of whom believe that a governmental-industrial-military complex exercises tyrannical power over the rest of the country. The issue is worth serious discussion, and a few statistics and analytical remarks may serve as a beginning.

In the United States, the number of independent entrepreneurs (men owning and operating their own business) dropped from 11.4 percent of the labor force in 1870 to 6 percent in 1954. Even more significant, the relative power of this group has declined drastically, as is demonstrated by a study of the nation's 200 largest corporations, which control nearly half of its corporate wealth.[4] The study shows that 44 percent of these companies are now controlled or directed by hired managers rather than by their owners. Ownership of the corporations has become more broadly based through the issuance of stocks; and professional managers, rather than stockholders, make the decisions. Other studies reveal that, increasingly, hired managers, rather than the children of owners or founders, run the firms. Ownership and managership of corporations tend to be separate, with the independent entrepreneur who is both owner and manager becoming a rarity. The trend is made more complex, however, by the practice, among high-ranking managers, of obtaining stock options which give them partial ownership of the firms that employ them.

Regardless of how little stock they may own, professional managers wield great power. They can, for instance, set their own salaries. Not surprisingly, these are very high, especially when compared to the salaries paid to men with comparable education and ability employed in nonbusiness spheres. Some top American executives reportedly receive salaries of over one million dollars per year, and salaries of over $100,000 per year are common. These highly advantaged managers seem to be replacing some of the big business owners in the ranks of Mills's power elite. Perhaps a symptom of this trend is the tendency for high government offices to be awarded to elite managers, whereas formerly they went to big business owners. Charles Wilson, former president of General Motors Corporation, became President Eisenhower's Secretary of Defense; more recently, Robert McNamara, former president of Ford Motor Company, held the same post under Presidents Kennedy and Johnson, and Carter appointees Blumenthal and Miller held high corporation posts. This may signal a tendency toward more universalism in recruiting members of the power elite, since hired managers are more likely to reach the top through ability than are individuals who simply inherit ownership. At the same time, according to one study, approximately 50 percent of the managers themselves come from the propertied or wealthy class.

Membership in the political elite may also be financially rewarding. A study of twenty American city "bosses" carried out a generation ago showed that, although none came from wealthy families, at least nine left estates valued at a million dollars or more, and only three had failed to accumulate a substantial fortune. To take an example at a higher level: President Johnson, though a politician and not a businessman most of his life, managed to amass approximately nine million dollars by 1964.

Such wealth is not ordinarily acquired by chicanery or corruption; perfectly legal opportunities to accumulate wealth are afforded by political office. In recent years, however, these opportunities have declined, owing to the increasing bureaucratization of government and the civil service. As recruiting and operating procedures have been depersonalized, opportunities for politicians to turn personal power into profit have decreased. A great deal of power has moved from the politicians to the bureaucrats. Just as the managerial elite—the business bureaucrats—are replacing Mills's entrepreneurs, so are government bureaucrats tending to replace politicians with the power elite.

What of the military, the third faction of the power elite? Has the almost continuous military crisis of current times placed great power in the hands of the military? The answer is, of course, yes, but it must be recognized that the military have exercised marked restraint in certain areas. By contrast to most new nations, America has experienced neither military coups nor blatant corruption by the military. This is especially striking in view of their remarkably low salaries, which are more comparable to educators than to business executives. These facts suggest that the picture of the military as exclusively power hungry is exaggerated.

Certainly the bureaucratic-managerial elite do command great power, and Mills is correct in pointing to the potential dangers of tyranny. On the other hand, Mills underemphasizes both internal and external restraints on the power of this elite. It is not naive and Pollyannaish to assume that the religious and ideological traditions that have shaped American culture have exercised some influence on the consciences of the elite, causing them to restrain at least some of their lust for power in deference to the rights of the majority. It must also be kept in mind that the military, the government, and big business are not a single organization, but a cluster of many, each with its own interests. Competition among diverse interests is bound to check and balance the selfish interests of any single organization. Finally, although the power elite doubtless are to a degree a chummy clique of kinsmen and former Ivy League classmates, universalistic selection criteria probably have a sharper cutting edge than Mills admits. In a certain measure, incompetent and irrational individuals are doubtless lopped from the circle of the power elite.

Despite tendencies to exaggeration, a radical analysis such as Mills's helps toward a more penetrating and objective view of the power structure than is afforded by conventional opinion. Mills, for example, touches among other things on the important American trend toward ever greater bureaucratization and centralization—some cultural correlates of which we shall now examine.

Trends in American Culture

Instrumental activism and *institutionalized individualism* are, according to the social theorist Talcott Parsons, the two fundamental American values.[5] Parsons believes that both are rooted in the New England Puritanism that so heavily influenced American culture.

Activism refers to the American conviction that society should aggressively exploit its environment, rather than passively adjust to it. *Instrumental* refers to the American view that society is an instrument made to serve the ends of its members, rather than an end in itself. According to Parsons, American values of instrumental activism are most clearly expressed in the drive to produce *generalized resources,* i.e., resources (human as well as material) potentially mobilizable to achieve a wide variety of goals. Americans frantically produce anything and everything, from hula hoops to electronic computers, without much concern about the way these resources will ultimately serve society. To produce is good, for it is activism, and society should serve this activism rather than vice versa. The underlying Soviet value—that production should serve social goals defined by five-year plans—is distinctly un-American.

Instrumental activism can be traced to the Puritan traditions of early America, which held that society was not an end in itself, but merely an instrument to be employed by man in serving God. Man, aided by society, was called to produce and create incessantly in order to build on earth a kingdom like God's Kingdom. Today, although the Puritan beliefs are fast disappearing, the drive to produce and to employ society as an instrument toward production, remains. Some critics of the sprawling affluent society, which has resulted from the unchanneled productivity, exhort Americans to harness their productivity to specific social goals and policies. Although America is moving in this direction, it is far from a socialistic society.

Institutionalized individualism can also be traced to Puritan roots. The Puritans saw each moral individual as called on by God to undertake a special task. This notion encouraged a society of specialized roles, each performed according to the individual's interpretation of God's special command to him. Though the individual might join a group, God, not the group, dictated his calling. The individual joined the group voluntarily, and was free to leave if it did not facilitate his service to God. A secularized version of this pattern is reflected in America's bewildering assortment of voluntary groups, any of which the individual may join or leave according to his special needs.

American individualism is *institutional* in that it functions within the context of organizations. Americans organize everything: production, business, war, politics, child rearing, Sunday school, bowling. America has nourished the Red Cross, United Fund, Heart Association, Cancer Society, and Community Chest, to name only a few organizations within the single sphere of charity. When Americans think of a job to be done, their next thought is, "Let's organize." This attitude reflects not a Romantic view that the individual is the be-all and end-all, but a Puritan view that the individual is an instrument toward some larger end for which he must organize social instruments even as he follows his own conscience.

Instrumental activism and institutionalized individualism clearly are basic and important American values. Yet social commentators warn of deviations from this cherished pattern.

The Organization Man Syndrome[6]

In *The Organization Man,* William H. Whyte, Jr. argues that the Protestant Ethic had already begun to decline in America by the turn of the century. Whyte maintains that as the big business and big government bureaucratic Organization grew and spread, the Protestant Ethic became even more irrelevant to work and life. The employee does not need Protestant attitudes of thrift, for the Organization is thrifty for him; the personnel and payroll departments automatically provide pension plans, group health plans, and low interest loans. Even more significantly, the total orientation of the Organization is toward spending, not thrift. Whyte argues that one of the talents most in demand is that of persuading the public to deviate from the Protestant Ethic and spend.

The Organization Man directly reverses the Protestant Ethic by feeling guilty not about sloth, but about work. Work brings ulcers or (as in *The Man in the Gray Flannel Suit*) neglect of family. Work should be carefully separated from the rest of life, rather than be the whole of life as the Calvinists believed. The Organization Man reserves weekends for leisure activities in the club, the boat, or the suburban home. Rugged Protestant individualism is also out, says Whyte. Conferences, committees, and administration are the keys to success within the Organization. Achievement is through harmony with others, not through lonely struggle.

Whyte admits that the small businessman is likely even today to adhere to the doctrines derived from the Protestant Ethic of free enterprise and rugged individualism, but he asserts that small business is of decreasing importance in the American economy. The small businessman is fighting a losing battle against the Organization, and he can smell the future as well as anyone else. The bland young man the Organization sent to town to manage the plant is almost damnably inoffensive; he didn't rent the old place on the hill but a smaller house, he drives an Olds instead of a Caddy, and when he comes to the Thursday luncheons he listens more than he talks. But he's the future just the same.[7]

A similar decline of Protestant Ethic individualism is observed by another classical commentator, David Riesman, but Riesman sees the mass media as the culprit that has transformed the American character from an inner-directed Protestant Ethic type toward an other-directed Organization Man type.

According to Riesman, in the inner-directed Protestant societies after 1600, the medium of print concentrated especially on success in business. Benjamin Franklin's *Poor Richard's Almanack*—the text selected by Max Weber as a typical self-inspirational document of the period of the Protestant Ethic—taught attitudes conducive to commercial achievement. Riesman considers even Defoe's *Robinson Crusoe*, with its elaborate descriptions of food, clothing, shelter, and money transactions, to have encouraged a business-like approach to life. Pious biographies as well as fictional works encouraged a spirit of Calvinist capitalism. A biography of George Washington preached that if a child worked hard, did not lie, and kept a firm character, he would succeed. The story of Booker T. Washington provided a similar model for the black child.

With the advent of other-directed values in American culture, observes Riesman, child-oriented media changed. Rather than train children to be thrifty and productive, the new media trained "the young for the frontiers of consumption—to tell the difference between Pepsi-Cola and Coca-Cola. . . ."[8] And they taught conformity. To mark this shift in attitude, Riesman cites the old nursery rhyme:

> *This little pig went to market; This little pig stayed at home.*
> *This little pig had roast beef;*
> *This little pig had none.*
> *This little pig went wee-wee-wee*
> *All the way home.*

In the Protestant Ethic era, suggests Riesman, this rhyme symbolized inner-directed individualism. In the other-directed era of the twentieth century, however, "all the little pigs go to market; none stay home; all have roast beef, if any do; and all say 'we-we.' "[9]

Reisman notes that the child-reader of the other-directed era is rarely alone. Before the spread of television, he was typically lying on the floor with his peers, trading comics, or listening to the "Lone Ranger" on the radio. Riesman feels that the other-directed child is too aware of his real-life peers to identify deeply with fictional heroes in the way the inner-directed child could—a change reflected in the media of the two eras:

> Think of the Count of Monte Cristo's years in jail, his suffering, his incredible patience, and the industry and study of the abbé's teaching. . . . he is an old man when, after many chapters, he wins.[10]

By contrast, the comic book or radio drama detective or superfigure might get roughed up and kicked around during the story, but he did not undergo a deep and gradual development of character in the process. Therefore, unlike the story of the Count of Monte Cristo, comic book and radio tales did not encourage their audiences vicariously to undergo sustained transformations of character.

Extending Riesman's arguments to today, much of what he says would seem to apply to television. Characters do not ordinarily mature and develop in the television drama, which typically covers only one episode in a life. Not only is television often viewed by groups, but the heroes themselves often are groups (e.g., teams of scientists or a family of cowboys). Presumably, this emphasis on the group reflects and encourages collectivism, an attitude of other-direction rather than individualism.

Riesman's analysis concentrated on media that are enjoyed passively. More active modes of entertainment, however, seem to reflect the same trend toward other-direction. Thus, in suburbia lives the "participative purist,"[11] the enthusiastic joiner of disco, stereo, and raquetball games. Even a seemingly private hobby such as painting may surrender to the guidance of the painting association. Children are organized at play through Little League baseball, eurythmics, and violin instruction by the Suzuki *group* method; bureaucratized recreation replaces the old hopscotch, marbles, and hide-and-seek; and universities offer degrees in "recreation administration."

Perusal of *Dissent, Partisan Review, Harper's, The Atlantic Monthly, Saturday Review,* and *Esquire* will unearth abundant commentary on the other-direction, bureaucratization, popularization, and commercialization. Loss of individuality and the rise of a herdlike conformism are observed. Cheapening and vulgarization of culture and character are seen as the result. These two trends are perceived as mutually supportive: Through constant exposure to cheap culture, the public is deprived of its critical capacities and is thereby prepared for an unthinking conformity to the group and ultimately to totalitarian power elites.

Many of the criticisms and fears are, of course, justified. Many of the remarkable qualities of Puritan early America *are* disappearing with the rise of other-direction and the Organization. The strident voices of the critics, however, should not obscure alternative interpretations such as the one presented by Winston White in his *Beyond Conformity.*

White takes issue with the social critics for their assumption of a *zero-sum* social system, that is, one in which the quantity of choices available within the society and culture is fixed, so that a given trend's gain is automatically another's loss. In this view, loss of individuality follows directly from increase in conformity. If only X amount of individuality is available, an increase in conformity necessarily means a decrease in that X amount of individuality. As an alternative to the zero-sum assumption, White suggests an interpretation much like the theory of modernization. Societies evolve toward greater and greater functional specialization and differentiation. In primitive society, a single unit (e.g., a lineage or clan) may perform all functions (economic, political, religious, etc.); therefore, primitive society is essentially a set of identical, unspecialized units (e.g., a set of clans). Modern society, on the other hand, is a coordinated system of dissimilar units, each with its own specialty—religious, economic, educational, political, etc.—and these units cooperate to form a workable system. Primitive man has basically one choice open to him: to be a nonspecialist and perform all functions that others of his age and sex perform. Modern man, on the other hand, can choose to specialize in religion, education, politics, art, or any other field. About the only choice not open to modern man is to be a nonspecialist.

This modern pattern increases the range of choices open to the individual and also increases the flexibility of society as a whole. Modern society, consisting of a variety of relatively independent units, can shuffle these into new combinations—say, religious businesses or educational churches.

True, modern man loses freedoms that primitive man enjoyed. White argues, however, that the freedoms lost are of a lower order than the freedoms gained. The modern worker loses the primitive man's freedom to schedule his own hours on the job, but he gains the freedom to change the job itself. He also gains freedom to choose his own activities after working hours; he can theoretically devote his leisure hours to any of a range of creative endeavors. Organization and standardization of the lower-order categories of life—i.e., work schedules and bureaucratic procedures—free the individual to devote his time and energy to higher-order creativity and development. Thus, far from depriving the individual of his individuality, White concludes, the low-order conformism demanded by bureaucracy and the Organization sets the stage for creative individuality on a wide scale.

A final question that White raises is whether the increasing complexity of modern society and the increasing opportunity for high-order creativity may not force man drastically to transform his personality. Basic human character itself may change, perhaps toward a more complex, creative, and sophisticated type.

The Media Explosion

"The electric light," said Marshall McLuhan, "may prove illuminating."[12] Although the electric light does not say anything (unless it should spell out words on a sign), it carries a message. That is, the light affects minds and introduces "a change in scale, pace, or pattern"[13] into human affairs. The light bulb is simply one of many media—radio, television, movies, telephones, typewriters, computers—which, according to McLuhan, have impact on thought and life simply by virtue of their distinctive forms. "The medium is the message!"[14] shouts McLuhan. He means that, regardless of the particular words uttered, stories told, or lessons taught via a given medium, that medium carries a distinctive punch and impact solely because of its *form*.

Print, for example, has a distinctive form. In the West, print is arranged in straight lines across a page. McLuhan asserts that with the introduction of print in the West, men's lives were flooded with printed lines, and men began to think linearly. Such linearity is reflected in Western patterns of designing cities, economies, and wars: "For the West, literacy has long been pipes and taps and streets and assembly lines and inventories."[15] "Print taught men to say, 'Damn the torpedoes, Full steam ahead.'"[16]

McLuhan asserts that because in the West physics and mathematics are taught by print, Western physicists are barely capable of comprehending nonlinear notions of time and space. They find it difficult to understand post-Newtonian physics. In order to overcome linear biases, McLuhan proposes the teaching of physics by telephone. The telephone is oral and oral media induce configurational, participational orientations, as opposed to the linear, analytical ones of print. Oral media absorb the fullness of one's being rather than concentrating a mere segment of one's attention along a sequential line of print.

The oral, participational, configurational orientation is spreading in the West thanks to television, McLuhan argues. The TV image is not as clear as the movie image, for it is composed of roughly connected dots on the screen. The viewer is urged to "close" the spaces between the dots by a "convulsive sensory participation that is profoundly kinetic and tactile."[17] (For McLuhan, tactility is, like the auditory and oral, participational and configurational.) Television viewers presumably feel moved mentally to crawl inside the set and gambol in the spaces between the dots.

As evidence that television induces a sense of participation, McLuhan cites the fact that, although movie fans are fascinated with the private lives of movie stars, television viewers show little interest in the private lives of television stars. Even though they identify with a particular TV character, they are so strongly involved with his on-screen roles that they would even prefer not to see the real person behind the character. This, at least, is McLuhan's theory. Like many of his observations, these "facts" about television are open to alternative explanations. Might not the difference between movie and television fans stem from differences in programming? Television stars frequently play in serials, movie stars commonly appear in one-shot stories. Playing in a variety of one-shot stories, the movie star naturally stands above any single role as a personality in his own right. The television star who plays a single character in a serial does not so easily transcend his screen personality. And television's availability at home is sufficient to explain why it should lend itself to serials. Its fuzzy image is not necessary to explain the viewer's identification with the characters on screen.

Although McLuhan's interpretation of television may be questioned, he has been suggestive in his perception of a configurational, participational attitude introduced with the 1960's counter-culture. America reached the end of the line! Lineality was out, along with the Protestant Ethic and the straight and narrow path. The lonely, inner-direction of the Calvinist gave way to gregarious, other-directed participationality. The trend was reflected in the hirsute pattern. Young men and women grew great manes of hair in which they engulf themselves, rejecting the antiseptic crew cuts of linear epochs. The tiny "wrap-around" automobiles reflect a similar shift in attitude. In the American "Big Buick," one sat in cold and solitary splendor, while in the Volkswagen, one enjoys cozy, intimate participationality. Best of all, with the new participationality, B.O. was back. "B.O., the unique signature and declaration of human individuality, is a bad word in literate society," but since odor is the "most iconic" of the human senses in that it involves the "entire human sensorium,"[18] it should naturally come on strong in an era of participationality.

"The World's a sage," declares McLuhan alluding to the fast flow of information in the world of today. He forecasts that the world will become a giant village whose inhabitants are cozily plugged in on one another via the electronic media.[19] Early-modern society may have been organized as a system of specialized "lines" of work, but in the world village specialized units will melt into a communal participationality of sensuous delight. Of course, linear thinkers might protest that without rationality, specialization, universalism, and the other modern values, technology cannot advance and complex technology cannot function. By this argument, McLuhan's electronic village will institute antimodern values that would soon force its technological base to crumble; the villagers would not long enjoy their communal bliss, for all those electric circuits would soon break down. Yet this may be an overly conservative view. Self-repairing machines may be developed, or perhaps an elite of ascetic eunuchs could administer the orgy which the rest of society would enjoy, as in Aldous Huxley's *Ape and Essence.*

Certainly the values governing McLuhan's new society would differ from those of the Protestant Ethic. The Calvinist, suppressing carnal appetites to attain salvation and restraining the acquisitive instinct to insure profit, forwent immediate gratification in the interest of long-range goals. Future, plans, and career were important American symbols derived from Calvinism. But this is no longer the case, according to McLuhan, for with television has come a new emphasis on immediate, depth participation and a de-emphasis on linear paths toward future goals: "The TV child cannot see ahead."[20] This interpretation agrees in part with Riesman's. What Riesman had to say about radio failing to draw the viewer through the same sustained progression as the classical novel could also be applied to television. The television drama is episodic, a succession of "nows."

In McLuhan's new, television-schooled, electronically integrated society, there will be no distance between present situation and future goal. The automated and computerized world will resemble Al Capp's schmoo. One had only to look at the schmoo and "think longingly of pork chops or caviar," and the schmoo ecstatically transformed itself into the object of desire. Similarly, the new man will program his wishes into the computer, and they will be immediately fulfilled. No time lag will exist between wish and outcome. The world will be one of immediacy and simultaneity.

To be sure, many objections can be raised against McLuhan's theories. The assertion that print gave birth to linear thinking in the West is surely an exaggeration. In the first place, non-Western print (e.g., Arabic or Chinese) is also linear, yet to these cultures McLuhan often attributes nonlinear thought. Secondly, the West possessed linear thought long before print. The linear grammatical structure of Western languages and the linear conceptions of time and history found in Judeo-Christian thought existed many centuries before Gutenberg. Nevertheless, many of McLuhan's assertions fit into our framework. The Protestant Reformation *was* connected with the rise of print and reading (especially of the Bible). The imagery of Protestantism *was* very linear, as in the progress of the pilgrim, the voyage of the ship of state, and the straight and narrow path toward success and salvation. And the trend toward immediate participation does currently seem a reality. Certainly, McLuhan is tracing a significant transformation of early-modern patterning. One "line" of analysis that he does not pursue, however, is that of religious systems which may serve to render this new world meaningful. One of the most dramatic postwar examples of a trend toward such a system is the movement that proclaimed the Death of God.

The Death of God Movement

Historic Christianity filled the gulf between God and man with a sacred hierarchy of offices, symbols, and rites. Calvinistic Christianity swept away and desanctified this mediating hierarchy, concentrating all sacredness on a single symbol, God. The Death of God movement sought to further the progress of religion by removing sacredness from even this symbol. To the young and radical "Atheistic Christian" theologians who proclaimed the death of God, no symbol, not even the symbol of God, is sacred, because every symbol is a mere product of the human mind. Therefore, to regard God or any other symbol as sacred is idolatry. Jesus fought idols with vigor, and the Atheistic Christians, carrying his campaign further, would topple what they consider the God idol.

Repudiating God, the Atheistic Christians also repudiate the traditionally sacred Christian goals of Heaven and salvation. They place their hope in immediate situations, not in distant goals, and preach that the Christian should operate from situation to situation in search of immediate participational experience. They see life as a floating crap game, with the Christian as a gambler who wagers anew each day. Enduring human relationships such as the *I–Thou* bond are idolatrous, as well as inconvenient since they promote plans and promises that distract from the immediate experience. The *I–You* encounter on the street is more valuable.

Emphasizing the immediate present at the expense of the distant future, the Atheistic Christian redefines the thrust of the Protestant Ethic. The Calvinist is under continuous pressure to progress toward the idealized future, which holds Heaven, salvation, and the Kingdom of God. To move toward that future and to transform the present in its image is man's calling. More important than immediate encounters—be they sensory, social, or aesthetic—is the fulfillment of that calling. Immediate participationality is at best distracting, at worst sinful and productive of eternal damnation. McLuhan's new society is hardly sanctioned by the Protestant Ethic; perhaps a theology of God's Death could come closer to providing a sanction.

For a more concrete view of the Atheistic Christians, let us briefly summarize some distinctive ideas of the movement's leading figures, including those of Gabriel Vahanian, Harvey Cox, Thomas J. J. Altizer, William Hamilton, and Paul M. van Buren.*

Gabriel Vahanian illustrates God's irrelevance to modern culture by referring to the opening scene of Fellini's film, *La Dolce Vita*, in which a huge crucifix suspended from a helicopter hovers incongruously over an indifferent sunbathing woman below. Vahanian and Harvey Cox argue that the transcendental essence formerly symbolized by God and His Kingdom is now manifest in the secular world—in art, in social change, and in the fleeting I–You encounters of the modern secular city. Embracing this world in all his participational immediacy, man must evaluate and appreciate human relationships for their own sake, without reference to abstract, God-given standards. Both Vahanian and Cox seek a transcendent being, but a being to be encountered in the pulsating secular life "where the action is."[21]

Professing the principle of the *coincidence of opposites,* Thomas Altizer concludes that the way to encounter the otherworld is to welcome fully this world. To discover the transcendent, man should deny the transcendent. As stated by the poet and mystic William Blake, a man should dare to "name God as Satan" and to "identify the transcendent Lord as the ultimate source of alienation and repression."[22] According to the principle of the coincidence of opposites, this procedure will result in the discovery of the true God. Altizer, therefore, does not deny the existence of the transcendent, but simply claims (as did mystics such as Meister Eckhart) that the transcendent exists beyond the conventional symbol, God. He differs from the mystics in that he hopes to discover and know this transcendental being not by probing the inner recesses of the soul or by direct communion with the ultimate, but by embracing the world in all its chaos, filth, and flux.

William Hamilton calls for a new optimism that will "say Yes to the world of rapid change, new technologies, automation, and the mass media."[23] In these realms may lurk Jesus. Hamilton, therefore, calls on man to move from his anguished quest for salvation toward a confident, optimistic stance "in the world, in the city, with both the needy neighbor and the enemy." For "Jesus is in the world as masked."[24]

Paul van Buren believes that modern life is irrevocably pluralistic

*The following quotations from the Atheistic Christians were, for convenience, taken from a single source, John Warwick Montgomery's *The "Is God Dead?" Controversy.* Although Montgomery's book is polemical, a survey of various writings by the Atheistic Christians indicates that these particular passages accurately reflect their thought.

and relativistic, the source of a multitude of "language games." Theology is simply one of these languages and is appropriate in some situations, irrelevant in others. It does not speak about God, but is "a dated way, among a number of ways," of talking about "man and human life and human history."[25] What theology says can also be said by other languages, such as psychology. Thus, van Buren interprets Gospel accounts as a reporting of psychological experiences—for example, the gaining of new insights into life's meaning by the disciples after Christ's death.

The Death of God movement derived in part from a sense of estrangement and alienation from traditional conceptions of the deity. The Death of God theologians felt that these traditional forms were irrelevant to modern conditions. Although their views were not shared by many practicing believers, their movement points to a basic problem of religion in the modern world which is experienced by many, especially the young: the problem of waning belief in traditional sacred forms. A response of modern religious movements has been to seek the experiential reality presumed to exist behind or beyond the forms. This endeavor is exemplified by such seemingly varied groups as the Pentecostals and Charismatics, the Eastern-influenced Hare Krishna and Transcendental Meditation, and the Unification Church. The reality sought by such movements is mystical, an inner truth which generates a variety of forms; thus a Pentecostal song responds to the questioning of *objective* forms with a *subjective* answer: "If God is Dead, then what is this living in my soul?" Though new cults and movements have emerged, none depicts the problem of desacralization of objective religious forms more pointedly than the slogan "God is Dead." The study of this image continues to provide insight into the most fundamental processes of modern times.

Overview

In many respects, American society is simply a perfection (or monstrous exaggeration) of trends toward modernization: It maximizes characteristics far less pronounced in premodern societies, such as specialization of units, specificity of social relationships, centralization, bureaucratization, universalization, conjugalization, technological advance, mobility, and rapidity of change.

Consider bureaucratization. Nonmodern societies, of course, developed extensive and effective bureaucracies. Such bureaucracies—for example, the Mesopotamian city-state, the Buddhist state-church, the Chinese scholar-bureaucrat system—made possible the integration and control of large populations. Yet the nonmodern bureaucracies never administered more than a fraction of a society's activities. Modern American bureaucracies administer a much larger proportion of American activities.

At the same time, American bureaucrats perform roles much more specialized than did nonmodern bureaucrats. An archaic priest-councillor or temple scribe experienced many facets of his life in terms of his office. Whom he married, where he resided, what recreation he indulged in, were strongly determined by his office. It was a diffuse status—covering many strands of life. The American bureaucrat's office is much more specific and specialized; his nonbureaucratic roles are much more separate from his bureaucratic one.

The great specialization and specificity of the American bureaucratic role make possible efficient bureaucratic organization toward some single, limited goal. A firm specializing in the manufacture of toothpicks can hire and fire solely on the basis of the individual's talent and interest in making toothpicks. It is acceptable to ignore other personal characteristics since the concept and pattern of the specialized, specific bureaucratic role is well established in American society and culture.

American society is composed of a variety of more or less autonomous specialized organizations, each built to cope effectively with a particular need or problem. Such a system of specialized organizations is far more flexible than, for example, an archaic one consisting of a single politico-religious organization. The archaic system's functions are so intimately entwined that change in any one function provokes turbulence and confusion throughout the system. The tendency is, therefore, to avoid change by being inflexible.

The flexibility of America's bureaucratic system depends on several patterns rarely considered by business or government planners. For example, the nuclear family, the typical American pattern, is more mobile than the extended family of the family-farm type. Business and government would experience much greater difficulty in transferring employees if the extended family of early America rather than the nuclear family of today were prominent.

Individuals, as well as families, move freely about the American landscape. Partly because of the incessant creation of new specialties, few parents expect their children to inherit their jobs. Many children leave home and their home town in search of jobs different from those of their parents. Such mobility is aided by the highly bureaucratized school system, which provides universalistic systems of recruitment and transmits skills, knowledge, and values that equip the youth, mentally and emotionally, for a wide range of American occupations. A great challenge to the schools is to keep the bureaucratization from smothering human capacities while maintaining sufficiently universalistic and centralized standards for social mobility to remain relatively easy.

The seemingly relentless modernizing thrust of American culture has frequently engendered opposing movements. Examples could be drawn from the nineteenth century communes and sects, the Agrarians of the South, and others; but the most recent is the so-called counter-culture of the 1960's.

During the sixties, the hippies and yippies, the New Left, and radical student organizations appeared to embody changes in the national character as well as particular political grievances.

The student protestors, for example, demanded not only the old, liberal quantitative achievements of wider distribution of privilege, wealth, and freedom, but also qualitative advances in human experience. They called for creative, participatory, depth encounters in art and life to replace the shallow efficiency of the technocracy. They revolted against uniformity and standardization, worshipping in its place the exotic and unique, even the quaint and the queer. They foresaw a life of continual openness and development, such that the individual's unfolding never ceases, and he is always "with it" and in step with the present. They proposed a participational democracy through which they themselves would take part in the decisions that affect their own education and maturation. They craved human relationships which, though short-lived, were meaningful and deeply involving of the whole self.*

By the 1970's, the cultural pendulum had seemingly swung back toward the center. Mainline American values reasserted themselves. In a time of declining affluence, ideologies of productivity, including a kind of neo-Protestant Ethic, were preached again. Hippies became Organization Men, getting shaves and haircuts and going to law or business school, as radicalism to some extent gave way to professionalism. The counterculture nonetheless left its imprint on American culture—in a sensitivity for subtleties of human relationships, a concern for a balanced rather than exploitative relation to the environment, and probably a greater openness to ethnic and cultural diversity.

What was the relation of these trends and countertrends to religion? An illustrative answer is given by the case of the Death of God.

Consider the relationship of God's Death to bureaucracy. Although

---

*This formulation follows Kenneth Keniston, "You Have to Grow Up in Scarsdale to Know How Bad Things Really Are," pp. 122–39. Although the 1970s saw some dilution of student values rampant in the 1960s, the basic pattern of opposition to the industrial technocracy remains and, of course, has characterized a stream of western student culture since the nineteenth century.

the Atheistic Christians explicitly side with the antibureaucratic radicals of America, their theology, ironically, sanctifies bureaucratic values by calling for the removal of a personal deity. Bureaucracy also calls for a depersonalization (since regulations, manuals, and examinations replace personalistic modes of administering and recruiting). Perhaps the Organization Man who comes to think in depersonalized, bureaucratic categories would find very meaningful a religion that denies the existence of a personal deity.

God's Death, however, carries broader implications. The reformist, flexible, self-revising character of American society is, we have suggested, inspired in part by the Calvinist belief in a duality between this world and the otherworld such that this world must be constantly remodelled to fit the other. Since the time of Kant, this dualistic world view has been repeatedly challenged. The notion has emerged that, instead of merely two worlds, as many worlds exist as man can apprehend. Why stop with imagining merely a Heaven and a Hell? Why not imagine an infinity of worlds? The Atheistic Christians encourage this view by offering to free men from the preoccupation with any single symbol, such as God, or Heaven, or Hell. They maintain that these symbols possess no special sanctity, and that others might just as well be imagined. Incessant production of new images of transcendent worlds would seem to be the consequence of current theological trends.

Such constant cultural ferment and creativity might, paradoxically, yield social stagnation. The Calvinist could strive continuously for a better world because he had a secure place to stand. Rigidly adhering to an image of God's Kingdom, which he perceived as an eternal and unchanging model of the ultimate, he insisted that the world change. Avant-garde proponents of cultural creativity must consider the possibility that by constantly multiplying images of the ideal, they deprive men of a constant cultural ideal that can inspire continuous social reform. Stagnation is not, of course, inevitable. Rapid change of ideal images, any one of which can arouse temporary passion to remake the social order, seems more likely.

Today less is heard of the Death of God, which in any event was confined largely to academic theologians, than of popular movements which affirm rather than deny religious symbols. Among these are the Jesus cults, Pentecostalism, and various endeavors at meditation. These movements are not, however, in opposition to the viewpoint of the Atheistic Christians, but carry forward a variety of implications of their school. To reject the belief in a god who exists outside the self is to open the way for a search within. Introspection and inner exploration is at the heart of the new movements among the young; as one of their spokesmen put it, "The New Religion is finding out about yourself." Modern religion is significant in that the faithful worship not the symbols that man has created but the very consciousness of man himself.

Topics for Discussion

A central topic for discussion suggested by this chapter is the place of sociocultural analysis in *modern* contexts. Consider the following argument. Core values of modern society call for endless evaluation and revision of the society itself. Therefore, scientific analysis of the society is religious worship in the sense that it expresses the ultimate values of the social scientist's society. If science is a rite expressing modern social values, traditional social analysts were less religious than modern social scientists. For example, the ancient Indian grammarian Panini was not, by his analytical performances, worshipping core values of his society. His society's values were antianalytical. Unlike the modern social scientist, Panini was a radical and a nonconformist.

But are the core values of modern society themselves so profoundly antireligious that to call the expression of these values "worship" is sacrilege? After all, the genuinely religious attitude is one of unconditional commitment. To regard a symbol as sacred or ultimate is to be unconditionally committed to that symbol, to sacrifice all for its sake. Modern men tend to regard all symbols as conditional. God and Heaven are seen as human creations, hence dependent on human conditions. Social scientists such as Marx and Freud argue that as these conditions change, the symbolism of religion also changes. Should social science be seen, then, as undermining unconditional commitment to all symbols by revealing them as products of changing conditions? If the answer is yes, social analysis, far from constituting worship, should be regarded as a profoundly antireligious action. The worshipful attitude that sometimes pervades the analytic endeavor would be viewed as merely an abortive clutching after ultimate commitments within a framework of thought that renders such commitment logically impossible.

Suggested Readings

American Culture

The American People: A Study in National Character (paperback, 1964) by Geoffrey Gorer. A readable and perceptive anthropological analysis of American life by a British anthropologist.

And Keep Your Powder Dry (paperback, 1965) by Margaret Mead. Readable and perceptive anthropological analysis of American life by a well-known American anthropologist.

American Life: Dream and Reality (paperback, 1964) by W. Lloyd Warner. American society and symbolism viewed from a Durkheimian perspective by an expert on the Australian aborigine.

"The Dominant Value Profile of American Culture" (1955) by Cora DuBois.

"National and Regional Cultural Values in the United States" (1955) by John Gillin.

"The American Cultural Configuration," in *Anthropology: An Introduction* (1965) by Lowell D. Holmes.

"Body Ritual Among the Nacirema" (1956) by Horace Miner. Useful if somewhat heavy-handed satire on American culture.

Culture Against Man (paperback, 1963) by Jules Henry. Provocative and bitter anthropological critique of American culture.

"Population Growth in the United States" (1965) by Donald J. Bogue. A readable essay on population trends.

The Nacirema: Readings in American Culture (1975) by James Spradley and Michael Rynkiewich.

The Changing Shape of American Society and Culture

The Power Elite (paperback, 1956) by C. Wright Mills.

The Lonely Crowd: A Study of Changing American Character (abridged paperback, 1953) by David Riesman, Nathan Glazer, and Reuel Denney.

The Organization Man (paperback, 1957) by William H. Whyte, Jr.

Mass Culture (paperback, 1957) edited by Bernard Rosenberg and David Manning White.

Beyond Conformity (1961) by Winston White.

The Kandy-Kolored Tangerine-Flake Streamline Baby (paperback, 1966) by Tom Wolfe. A particularly enjoyable commentary.

America as a Civilization (paperback, 1957) by Max Lerner. An encyclopedic synthesis with an extensive bibliography.

The First New Nation: The United States in Historical and Comparative Perspective (1967) by Seymour Martin Lipset. Elaborates many of the present authors' points about America.

Gamesmanship (1976) by Michael Maccoby. In the tradition of *The Organization Man.*

A Religious History of the American People (1972) by Sidney Ahlstrom.

The McLuhan Thesis

Understanding Media (paperback, 1964) by Marshall McLuhan. A basic source.

The Medium Is the Massage (paperback, 1967) by Marshall McLuhan and Quentin Fiore. Presents the McLuhan thesis through pictures as well as words.

"The Medium Is the Massage" (Columbia Stereo (C5 9501). To insure that the message is properly mediumed, McLuhan has made it audible in this bizarre and entertaining phonograph record.

The Death of God

The "Is God Dead?" Controversy (paperback, 1966) by John Warwick Montgomery.

The Meaning of the Death of God (1967) edited by Bernard Murchland.

The Death of God Debate (paperback, 1967) edited by Jackson Lee Ice and John J. Carey.

General Problems of Rapid Change in America

Future Shock (1971) by Alvin Toffler.

The Greening of America (1971) by Charles A. Reich.

A Runaway World? (1968) by Edmund Leach. An interesting comparison to the books by Toffler and Reich because it concentrates on Britain rather than America.

The Cultural Contradictions of Capitalism (1975) by Daniel Bell.

Ecological Problems

The American Population Debate (1971) edited by Daniel Callahan. Provides a rich and stimulating assortment of viewpoints on the consequences for American life of population increase and environmental decline.

Films

Special note should be taken of excellent portrayals of diverse American regional, ethnic, and religious patterns. Examples:

Pizza-pizza Daddy-O. Live portrayal of a rhyming game of black children.

The Amish. Depicts this important American religious group.

Born for Hard Luck. Beguiling autobiographical portrait by a black medicine-show musician.

For a full listing, see *American Folklore Films and Videotapes: An Index,* ed. William Ferris and Judy Peiser.

chapter 10

Sociocultural Evolution and the Future

Evolutionary theory has provided a viewpoint and framework in terms of which to confront various issues, generalizations, cultures, and behavioral processes. If nothing else, it is a useful pedagogical and organizational device. But it may be more than this. If its premises are valid, evolutionary theory should lead toward a better comprehension of world trends and even help predict the shape of the future.

Two broad evolutionary trends can be discerned. The first is apparent in the increased maximization, with the passage of time, of such features as specialization of units, specification of social relations, bureaucratization, centralization, mobility, and changeability. From this standpoint, the evolutionary process has been a gradual, but continuously accelerating, spread and intensification of modern traits. Assuming that this process will continue, the future will display these traits of modernity more extensively and intensively than the present does.

The second trend is evolution by a series of "leaps" from one level to another. Instead of merely spreading and intensifying a *fixed* set of traits, evolution has created a series of patterns, each displaying radically *different* traits. Archaic patterns differ radically from primitive ones, historic from archaic, early-modern from historic, modern from early-modern. Since each level is so radically different from the others, it is particularly difficult to predict what the patterning of the next level will be.

Continuous Evolutionary Trends

By simply assuming that the spread and intensification of modern traits will continue into the future—that the future will be like the present but that there will be "more of it"—we can hazard numerous speculation about the future. Several caveats should be issued, however. First, the very traits and dimensions that we have employed in constructing an evolutionary scheme are conditioned by our present position in the evolutionary process. Our view of the future is severely limited by our image of present and past. For example, we imagine the future in terms of images such as "world government," yet "government" may well appear to future theorists as outmoded an image as the medieval "social body" appears to us today.

Secondly, one of the very features that is increasingly salient renders the task of prediction increasingly difficult. The rate of sociocultural change is increasing. Because patterns are changing faster and faster, they are more and more difficult to perceive and analyze. A related trend is toward greater freedom of choice. The freer men are to choose, the more complex becomes the task of predicting what they will choose.

Finally, the assumption that certain evolutionary trends are continuous is an oversimplification. All evolutionary changes are in kind as well as in degree. Nevertheless, it is useful and defensible to treat some trends as merely quantitative, as simply tending toward more specialization, greater centralization, and faster change.

Rates of Change

The trend of sociocultural evolution throughout human history has been toward a faster overall rate of change. The trend is clearest in the realm of technology, but it is also apparent in other spheres of life. Especially with the advent of early-modern society, change becomes a positive value. Early-modern science, education, and government are built to insure incessant and rapid change, and since the early-modern pattern is still spreading around the world, the world's overall rate of change will continue to increase—barring holocaust and catastrophe.

The dynamism of early-modern society was inspired in part by a cultural pattern delineating a single, transcendent cosmos in whose image the world must be incessantly reordered and reformed. With the Death of God movement and associated cultural developments, the single transcendent cosmos of early-modern culture is being replaced with a multiplicity of transcendental images. This multiplicity might encourage a confusion resulting in stagnation. More likely, however, it will result in wild diversification of reformist impulses, as swarms of provocative images are propagated by prophets of every conceivable type.

Advances in mass communications and world transportation can be expected to encourage cultural exchange and hybrid union, with associated increases in excitement and creativity. Exploding population alone will insure a large number of creative minds, and if all these minds remain on earth (instead of migrating to another planet), the density of high-level thought guarantees continuous cross-fertilization and ferment.

To what point can change accelerate before man reaches his limit of tolerance? Sociocultural patterns threaten to set a pace that the human organism itself cannot endure. Advances in genetics, neurology, and psychology may increase the organism's capacity to tolerate rapid change. Yet even if the organism can adapt, can the society do so? So far man has managed to evolve social and technological systems to meet each new demand for faster change. Bureaucratic organization, high-speed automation, and computers are among the significant responses to such demands. Some problems, however, are difficult to solve organizationally or technologically. One of these is the "generation gap." The world changes so fast that parents must rear their children for an unknown future. The alternative is to train children for a way of life that is extinct by the time they are adolescent. Trained in this manner, adolescents feel confused and alienated. They protest, revolt, and in other ways incite social change and ferment—perpetuating the very conditions that produced their alienation. Social planning could break this cycle by providing parents with a firm view of the future. Yet rigid social planning may hamper a society's ability to adapt to rapidly changing environments.

Social Differentiation and Specialization

The general trend of history is toward societies that are increasingly differentiated into specialized units. This trend aids adaptation to accelerating change. As specialties and skills change and multiply faster and faster, it becomes impossible for the individual to master all of them; and the mastery is accordingly divided among numerous specialists and specialized groups.

The consequence for the individual is that he divides his time and energy among increasingly specialized and disconnected roles. His existence becomes more and more fragmented. How does this affect him? How far can fragmentation go before it reaches the limits of psychic tolerance? Men are, apparently, evolving new modes of neurosis in response to social fragmentation. Obsessive-compulsive neurosis was a frequent response to early-modern fragmentation in the West; the obsessive-compulsive's preoccupation with scheduling of roles and with separating technical jobs from emotional pleasures was simply an exaggeration of early-modern values. Neurotics today, however, complain of other symptoms. They feel "alienated," they feel they have no "identity," and they find no "meaning in life." These are perhaps more serious symptoms than the old ones in the sense that the neurotic individuals are, at a deep level of the psyche, reacting *against* the fragmented society instead of overconforming to its values.

A workable, viable society requires a degree of mutual empathy and solidarity among its members. In the primitive village, rites draw all villagers into a mutual empathy and solidarity. In the archaic community, public dramas serve the same function. In modern society, such rites and dramas unfortunately do not, perhaps cannot, flourish. Groups and individuals are too differentiated to join together as a total community on the village green.

Mass media partially fill the vacuum left by the demise of ritual and drama; but the media do not provide the kind of empathetic experience the rites offered. The rite or drama, occurring within a community of diffusely bound individuals, projected a diffuse empathy—an empathy with others that touched many levels of the self. The media, in a society bound together by one-dimensional ties, provide only shallow empathy. The contrast between the modern man's empathy with a stranger on a screen and the primitive's empathy with a kinsman during a rite is clear. It is possible that the more one-dimensional social relations become, the more shallow empathetic experience will become? Future empathy might shrink into a ghastly shadow of what we know even today. In the film *Barbarella*, for example, future sexual union is depicted as touching hands after taking a pill. But as this film also suggests, technological advance might allow the dispensing of specialized empathy in highly condensed doses.

Centralization and Bureaucratization

Social differentiation is always accompanied by a balancing trend toward centralization and bureaucratization, so that the differentiated units will perform in harmony. Therefore, if the world becomes more differentiated, it will likely also become more centralized and bureaucratized.

As this occurs, the individual will probably become more alienated. The more levels between the coordinating center of bureaucracy and the specialist bureaucrat, the more alienated the individual is likely to feel (as vividly illustrated in Kafka's *The Trial*). The alienation that comes with increasing bureaucratization is, of course, an old problem, and it will doubtless continue to be one. As in the present, future solutions will oscillate between anarchy and fascism, both of which aim at restoring a sense of belonging that bureaucracy destroys. The new dimension of future fascism will doubtless be an elaborate technology of tyranny. As science fiction predicts, electronic devices may control the public mind with great precision.

Will the future world centralize itself into a single society? Multinational governmental or economic unions such as NATO, the Warsaw Pact, the European Common Market, and the United Nations are indicative of a trend in that direction. But these organizations themselves raise questions about the chances for a world society. In the United Nations, for instance, the poor nations are at a disadvantage, and this is likely to be so in any world organization. Unfortunately, despite great strides by the poor nations, they are becoming relatively poorer as the rich nations become richer. Development of the underdeveloped nations must proceed at a much faster rate than it is doing in order to produce a union of equal nations.

It is conceivable that there could emerge some radically new governmental system which manages to coordinate unequal nations in a viable union, or perhaps such unity could be achieved by a system other than a governmental one. One thinks of possible advances in the media of exchange. The invention of money allowed fantastic innovations in economic exchange; perhaps some supergeneralized medium could do the same for international relations. One can imagine a political credit card that would allow politicians to move effortlessly among the nations, arranging pacts, treaties, and coalitions as easily as a housewife shops in a supermarket. To unite or not to unite with a given nation would be decided instantly by the assessment (facilitated by lightning-fast computers) of how much political credit the nation possesses at the moment of decision. Laborious negotiations would be a thing of the past, as would wars. This whimsy rests, of course, on an oversimplified analogy between economic and political media of exchange. Still, it is quite possible that treaties and diplomacy as they are currently known will give way to a much more flexible and quantitative system.

Family and Kinship

The importance of kinship units and of the parent-child bond on which such units are based is declining. Since this trend is connected to the trends of increased universalism, specialization, and centralization, if these continue, it will too.

Even in the last decades, the family in modern society has decreased its contribution to the education of the child—just about the only important function still served by the modern family. Children enter nursery school at an increasingly early age and stay in school to an increasingly advanced age. Eventually, the task of educating the child for an unknown future may simply prove too much for parents, and the child's education may be placed fully in the hands of specialized and bureaucratized organizations, guided by the latest research and expertise. Motivational problems might arise, as studies of children raised in orphanages suggest. Perhaps a compromise arrangement could be established, with the child allowed to sleep at home in order to receive and reciprocate parental love, but the parent forbidden by law to attempt to educate the child. The parent might then be merely a pal, entrusting the difficult task of educating the child in skills, knowledge, character, and ethics to the experts.

Relieved of their child-rearing responsibilities, man and wife would also be relieved of a keystone of marital permanence and stability: shared obligation to a child. Marital permanence would be much less important; marriage would no longer be a sacrament, nor even a long-term contract. Perhaps it would become no more than a courtship or date, and today's computerized dating systems could be extended to include all men and women, of all ages, all over the world.

Personal Identity

With sociocultural evolution the self has become a more and more distinct unit. Presumably this trend will continue; but what will this future self be like? Some current social commentators maintain that the ascetic, goal-directed Protestant Ethic character, supposedly dominant in earlier times, is being supplanted by a hedonistic, participational, sensuous character—what the Calvinists would call a good-for-nothing type. This may be partly true, but the evolutionary argument suggests an alternative diagnosis.

With evolution, the self becomes more distinct and it also assumes more responsibility for its own deeds. The individual may indeed cease to suppress sensual drives, but he will not simply remove his trousers and indulge his drives whenever a suitable object appears. Instead, assuming that the evolutionary trend toward rationality continues, he will *rationally* decide when, where, and how to indulge his drives whenever a suitable object appears. Instead, assuming that the evolutionary trend toward rationality continues, he will *rationally* decide when, where, and how to indulge his *irrational* drives. This is not to say that technical measurements and calculations will go into each decision of whether or not to copulate, but it does imply that the individual will feel compelled to consider carefully whether a particular experience will properly develop the self and contribute to his work. None of the Protestant Ethic taboos will be available to provide the individual with an absolute and categorical "no," so the individual must decide "yes" or "no" on rational grounds. Such freedom of choice is hardly likely to yield a joyous animal spontaneity.

The Future and Levels of Sociocultural Evolution

Certainly the predictions hazarded so far are tentative, general, and to some extent fanciful. But if the extrapolations from continuing trends must be speculative, forecasts about the nature of an utterly new level of sociocultural patterning must be even more so. If a trend can be anticipated to continue, it is reasonably safe to extrapolate from that trend and predict "the present, but more of it." But if the next level of sociocultural evolution is to be drastically different from the present one—different not merely in degree but in kind—simply predicting more of the present would be grossly misleading.

Let us imagine a Martian who, during his visit to the earth, rides in an automobile. He observes the driver shift into first, then second, then third gear. On the principle of "the present, but more of it," the Martian would predict that the trend will continue, and that the driver will shift into fourth, fifth, sixth . . . *n* gears. His prediction would, of course, be incorrect. If he is intelligent, however, he will base his prediction on more than mere observation of a trend. He will inquire about the mechanism that operates the automobile. With sufficient understanding of the mechanism, he could predict that stubbornly trying to shift a three-gear automobile into fourth gear would result in a new pattern, that is, a breakdown. He might even be able to predict the particulars of this new pattern: what happens to the clutch, the gears, the engine.

This analogy warns that plotting a trend in "history so far" is simply not adequate for predicting the character of an emerging sociocultural level (a breakdown or breakthrough). At the same time, it suggests that understanding the mechanism by which society moves from one level to the next may substantially aid such prediction.

Ordinarily, the three analytical distinguishable life processes that we have called *cultural, social,* and *psychological* are more or less in harmony. The patterning of values, symbols, and ideas in terms of which the individual defines his existence, the patterning of his society, and his own personal patterning are mutually supportive. Myth, self, and kinship reflect and reinforce each other among the Australian aborigine, as do cosmology, self, and kingship among the ancient Egyptians.

Nevertheless, there have been epochs when the cultural, the social, and the psychological were not in harmony. The city's commercial clamor did not harmonize with medieval man's organic imagery and pastoral disposition. For the Organization Man, the American dream is not in accord with other-directed passivity and the bureaucratic maze. Sensing such discrepancies, the populace is disquieted and expresses this disquietude in riots, crime, withdrawal, neurosis, millenarianism, and civil disobedience. Men speak of chaos, anxiety, and meaninglessness. Out of the chaos emerge new ideologies, cosmologies, theologies, and myths that can make sense of the forces of society and give them order, and that can harness and integrate the urges of the self.

How and why do cultural, social, and psychological systems get out of mesh? And how does such disharmony excite radical, i.e., evolutionary, sociocultural change? Despite the importance of the questions, surprisingly little is known about the precise mechanisms that bring about the disharmony; nor is it clear precisely how much is tolerable before radical change must occur. Yet both the disharmony and the change have appeared throughout human history, in circumstances so varied that they must derive from characteristics intrinsic to sociocultural systems and to the human condition itself.

Cultural systems and social systems differ in their manner of integration. The beliefs, values, and ideas in terms of which men direct their actions, interpret their experiences, and render their lives meaningful are integrated by a unity of style and a consistency of logic. Mathematical systems, artistic compositions, religious theologies, even political ideologies and informal philosophies of life work toward such integration. These cultural systems tend toward *logico-meaningful* integration. The roles, groups, and relationships involved in ongoing processes of interaction, alliance, and conflict tend more toward *causal-functional* integration. They are connected in sequences of cause and effect, condition and consequence, and by interdependencies of supply and demand, goal and function. Social systems such as economies, governments, communities, and societies tend toward causal-functional integration.

Tendencies toward logico-meaningful integration are inevitably in disharmony with tendencies toward causal-functional integration. The idealist's drive toward an aesthetically pleasing and logically consistent five-year plan interferes with the practical arrangements necessary for an economy that *works*. The true believer's premise that "devotion to the otherworld is the only moral act" cannot be applied with perfect consistency to all men if the operational requirements of a functioning society—for example, that commerce proceed and that procreation occur—are to be met.

Perceiving the discrepancy between the two modes of integration, the individual feels disillusionment, even nostalgia—a feeling due partly to the psychology of growing up. Especially in complex modern societies, the individual tends to acquire basic culture—beliefs, values, religion, world view—mainly in childhood, whereas he tends to learn adult roles—that of job holder, family head, property owner—mainly in adulthood. These tendencies may suggest why cultural systems and their characteristic modes of thought and patterning recall the warmth, innocence, and magic of childhood, social systems the harsh realities of adulthood. A special sadness and a sense of loss of childhood and of youth may be evoked, at varying levels of consciousness, by the realization that the cultural (the logico-meaningful) must be compromised and sacrificed for the sake of the working system (the causal-functional). The process of growing up is not, of course, the only psychological dynamic that lends poignance to the perception of disonance between the cultural and social systems, but it is an important one, for the adult's attitude is rooted in the earliest experiences of life. Because of this and other psychological processes, the drive to order social reality, to render it meaningful by subsuming it within a cultural framework, is a fundamental force within the human personality.

The drive toward meaningfulness is often expressed by a belief that culture is constant, even as society changes. As with the aborigines, mythical, totemic, and other symbolic frameworks are imagined as eternal, constant, and static systems in terms of which ongoing and changing events of society can be classified, hence rendered orderly and meaningful. In actual fact, of course, neither culture nor society is entirely static. Instead, societies are constantly changed to match cultural ideals. And all societies boast specialists in elaborating and modifying the cultural order to accommodate social changes. In primitive societies, this is the task of the teller of tales; in modern society, of theologians, scientists, educators, and politicians. Paradoxically, the very attempt to elaborate the cultural that it may better fit the social may intensify the dissonance between the two, because cultural elaboration proceeds logico-meaningfully, social change proceeds causal-functionally.

External factors may also contribute to the cultural-social dissonance.

When modern and nonmodern societies come in contact, modern elements are invariably introduced in the nonmodern societies—whether deliberately, as by missionization, colonization, and foreign aid, or unintentionally, as by trade and tourism. For the recipient society, the new elements abruptly create discrepancies between cultural traditions and contemporary realities. For example, myths may venerate stone axes, but now the natives are actually using steel knives. Theologies may rank the priestly caste above the artisan caste, but in daily lfie it is the talents of the latter that, because of the influx of new machinery, are in demand. The resulting discrepancies between traditional culture and modern society precipitate tensions which find myriad expressions—an important one being religio-political movements that attempt radical modernization.

Whether precipitated by external contacts (as in the case with most of the movements of radical social and cultural reformulation that are emerging among colonized peoples) or by internal dynamics (as was broadly the case with the Protestant Reformation), these religio-political movements display certain common features. Either they dig deep into native traditions to select old elements suitable for a new order, as in the Reformation's claim to reestablish the original and pristine Christianity; or they project a fantasied future utopia, as in the millenarian movements of the Middle Ages and in political religions such as Communism. In both instances, the results are the same: the undermining of established values, the creation of new loyalties, the harnessing of dormant energies, and the shaping of modern forms of consciousness. Some of the movements (e.g., those that originated the historic religions) have deeply affected the whole of human history, others have so far had only local effects. All have contributed some sense of order and meaning to an existence suddenly rendered complex by modernization.

We may now draw on some of the above considerations, as well as others mentioned throughout the book, to formulate a basic mechanism of sociocultural evolution. We suggest that *each new cultural pattern that renders meaningful an advance in social modernity and complexity "transcendentalizes" the old cultural pattern from which it derives.* The mechanism of transcendentalization has already been exemplified by the various stages of evolution. Archaic Egypt, Mesopotamia, Swaziland, and Southeast Asia replaced primitive cosmic orders, existing in their respective regions, with more transcendent ones; their gods and god-kings transcended man and his world more than did the primitive spirits, totems, and heroes. Historic Buddhism, Islam, and Christianity replaced archaic cosmologies, whose gods and god-kings lived in the world, with conceptions of gods and ultimate orders existing outside and above the world, in a transcendent otherworld. Calvinism rendered this otherworld even more transcendent by sweeping away the mediating hierarchies, which, under historic Christianity, had connected it to this world. And now modern religion, represented by such schools as the Death of God, bids to transcendentalize the cosmic even more, pushing it to a level above God, Heaven, and the other idolatrous symbols of traditional Protestantism.

At each new level, there was an increase in social complexity. Therefore, it is reasonable to expect that the cosmic (cultural) order should be transcendentalized to render meaningful the new complexity and chaos of social existence. The old cosmology is too much wedded to the differentiated complexity of this existence to stand above it and subsume it, thereby rendering it meaningful. A broad prediction of the future, then, is that from current advances in modernization and complexity of society will emerge a cosmology more transcendent than any yet imagined. Otherwise the basic human drive toward meaning will be thwarted.

The Death of God disciples suggest one direction of this future transcendentalization: the placing of ultimate being far above and beyond God and other concrete symbols. Whatever form is assumed by the substance of such a religion, it will not be a visible, personified form, such as God or the Virgin Mary. Indeed, this substance may have no form at all; it will be that which the visible symbols have heretofore represented. Discovery of this "that," this ultimate essence, will be the aim of believers.

Given the positivist warp of modern culture, it is unlikely that believers will accept an ultimate essence inhabiting some fourth dimension unknowable except by mystics. Nor will they be satisfied by tracing the ultimate to a set of nerve endings and brain cells in the neurologist's laboratory. At present, the clearest trend, suggested at the close of the last chapter, is toward a searching within the self. Yet the self as a unit of consciousness is no more visible than the mystic's fourth dimension. Accordingly, should this mysterious self become an object of worship, many cults and theories, speculating about its nature and destiny, will arise. As the cults and theories multiply, the self will become ever more mysterious and complex, expanding in rhythm with the worship lavished upon it by those faithful who seek the transcendent within the self. As seeker seeks to transcendentalize the sought, and the sought is within the seeker's self, this self will assume an odd shape. A world of such *selves* could be radically different from the world we know today.

Notes*

Preface

1. Robert N. Bellah, "Religious Evolution."
2. V. Gordon Childe, *Man Makes Himself*, chapter 5.
3. Abraham Kaplan, *The Conduct of Inquiry*, p. 11.

Chapter 1

1. Raymond Firth, *We, the Tikopia*, p. 2.
2. Walter Goldschmidt (ed.), *Exploring the Ways of Mankind*, p. 15.
3. Lynn White, Jr., "World View and Technology in the European Middle Ages," p. 2.
4. Weston LaBarre, "The Cultural Basis of Emotions and Gestures," pp. 49–68.
5. Clyde Kluckhohn, *Mirror for Man*, pp. 153–54.
6. Kluckhohn, p. 155.

*Full facts of publication for sources cited in the notes are supplied in the bibliography.

7. This broadcast was reported in *True: The Man's Magazine,* 49 (September 1968), p. 20.
8. Edward T. Hall, *The Silent Language,* chapters 1, 4, 9, 10.
9. James George Frazer, *The Golden Bough,* pp. 12–52.
10. Dorothy Lee, "Lineal and Nonlineal Codifications of Reality," p. 97.
11. John Gillin, *The Ways of Men,* pp. 295–96.
12. Hall, chapter 9.
13. Marion J. Levy, Jr., *Modernization and the Structure of Societies,* vol. I, p. 29.
14. The Navaho and Hopi examples cited come from Weston LaBarre, *The Human Animal,* pp. 197–98.
15. John B. Carroll and Joseph B. Casagrande, "The Function of Language Classifications in Behavior."
16. From a letter by Franklin to the Abbé Morellet, quoted in Robert K. Merton, *Social Theory and Social Structure,* p. 38.
17. George Herbert Mead, "The Psychology of Punitive Justice," p. 591.
18. George Devereux, "Art and Mythology."
19. Tom Wolfe, *The Kandy-Kolored Tangerine-Flake Streamline Baby,* pp. 42–43.
20. Dorothy Baker, *Young Man with a Horn.*

Chapter 2

1. See chapter eight for a fuller discussion of the "great chain of being" metaphor.
2. This discussion of the development of geology draws on Charles C. Gillespie, *From Genesis to Geology.*
3. Godfrey Lienhardt, *Social Anthropology,* p. 13.
4. See I. C. Jarvie, *The Revolution in Anthropology,* for an assessment of the significance of the shift from an evolutionary anthropology to a functionalist one based on intensive fieldwork.
5. E. R. Leach, *Rethinking Anthropology,* pp. 1–27; and Dell Hymes (ed.), *Reinventing Anthropology.*
6. E. O. Wilson, *Sociobiology: The New Synthesis;* and A. P. Vayda (ed.), *Environment and Cultural Behavior.*

Chapter 3

1. The transcription of Thai used here follows that developed by Mary R. Haas and Heng R. Subhanka, *Spoken Thai* (Washington, D.C., 1945).
2. Robin Fox, *Kinship and Marriage,* is a good introduction to this literature.
3. It is conventional to use the symbol "Z" for "sister" to avoid confusion with the use of the symbol "S" used for "son."
4. A useful survey of some anthropological views of religion are found in E. E. Evans-Pritchard, *Theories of Primitive Religion.*

Chapter 4

1. Godfrey Lienhardt, *Social Anthropology,* p. 14.
2. Marvin Harris, *The Rise of Anthropological Theory,* pp. 171–73.
3. L. T. Hobhouse, G. C. Wheeler, and M. Ginsburg, *The Material Culture and Social Institutions of the Simple Peoples* (London, 1915). Quoted in Lienhardt, *Social Anthropology,* p. 43.
4. Personal communication, Marion J. Levy, Jr.
5. Much of this section is based on Levy, *Modernization and the Structure of Societies.*
6. These levels are derived from Robert Bellah, "Religious Evolution."
7. Bronislaw Malinowski, *Argonauts of the Western Pacific.*
8. Daniel Lerner, *The Passing of Traditional Society.* The subsequent examples of empathy in the Near East come from this work.
9. J. K. Campbell, *Honour, Family, and Patronage,* pp. 217–47.
10. Campbell, pp. 59–88.
11. Campbell, p. 145.
12. James L. Peacock, *Rites of Modernization,* chapter 15.
13. Bellah, "Religious Evolution."
14. This section to this point follows S. N. Eisenstadt, *Modernization: Protest and Change.*
15. Anthony F. C. Wallace, "Revitalization Movements." This discussion of the movements follows Wallace.
16. The remainder of this section is indebted to Robert N. Bellah, *Beyond Belief,* pp. 279–82.
17. Ernest Nagel, *The Structure of Science,* pp. 107–17.
18. Robert Redfield, *The Primitive World and Its Transformations,* chapter 5.
19. Harold F. Blum, "On the Origin and Evolution of Human Culture," pp. 211, 219.

Chapter 5

1. This paragraph and the diagram follow Robin Fox, *Kinship and Marriage,* p. 183.
2. This section follows W. E. H. Stanner, "The Dreaming."
3. Stanner, p. 514.
4. Stanner, p. 517.
5. Claude Lévi-Strauss, *The Savage Mind,* p. 89.
6. A. P. Elkin, *The Australian Aborigines,* p. 211.
7. Lévi-Strauss, *The Savage Mind,* pp. 233–34.
8. Edmund Leath, *Political Systems of Highland Burma,* pp. 73–74.
9. See Rodney Needham, *Structure and Sentiment.*
10. Godfrey Lienhardt, *Social Anthropology,* p. 113.
11. Needham, p. 96.
12. Needham, p. 99.
13. This account is taken from Victor W. Turner, "A Ndembu Doctor in Practice," pp. 230–63.

14. Turner, pp. 260–61.
15. Max Gluckman, "Les Rites de Passage," p. 24.
16. Leach, *Political Systems of Highland Burma.*
17. Harold F. Blum, "On the Origin and Evolution of Human Culture," pp. 211, 219.

Chapter 6

1. This section follows the research of Hilda Kuper, reported in *An African Aristocracy.*
2. Kuper, p. 69.
3. Kuper, p. 141.
4. Kuper, p. 203.
5. Kuper, p. 204.
6. Kuper, p. 205.
7. Kuper, p. 217.
8. Kuper, p. 217.
9. Kuper, pp. 217–18.
10. Kuper, p. 206.
11. Max Gluckman, "Rituals of Rebellion in Southeast Africa."
12. T. O. Beidelman, "Swazi Royal Ritual."
13. Beidelman, p. 397.
14. Most of the following material on Egypt comes from John A. Wilson, *The Culture of Ancient Egypt.* The material on Mesopotamia comes from a variety of sources, especially Sabatino Moscati, *The Face of the Ancient Orient.* Some suggestions for comparing the Egyptian and Mesopotamian patterns derive from Talcott Parsons, *Societies: Evolutionary and Comparative Perspectives,* chapter 4.
15. Wilson, *The Culture of Ancient Egypt,* p. 48.
16. Wilson, p. 49.
17. See Thorkild Jacobsen, "Mesopotamia."
18. Jacobsen, pp. 189ff.
19. Much of the material presented here can be found in Robbins Burling, *Hill Farms and Padi Fields,* chapters 4 and 5.
20. Burling, p. 66.
21. Karl A. Wittfogel, *Oriental Despotism.*
22. Robert J. Braidwood and Gordon R. Willey (eds.), *Courses Toward Urban Life,* pp. 350–58.

Chapter 7

1. Much of the material on Buddhism and Thailand comes from A. Thomas Kirsch, "Phu Thai Religious Syncretism."
2. The following remarks on Indian prehistory follow Sir Mortimer Wheeler, *Early India and Pakistan: To Ashoka.* The analysis of Hinduism owes much to Max Weber, *The Religion of India,* and Talcott Parsons, *Societies,* chapter 5.

3. The following analysis of Islam is primarily based on Gustave von Grunebaum, *Medieval Islam.*
4. Carl Brockelmann, *History of the Islamic Peoples,* pp. 8ff.
5. von Grunebaum, *Medieval Islam,* p. 215.

Chapter 8

1. Michael Walzer, *The Revolution of the Saints,* p. 167.
2. The following account of Weber's Protestant Ethic Thesis owes much to Talcott Parsons, *The Structure of Social Action,* part III. The other major source is Max Weber, *The Protestant Ethic and the Spirit of Capitalism.*
3. Weber, *Protestant Ethic,* p. 51.
4. Weber, p. 116.
5. Reinhard Bendix, *Max Weber: An Intellectual Portrait,* p. 72.
6. Sinclair Lewis, *Dodsworth,* p. 10.
7. Several of the following criticisms are expressed in Kurt Samuelsson, *Religion and Economic Action.*
8. Samuelsson, pp. 27–42.
9. Marion J. Levy, Jr., "Some Aspects of 'Individualism' and the Problem of Modernization in China and Japan," p. 230.
10. Robert N. Bellah, *Tokugawa Religion,* p. 2. The following discussion derives from this work.
11. David E. Apter, *The Politics of Modernization,* chapter 8.
12. The interpretation of Indonesia presented here basically follows Herbert Feith, "The Dynamics of Guided Democracy." However, most comments and examples regarding Sukarno's imagery and the role of youth come from direct observation by Peacock during a 1962–1963 sojourn in Indonesia.
13. Feith, p. 313.
14. Feith, p. 325.
15. These images are taken from several utterances by Sukarno, some of which are briefly described in James L. Peacock, *Rites of Modernization,* p. 101, note 9.

Chapter 9

1. These and other statistics cited in this chapter are, except where noted otherwise, taken from Gerhard Lenski, *Power and Privilege.*
2. Donald J. Bogue, "Population Growth in the United States," p. 385.
3. Full exposition of Mills's argument appears in his *The Power Elite.*
4. These statistics, those that follow, and some of the implications drawn from them derive from Lenski, *Power and Privilege,* pp. 347–63.
5. Parsons set forth this analysis in the course of lectures on the "Social Structure of the United States" at Harvard University in 1964.

6. The following argument is taken from William H. Whyte, Jr., *The Organization Man,* pp. 4–24.
7. Whyte, p. 22.
8. David Reisman, Nathan Glazer, and Reuel Denney, *The Lonely Crowd,* p. 122.
9. Riesman, p. 122.
10. Riesman, p. 127.
11. Reuel Denney, *The Astonished Muse,* p. 28.
12. Marshall McLuhan, *Understanding Media,* p. 8.
13. McLuhan, p. 8.
14. McLuhan, pp. 7–21.
15. McLuhan, p. 86.
16. McLuhan, p. 178.
17. McLuhan, p. 314.
18. McLuhan, p. 136.
19. McLuhan, p. 332.
20. McLuhan, p. 346.
21. Cited in John Warwick Montgomery, *The "Is God Dead?" Controversy,* p. 21.
22. Cited in Montgomery, p. 24.
23. Cited in Montgomery, p. 29.
24. Cited in Montgomery, p. 29.
25. Cited in Montgomery, p. 33.

Bibliography

An asterisk (*) at the beginning of an entry means either that the edition cited is in paperback or that it is available in paperback.

ADAMS, RICHARD E. W. *Prehistoric Mesoamerica.* Boston: Little, Brown, 1977.

AHLSTROM, SIDNEY. *A Religious History of the American People.* New Haven, Conn.: Yale University Press, 1972.

*ALLAND, ALEXANDER. *Evolution and Human Behavior: An Introduction to Darwinian Anthropology.* New York: Anchor Press, 1973.

*APTER, DAVID E. *The Politics of Modernization.* Chicago: University of Chicago Press, 1965.

BAKER, DOROTHY. *Young Man with a Horn.* Boston: Houghton Mifflin, 1938.

BALANDIER, GEORGES. *Political Anthropology.* New York: Pantheon Books, 1970.

BALDUS, H. "Curt Nimuendaju, 1883–1945." *American Anthropologist* 48 (1946):238–243.

*BEATTIE, JOHN. *Bunyoro: An African Kingdom.* New York: Holt, Rinehart and Winston, 1960.

BEIDELMAN, T. O. "Swazi Royal Ritual." *Africa* 36 (1966):373–405.

BELL, DANIEL. *The Cultural Contradictions of Capitalism.* New York: Basic Books, 1975.

BELLAH, ROBERT N. "Reflections on the Protestant Ethic Analogy in Asia." *Journal of Social Issues* 19 (1963):52–60.

———. "Religious Evolution." *American Sociological Review* 29 (1964):358–74.

———. *Tokugawa Religion: The Values of Pre-Industrial Japan.* New York: Free Press, 1957.

———. *Beyond Belief: Essays on Religion in a Post-Traditional World.* New York: Harper & Row, 1970.

———, ed. *Religion and Progress in Modern Asia.* New York: Free Press, 1965.

*BENDIX, REINHARD. *Max Weber: An Intellectual Portrait.* Garden City, N. Y.: Doubleday, 1962.

*BERGER, PETER. *The Homeless Mind.* New York: Random House, 1973.

BIRDSELL, J. B. *Human Evolution.* Chicago: Rand McNally, 1972.

BLOOMFIELD, LEONARD. *Language.* New York: Holt, 1933.

*BLUM, HAROLD F. "On the Origin and Evolution of Human Culture." In Wilbert E. Moore and Robert M. Cook, eds., *Readings on Social Change.* Englewood Cliffs, N.J.: Prentice-Hall, 1967.

BOGUE, DONALD J. "Population Growth in the United States." In Edward C. McDonagh and Jon E. Simpson, eds., *Social Problems: Persistent Challenges.* New York: Holt, Rinehart and Winston, 1965.

BOHANNAN, PAUL J. *Justice and Judgment Among the Tiv.* London: Oxford University Press, 1957.

———. *Social Anthropology.* New York: Holt, Rinehart and Winston, 1963.

———, and M. GLAZER, eds. *High Points in Anthropology.* New York: Knopf, 1973.

*BOWEN, ELENORE S. *Return to Laughter.* Garden City, N.Y.: Doubleday, 1964.

*BRACE, C. LORING. *The Stages of Human Evolution: Human and Cultural Origins.* Englewood Cliffs, N.J.: Prentice-Hall, 1967.

BRAIDWOOD, ROBERT J., and GORDON R. WILLEY, eds. *Courses Toward Urban Life: Archaeological Considerations of Some Cultural Alternatives.* Chicago: Aldine-Atherton, 1962. (Viking Fund Publications in Anthropology, 32)

*BRINTON, CRANE, ed. *The Age of Reason Reader.* New York: Viking Press, 1973.

*BROCKELMANN, CARL. *History of the Islamic Peoples.* New York: Putnam, 1960.

BUETTNER-JANUSCH, J. *Physical Anthropology: A Perspective.* New York: John Wiley, 1973.

BUNZEL, RUTH. "Introduction to Zuni Ceremonialism." In *47th Annual Report of the Bureau of American Ethnology.* Washington, D.C.: U.S. Government Printing Office, 1932.

*BURLING, ROBBINS. *Hill Farms and Padi Fields: Life in Mainland Southeast Asia.* Englewood Cliffs, N.J.: Prentice-Hall, 1965.

*BURROW, J. W. *Evolution and Society: A Study in Victorian Social Theory.* Cambridge, England: Cambridge University Press, 1970.

*CALLAHAN, DANIEL, ed. *The American Population Debate.* Garden City, N.Y.: Doubleday, 1971.

CAMPBELL, JOHN K. *Honour, Family and Patronage.* New York: Oxford University Press, 1964.

CARROLL, JOHN B., and JOSEPH B. CASAGRANDE. "The Function of Language Classifications in Behavior." In Alfred G. Smith, ed., *Communication and Culture: Readings in the Codes of Human Interaction.* New York: Holt, Rinehart and Winston, 1966.

*CASAGRANDE, JOSEPH B., ed. *In the Company of Man: Twenty Portraits of Anthropological Informants.* New York: Harper & Row, 1964.

*CHILDE, V. GORDON. *Man Makes Himself.* New York: New American Library, 1956.

*————. *Social Evolution.* Cleveland: World, 1951.

*————. *What Happened in History.* Baltimore: Penguin, 1946.

*CLARK, W. E. LE GROS. *History of the Primates.* Chicago: University of Chicago Press, 1965.

*COE MICHAEL D. *Mexico.* New York: Praeger, 1962.

COEDÉS, GEORGE. *Angkor: An Introduction.* New York: OXford University Press, 1963.

————. *The Making of Southeast Asia.* Berkeley: University of California Press, 1966.

COHN, BERNARD S. *India: The Social Anthropology of a Civilization.* Englewood Cliffs, N.J.: Prentice-Hall, 1971.

*COHN, NORMAN. *The Pursuit of the Millenium.* New York: Harper & Row, 1961.

COOK, SCOTT. "Economic Anthropology: Problems in Theory, Method, and Analysis." In John J. Honigmann, ed., *Handbook of Social and Cultural Anthropology.* Chicago: Rand McNally, 1973.

*COX, HARVEY. *The Secular City.* New York: Macmillan, 1965.

*CRANE, JULIA and MICHAEL ANGROSINO. *Field Projects in Anthropology: A Student Handbook.* Morristown, N.J.: General Learning Press, 1974.

*DANIEL, GLYN. *Origin and Growth of Archaeology.* New York: Thomas Y. Crowell, 1971.

DARNELL, REGNA. *Readings in the History of Anthropology.* New York: Harper & Row, 1974.

*DEETZ, JAMES. *Invitation to Archaeology.* New York: The Natural History Press, 1967.

*DENNEY, REUEL. *The Astonished Muse.* Chicago: University of Chicago Press, 1957.

DEVEREUX, GEORGE. "Art and Mythology: A General Theory." In Bert Kaplan, ed., *Studying Personality Cross-Culturally.* New York: Harper & Row, 1961.

DEWEY, ALICE G. *Peasant Marketing in Java.* New York: Free Press, 1962.

DOUGLAS, MARY. *Purity and Danger: An Analysis of Concepts of Pollution and Taboo.* New York: Praeger, 1966.

DuBois, Cora. "The Dominant Value Profile of American Culture." *American Anthropologist* 57 (1955):1232–39.

*Durkheim, Emile. *The Elementary Forms of the Religious Life.* New York: Free Press, 1965.

*———, and Marcel Mauss. *Primitive Classification.* Chicago: University of Chicago Press, 1963.

*Edgerton, Robert and L. L. Langess. *Methods and Styles in the Study of Culture.* San Francisco: Chandler & Sharp, 1974.

*Eiseley, Loren. *Darwin's Century: Evolution and the Men Who Discovered It.* New York: Anchor Books, 1961.

Eisenstadt, S. N. *Modernization: Protest and Change.* Englewood Cliffs, N.J.: Prentice-Hall, 1966.

*Eisenstadt, S. N., ed. *The Protestant Ethic and Modernization: A Comparative View.* New York: Basic Books, 1968.

*Elkin, A. P. *The Australian Aborigines.* London: Angus and Robertson, 1966.

Evans-Pritchard, E. E. *Kinship and Marriage Among the Nuer.* London: Oxford University Press, 1951.

*———. *The Nuer.* London: Oxford University Press, 1940.

———. *Nuer Religion.* London: Oxford University Press, 1956.

*———. *Social Anthropology and Other Essays.* New York: Free Press, 1964.

*———. *Theories of Primitive Religion.* London: Oxford University Press, 1965.

Fagan, Brian M. *In the Beginning: An Introduction to Archaeology.* Boston: Little, Brown, 1975.

*Fallers, Lloyd. *Bantu Bureaucracy.* Chicago: University of Chicago Press, 1965.

Fei, Hsiao-t'ung. *Peasant Life in China: A Field Study of Country Life in the Yangtze Valley.* New York: Oxford University Press, 1946.

Feith, Herbert. "The Dynamics of Guided Democracy." In Ruth T. McVey, ed., *Indonesia.* New Haven, Conn.: Human Relations Area Files Press, 1963.

Ferris, William and Judy Peiser, eds. *American Folklore Films and Videotapes: An Index.* Memphis, Tenn.: Center for Southern Folklore, 1976.

Firth, Raymond. *Primitive Polynesian Economics.* London: Routledge, 1939.

*———. *We, the Tikopia: A Sociological Study of Kinship in Primitive Polynesia,* 2nd abr. ed. Boston: Beacon Press, 1963.

*———, ed. *Man and Culture: An Evaluation of the Work of Bronislaw Malinwoski.* New York: Harper Torchbooks, 1964.

———. *Symbols: Public and Private.* Ithaca, N.Y.: Cornell University Press, 1973.

*Forde, Daryll, ed. *African Worlds: Studies in the Cosmological Ideas and Social Values of African Peoples.* London: Oxford University Press, 1954.

Fortes, Meyer. "The Structure of Unilineal Descent Groups." *American Anthropologist* 55 (1953):17–41.

*———, and E. E. EVANS-PRITCHARD, eds. *African Political Systems*. London: Oxford University Press, 1940.

*FOX, ROBIN. *Kinship and Marriage*. Baltimore: Penguin, 1967.

*FRANKFORT, HENRI. *Ancient Egyptian Religion*. New York: Harper & Row, 1961.

———. *Kingship and the Gods*. Chicago: University of Chicago Press, 1948.

*———, et al. *Before Philosophy: The Intellectual Adventure of Ancient Man*. Baltimore: Penguin, 1967.

*FRAZER, JAMES GEORGE. *The Golden Bough: Study in Magic and Religion*, abr. ed. New York: Macmillan, 1958.

*FRIED, MORTON H. *The Evolution of Political Society*. New York: Random House, 1967.

*FROMKIN, VICTORIA and ROBERT RODMAN. *An Introduction to Language*. New York: Holt, Rinehart, and Winston, 1974.

GEERTZ, CLIFFORD. *Islam Observed: Religious Development in Morocco and Indonesia*. New Haven, Conn.: Yale University Press, 1968.

*———. *Peddlers and Princes: Social Change and Economic Modernization in Two Indonesian Towns*. Chicago: University of Chicago Press, 1963.

*———. "Religion as a Cultural System." In Michael Banton, ed., *Anthropological Approaches to the Study of Religion*. London: Tavistock, 1966.

*———. *The Religion of Java*. New York: Free Press, 1964.

———, ed. *Old Societies and New States*. New York: Free Press, 1963.

GEERTZ, HILDRED. *The Javanese Family: A Study of Kinship and Socialization*. New York: Free Press, 1961.

*GIBB, H. A. R. *Mohammedanism: An Historical Survey*. New York: Oxford University Press, 1962.

GILLIN, JOHN. "National and Regional Cultural Values in the United States." *Social Forces* 34 (1955):107–13.

———. *The Ways of Men: An Introduction to Anthropology*. New York: Appleton-Century-Crofts, 1948.

*GILLISPIE, CHARLES C. *From Genesis to Geology: A Study in the Relations of Scientific Thought, Natural Theology, and Social Opinion in Great Britain, 1790–1859*. New York: Harper Torchbooks, 1959.

GLUCKMAN, MAX. *The Ideas in Barotse Jurisprudence*. New Haven, Conn.: Yale University Press, 1965.

———. *The Judicial Process Among the Barotse of Northern Rhodesia*. New York: Free Press, 1955.

———. "Les Rites de Passage." In Max Gluckman, ed., *Essays on the Ritual of Social Relations*. Manchester: Manchester University Press, 1962.

———. "Rituals of Rebellion in Southeast Africa." In Max Gluckman, ed., *Order and Rebellion in Tribal Africa*. New York: Free Press, 1963. (Bobbs-Merrill reprint A-368)

GODELIER, MAURICE. *Perspectives in Marxist Anthropology*. New York: Cambridge University Press, 1977.

GOLDSCHMIDT, WALTER, ed. *Exploring the Ways of Mankind.* New York: Holt, Rinehart and Winston, 1960.

GOLDE, PEGGY. *Women in the Field,* Chicago: Aldine-Atherton, 1970.

*GOODE, WILLIAM J. *Religion Among the Primitives.* New York: Free Press, 1964.

———. *World Revolution and Family Patterns.* New York: Free Press, 1963.

GOODENOUGH, WARD H. "Residence Rules." *Southwestern Journal of Anthropology* 12 (1956):22–37.

GOODY, JACK, ed. *The Developmental Cycle in Domestic Groups.* London: Cambridge University Press, 1958. (Cambridge Papers in Social Anthropology, 1)

*———. *Kinship: Selected Readings.* Baltimore: Penguin Books, 1971.

*GORER, GEOFFREY. *The American People: A Study in National Character.* New York: Norton, 1964.

*GRANET, MARCEL. *Chinese Civilization.* New York: Meridian Books, 1958.

*GREEN, ROBERT, ed. *Protestantism and Capitalism: The Weber Thesis and Its Critics.* Boston: Heath, 1959.

*GREENBERG, JOSEPH H. *Anthropological Linguistics: An Introduction.* New York: Random House, 1968.

*GREENE, JOHN C. *The Death of Adam: Evolution and its Impact on Western Thought.* New York: Mentor Books, 1961.

HAAS, MARY R. and HENG R. SUBHANKA. *Spoken Thai.* Washington, D.C.: Linguistic Society of America, 1945.

HADDON, ALFRED C. *A History of Anthropology.* New York: Putnam, 1910.

*HALL, EDWARD T. *The Silent Language.* Greenwich, Conn.: Fawcett, 1961.

HARRIS, MARVIN. *The Rise of Anthropological Theory.* New York: Thomas Y. Crowell, 1968.

———. *Cows, Pigs, Wars, and Witches: The Riddles of Culture.* New York: Vintage Books, 1974.

*HART, C. W. M., and ARNOLD R. PILING. *The Tiwi of North Australia.* New York: Holt, Rinehart and Winston, 1960.

*HATCH, ELVIN. *Theories of Man and Culture.* New York: Columbia University Press, 1973.

*HAYS, H. R. *From Ape to Angel.* New York: Putnam, 1964.

HEIDER, KARL G. *Films for Anthropological Teaching.* Cambridge, Mass.: Program in Ethnographic Film, 1968.

HEINE-GELDERN, ROBERT. *Conceptions of State and Kingship in Southeast Asia.* Ithaca, N.Y.: Cornell University Southeast Asia Program, 1956. (Data paper, 18)

HEIZER, ROBERT, and FRANK HOLE. *Prehistoric Archaeology: A Brief Introduction.* New York: Holt, Rinehart, and Winston, 1969.

HELM, JUNE, ed. *Pioneers of American Anthropology.* Seattle: University of Washington Press, 1966.

*HENRY, JULES. *Culture Against Man.* New York: Random House, 1963.

*HERBERG, WILL. *Protestant, Catholic, Jew.* Garden City, N.Y.: Doubleday, 1955.

*HERSKOVITS, MELVILLE J. *Economic Anthropology.* New York: Norton, 1965.

HOCKETT, CHARLES F. *A Course in Modern Linguistics.* New York: Macmillan, 1958.

——, and ROBERT ASCHER. "The Human Revolution." *Current Anthropology* 5 (1964):135–68.

*HODGEN, MARGARET T. *Early Anthropology in the Sixteenth and Seventeenth Centuries.* Philadelphia: University of Pennsylvania Press, 1971.

HODGSON, MARSHALL. *The Venture of Islam.* Chicago: University of Chicago Press, 1974.

*HOEBEL, E. ADAMSON. *The Law of Primitive Man: A Study in Comparative Legal Dynamics.* New York: Atheneum, 1968.

HOLMES, LOWELL D. *Anthropology: An Introduction.* New York: Ronald, 1965.

HOMANS, GEORGE C., and DAVID M. SCHNEIDER. *Marriage, Authority, and Final Causes.* New York: Free Press, 1955.

HONIGMANN, JOHN J. *Personality in Culture.* New York: Harper & Row, 1967.

——. *The Development of Anthropological Ideas.* Homewood, Ill.: Dorsey Press, 1976.

*HSU, FRANCIS L. K. *Under the Ancestor's Shadow.* Garden City, N.Y.: Doubleday, 1948.

——, ed. *Psychological Anthropology: Approaches to Culture and Personality.* Homewood, Ill.: Dorsey Press, 1961.

HUBERT, HENRI, and MARCEL MAUSS. *Sacrifice: Its Nature and Function.* Chicago: University of Chicago Press, 1964.

HYMES, DELL, ed. *Language in Culture and Society: A Reader in Linguistics and Anthropology.* New York: Harper & Row, 1964.

——, ed. *Reinventing Anthropology.* New York: Pantheon Books, 1972.

*ICE, JACKSON LEE, and JOHN J. CAREY, eds. *The Death of God Debate.* Philadelphia: The Westminster Press, 1967.

*JACOBSEN, THORKILD. "Mesopotamia." In Henri Frankfort et al., *Before Philosophy.* Baltimore: Penguin, 1967.

JARVIE, I. C. *The Revolution in Anthropology.* London: Routledge, 1967.

JOHNSON, HARRY M. *Sociology: A Systematic Introduction.* New York: Harcourt Brace Jovanovich, 1960.

*KAPLAN, ABRAHAM. *The Conduct of Inquiry: Methodology for Behavioral Science.* San Francisco: Chandler, 1964.

*KARDINER, ABRAM, and EDWARD PREBLE. *They Studied Man.* New York: New American Library, 1965.

KATEB, G. *Utopia and Its Enemies.* New York: Schocken Books, 1972.

KENISTON, KENNETH. "You Have to Grow Up in Scarsdale to Know How Bad Things Really Are." *New York Times Magazine* (April 27, 1969):27–28, 122–30.

KIRSCH, A. THOMAS. "Phu Thai Religious Syncretism." Unpublished doctoral thesis, Harvard University, 1967.

———. *Feasting and Social Oscillation.* Ithaca, N.Y.: Cornell University Press, 1973.

*KLUCKHOHN, CLYDE. *Mirror for Man: The Relation of Anthropology to Modern Life.* Greenwich, Conn.: Fawcett, 1968.

*———, and DOROTHEA LEIGHTON. *The Navaho,* rev. ed. Garden City, N.Y.: Doubleday, 1962.

KROEBER, ALFRED L. *Anthropology,* rev. ed. New York: Harcourt Brace Jovanovich, 1948.

———. *Configurations of Culture Growth.* Berkeley: University of California Press, 1944.

*———, and CLYDE KLUCKHOHN. *Culture: A Critical Review of Concepts and Definitions.* New York: Random House, 1963.

KUPER, ADAM. *Anthropologists and Anthropology: The British School, 1922-1972.* London: Allen Lane, 1973.

KUPER, HILDA. *An African Aristocracy: Rank Among the Swazi.* London: Oxford University Press, 1965.

*———. *The Swazi: A South African Kingdom.* New York: Holt, Rinehart and Winston, 1963.

LABARRE, WESTON. "The Cultural Basis of Emotions and Gestures." *Journal of Personality* 16 (1947):49-68.

*———. *The Human Animal.* Chicago: University of Chicago Press, 1960.

*———. *The Ghost Dance: The Origins of Religion.* New York: Dell Publishing Co., 1972.

LANDON, KENNETH. *Southeast Asia: Crossroad of Religions.* Chicago: University of Chicago Press, 1949.

*LANNING, EDWARD P. *Peru Before the Incas.* Englewood Cliffs, N.J.: Prentice-Hall, 1967.

*LEACH, EDMUND. *Political Systems of Highland Burma.* Boston: Beacon Press, 1965.

*———. *Rethinking Anthropology.* New York: Humanities Press, 1966. (London School of Economics Monographs on Social Anthropology #22)

*———. "The Structural Implications of Matrilateral Cross-Cousin Marriage," *Rethinking Anthropology.* New York: Humanities Press, 1966.

———. *A Runaway World? The BBC Reith Lectures 1967.* New York: Oxford University Press, 1968.

LEE, DOROTHY. "Lineal and Nonlineal Codifications of Reality." *Psychosomatic Medicine* 12 (1950):89-97.

*LEHMAN, F. K. *The Structure of Chin Society.* Urbana: University of Illinois Press, 1963.

LENSKI, GERHARD. *Human Societies: A New Introduction to Sociology.* New York: McGraw-Hill, 1970.

————. *Power and Privilege: A Theory of Social Stratification.* New York: McGraw-Hill, 1966.

*————. *The Religious Factor: A Sociological Study of Religion's Impact on Politics, Economics and Family Life.* Garden City, N.Y.: Doubleday, 1963.

*LERNER, DANIEL. *The Passing of Traditional Society: Modernizing the Middle East.* New York: Free Press, 1965.

*LERNER, MAX. *America as a Civilization.* New York: Simon & Schuster, 1957.

LESSA, WILLIAM A., and EVON Z. VOGT, eds. *Reader in Comparative Religion*, 2nd ed. New York: Harper & Row, 1965.

*LEVINE, ROBERT. *Culture, Behavior and Personality.* Chicago: Aldine-Atherton, 1973.

*LÉVI-STRAUSS, CLAUDE. *The Elementary Structures of Kinship.* London: Eyre and Spottiswoode, 1969.

*————. "The Family." In Harry L. Shapiro, ed., *Man, Culture, and Society.* New York: Oxford University Press, 1956.

————. "The Future of Kinship Studies." *Proceedings of the Royal Anthropological Institute* (1965):13–22.

*————. *The Savage Mind.* Chicago: University of Chicago Pre-s, 1966.

*————. *Totemism.* Boston: Beacon Press, 1963.

*————. *Tristes Tropiques.* New York: Atheneum, 1964.

LEVY, MARION J. JR. "Contrasting Factors in the Modernization of China and Japan." *Economic Development and Culture Change* 2 (1953);161–97.

*————. *The Family Revolution in Modern China.* New York: Atheneum, 1968.

*————. *Modernization and the Structure of Societies: A Setting for the Study of International Affairs*, 2 vols. Princeton, N.J.: Princeton University Press, 1966.

*————. "Social Patterns (Structures) and Problems of Modernization." In Wilbert E. Moore and Robert M. Cook, eds. *Readings on Social Change.* Englewood Cliffs, N.J.: Prentice-Hall, 1967.

————. "Some Aspects of 'Individualism' and the Problem of Modernization in China and Japan." *Journal of Educational Development and Cultural Change* 10 (1962):225–40.

*LEVY, REUBEN. *The Social Structure of Islam.* New York: Cambridge University University Press, 1962.

LEWIS, I. M. *Ecstatic Religion: An Anthropological Study of Spirit Possession and Shamanism.* Baltimore: Penguin, 1971.

*LEWIS, SINCLAIR. *Dodsworth.* New York: Harcourt Brace Jovanovich, 1929.

LIENHARDT, GODFREY. *Divinity and Experience: The Religion of the Dinka.* London: Oxford University Press. 1961.

*————. *Social Anthropology.* London: Oxford University Press, 1965.

*LIPSET, SEYMOUR MARTIN. *The First New Nation: The United States in Historical and Comparative Perspective.* Garden City, N.Y.: Doubleday, 1967.

LLEWELLYN, K. N., and HOEBEL, E. ADAMSON. *The Cheyenne Way: Conflict and Case*

Law in Primitive Jurisprudence. Norman: University of Oklahoma Press, 1941.

LOWIE, ROBERT H. *The History of Ethnological Theory.* New York: Holt, 1937.

*MCCLELLAND, DAVID C. *The Achieving Society.* New York: Free Press, 1967.

MACCOBY, MICHAEL. *The Gamesman: The New Corporate Leaders.* New York: Simon & Schuster, 1976.

*MCDONAGH, EDWARD C., and JON E. SIMPSON, eds. *Social Problems: Persistent Challenges.* New York: Holt, Rinehart and Winston, 1966.

*MCLUHAN, MARSHALL. *Understanding Media.* New York: McGraw-Hill, 1964.

*————, and QUENTIN FIORE. *The Medium Is the Massage.* New York: Bantam Books, 1967.

MCVEY, RUTH T., and KARL J. PELZER, eds. *Indonesia.* New Haven, Conn.: Human Relations Area Files Press, 1963.

*MAINE, HENRY. *Ancient Law: Its Connection with the Early History of Society and Its Relations to Modern Ideas.* Boston: Beacon Press, 1963.

*MALEFIJT, ANNEMARIE DE WAAL. *Images of Man: A History of Anthropological Thought.* New York: Knopf, 1974.

*MALINOWSKI, BRONISLAW. *Argonauts of the Western Pacific: An Account of Native Enterprise and Adventure in the Archipelagoes of Melanesian New Guinea.* New York: Dutton, 1961.

*————. "Myth in Primitive Psychology," *Magic, Science and Religion, and Other Essays.* Garden City, N.Y.: Doubleday, 1954.

*————. *Sex and Repression in Savage Society.* Cleveland: World, 1968.

*MATOSSIAN, MARY. "The Ideologies of Delayed Industrialization: Some Tensions and Ambiguities." In J. H. Kautsky, ed., *Political Change in Underdeveloped Countries: Nationalism and Communism.* New York: John Wiley, 1962.

*MAUSS, MARCEL. *The Gift: Forms and Functions of Exchange in Archaic Societies.* New York: Norton, 1967.

MEAD, GEORGE HERBERT. "The Psychology of Punitive Justice." *American Journal of Sociology* 23 (1918):577–602.

*MEAD, MARGARET. *And Keep Your Powder Dry.* New York: Apollo Editions, 1965.

*————. *Ruth Benedict.* New York: Columbia University Press, 1974.

MERTON, ROBERT. *Social Theory and Social Structure.* New York: Free Press, 1957.

MICHAEL, DONALD N. "The Problems of Automation." In Edward C. McDonagh and Jon E. Simpson, eds., *Social Problems: Persistent Challenges.* New York: Holt, Rinehart and Winston, 1966.

MIDDLETON, JOHN, and DAVID TAIT, eds. *Tribes Without Rulers.* London: Routledge, 1958.

*MILLS, C. WRIGHT. *The Power Elite.* New York: Oxford University Press, 1956.

MINER, HORACE. "Body Ritual Among the Nacirema." *American Anthropologist* 58 (1956):503–7.

*Mirsky, Jeannette, and Nevins, Allan. *The World of Eli Whitney.* New York: Macmillan. 1952.

Montgomery, John Warwick. *The "Is God Dead?" Controversy.* Grand Rapids, Mich.: Zondervan, 1966.

*Moore, Wilbert, and Robert M. Cook, eds. *Readings on Social Change.* Englewood Cliffs, N.J.: Prentice-Hall, 1967.

*Morgan, Lewis Henry. *Ancient Society.* Cleveland: World, 1963.

*Moscati, Sabatino. *The Face of the Ancient Orient.* Garden City, N.'.: Doubleday, 1962.

*Murchland, Bernard, ed. *The Meaning of the Death of God.* New York: Random House, 1967.

*Murdock, George Peter. *Social Structure.* New York: Free Press, 1965.

*Murra, John, ed. *American Anthropology: The Early Years.* St. Paul and New York: West Publishing Co., 1974. Proceedings of the American Ethnological Society, 1976.

Nagel, Ernest. *The Structure of Science: Problems in the Logic of Scientific Explanation.* New York: Harcourt Brace Jovanovich, 1961.

Nash, Manning. *The Golden Road to Modernity.* New York: John Wiley, 1965.

———, ed. *Anthropological Studies in Theravada Buddhism.* New Haven, Conn.: Yale University Southeast Asia Studies, 1966. (Cultural Report, 13)

Needham, Rodney. *Structure and Sentiment.* Chicago: University of Chicago Press, 1962.

Norbeck, Edward. *Religion in Primitive Society.* New York: Harper & Row, 1961.

*Parsons, Talcott. *Societies: Evolutionary and Comparative Perspectives.* Englewood Cliffs, N.J.: Prentice-Hall, 1966.

*———. *The Structure of Social Action.* New York: Free Press, 1968.

———, Edward Shils, Kaspar D. Naegele, and Jesse R. Pitts, eds. *Theories of Society: Foundations of Modern Sociological Theory,* 2 vols. New York: Free Press, 1961.

Peacock, James L. "Mystics and Merchants in Fourteenth Century Germany." *Journal for the Scientific Study of Religion* 8 (1969):47–59.

———. *Rites of Modernization: Symbolic and Social Aspects of Indonesian Proletarian Drama.* Chicago: University of Chicago Press, 1968.

———. "Ethics, Economics, and Society in Evolutionary Perspective." In Ivan Hill, ed., *The Ethical Basis of Economic Freedom.* Chapel Hill, N.C.: American Viewpoint, 1976.

———. *Consciousness and Change: Symbolic Anthropology in Evolutionary Perspective.* New York: John Wiley, 1975.

*Penniman, T. K. *A Hundred Years of Anthropology,* rev. ed. New York: Morrow, 1974.

*Peterson, Frederick, *Ancient Mexico.* New York: Putnam, 1959.

Phillips, Herbert P. *Thai Peasant Personality.* Berkeley: University of California Press, 1965.

*PIGGOTT, STUART. *Approach to Archaeology.* New York: McGraw-Hill, 1965.

POCOCK, DAVID. *Mind, Body, and Wealth.* Totowa, N.J.: Rowman and Littlefield 1973.

*POTTER, J. M., M. N. DIAZ, and G. M. FOSTER, eds. *Peasant Society: A Reader.* Boston: Little, Brown, 1967.

POWDERMAKER, HORTENSE. *After Freedom: A Cultural Study in the Deep South.* New York: Atheneum, 1968.

*RADCLIFFE-BROWN, A. R., and DARYLL FORDE, eds. *African Systems of Kinship and Marriage.* London: Oxford University Press, 1950.

RADIN, PAUL. *Primitive Man as Philosopher,* 2nd rev. ed. New York: Dover, 1957.

RAPPAPORT, ROY. "Nature, Culture, and Ecological Anthropology." In Harry L. Shapiro, ed., *Man, Culture, and Society.* New York: Oxford University Press, 1971.

*REDFIELD, ROBERT. *The Primitive World and Its Transformations.* Ithaca, N.Y.: Cornell University Press, 1953.

*REICH, CHARLES A. *The Greening of America.* New York: Bantam Books, 1971.

RICHERSON, PETER and J. McEVOY, eds. *Human Ecology, An Environmental Approach.* North Scituate, Mass.: Duxbury, 1976.

*RIESMAN, DAVID, NATHAN GLAZER, and REUEL DENNEY. *The Lonely Crowd: A Study of Changing American Character,* abr. ed. Garden City, N.Y.: Doubleday, 1953.

*ROSENBERG, BERNARD, and DAVID MANNING WHITE, eds. *Mass Culture.* New York: Free Press, 1957.

*SAGGS, H. W. F. *The Greatness That Was Babylon.* New York: New American Library, 1968.

SAHLINS, MARSHALL. *Culture and Practical Reason.* Chicago: University of Chicago Press, 1976.

*SAMUELSSON, KURT. *Religion and Economic Action: A Critique of Max Weber.* Stockholm: Scandinavian University Books, 1961.

*SAPIR, EDWARD. *Language.* New York: Harcourt, Brace, 1921.

*SCHNEIDER, DAVID M. *American Kinship: A Cultural Account.* Englewood Cliffs, N.J.: Prentice-Hall, 1968.

———, and KATHLEEN GOUGH eds. *Matrilineal Kinship.* Berkeley: University of California Press, 1961.

SCHUSKY, ERNEST LESTER. *Manual for Kinship Analysis.* New York: Holt, Rinehart and Winston, 1972.

*SERVICE, ELMAN R. *Primitive Social Organization.* New York: Random House, 1962.

———. *Origin of the State and Civilization.* New York: Norton, 1975.

*SIGMUND, PAUL E. *The Ideologies of the Developing Nations.* New York: Praeger, 1963.

SINGER, MILTON. *When A Great Tradition Modernizes.* New York: Praeger, 1972.

SLOTKIN, J. S. *Readings in Early Anthropology.* Chicago: Aldine-Atherton, 1965.

*SPIRO, MELFORD E., *Burmese Supernaturalism*. Englewood Cliffs, N.J.: Prentice-Hall, 1967.

SPRADLEY, JAMES, and DAVID McCURDY. *The Cultural Experience*. Chicago: Science Research Associates, 1972.

SPRADLEY, JAMES, and MICHAEL A. RYNKIEWICH. *The Nacirema: Readings on American Culture*. Boston: Little, Brown, 1975.

*SPUHLER JAMES N., ed. *The Evolution of Man's Capacity for Culture*. Detroit: Wayne University Press, 1959.

STANNER, W. E. H. "The Dreaming." In W. A. Lessa and E. Z. Vogt, eds. *Reader in Comparative Religion*, 2nd ed. New York: Harper & Row, 1965.

STANTON, WILLIAM S. *The Leopard's Spots: Scientific Attitudes Toward Race in America*. Chicago: University of Chicago Press, 1960.

*STEBBINS, G. LEDYARD. "Pitfalls and Guideposts in Comparing Organic and Social Evolution." In Wilbert E. Moore and Robert M. Cook, eds. *Readings on Social Change*. Englewood Cliffs, N.J.: Prentice-Hall, 1967.

STEVENSON, H. N. C. *The Economics of the Central Chin Tribes*. Bombay: Times of India Press, 1943.

STEWARD, JULIAN H. *The Theory of Culture Change: The Methodology of Multilineal Evolution*. Urbana: University of Illinois Press, 1955.

———. *Alfred Kroeber*. New York: Columbia University Press, 1973.

STOCKING, GEORGE W. JR. *Race, Culture and Evolution: Essays in the History of Anthropology*. New York: Free Press, 1968.

———, ed. *The Shaping of American Anthropology, 1883–1911: A Boas Reader*. New York: Basic Books, 1974.

*SWANSON, GUY E. *The Birth of the Gods: The Origin of Primitive Belief*. Ann Arbor: University of Michigan Press, 1960.

*TAWNEY, RICHARD. *Religion and the Rise of Capitalism: A Historical Study*. New York: New American Library, 1961.

*TOFFLER, ALVIN. *Future Shock*. New York: Bantam Books, 1971.

TONKINSON, ROBERT. *The Jigalong Mob: Aboriginal Victors of the Desert Crusade*. Menlo Park, Calif.: Cummings, 1974.

True: The Man's Magazine 49 (September 1968).

TURNER, VICTOR W. *The Drums of Affliction: A Study of Religious Processes Among the Ndembu of Zambia*. London: Oxford University Press, 1968.

———. *The Forest of Symbols: Aspects of Ndembu Ritual*. Ithaca, N.Y.: Cornell University Press, 1967.

———. "A Ndembu Doctor in Practice." In Ari Kiev, ed., *Magic, Faith and Healing: Studies in Primitive Psychiatry Today*. New York: Free Press, 1964.

———. *Schism and Continuity in an African Society*. Manchester: Manchester University Press, 1957.

UNDERHILL, RUTH M. *Ceremonial Patterns in the Greater Southwest*. New York: Augustin, 1948. (Monographs of the American Ethnological Society, 13)

VAYDA, ANDREW. "An Ecological Approach in Cultural Anthropology." In

Morton Fried, ed., *Explorations in Anthropology.* New York: Thomas Y. Crowell, 1973.

————, ed. *Environment and Culture Behavior.* Garden City, N.Y.: Natural History Press, 1969.

VERGOUWEN, J. C. *The Social Organization and Customary Law of the Toba-Batak of Northern Sumatra.* The Hague: Nijhoff, 1964.

VOGET, FRED. *A History of Ethnology.* New York: Holt, Rinehart and Winston, 1975.

*VON GRUNEBAUM, GUSTAVE E. *Medieval Islam.* Chicago: University of Chicago Press, 1961.

WALES H. G. QUATRITCH. *Ancient Siamese Government and Administration.* New York: Paragon, 1965.

WALLACE, ANTHONY F. C. *Religion: An Anthropological View.* New York: Random House, 1966.

————. "Revitalization Movements." *American Anthropologist* 58 (1956):264–81.

*WALZER, MICHAEL. *The Revolution of the Saints: A Study in the Origins of Radical Politics.* New York: Atheneum, 1968.

*WARNER, W. LLOYD. *American Life: Dream and Reality.* Chicago: University of Chicago Press, 1964.

*————. *Black Civilization.* New York: Harper & Row, 1964.

*WEBER, MAX. *The Protestant Ethic and the Spirit of Capitalism.* New York: Scribner, 1958.

*————. *The Religion of China.* New York: Free Press, 1951.

*————. *The Religion of India.* New York: Free Press, 1958.

*WEST, JAMES. *Plainsville, U.S.A.* New York: Columbia University Press, 1945.

WHEELER, SIR ROBERT ERIC MORTIMER. *Early India and Pakistan: To Ashoka.* New York: Praeger, 1959.

*WHITE JON E. M. *Everyday Life in Ancient Egypt.* New York: Putnam, 1967.

*WHITE, LESLIE A. *The Evolution of Culture.* New York: McGraw-Hill, 1959.

*WHITE, LYNN JR. *Medieval Technology and Social Change.* New York: Oxford University Press, 1962.

————. "World View and Technology in the European Middle Ages." Paper presented at Wenner-Gren Summer Symposium no. 41, Burg Wartenstein, Austria, August, 1968.

WHITE, WINSTON. *Beyond Conformity.* New York: Free Press, 1961.

*WHORF, BENJAMIN LEE. *Language, Thought, and Reality: Selected Writings of Benjamin Lee Whorf,* ed. John B. Carroll. Cambridge, Mass.: M.I.T. Press, 1956.

*WHYTE, WILLIAM H. JR. *The Organization Man.* New York: Simon & Schuster, 1957.

WILLEY, GORDON R. *An Introduction to American Archaeology,* vol. I: *North and Middle America.* Englewood Cliffs, N.J.: Prentice-Hall, 1966.

WILSON, E. O. *Sociobiology: The New Synthesis.* Cambridge, Mass.: Harvard University Press, 1975.

*WILSON, JOHN A. *The Culture of Ancient Egypt.* Chicago: University of Chicago Press, 1956.

*WITTFOGEL, KARL A. *Oriental Despotism.* New Haven, Conn.: Yale University Press, 1957.

*WOLF, ERIC. *Peasants.* Englewood Cliffs, N.J.: Prentice-Hall, 1966.

*WOLFE, TOM. *The Kandy-Kolored Tangerine-Flake Streamline Baby.* New York: Pocket Books, 1966.

WORSLEY, PETER. *The Trumpet Shall Sound.* London: MacGibbon and Kee, 1957.

ZIMMER, HEINRICH. *Philosophies of India.* New York: Meridian Books, 1956.

Film Bibliography

The Amish (Gateway Film Production).
The Ancient Egyptian (International Film Foundation).
Ancient Mesopotamia (New York University).
Apu Trilogy: Pather Panchalli, Aparajito, The World of Apu (Audio Film Center).
The Baboon Troop (Amboseli Reserve).
Bear and the Hunter.
Born for Hard Luck (Tom Davenport Films).
Dead Birds (Contemporary Films; University of California).
Djalambu (Australian Institute of Aboriginal Studies).
Dynamics of Male Dominance in a Baboon Troop. (Educational Services).
Excavations at La Venta (University of California at Berkeley).
The Exiles (Contemporary Films).
Fincho (Audio Film Center).
Four Families (New York University).
Glooscap County (Canadian Consulate).
The Great Unfenced (Contemporary Films).
The Hunters (Contemporary Films; New York University).
Journey to Mecca (Radim Films).
The Loon's Necklace (New York University; University of California).
Mecca, the Forbidden City (S. Diamond Film Dist.).

Moulay Idriss (Radim Films).
The Navaho as Filmmaker.
North Indian Village (International Film Bureau; University of California).
The Nuer (McGraw-Hill).
Pizza, Pizza, Daddy-O (San Fernando Valley State College; University of California).
Primitive People (University of California).
Tjuringa: The Story of Stone Age Man (Australian News and Information Bureau).
Trance and Dance in Bali (New York University; University of California).
Trobriand Cricket: An Ingenious Response to Colonialism (University of California).
Trobriand Islanders (University of California).
The Village (University of California).
Walkabout: A Journey with the Aborigines (Australian News and Information Bureau).

Addresses of Film Distributors

Audio Film Center, Inc.
10 Fiske Place
Mount Vernon, N.Y. 10550

The Secretary
Australian Institute of Aboriginal Studies
P.O. Box 553
Canberra, A.C.T., Australia

Australian News and Information Bureau

> Films Officer
> 636 Fifth Avenue
> New York, N.Y. 10020

> Press and Information Officer
> Australian Consulate General
> 350 Post Street
> San Francisco, Calif. 94108

Canadian Consulate

University of California Extension Media Center
2223 Fulton Street
Berkeley, Calif. 94720

Contemporary Films, Inc.
> 267 West 25th Street, New York, N.Y. 10001
> 614 Davis Street, Evanston, Ill. 60201
> 1211 Polk Street, San Francisco, Calif. 94109

Tom Davenport Films
Pearlstone Street
Delaplane, Va. 22025

S. Diamond Film Dist.
19208-8 Hamlin Street
Reseda, Calif. 91335

Educational Services, Inc.
39 Chapel Street
Newton, Mass. 02158

Gateway Film Productions
St. Lawrence House, 29/31 Broad Street
Briston, BS1 2HF England

International Film Bureau, Inc.
332 South Michigan Avenue
Chicago, Ill. 60604

International Film Foundation
475 Fifth Avenue
Suite 916
New York, N.Y. 10017

The Film Library
New York University
26 Washington Place
New York, N.Y. 10003

Radim Films, Inc.
220 West 42nd Street
New York, N.Y. 10036

Glossary

actual pattern: a pattern of behavior formulated by the objective scientific observer but not necessarily recognized by the performer. *Cf.* IDEAL PATTERN.

affine: a person related to another by marriage, e.g., an "in-law." *Cf.* KINSMAN.

age-grade: a group or status that includes all members of a society of a given age and sex.

avoidance custom: culturally prescribed inhibition of social contact.

bilateral kinship: a relationship established according to a pattern of tracing descent more or less equally through both paternal and maternal lines. *Cf.* UNILINEAL KINSHIP.

bureaucracy: an organization in which positions are ranked along explicit lines of authority and responsibility, one staffed according to universalistic standards and requiring of its personnel the performance of explicitly defined duties.

centralization: a trend toward coordinating the units of society under a central control.

circulating connubium: a system whereby prescribed marriage of matrilateral cross-cousins results in a regular exchange of women and goods between unilineal descent groups.

clan: a sizable unilineal descent group, ordinarily composed of a number of related lineages.

classificatory kinship terms: label given by Lewis Henry Morgan to a nomenclature in which a single term is applied to several kin types (lineal and collateral, maternal and paternal, etc.), with the effect of lumping them into one category; e.g., the English term "uncle" is classificatory in that it may refer either to a maternal or to a paternal relative. *Cf.* DESCRIPTIVE KINSHIP TERMS.

couvade: the custom of a man displaying the symptoms of pregnancy and/or birth while his wife is pregnant and/or giving birth.

cross-cousin: a child of one's parents' siblings of unlike sex, e.g., one's mother's *brother's* daughter, one's father's *sister's* daughter. *Cf.* PARALLEL COUSIN.

cultural relativism: the view that a society should be evaluated only in terms of the standards held by that society.

culture: a system of logically related ideas and values shared by members of a social system.

descriptive kinship terms: label given by Lewis Henry Morgan to a nomenclature in which distinct terms or combinations of basic terms are used to designate specific relationships; e.g., the terms "father" and "father's brother" distinguish lineal form collateral kin. *Cf.* CLASSIFICATORY KINSHIP TERMS.

diffuseness: the tendency to leave implicit the rights and obligations entailed by a given social relationship. *Cf.* SPECIFICITY.

endogamy: the custom of mating or marrying within a kinship or residential group. *Cf.* EXOGAMY.

ethical centralization: the development of a single ethic that is regarded as applying to all situations. *Cf.* SITUATIONALISM.

ethnocentrism: the interpretation of native behavior from the viewpoint of the observer's society rather than from the viewpoint of the native's society.

evolutionary theory: a conceptual scheme designed to expound how systems develop in determinate directions through persistent processes of change.

exogamy: the custom of mating with or marrying individuals from outside one's own kinship or residential group. *Cf.* ENDOGAMY.

extended family household: a residence unit composed not only of a couple and their offspring but of additional relatives as well. *Cf.* NUCLEAR FAMILY HOUSEHOLD.

fictive kinship: the application of kinship terminology and/or behavior to non-kinsmen.

formal pattern: a pattern regarded by members of a group as defining the only proper way to behave. *Cf.* TECHNICAL PATTERN.

functional pattern: a pattern of conditions and consequences formulated by the analyst with reference to a given society. *Cf.* LOGICAL PATTERN.

ideal pattern: a conception of morally desirable behavior formulated by members of a society but not necessarily paralleled by their actual patterns of behavior. *Cf.* ACTUAL PATTERN.

incest: culturally prohibited mating or marriage between kinsmen.

invisible functions: consequences or implications (of sociocultural patterns) not consciously perceived by natives of the society.

irrigated agriculture: a system of farming whereby crops are watered by artificial means.

kinsman: a person related to another by ties of common descent. *Cf.* AFFINE.

levirate: a custom whereby the brother of a deceased husband marries his widow.

lineage: a relatively small unilineal descent group. *Cf.* CLAN.

logical pattern: a pattern formulated by the analyst with reference to a given society, in which he relates to rules of behavior practices he sees as derived from them. *Cf.* FUNCTIONAL PATTERN.

matrilateral cross-cousin marriage: a pattern that allows or encourages a man's marriage to his mother's brother's daughter, but prohibits or discourages his marriage to his father's sister's daughter.

matrilineal: pertaining to descent traced solely or primarily through the mother and her female relatives. *Cf.* PATRILINEAL.

matrilocal residence: the settling of the newly married couple in or near the household of the wife's parents. *Cf.* NEOLOCAL; PATRILOCAL.

neolocal residence: the settling of the newly married couple in a domicile separate from the households of both the husband's and the wife's parents. *Cf.* MATRILOCAL; PATRILOCAL.

nuclear family household: a residence unit confined to a couple and their offspring. *Cf.* EXTENDED FAMILY HOUSEHOLD.

parallel cousin: a child of one's parents' siblings of like sex, e.g., one's mother's *sister's* daughter, one's father's *brother's* daughter. *Cf.* CROSS-COUSIN.

particularism: the pattern of evaluating individuals on the basis of their inherited status or kinship relationships rather than on the basis of their merit, skill, or accomplishments. *Cf.* UNIVERSALISM.

patrilineal: pertaining to descent traced solely or primarily through the father and his male relatives. *Cf.* MATRILINEAL.

patrilocal residence: the settling of the newly married couple in or near the household of the husband's parents. *Cf.* MATRILOCAL; NEOLOCAL.

personality: the system of behavioral components of an individual person.

polygyny: the custom of marriage between one man and two or more women simultaneously.

rationality: the tendency to justify or explain actions by emphasizing their efficient contribution to ends. *Cf.* TRADITIONALISM.

ritual of rebellion: culturally permitted symbolic expression of hostility and ambivalence toward institutionalized authority.

ritual of social relations: stylized ceremonials in which participants play the same roles toward one another that they play in ordinary life, thereby insuring that supernatural processes will tend to desirable ends for the society—purification, protection, prosperity.

silent pattern: a pattern that the natives of a society follow but cannot or do not verbalize.

situationalism: the practice of applying different ethical rules to different situations. *Cf.* ETHICAL CENTRALIZATION.

slash and burn agriculture: a system of farming entailing the cutting and burning of forest cover in order to prepare fields for planting and to increase their fertility.

social differentiation: the separation of social units from one another.

social system: a system of interacting roles and groups.

sorarate: a custom whereby a widower marries the sister of his deceased wife.

specialization: the concentration of efforts toward a limited end.

specificity: the tendency to define explicitly the rights and obligations entailed by a given social relationship. *Cf.* DIFFUSENESS.

syncretism: the blending of historically distinct traditions.

technical pattern: a pattern regarded by members of a group as defining one of several possible means to achieve some designated goal. *Cf.* FORMAL PATœ TERN.

teological fallacy: the assumption that every pattern which serves a given function was deliberately designed by someone to serve that function.

totem: an object, often a plant or animal, identified with, and venerated by, an individual or group.

traditionalism: the tendency to justify or explain actions by emphasizing their conformity to accepted and long-standing patterns. *Cf.* RATIONALITY.

unilineal descent group: a group composed of individuals who trace common kinship through either maternal or paternal lines exclusively.

unilineal kinship: a relationship established according to a pattern of tracing descent more or less exclusively through either paternal or maternal lines. *Cf.* BILATERAL KINSHIP.

universalism: the pattern of evaluating individuals on the basis of their merit, skill, or accomplishments rather than on the basis of their inherited status or kinship relationships. *Cf.* PARTICULARISM.

Index